The Gladsome Light
of
Jurisprudence

Recent Titles in
Contributions in Legal Studies
Series Editor: Paul L. Murphy

The Gladsome Light
of
Jurisprudence

Learning the Law in England
and the United States
in the 18th and 19th Centuries

Edited and Compiled by
Michael H. Hoeflich

Contributions in Legal Studies, Number 49

Greenwood Press
New York • Westport, Connecticut • London

Library of Congress Cataloging-in-Publication Data

The Gladsome light of jurisprudence : learning the law in England and
    the United States in the 18th and 19th centuries / edited and
    compiled by Michael H. Hoeflich.
        p.   cm. – (Contributions in legal studies, ISSN 0147-1074 ;
    no. 49)
      Bibliography: p.
      Includes index.
      ISBN 0-313-26437-6 (lib. bdg. : alk. paper)
      1. Law – Study and teaching – Great Britain – History.   2. Law – Study
    and teaching – United States – History.   I. Hoeflich, Michael H.
    II. Series.
    K100.Z9G55   1988
    340'.07'1142 – dc19   88-15427

British Library Cataloging in Publication Data is available.

Library of Congress Catalog Card Number: 88-15427
ISBN: 0-313-26437-6
ISSN: 0147-1074

First published in 1988

Greenwood Press, Inc.
88 Post Road West, Westport, Connecticut 06881

Printed in the United States of America

The paper used in this book complies with the
Permanent Paper Standard issued by the National
Information Standards Organization (Z39.48-1984).

10 9 8 7 6 5 4 3 2 1

Contents

Preface

Legal education in the United States is at a crossroads today. As the world changes rapidly we continue to utilize a method of instruction developed in the Nineteenth Century within an intellectual and societal context long dead. It is now necessary to look forward to the next millennium and to develop a pedagogical method suitable for the Twenty-First Century. To do that, however it might be useful to refresh our memories of how present day legal education came into being. It is in that spirit that the readings in this book are put forward.

The collection of the material contained in this volume has been long and difficult. For financial support during this project I wish to thank the National Endowment for the Humanities, the Research Board of the University of Illinois at Urbana-Champaign, the Workman Research Fund at the College of Law at UIUC, and the Illinois Bar Foundation. Obviously, libraries and librarians have played a major role in this project and I must express my gratitude to the Huntington Library in San Marino, California, the Newberry Library in Chicago, Illinois, the Cambridge University Library, the Edinburgh University Library, the Glasgow University Library, and, above all, the University Library and the Law Library at the College of Law at UIUC. Special thanks are due to Joe Luttrell, owner and proprietor of Meyer Boswell Books who has both the skills of a bookseller and the sensitivities of a scholar and has been of infinite help. Individual thanks, too, are due to my friends and colleagues, Rick Surles, Tim Kearley, and Scott Finet of the Law Library at UIUC, David Coombe of the Tulane Law School Library, and John Cairns, of Edinburgh University, my friend and expert finder of seemingly lost texts. Finally, I want to thank my research assistants, John Thies, Laura Clower, and Patricia Norcott and my secretary, Jan Sanderson, who has put up with more than I could ask.

The Gladsome Light
of
Jurisprudence

– 1 –

Introduction

Lawyers as a professional group have occupied a special place in Anglo-American society since the late Thirteenth Century. (1) In few other societies throughout history has one group occupied so consistently a position of power and prestige. It is, therefore, particularly interesting that there has been so much variation in standards for training and entrance to the legal profession in the Anglo-American world during this period. It is, perhaps, even more significant that while there has been considerable debate about the proper means and approaches to the process of learning the law since the beginning of the English legal profession in the Thirteenth Century there has been remarkably little historical perspective interjected into that debate. On the contrary, the debates over legal education and method have been remarkably ahistorical. For instance, in the past few years there has been a virulent split amongst professional teachers of law in the United States as to the proper ideological content of legal education. (2) These debates have recognized that this same concern was voiced in the debate between the formalists and the realists in the United States during the 1920's but they wholly ignore the countless times such concern was at issue in legal circles the Anglo-American world in the preceeding two centuries (not to mention the role such concerns played in Germany during the Nazi era). (3) Such ahistorical parochialism is inexcusable, but it may be understandable. Most lawyers and law professors are not legal historians and know very little about history generally. This, in itself, is somewhat ironical, since most lawyers have some interest in history – if only in the sense that the relationship between history and precedent is close – as well as some interest in their own profession. Indeed, a sense of professional identity is one of the requisites for the professionalisation of a group (4) and a knowledge of history tends to be a key component of such a sense of identity.

Thus, I have collected in this book brief essays and extracts from longer essays and books, all of which are part of what is today an underappreciated genre of legal literature from an underappreciated period of legal history, those which are representative of the Eighteenth and Nineteenth Century concern with identifying the proper method of learning the law or, as Edward Coke so felicitously called it, entering upon the "gladsome light of jurisprudence." (5)

Models of Legal Education

Broadly speaking there have been only two methods used to teach law during the past six hundred years. The first model for legal education - and the one used earliest and most often - is the apprenticeship model. This method is quite simple. The young legal tyro attaches himself to an established practitioner and, observing that practitioner at work, learns the ins and outs of the profession. The second model, which has long been dominant on the Continent and which has held first place in England and the United States since the third quarter of the Nineteenth Century is the school model. In this scheme, the young would-be lawyer attends a school whose purpose is to instruct and train such young men and women in those skills that will permit them to become practitioners upon finishing their course. The two models, of course, are not mutually exclusive. Similarly, there are wide variations as to the specific content of each model. But, within the past six hundred years, there has been remarkable unanimity amongst those who have concerned themselves with legal training that these are the principal models within which to work. (6)
Quite early in the history of the legal profession in England a standard path for professional legal training was established. On the Continent those who aspired to be lawyers, either civil or canon, attended one of the great medieval universities and there studied law, ultimately to receive the doctor utriusque juris degree. (7) In England law teaching was also undertaken at the two great medieval universities, Oxford and Cambridge. Beginning with the legendary lectures of Vacarius at Oxford in the Twelfth Century, (8) there has been a continuous tradition of university lectures on the Roman and Civil law. However, Roman and Civil law were not fully received in England and eventually came to play only a minor role in English jurisprudence. (9) Common law, the dominant source of English law throughout the medieval and early modern period, did not gain a serious foothold in the universities until the late Eighteenth Century. Until then, the universities were the sole property of the English Civilians. (10) The Common lawyers, rather than use the universities as centers for training new lawyers, formed instead a series of guild-like societies centered in London which came to be called the Inns of Court. (11)
The Inns provided a mixture of both models of training for their students. The medieval and early modern Inns were both teaching and apprenticeship centers. A young would-be lawyer would join an Inn and often reside

therein and frequently dine there as well. (12)   In this way, the young legal tyro would observe older members - established practitioners - in both social and professional settings and learn proper deportment.   The Inns also provided lectures on legal topics (called readings) and mock trials (called moots) by which the young members would learn their calling. (13)   The Inns also provided an opportunity (because they were proximate to the law courts) for the young members to serve as clerks to established practitioners and to observe the senior members at work in court. Finally, the Inns regulated formal admission to the profession and, thereby, could enforce educational standards. (14)

The Inns of Court system had both advantages and disadvantages.   Perhaps primary amongst the advantages was the close control this system allowed the practising Bar upon legal education, since the principal professional organization was itself the primary source of training. This model also permitted students to observe not only a single practitioner or small groups of practitioners to whom they had attached themselves as clerks, but also to have extensive contact with all the members, senior and junior, of their Inn.   Indeed, this close social and professional contact amongst members of each Inn and the corresponding impact of this close society upon practice helped, during the early modern period, the process of subject specialization amongst the Inns. (15)   As practitioners with particular legal specialities would come to congregate as members of a particular Inn, so students interested in that specialty would join that Inn.

The system had also some distinct disadvantages. First, the Inns were isolated from the universities, both of which were at some distance from London and the law courts. (16)   This meant that intellectual activity at the universities would not necessarily have any influence upon the Inns and their members.   For instance, one might argue that the systematizing movement in philosophy based upon the work of Descartes and Leibniz and other mathematicians, which was influential at the universities during the Seventeenth Century, failed to capture the imagination of the Common lawyers for quite some period because the connections between the universities and the Inns were simply lacking. (17)   On the other hand, during certain periods it was London not Oxford nor Cambridge which was the intellectual center of England.   Thus, the Seventeenth Century scientific revolution was centered at London and had widespread influence amongst the lawyers at the Inns of Courts. (18)   Similarly much of the most creative activity in the theater in the Seventeenth Century was London-based and it is not at all surprising to discover extensive use of the Inns themselves as sites for production. (19)

A major disadvantage of the Inns, however, which was related, in part, to their isolation from the universities was the extent to which the system tended to make the Common lawyers isolated and highly introverted.   The Civilians, for instance, did have their own Inn, but they also were all university trained.   Thus, they were forced to be part of the larger intellectual society and had both social and professional contacts in London and at the universities. (20) The Common lawyers, on the other hand, were very much creatures of their Inns, joining them at an early age and remaining in their comfortable but isolated environs for the whole of their lives. It seems quite likely that this isolation helped to insulate the Common lawyers from Continental influences and helped the Common law avoid influence from Continental legal systems. (21)

The other major disadvantage to the Inns of Court which began to be apparent in the late Seventeenth Century was the effect of the need to train at the Inns upon colonial lawyers. Would-be lawyers in the American colonies during the Eighteenth Century, for example, found themselves faced with the choice of undertaking the arduous and expensive trip across the Atlantic or of finding some form of domestic training. (22) So long as the legal profession insisted upon the primacy of the Inns at London, the potential for losing influence in the colonies was great.

Thus it was that while the traditional Continental form of legal training was university based, in England both models coexisted. The training of Civilians mirrored the Continental model and was centered at the English universities. The Common lawyers enjoyed a hybrid of apprenticeship and law school training, but divorced from the universities and centered at the Inns of Court.

In the American colonies, the difficulty of the transatlantic voyage led to the need to establish an alternative path to the law for would be lawyers. There were always some colonials with the sense of adventure and monetary resources to take the trip to London, but for most a stay at the Inns was simply too much to ask. (23) Interestingly, no new Inn was established in the colonies, presumably because of opposition to such a possibility by the Inns at London. Also, it is interesting that legal education was not made a part of the curriculum at the first colonial colleges such as Harvard. Rather these institutions saw themselves primarily as the training ground for ministers, not lawyers. (24) Thus, the model for legal training that came to be predominant in the American colonies during the Seventeenth and Eighteenth Centuries was the pure apprenticeship model. (25) A would-be young lawyer would find an established practitioner and become a clerk in his office for a period of years. (26) By observation and by actual work in the office the candidate for the Bar would acquire a working knowledge of law practice and eventually become a member of the Bar himself. Such a clerk would have no academic study in the law, other than through his own reading. In the Sixteenth Century colonial law office such outside reading would most likely have been very limited; perhaps, the young clerk might read Coke and some books of pleadings. (27) By the late Eighteenth Century Blackstone's great Commentaries and a few treatises would have begun to be available for study as well. (28)

All in all, however, colonial legal education was really a hit or miss affair. If a young student chose as

his master a lawyer seriously interested in training his
clerks and one who himself was well-versed in the law,
then he might, after several years, have learned a good
deal. If, however, he did not find a helpful master, then
his period of apprenticeship would be next to useless and
the young would-be lawyer would be doomed to enter upon
his own professional career with little knowledge.

Indeed, by the Eighteenth Century, legal training in
both England and the American colonies was in trouble. In
England the isolation of the Inns and the monopoly the
Inns exercised over admission to the legal profession (at
least as regards the Common law) had led to a period of
complacency, declining standards, the abandonment of
serious readings and moots, and easy entrance to the Bar.
(29) In the American colonies, the absence of an Inn or
college-related legal education combined with the
haphazard nature of legal training on the apprenticeship
model had led to similar problems. (30) By the second
half of the Eighteenth Century the need for reform was
becoming more and more clear.

The reaction in England and the newly formed United
States at the end of the Eighteenth Century to the serious
state of legal training was interesting. In England the
reaction was one of the realization that there was a need
for reform, but the realization was slow in coming and the
implementation of reform programs even slower. Some few
tentative steps, however, were taken in new directions.
The major reform step, of course, was the foundation at
Oxford, by virtue of the Viner bequest, of the Vinerian
Chair in English Law and the appointment of its first
incumbent, William Blackstone. (31) This development was
crucial on a number of counts. The Vinerian Chair was the
first foothold established for English law at the
universities and served as a model for the establishment
of similar foundations at Cambridge, and later, at London.
(32) Second, and far more important, it provided the
impetus for Blackstone to undertake his scholarly writing
and produce not only his Commentaries but also his
enormously important Discourse on the Study of Law, a
short essay which exercised substantial influence on
pedagogical theory for a century after its publication.
(33)

Unfortunately, the foundation of chairs in English
law did not accomplish, over the long term, all that their
proponents had hoped. Blackstone's successors were men of
lesser talent as were the first Cambridge professors. (34)
Indeed, it was not until Andrew Amos was appointed at
London, a full half century later that English law was
well taught at the universities. (35) Also, one must
always keep in mind that the first lectures on English law
at the universities were not intended for students bent on
a professional career. Blackstone and his early
successors aimed to provide young gentlemen with some
knowledge of law so that they might be better citizens and
parliamentarians or justices of the peace, not so that
they might be practising lawyers. This they still left to
the Inns. (36) Unfortunately, the Inns of Court were in a
state of disarray and the activity at Oxford and Cambridge

had little effect upon them. In fact, reform of English
professional legal education did not get fully underway
until the mid-Nineteenth Century with the appointment of
parliamentary commissions to examine law teaching at the
universities in 1846 and at the Inns of Court in 1855.
(37)   Nevertheless, the period from 1750 until 1850 was
one during which many lawyers and others interested in the
law in England took the opportunity to consider the need
for educational reform.   The period is, not surprisingly,
therefore, marked by a profusion of articles and pamphlets
on legal study and preparation for the Bar.
      During this same period legal education in the new
United States was undergoing far more furious and quick
paced change. (38)   Again, it is, perhaps, in part
attributable to the inconvenience of crossing the Atlantic
combined with the new hostility to all things English that
helped to bring about this reform.   Important, too, during
this period was the increasing influence of European
rather than English models on the American profession and
the concomitant growth of the idea that leagl education
should be university-based. (39)   At any rate it is during
the last two decades of the Eighteenth Century that the
first law professorships were founded at American colleges
and universities, such as at Mr. Jefferson's newly founded
University of Virginia, at William & Mary, at Columbia
College in New York, at the University of Pennsylvania,
and at other collegiate institutions. (40)   For the most
part, these foundations cannot be called law schools.
Rather, they resembled the Vinerian Chair at Oxford in
being single professorships oriented towards the teaching
of undergraduates who might go on to become lawyers after
graduation through office apprenticeship. (41)
      Indeed, throughout the later Eighteenth and well past
the middle of the Nineteenth Century, office
apprenticeship continued to be the most common form of
legal training in the United States, though it was, as the
Nineteenth Century progressed, frequently preceeded by a
period of instruction in law at a college or university
affiliated law department. (42)
      The first wave of law schools, properly so-called,
were established in the period from 1810 until 1860. (43)
This was the period of the establishment and growth of the
Dane Law College at Harvard under the leadership of Joseph
Story and Simon Greenleaf, of the law school at
Transylvania University at Lexington, Kentucky under the
tutelage of James Bledsoe and Daniel Mayes, of the law
school at Litchfield under Tapping Reeve and James Gould,
of the Tulane Law School under the German emigre,
Christian Roselius, as well as the reestablishment of a
law school at Columbia College and the ill-fated attempt
to begin a law school at New York University under
Benjamin F. Butler. (44)
      During this same period several practitioner law
schools using creative types of method were also
established.   For instance, a school was founded at
Needham, Virginia, designed to give part-time instruction
by way of moot court exercises to law clerks already
studying in practitioners' offices. (45)   In the South a

movement grew for a different type of institution, a "legal University." (46)   And, of course, law clerkships in practicing lawyers' offices continued to be common.

In short, the antebellum period in the United States was a period of experimentation in legal education, much as it was in other areas. By no means was there even the slightest hint as to a community consensus on the best form of legal training. For such a consensus, it is necessary to look to the period after the Civil War when the Harvard model as developed by C.C. Langdell and James Barr Ames became the predominant model for legal education through a combination of merit and marketing. (47)

Because the Harvard model has succeeded so well in this century, there is a tendency to forget that prior to 1870 there was great variation in the form of legal training offerred to would-be young lawyers in the United States and Great Britain. But great variation there was and the written contributions to the debates on legal training are numerous from the century preceding Langdell's tenure at Harvard. It is, perhaps, especially important now, when the Harvard model of legal education is beginning to show signs of age and impatience with it is growing amongst the ranks of professional law teachers, to begin again the debate that Langdell and his proselytes quelled and to do so with an eye to history.

Approaches to Legal Method

One essential part of the antebellum debate over legal education concerned legal method. Again, today we have what we tend to think of as a standard approach to the law, which we generally refer to as the case method. In one sense, what we mean by case-method is that students are to learn the law through the close study, analysis, and explication of leading cases in the various recognized fields of legal study. (48)   But we also mean more than this, for what we expect students to do with the cases is to extract from them a principle or priciples which may furnish the rule of decision in other factually analogous situations when applied deductively. (49)   In effect, the case method involves both a teaching method and an approach to legal reasoning which combines inductive empiricism (actual cases form the first substance of inquiry and analysis from which principles are derived inductively) and deductive logic (once derived, principles are applied deductively).   This approach to legal reasoning has become characteristic and is often referred to as "scientific." (50)

The origin of the case-method is usually ascribed to the Langdellian period at Harvard, but, in fact, it has been an integral part of the Western legal tradition since at least the Seventeenth Century and the work of Leibniz and Descartes. (51)   There has been surprisingly little debate on the validity of this method until the past few years, when its allegedly value neutral approach to law has been called into question and the argument has been put forward for the abandonment of logic in favor of

ideology and passion. (52)   What was a debatable point
during the late Eighteenth and early Nineteenth Century,
however, was whether it was necessary for would-be lawyers
to acquire any skills in formal legal reasoning at all.
    This debate was, in fact, a debate over the
profession's self-image, over whether law was an art or a
science.   It derived, in part, from the two alternative
models of legal training. The substance of the debate was
simple. When one studied law in an office or at the Inns
through readings and moots, one did not obtain a
systematic and principled view of the law. One saw law,
rather, as a craft, to be learned by observation and
replication. One did not, so the critics of this method
argued, gain an overview or a philosophical approach to
the law. (53) The virtue of academic instruction in law,
so the argument went, was that it did teach law as a
principled subject, one with a philosophical foundation
and with connections, intellectual and professional, to
other academic disciplines. The proponents of law as a
philosophically coherent structure tended to support such
intellectual movements in the law as reception and
codification. (54)   They tended to dismiss those who
emphasized the craft aspects of the law, special pleading,
drafting, the intricacies of conveyancing, as mere
pettyfoggers. (55) Those who espoused the craft view of
the law dismissed the academics as mere academics with
little experience of the realities of the law as
practiced. What one had here, fundamentally, was a debate
between those who espoused a pragmatic view of the
profession and resisted its more intellectual side with
those who castigated practitioners as mere technicians who
acted dumbly and without insight. One sees a tradition in
the literature about legal education from Hale and
Blackstone through Mayes and others arguing for this more
academic approach to law and legal education.
Nevertheless, the more pragmatic approach, exemplified,
for instance, by the writings of Samuel Warren, also
continued to be strong throughout the Nineteenth Century.
Indeed, to some extent, the debate continues today,
although now within the ranks of academic lawyers in the
form of a debate over the place of clinical legal
education in law schools. (56)

The Literature about Learning the Law

    At the present time there is a mini-industry centered
about legal education and learning the law. This is not
surprising, since we now have had a fully developed
full-time law professoriate for over a century in the
United States and in England. (57) As everyone knows,
wherever there are academics, literature and scholarly
journals are sure to follow. But there was another
period, roughly from the first quarter of the Eighteenth
Century until the last quarter of the Nineteenth Century,
which also witnessed an outpouring of literature about
learning the law and formal legal education. As I noted
earlier, this literature is attributable to the reform

movements then sweeping the profession and the debates these movements inevitably provoked.

The Eighteenth and Nineteenth Century literature on legal training can be classified into several types. First, is the polemic against practical, office-based education (including education solely at the Inns of Court) and in favor of the introduction of serious legal education at the universities. Second, is the literature against such university-based education and in favor of pragmatic, non-elitist training. The third type of literature which one finds is the proposal for new types of legal education, some of which are quite utopian and others of which are really quite reasonable. The fourth type is related to the first and tends to be polemic in favor of the introduction of system and method into the law and legal training, often through the teaching of logic, moral philosophy or Roman law. Much of the literature of this period fits within more than one of these categories, but the categories do help us to understand the concerns of the authors in capsule format.

One of the great difficulties in becoming acquainted with the literature produced during this period is the relative rarity of most of these items today. Law books as books suffer from two great failings. First, they tend to be used a great deal when current and, therefore, tend to wear out and be discarded. Second, law books tend to lose currency quickly and are, therefore, discarded by their owners as obsolete and useless. Thus it is that many volumes that may have been common a century or two ago are now quite difficult to obtain, even for a major research library. This means that even those few individuals who may feel motivated to look at such things as Mayes' Address of 1834 or Benjamin Butler's Proposal of 1834 are unable to do so because of the unavailability of the texts. It is this which has motivated me to put together this collection of texts. It is meant to amuse, to instruct, and, perhaps, to instill in its readers some sense of the history of the legal profession and legal instruction and training for the Bar.

A Note on the Selection of Texts

The basis upon which the texts in this volume have been selected is simple. In order to be included, a text had to be representative of the thought of its time or viewed by contemporaries as significant. To a lesser extent, the rarity of a text today contributed to its inclusion as well. Where texts were short enough themselves to be included without abridgement, I have so included them. Where they were simply too long, I have attempted to include either an abridged version or extracts from the whole which give the reader both a sense of the argument made and the style of the author. The latest text included in this collection is Oliver Wendell Holmes' "The Use of Law Schools" first published in 1896. While it would certainly be possible to include texts published in the Twentieth Century, I believe that,

generally, these are still easily available and thus
reprinting is unnecessary.

In general, footnotes in the original have not been
retained in the version reprinted here, but original
spelling, underlining and punctuation has been. A select
bibliography is included at the end of the book, as is a
full bibliographical description of each text and, where
possible, biographical details of the authors.

NOTES

1.   See, P. Brand, The Origins of the English Legal
Professsion, 5 LAW & HISTORY Rev. 31 (1987); see, also,
J.H. BAKER, THE LEGAL PROFESSION AND THE COMMON LAW
(1986); W. PREST, THE RISE OF THE BARRISTERS (1986).

2.   I refer here to the Critical Legal Studies Movement;
on this see, R. Unger, THE CRITICAL LEGAL STUDIES MOVEMENT
(1986).

3.   See my unpublished lecture "Legal History & Ideology"
presented at the AALS Mini-Workshop on Legal History held
at New Orleans, Louisiana in January 1986; for a
frightening example of this, see H. MEYER, RASSE UND RECHT
BEI DEN GERMANEN UND INDOGERMANEN (1937).

4.   See, P. Wright, What is a Profession?, 29 CAN. B. REV.
748 (1951).

5.   The phrase is from 2 E. COKE, THE FIRST PART OF THE
INSTITUTES OF THE LAW OF ENGLAND, Epilogus (18th ed.,
1823).

6.   See, for instance, The Seminal Work of A. Harno, LEGAL
EDUCATION IN THE UNITED STATES 1-34 (1953); see, also,
A.H. CHROUST, THE RISE OF THE LEGAL PROFESSION IN AMERICA
(1965); R. COCKS, FOUNDATIONS OF THE MODERN BAR (1983); C.
Warren, A HISTORY OF THE AMERICAN BAR (1913).

7.   I.e. "doctor of both laws [civil and canon]"; on the
interaction of Civil and Canon law in the Middle Ages,
see, H. Berman, LAW AND REVOLUTION: THE FORMATION OF THE
WESTERN LEGAL TRADITION (1983) and on law schools during
the Middle Ages, BERMAN, OP.Cit. at 127-164; see, also, D.
Clark, The Medieval Origins of Modern Legal Education:
Between Church and State, forthcoming in the
RABELSZEITSCHRIFT (1987).

8.   On Vacarius' lectures at Oxford, see, L. Boyle, The
Beginnings of Legal Studies at Oxford, 14 VIATOR 107
(1983); see, also, H.G. Richardson, The Oxford Law School
Under John, 57 L.Q.R. 319 (1941).

9.   There is a vast literature on the reception of Roman
law in England; see, the still useful work of T.E.
SCRUTTON, THE INFLUENCE OF THE ROMAN LAW ON THE LAW OF
ENGLAND (1885).

10.   The best study of the English Civilians is B. LEVACK, THE CIVIL LAWYERS IN ENGLAND 1603-1641 (1973); see, also, D.R. Coquilette, Legal Ideology and Incorporation I: The English Civilian Writers, 1523-1607, 61 B.U.L. REV. 1 (1981); Ibid., Legal Ideology and Incorporation II: Sir Thomas Ridley, Charles Mallory, and the Literary Battle for the Law Merchant, 1607-1676, 61 B.U.L. Rev. 314 (1981); Ibid., Ideology and Incorporation III: Reason Regulated - The Post-Restoration English Civilian, 1653-1735, 67 B.U.L. REV. 289 (1987); B. Levack, The English Civilians, 1500-1750, in W. PREST, LAWYERS IN EARLY MODERN EUROPE AND AMERICA 108-128 (1981).

11.   On the early history of the Inns of Court, see, esp., the essays in J.H. BAKER, THE LEGAL PROFESSION AND THE COMMON LAW (1986).

12.   See, J.H. BAKER, OP. CIT., n. 11, above.

13.   A selection of these have been edited in S. THORNE, READINGS AND MOOTS AT THE INNS OF COURT IN THE FIFTEENTH CENTURY (1954).

14.   W. HOLDSWORTH, 12 A HISTORY OF ENGLISH LAW 18-33 (1938).

15.   Thus, Certain Inns became associated with a particular type of practice, eg. Inns of Chancery; for a description of the Chancery Inns; see, eg., 12 W. HOLDSWORTH 40-46 (1938).

16.   Indeed, the distance of Oxford and Cambridge from London and the Law Courts made it especially difficult to find lawyers to come up to the universities to teach since this would, of necessity, have required them to give up full-time practice.

17.   On this movement, see, Hoeflich, Law & Geometry: Legal Science from Leibniz to Langdell, 30 Am. J. LEG. HIST. 95 (1986).

18.   B. SHAPIRO, PROBABILITY AND CERTAINTY IN SEVENTEENTH-CENTURY ENGLAND 163-193 (1983); B. Shapiro, Law and Science in Seventeenth Century England, 21 STAN. L. REV. 738 (1969).

19.   See, for instance, D.S. BLAND, THREE REVELS FROM THE INNS OF COURT (1984).

20.   See, B. LEVACK, THE CIVIL LAWYERS IN ENGLAND 1603-1641 (1973); B. Levack, The English Civilians, 1500-1750, in W. PREST, LAWYERS IN EARLY MODERN EUROPE AND AMERICA 108-128 (1981).

21.   In Scotland, where legal education was always university-based, on the other hand, and, as where the system is a hybrid Common law/Civil law System, there have

been extensive European influences on the Legal profession over the centuries, see, H. Murdoch, The Advocates, the Law in the Nation in Early Modern Scotland, in W. PREST, LAWYERS IN EARLY MODERN EUROPE AND AMERICA 147-163 (1981); J. Cairns, The Formation of the Scotish Legal Mind in the Eighteenth Century: Themes of Humanism and Enlightment in the Admission of Advocates, in N. MACCORMICK & P. BIRKS, THE LEGAL MIND: ESSAYS FOR TONY HONORE (1986) and his as yet unpublished essay, J. Cairns, "Scottish University Education in Law in the Eighteenth Century; the Vocation of the Age for Roman Law"; see also, Hoeflich, Art. Cit., n. 17, above.

22.   For a good survey of colonial legal education, see, C. WARREN, A HISTORY OF THE AMERICAN BAR 157-187 (1913) and P. HAMLIN, LEGAL EDUCATION IN COLONIAL NEW YORK (1939); see, also, C. Consalus, Legal Education During the Colonial Period, 1663-1776, 29 JL. LEG. ED. 295 (1978).

23.   See, for instance, the letter from John Rutledge to his brother Edward, a student at the Turner Temple written in July 1769 as included in a letter from Mitchell King to Francis Lieber now in the Huntington Library, Ms. LI 2530.

24.   See, S.E. Morison, The Founding of Harvard College (1968).

25.   See, words cited, n. 22, above; see, also, C. McKirdy, The Lawyer as Apprentice: Legal Education in Eighteenth Century Massachusetts, 28 JL. LEG. ED. 124 (1976).

26.   An excellent example of this is provided in John Adams' diaries; see,

27.   See, C. WARREN, OP.CIT., n. 22, above.

28.   On Blackstone's Commentaries as an educational tool see D. Nolan, Sir William Blackstone and The New American Republic: A Study of Intellectual Impact 51 N.Y.U.L. REV. 731 (1976); P. Lucas, Blackstone and the Reform of the Legal Profession, ENG. HIST. REV. 456 (1962); see, also, 12 W. HOLDSWORTH, A HISTORY OF ENGLISH LAW 702-736 (1938).

29.   12 W. HOLDSWORTH, A HISTORY OF ENGLISH LAW 77-91 (1938).

30.   2A.H. CHROUST THE RISE OF THE LEGAL PROFESSION IN AMERICA 174-175 (1965); see also works cited n. 22, above.

31.   See H.G. HANBURY, THE VINERIAN CHAIR AND LEGAL EDUCATION (1958); F.H. LAWSON, THE OXFORD LAW SCHOOL 1850-1956 1-33 (1968); 12 W. HOLDSWORTH, A HISTORY OF ENGLISH LAW 95-101 (1938); L. Sutherland, William Blackstone and the Legal Chair at Oxford, in R. WELLER & A. RIBIERO, EVIDENCE IN LITERARY SCHOLARSHIP 229 (1979).

32.   H.G. HANBURY, THE VINERIAN CHAIR AND LEGAL EDUCATION
(1958) 52-78.

33.   Reprinted, below, at pp. 53-73.

34.   H.G. HANBURY, OP.CIT., n.32, above, at 79-97.

35.   See, R. COCKS, FOUNDATIONS OF THE MODERN BAR 37-51
(1983); J. H. Baker, University College and Legal
Education, 30 CURRENT LEG. PROBS. 1 (1977).

36.   See the Report of the Parliamentary Commission on
Legal Education cited, below, at n. 37.

37.   REPORT FROM THE SELECT COMMITTEE ON LEGAL EDUCATION
(1846); REPORT OF THE COMMISSIONERS APPOINTED TO INQUIRE
INTO THE ARRANGEMENTS IN THE INNS OF COURT AND THE INNS OF
CHANCERY, FOR PROMOTING THE STUDY OF THE LAW AND
JURISPRUDENCE (1855).

38.   See, C. WARREN, A HISTORY OF THE AMERICAN BAR 341-365
(1913); 2 A.H. CHROUST, THE RISE OF THE LEGAL PROFESSION
IN AMERICA 173-223 (1965); A.Z. REED, TRAINING FOR THE
PUBLIC PROFESSION OF LAW 107-202 (1921).

39.   See, M.H. Hoeflich, Law & Geometry: Legal Science
from Leibniz to Langdell, 30 AM. JL. LEG. HIST. 1 (1986);
see, also, M.H. Hoeflich, The Americanization of English
Legal Education, forthcoming in JL. LEG. HIST. (1987).

40.   See, works cited, n. 38, above.

41.   See, works cited, n. 38, above.

42.   See, works cited, n. 38, above.

43.   See, works cited, n. 38, above; R. STEVENS, LAW
SCHOOL: LEGAL EDUCATION IN AMERICA FROM THE 1850s TO THE
1980s 3-19 (1983).

44.   See, works cited, n. 38, above.

45.   See, JOURNAL OF THE LAW SCHOOL, AND OF THE MOOT COURT
ATTACHED TO IT . . . (1822); on this school, see, A.
Dobie, A Private Law School in Old Virginia 16 VA. L. REV.
815 (1930).

46.   This proposal, entitled, "A Study of the Law" is
reprinted, below, at 201-213.

47.   See, above all, R. STEVENS, LAW SCHOOL: LEGAL
EDUCATION IN AMERICA FROM THE 1850s TO THE 1980s 35-91
(1983); see, also, J. SELIGMAN, THE HIGH CITADEL; A.J.
HARNO, LEGAL EDUCATION IN THE UNITED STATES 53-70 (1953);
see, also, A.Z. REED, TRAINING FOR THE PUBLIC PROFESSION
OF LAW 343-390 (1921).

48.   A.J. HARNO, LEGAL EDUCATION IN THE UNITED STATES 51-70 (1953); see, also, A.L. Goodhart, Case Law in England and America, 15 CORN. L.Q. 173 (1930).

49.   M.H. Hoeflich, Law & Geometry: Legal Science from Leibniz to Langdell 30 AM. JL. LEG. HIST. 1 (1986).

50.   See, M.H. Hoeflich, Art. Cit. n. 49, above.

51.   See, M.H. Hoeflich, Art. Cit. n. 49, above.

52.   See, R. UNGER, OP. CIT. n. 2, above.

53.   See, for instance, Blackstone's comments in his DISCOURSE ON THE STUDY OF LAW and Mayes' in his Inaugural Lecture, both reprinted below at pp. 53-73 and at pp. 145-164.

54.   See, M.H. Hoeflich, Art. Cit. n. 48, above.

55.   As did Mayes, for instance, reprinted below, at 145-164.

56.   There is a vast literature on clinical legal studies; see, for instance, AALS/ABA, CLINICAL LEGAL EDUCATION (1980).

57.   R. STEVENS, LAW SCHOOL: LEGAL EDUCATION FROM THE 1850s TO THE 1980s (1983).

– 2 –

Roger North

Discourse on the Study of the Laws
(ca. 1700–1730)

Of all the professions in the world, that pretend to
book-learning, none is so destitute of institution as that
of the common law. Academic studies, which take in that
of the civil law, have tutors and professors to aid them,
and the students are entertained in colleges, under a
discipline, in the midst of societies, that are or should
be devoted to study, which encourages, as well as
demonstrates such methods, in general, as everyone may
easily apply to his own particular use. But for the
Common Law, however, there are Societies, which have the
outward show, or pretence of collegiate institution; yet
in reality, nothing of that sort is now to be found in
them; and, whereas, in more ancient times, there were
exercises used in the Hall, they were more for probation
than institution; now even those are shrunk into mere
form, and that preserved only for conformity to rules,
that gentlemen by tale of appearances in exercises, rather
than any sort of performances, might be entitled to be
called to the Bar. But none of these called Masters, and
distinguished as Benchers, with the power of ordering, and
disposing all the common affairs of the Society, ever
pretended to take upon them the direction of the students,
either to put them, or lead them in any way, but each is
left to himself to enter at which end he fancies, or as
accident, inquiry, or conversation prompts. And such as
are willing, and inquisitive, may pick up some hints of
direction, but generally the first step is a blunder, and
what follows, loss of time, till even out of that, a sort
of righter understanding is gathered, whereby a gentleman
finds how to make better use of his time. And of those
who are so civil to assist a novice with their advice,
what method to take, few agree in the same, some say one
way,some another, and amongst them rarely any one that is
tolerably just. Nor is it so easy a matter to do it, that
everyone should pretend to advise, for most enter the
profession by chance, and all his life after is partial to
his own way, though none of the best; and it is a matter
of great judgment, which requires a true skill in books,
and men's capacities, so that I scarce think it is harder

to resolve very difficult cases in law, than it is to
direct a young gentleman what course he should take to
enable himself so to do. But since some directions in a
study so particular, and beside all common erudition, are
necessary, (for how should a student of himself find out
what to begin with, and they must be very mean intimations
coming from one of the profession, that are not better
than none at all;) and I, having been so frequently
solicited to assistances of this kind, and as often ready
to afford them in discourse, according to my capacity,
(but such discourses make but indifferent impression,
being of matters strange and new, and so are apt to sink,
and fade to nothing;) and yet being desirous to gratify
friends, as well as in due time to put forward some, I may
be a debtor to for such care, and for these ends to
preserve in my remembrance such notices, as at present
seem material, and considerable, I have undertaken in an
extempore way to set them down in writing, but cursorily,
and in no better method than that way of proceeding will
permit.
    First, as to the professions, in general, I think few
are ignorant how necessary they are to persons of the
second rate in families. The eldest is usually provided
for by settlements, and if the younger have any provision,
whether by settlement, or just disposition of parents, it
is seldom or never more than is judged sufficient for
education in some profession; concluding that for all the
future plenty and dignity of life, it must be expected
from a profession, and from no other means; and if there
be examples from good fortune, from mortality, or other
accidents happening to them, it is but as a lottery prize,
and none but fools are drawn in by the trumpet of it to
venture their all, in expectation of the like events. And
it is to be observed that there is a vast difference
between the circumstances of youth and age. The former
will pass and live merrily upon a common exhibition, and
fancy that will hold on, but it is a great mistake, for
age requires more a great deal, because it sets up for
authority, and dignity, which is not had without an
estate, and whatever good parts a man has, and howsoever
his company is desired, without an estate or gainful
profession he is but an underling, and must look poorly in
company of such as are better provided for. And that
which was gay, and seemed a full provision for a youth,
viz. a servant and perhaps a horse, with a few airs of
dressing, comes far short of the pretensions even of the
middle ages, which require settlement, plenty, and
economy, and so in process the former becomes little
better than a genteel vagabond, and at length ends in the
dismal apprehension of being burthensome, and fastidious
every where, and, in the no less horrid thought of being
good for nothing, draws on some wretched and abject
retirement. The true policy of life is to provide that
the latter part may be easy, and comfortable; for that has
disadvantages that require the counterpoise of good heart
and spirits; conscientia vitae bene ante actae; and the
Ancients accounted otium cum dignitate to be a full
compensation for the miseries even of old age. And which

way should a man secure this to himself, but from the
course of a profession?   It may be thought that the
assiduity and pains, required in the pursuit of success,
is too hard a task to be borne, but let it be considered
that it is better to bear the means, out of choice, and
enjoy the fruits in due time, than volens, nolens, to bear
the bad consequences of neglect, when it is out of all
possibility, by any means, or industry, to retrieve the
mistake.   There are two points undoubted, first, that no
great gain is without great pain, or (more explicitly)
that no person can reasonably expect success in a
profession, without industry, assiduity, and perseverance.
For the business is to exceed, or at least be a match for
others that do take pains, and how can that be done but by
taking more, or, at least, as much pains?   Professions
generally advance upon competition, and then the
consequence is plain.   Secondly, the pains and application
must be in the youth, and that gone, the opportunity is
lost.   A man has but one youth, and considering the
consequence of employing that well, he has reason to think
himself very rich; for that gone, all the wealth in the
world will not purchase another.   It would seem strange,
if experience did not confirm it, that a man's age should
be like the seasons of the year; for if you sow in
harvest, when are you to reap?   The spring is the time to
commit seeds to increase, and if a man gets not his skill
when young, he is like never to have any at all; for the
soil becomes arid as age advances, and whatsoever is
scattered upon it takes no thrift, but perishes and
starves.   Therefore, the thought of uneasiness in the way
of a profession must be conquered, and let perseverance in
a regular and steady pursuit be the object of an unshaken
resolution.   But that must not pass as granted, that the
pursuit of a profession is such a course of labour and
pain.   The spectre that frights so, stands at the
entrance; when that is put by, the walk will be easy, and,
at last, pleasant; for every day's work makes the next
easier, and when the work becomes, as in time it will be,
engaging, then the very exercise that was so very
laborious, will be rather a pleasure, and be at last an
habitually agreeable diversion, and entertainment of time;
and if the understanding and consequences are rightly
considered, reason itself will get the better of aversion:
for what can a man do better than that which he knows is
best for him?   But there is a great error in the common
apprehension that a profession is inconsistent with
pleasure; for I know no employment, but, undertaken and
pursued in fit time and manner, in fit times and manner,
also admits of many reasonable pleasures.   If idleness be
counted such, I own it is inconsistent with pains-taking
at any time; but most people have found the fatigue of
want of past-time more fastidious than the reasonable
pains that lead to a profession; and I am sure that it is
a great point gained in the course of a man's life, if he
is never at a loss as to the spending of his time, or
knowing what to do.
     As to the profession of the law, I must say of it in
general, that it requires the whole man, and must be his

north star, by which he is to direct his time, from the
beginning of his undertaking it, to the end of his life.
It is a business of that nature, that it will not be
discontinued, nor scarce endure a cessation; but he that
will reap the fruit expected from it, that is, raising of
an estate by the strength of that, must pursue the subject
without interruption, and he must not only read and talk,
but eat, drink, and sleep law; that is, he must purpose to
prosecute his studies daily, till he comes to practice,
and then to be never out of the way of business; but, as
the proverb is, semper tibi pendeat hamus, and all this
while all other studies, entertainments, and pleasures,
must be such as are consistent with the profession, at
least not averse or opposite to it.   This may be thought,
perhaps, a hard and discouraging sentence, as if a man
were condemned to the gallies during life, without hopes
of redemption, but this is a great mistake, as has been
touched before; for when I say daily, without intermission
or cessation, I do not mean every hour and minute in every
day, but only, as the philosophers meant by nulla dies
sine linea, no day is to pass without somewhat of study or
practice of the law, except such as order and necessity
will have exempted.   As to actual study, it doth not
demand so much of a day as it need to be esteemed a
labour.   I have heard some say, four hours in a morning
close application to books is enough for law.   Sir Henry
Finch used to say, study all the morning, and talk all the
afternoon.   Yet this does not suppose the rest of a man's
time is to be idle or lost.   For there are other studies
more pleasant which may be interwoven with the study of
the law with great emolument; as for instance, History,
and particularly that of England, which latter is to be
accounted, however pleasant to read, an appendix or
incident necessary to the study of the law: for it often
lays open the reasons and occasions that have been for
changes that have befallen the Common Law, either by
authority of Parliament, or of the Judges in Westminster
Hall.   And besides history, there are other sorts of
learning most reasonable for a lawyer to have some
knowledge of, though even superficial, as of the Civil
Law.   A man of the law would not be willing to stand mute
to the question, what is the difference between the Civil
and the Common Law; what is the Imperial Law, what the
Canon, what the Pandects, Codes, &c.   It is not at all
needful to study questions in these laws, but the rise and
progress of them, in gross, is but a necessary knowledge,
and so far taking up but little time, and had by mere
inspection of some books, and perusing their
introductions.   It may with ease and pleasure be
interlaced with the Common Law; and not only that for a
sort of use, but divers other sciences may be taken notice
of for diversion, or ornament, and pleasure.   I have known
Music, Geometry, and Natural Philosophy, as well as the
knowledge of Geography, States and Republics, in great
perfection, harboured in eodem subjecto with the body of
the Common Law, and consistent with as great practice and
preferments as have been known in the profession.   For if
it be considered what may be done in these idle times,

usually spent in useless talk, and the vain whiling of it
away, such acquests are not to be wondered at.   I grant
there must be a genius and zeal that way; it is not to be
forced, and then there is no greater pleasure.   Of this
the great Bacon was an instance, and surely it is a vast
advantage to be not only a common lawyer, but a general
scholar, as in latter times Selden was; for that you call
a mere lawyer, seldom reaches better preferment than to be
a puisne judge, if at all to be ever invited from his
chamber.   The profession of the law, comprehending the
whole in due order, refers to 1.   Reading; 2.
Common-placing; 3.   Conversing; 4.   Reporting; 5.
Practising.

   1.   The first is reading or study, and that is
referred to the books of law, which are, 1.   Institutions;
2.   Reports; 3.   Repertories; 4.   Formularies.   As for
statutes and records, they fall in with the others: for
the Acts of Parliament bringing change or alteration in
the Common Law, and the interpretation of them belonging
to the courts of law, they are taken notice of and
agitated as other points of law are, and with them to be
found in the books.

   1.   A student begins with books that are
institutionary, and of them, in the first place,
LITTLETON, the text of which is accounted law, and no
other book hath that authority.   It was originally
compiled for the initiation of a student, and is,
therefore, the most plain and intelligible, without any
sort of obscurity, and contains the fundamentals of law,
touching estates and contracts; and however fitted this
book is to the capacity of a beginner, the very adepts in
the law are not ashamed frequently to read it.   I knew a
Lord Keeper that read it every Christmas as long as he
lived.   So necessary is it to retain in memory the very
words of a book which is so authentic.   This implies the
small need this book has of a comment; for all such
attempts must make more obscure that which is of itself as
plain as possibly can be; and that, so titled by my Lord
Coke, which by the very word Comment, as supposing it
carries explanation (cujus contrarium verum est) hath
deceived many students to take it along with the text of
Littleton; but to very bad purpose, for it disturbs and
hinders the attention to the text of the book, which is
that principally to be regarded and remembered; and
further reasons shall be given of this elsewhere.   There
is another little book, called PERKINS; it contains a
collection of cases and distinctions put under several of
the chief heads of the law, as Feoffments, Grants, &c.
This is very useful to a student, for it practices his
attention to cases and niceties of the law, and shows upon
what small niceties and diversities things will turn; but
this book hath not authority equal with the other, and
many cases in it are not allowed for law; but, however,
for the reasons given, useful for a student, and the
rather, because it is ordinarily printed in the same
volume with Littleton, or so as may be pocketed, and
thereby fit for subsecive times, and lazy intervals to be
employed.   Here I must stay to observe the necessity of a

student's early application to learn the old law French, for these books, and most others of considerable authority, are delivered in it. Some may think that because the law French is no better than the old Norman corrupted, and now a deformed hotch-potch of the English and Latin mixed together, it is not fit for a polite spark to foul himself with; but this nicety is so desperate a mistake, that lawyer and law French are coincident; one will not stand without the other. All the ancient books that are necessary to be read and understood are in that dialect, and the law itself is not in its native dress, nor is, in truth, the same thing in English. During the English times, as they are called, when the Rump abolished Latin and French, divers books were translated, as the great work of Coke's Reports, &c.; but upon the revival of the law, those all died, and are now but waste paper. Even the modern Reports mostly are in French, and, as I said, all the ancient as well as divers authentic tracts, as FITZHERBERT'S Natura Brevium, STAUNFORD'S Pleas of the Crown, CROMPTON'S Jurisdiction of Courts, &c. are only to be had in French; and will any man pretend to be a lawyer without it, when that language should be as familiar to him as his mother-tongue? Now, it is not the least use of these initiatory books that they are to be read in French, for, thereby a student, with his slow steps, gains ground in the language as well as in the law, and, by that time as he shall be capable to understand other books, he will be capable to read them, therefore, I should absolutely interdict reading Littleton, &c. in any other than French, and, however it is translated, and the English con-columned with it, it should be used only as subsidiary, to give light to the French where it is obscure, and not as a text. For really the Law is scarce expressible properly in English, and, when it is done, it must be Françoise, or very uncouth. All moots and exercises, nay, many practices of the law, must be in French, at the bar of the courts of justice; as when Assizes or Appeals are arraigned, the Array, that is, Pannels of Juries challenged or excepted to, it must be done in French; so Counts, Bars, and such transactions as reach no farther than the Bench and Counsel, with the Officers, and not to the Country, (as Trials by Jury,) or to the Lay Gents (as we call our Clients) in motions and arguments of their suits, which they are concerned to understand, are to be done in Law French; also Replications at the Common Pleas Bar in real actions; and this is the meaning of those scraps of French so frequently heard in the Courts, which to explain is not the business here, but it is enough to show how necessary for a lawyer it is to be as ready as possible at his French, and how he must blush to be discovered incompetent. It is a language so religiously embraced by all good lawyers, that it is the custom for such to write their notes, or reports taken at the bar, as the shortest, and it is, in reality, the most apt way for expressing the Law, and that a little experience will show. For the assistance of students in this task of entering into a course of study of the law, and learning the language,

Rastall, one of our best authors, composed a book, which at first was printed in English and French, called the Terms of the Law, that lay in a little room, but it has been since, in every edition, enlarged, and makes a thick octavo; this is fit to lie by at reading, to the end when terms occur which are of art, as I may call them, and peculiar to the law, for comprehending a great deal in a word, as Avowry, Warranty, Brief, Attachment, &c. that book is ready to explain them, and at the same time instruct both in the subject and language; and the same be looked into at times and much information had out of it. At first gentlemen have a horrid aversion to French, and think it desperate hard to learn, but if the former, that is the aversion, be conquered by resolution, the other will be found a mistake, for such as have a preparation of Latin, and a moderate apprehension of modern French, soon master it. Few need more than a fortnight's application for enabling them to read, fluently and currently; but, in a word, whether sooner or later, it is necessary, and must be done. A man may be a wrangler, but never a lawyer, without a knowledge of the authentic books of the law in their genuine language. One great discouragement here is the multitude of abbreviations which makes law French to the eye appear as difficult as if it were Arabick, but this is because the particles and monosyllables, which frequently occur, are so abbreviated. But a small list of them, set down with a pen as they are found out, lying by, with a cast of the eye, readily helps, and in a few hours' time the memory receives and supplies all. It was the way of all writing, before printing, to abridge the labour of the pen, and the first printing followed the way of the manuscripts which in those times, was as familiar and easy as our alphabet. The law writings and books retain much of the old abbreviations, I cannot undertake to represent them all but a few are as follows:

b^s	.	bus.	$eè_t$ . .	estre
bns	.	biens	ff_t . . .	fait or fuit
c	.	ceo	ec^t . .	esteant.
e_t	.	est.	fktmt . .	frank tenement.
m^t	.	ment	oia . .	omnia
ss.	.	scilicet	oib^s . .	omnibus
tras	.	trespass		per
aps	.	apres		pro
acc	.	actio	q . .	que
covnt	.	covenant	rns . .	riens-respons
K^t	.	Knight	trs . .	terres
R_t	.	Roy	bre . .	brief
g^t	.	gist	hoe . .	home
huit	.	habuit	p^s . .	pres

These and many others will occur in the old books, and so in the latter also, which sense and common ingenuity will interpret, but if one will have recourse to the rest of them, let him look over TROTMAN'S Abridgment of COKE'S Reports, and he will find all that ever were used, it being affectedly done in that way for shortness. So let us leave the languages as supposed our own, without

hesitation, and go on to books and matters.   I have, at
present, named only Littleton, Perkins, and the Terms.
Now as we come farther into business, I must intimate that
a student is not to make his course so strict as to read
only one book till he has read it out, but to have divers
books going at the same time, some for principal studies,
and others for aid, and to relieve the time by somewhat of
change; as then may be had some small pieces, such as the
old Tenures which are short, and very apposite and
material.   These are scarce known to many students, but
very useful to be taken along at intervals with other
reading, for they will give a notion of the jurisdiction
and process the law upon the foot of antiquity, whence
only they are justly to be taken.   And generally in the
law, as well as in all other human literature, antiquity
is the foundation; for he that knows the elder, can
distinguish what is new, but he that deals only in the
new, cannot tell how fresh or stale his opinions are, nor
from whence they are derived.   I must not forget among the
subsidiary books, that of St. Germains called Doctor and
Student, because it is plain and intelligible, and the
points of law that are touched there are sound and well
stated.   There is recommended also the little book of
FORTESCUE de Laudibus Legum Angliae; along with which are
some accounts of the ancient law in Latin, added by Mr.
Selden, called the Sum of Hengham, but let such things be
entertained no longer than they have relish, for though it
is profitable to understand them, it is not reasonable to
throw away the first time about it, that should be better
employed: at length these will become intelligible of
course.   Next to LITTLETON without any Comment, I should
advise to take into solemn course PLOWDEN'S Commentaries,
and to join, at intervals FITZHERBERT'S Natura Brevium,
and CROMPTON'S Jurisdiction of Courts; there is also
STAUNFORD'S Pleas of the Crown, with the book at the end
De Prerogativa Regis, and MANWOOD'S Forest Law, all of
which are institutionary, and must be read at one time, or
another, so, as the fancy takes, this or that may have a
preference, and variety will be found a considerable
relief in a course of study.   The Natura Brevium gives
full light into the nature of most common law process, but
it is useful to have near at hand the Registrum Brevium,
because many processes are there, not in the Natura, and
no information, or description, can be so well to explain
a process, as the form itself, and for the same reason it
is good to have within reach some of the books of entries,
as RASTAL, COKE, &c.; for if you would understand what
counts, bars, pleas, replications, demurrers, and joining
issues, and the like are, there you may read the form of
them, which speaks all that is to be known of them.   But
Plowden is now sur la tap is, and that I would have read
all over.   I know it will seem tedious, because it is a
collection of the prolix stating cases at the bar, and the
no less extended arguments of the Serjeants' pleadings,
and the Judges' resolving them.   But therein is the profit
to the student, for these extended discourses make the
sense of what they speak clear, and very much variety of
law and authority is incidentally brought to embellish as

well as enforce your arguments, and all in a very proper
style and expression, most fit to make an early impression
in a student's memory, and after all the book carries much
authority in the law, and is cited for proof, being
authentic as any other book is. It will be expected now,
that I say what I think of the Year Books, which were
Reports taken by officers assigned for that purpose, and
registered under the order of years of the Kings' reigns
and terms. The number of the folios usually concludes
with the year, so they are thus called, an. 23 Ed. 3. fol.
4. About the time of Dyer there was little or no learning
of the law, but from Year Books, and there was scope
enough, for they swelled into ten considerable volumes, so
that those great pains-takers of the law, Fitzherbert and
Brook, thought it fit to abridge them, under titles which
indeed were but then common-place books carefully adjusted
or regulated. These are called the Grand Abridgments, but
of such I say no more, only this, that a student must have
a care of dealing in abridgments, indexes, and common
places, which are all his enemies; his business is with
the books themselves; and his own common place, if ever he
makes any, however imperfect it prove, is better for his
own use than all the others that are extant put together;
but I shall have to touch that afterwards. Now as
touching the Year Books, I cannot propose them all to be
read carefully, and in course, because I know the work is
too immense, and the age not studious enough to promise a
compensation for so much pains, nor is there any that
apply themselves so desperately to study, as that
requires. But I must say, that if there even riseth a
genius that shall have strength of body, and ambition of
mind, joined with a resolution to conquer the learning of
the law, he will not skip over the Year Books, but, as the
great Hales did, read them all, and moreover all the old
musty registers and records that he could come at, and he
thought useful to be understood. Industry and order in
the law ceased with order and peace in the State, for
after Noy, who was captain of the band, followed by Jones,
Windham, Rolls, Glynn, Maynard and Hales, all such as I
have described, and most of them survived the troubles,
and shone sufficiently after the Reformation, and showed
that preferment in the law may be acquired by great
learning, and ability, more surely than by fortune; for
those had none of her favours extraordinary; but when such
are not extant, fortune must choose; but still they, even
in that wheel, have a great advantage, that by study make
themselves capable of her favours, and who may lay hold of
such benefits when they proffer, without shame or
blushing, whereas there are, and ever will be, many, and
every day more and more, who cannot venture into advanced
parts of the law, for want of foundation. But, to return
to the books, I must own the task is much more
insupportable of taking them into course, because of the
superfetation of modern Reports published since the time
of Dyer to ours, the very names of which are a catalogue
of a large class, and it is fit that a lawyer should be
acquainted with them all, at least in some measure, for a
lawyer should know every decisive case reported in the

books, or blush at his defect.   And I must add, that if
the Year Books were taken into course, it must not be
here; it is too early; they are too abstruse and difficult
for a student to batter through, but thus much I must
require as necessary for a tolerable common lawyer, that
after Plowden, he take in hand the Year Book that is
called Hen. 7th; which is accounted the most explicit in
expression and matter, and very many of the chief law
matters now evidently known, were considered, debated, and
resolved there; and it gives an idea of the manner of
practice, and expression of the law in that time, and
enables a student to read the other books of the Annals,
or to understand them, if he has occasion to consult or
peruse any cases referred to there.   For these reasons,
that Year Book is recommended to students.   Together with
this may be read some of my Lord Coke's Institutionary
Pieces, as his Pleas of the Crown, Jurisdiction of Courts,
and Comments (these truly so) upon Magna Charta, and the
old statutes; these will bring a remission over the other,
and relieve the fatigue that will be found in dwelling too
long upon it.   When this is done, I should advise to enter
upon some of the more modern Reports, used to be
recommended, LEONARD'S, HOBART'S, MOOR and PALMERS', not
forgetting CROOK.   But I shall soon have too many, so we
stop after one or two of them, and then look back, where
we find two books which must not be omitted, that is,
THELWALL and DYER; the former has matters concerning the
old law of Franchises and Iters, not found in any other
book, and the latter is a sans peer for conciseness and
profound judgment.   DYER is a book that will bear a second
reading in course, after most of the other books of
Reports are dispatched, and the latter reading shall be
with more profit incomparably than the former.   When we
are got thus far, then it will be time to take in hand my
LORD COKE'S Reports; these will not come so well, before a
good foundation is laid out of the older books; this is a
considerable branch, and therefore should be carefully and
attentively treated, because the reputation of Coke, and
the wonderful and specious formality of his Reports, have
given them an authority in the law superior to most
others; and, to say truth, as he was a most affected
formalizer, his works are very apt for forming a student,
and his Institutes have very much useful learning.   It may
be wondered I have not yet noted him upon LITTLETON, but
the reason has been touched; but further now I must
observe, that it is the confusion of a student, and breeds
more disorder in his brains than any other book can, that
is not a mere index and abridgment; for this Commentary,
so called, is only a common-place book exhausted, and the
titles disposed, after the alphabetical order, into that
as may follow the text of Littleton, and bating the small
application to the text, more often impertinent than
otherwise.   The subject matter is extract of controversial
law, which a student ought to gather for himself; for he
will never thoroughly understand it, at least not retain
it in his mind, when it is of another's gathering.   No one
ever learnt a language by reading of a Dictionary; so no
man can be a lawyer by reading Indexes, Abridgments, and

Common Places such as this upon Littleton is. There are
many sorts of such Common Places called Abridgments, which
carry no other countenance: some under heads, as the
Grand Abridgment, and some under Maxims, as Wingate and my
Lord Bacon's, in a small piece, and Hugh's Boroughs, the
modern Cases and Resolutions under titles, Jenkin's Cases
adjudged. Shepherd has a body of law under titles; these
are all useful as Repertories, to consult and find out
where the authorities lie, and to furnish arguments, but
are by no means to be read or looked upon, but
occasionally as was said. It has been observed, that a
student never takes a just impression of law but from the
case itself, where it is most largely debated; for the
much altercation works it into his memory, whereas, if he
has the bare point adjudged, and nakedly delivered to him,
it enters at one ear, as they say, and goes out at the
other. The reason is, resolutions of law are mostly
independent of each other, and not like mathematical
propositions that have a perpetual connection, and this is
meant by that trite saying, proestat petere fontes quam
sectari rivulos. That of Coke upon Littleton being of a
mixed sort, is allowed to be read in course, after some
progress in the books of Reports, of which little account
as to order is to be given. And since there are such
abundance of these, it is enough to leave it to a
student's fancy to take where he pleaseth, so as he reads
them in fit manner; it is not of great import which, 1st,
2d, or 3d, nor is it a work here to give a character of
the Reports, though some are better than others; it may
suffice to say that KEEBLE only is esteemed under value;
GODBOLT, GOLDSBOROW and MARCH mean, but yet not to be
rejected; DYER, MOOR, YELVERTON, ANDERSON, PALMER, CROOK,
JONES, SIDERFIN, ROLLES, and several others of note are
not to be passed by. So to conclude this head of reading,
if more of the Year Books are taken in hand, they will
come well after Coke's Reports and the Institutes, but if
the obsolete law be any discouragement, I would as a cure
refer the student to read the Preface to Rolles' Grand
Abridgment.
        The next considerable article in our student's
process is common placing. It is so necessary, that
without a wonderful, I might say miraculous felicity of
memory, three parts of reading in four shall be utterly
lost to one who useth it not. Reading may form a
capacity, create a judgment, and perhaps in time make the
law pleasant as well as easy; but without common placing,
it will not obtain the useful part, that is, authority and
resort to books. It will often happen that a man shall
hear a question of law stated, and remember that he has
read some case or other very apposite to, if not the very
question in point resolved, somewhere in the books, and if
he would give all he is worth, he cannot recover where it
is to be found. This is a Crevecoeur, and it is not to be
imagined what a solicitude and loss of time this will
create in searching vainly where to find it out. Now he
that common places along with his reading, runs straight
to his book; and knowing the method, probably at first
finds it out. But if it be a matter that may with equal

propriety fall under several titles, then he has two or
more to look over, and perhaps divers, and not hit on the
right.   This is not loss but gain of time, for the very
perusing the common-place book, and the many entries there
which will be taken notice of, besides what is searched
for there, will refresh the memory in divers other points
that are not in his inquisition; for these entries being
his own, bring to his mind the case at large, the book,
and many other circumstances that occurred in his reading,
beside what was noted, and hath an unthought-of virtue in
improving, or at least retaining in, or, it may be
recovering in what one has once read; and in regard that
judgment grows with study and more with experience, it is
of more use to recover a case to the memory when the
judgment is ripe to esteem and value it, than it was at
first to read and set it down.   Now this advantage is not
had from perusing Indexes, Common-places, or Abridgments
of others, for there no more is known than what falls
under the eye, and that, perhaps, so short and imperfecT
that it breeds in the mind rather confusion than the
distinction and information of Law.   But, by accident, one
may light on notable discoveries of books and authorities
by such helps, but they are subservient to practice only,
but as to study they are pestiferous and treacherous
helps, and to be avoided rather than any way used.   this
is the use, or, in fitter terms, necessity of a
Common-place.   The next thing is the manner of conducting
it, and that, to students, is usually a profound secret;
for how should young men be inventors of methods that are
the result of art and consummate experience?   therefore I
propose first the furniture, which is a good, large, paper
book, as big (with some) as a church bible, but moderation
must have place with a beginner, who must conclude his
first attempts condemned to loss.   For as scribendo disces
scribere, so by essaying a common-place you learn to make
one, and whoever doth not bestow a fruitless beginning
shall never know a fruitful conclusion of his studies.
The next furniture is a set of titles, which must be had
either from some other common-place book, or from a
printed set of titles, and these must be wrote at the head
of pages, or rather columns, for three, or two at least,
in a page, are convenient, allowing spaces blank under
them, more or less, as the plenty of matter to fall under
the several titles is foreseen, more or less, wherein the
error, if any there be, is not material, provided the
student is not niggard of paper, and allow enough.   Thus
for the furniture.   Next I recommend the use of a small,
but legible and distinct hand, which in a common-place
book must be affected, for room will be required, and a
fair, French hand will eat upon it too fast; therefore, by
all means, practice a most minute character for the
purpose, and not illegible.   Then for the titles.   It is
the fault of affected methodists to derive matters from a
few generals, and so make most of your titles by way of
subdivision.   This is the fault of the printed titles, as
also of the table to Keeble's Statutes at large.   For
under the title Administration, you find the titles
Executors, Devastavit, Wills, Legacies, Probates, &c.

which is very faulty in respect to use, which requires all
or most to be distinct or general titles and few or no
subdivisions, or, at least, such only as are So apposite
as not to be mistakan; such as under Executors, Executors
de son tort, and the like. Whoever begins a common-place
book must be beholden to some friend for a list of titles,
and if they would be satisfied of the manner, I should
refer to Lincoln's-Inn Library, where the Lord Hale's
Common-place book is conserved, and that may be a pattern,
instar omnium.
     Then next, it is considerable to know the manner of
noting or entering in a common-place book; we find in the
laborious tables of many, only references, as to say where
an Executor shall be charged in his own estate and where
not. This is almost useless, for nothing is gathered from
perusing the entry, without perusing also the books, which
is great labour, and, perhaps, after all, nothing to the
purpose you enquire of, and also a great loss of time.
But a short note of the law, or sum of the book or case,
should be set down in print, by which you may know at
first view if it be to your purpose or not, as thus -- If
Executor assents to a legacy, and there be not assets, it
is a Devastavit; and then add the book by name and folio,
never omitting the name of the case. A good lawyer may
write at the end of his own Common-place book sparsa
coegi, for the business of a student in order to practice
is the collecting as many controverted points, nice
distinctions, and opinions, as well as resolutions of
judges, as he can. In which design his Common-place book
must be a succedaneum to his frail memory, and when he
finds the name and the case in his Common-place book he is
provided to wield the weapon as occasion requires, for
capping of books and book-cases by name is the great
ostentation of a put-case sudent and practising Lawyer,
and nothing more brings fame and credit to him. The end
and aim of a Lawyer is duplex, 1st to know, and 2d to
appear to know -- that latter brings in Clients, and the
former holds them. Such as are washy and feeble horses
will fail in conduct and argument as they in a journey,
and therefore all the art and assistance one can have in
this great work of being and appearing a good Lawyer is
but little enough.
     I think I next proposed conversing and mentioned the
advice of Sir Heneage Finch to study all the morning and
talk all the afternoon. I have heard Serjeant Maynard say
the law is Ars bablativa, meaning that all the learning in
the world will not set a man up in the bar practice
without a faculty of a ready utterance of it, and that is
acquired by a habit only, unless there be a natural
felicity of such; such as the family of the Finches are
eminent by. Where nature gives not, industry must
purchase. They say Demosthenes used to speak to the sea
with pebbles in his mouth to enable him to conquer an
impediment in his speech, and that the brutish noise of
the people might not with its importunity disturb him.
And he whose trade is speaking must not, whatever comes
on't, fail to speak, for that is a fault in the main much
worse than impertinence. When that is done, care must be

taken of subject matter; after that a man may let fly and his words be trusted; however, _audendum tamen_, time and practice will correct failings and acquire better performance. The expedient proposed for this is society, and 'tis said for every end of life desirable, for the fate of men's lives is too often determined to good or evil by their company, and as the choice of company is more nice and difficult, so are the hazards of young gentlemen's swinging into utter perdition greater; but a student of the law hath more than ordinary reason to be curious in his conversation, and to get such as are of his own pretension, that is, to study and improvement, and I will be bold to say that they shall improve one another by discourse as much as all their other study without it could improve them. There is seldom a time but in every Inn of Court there is a studious sober company that are select to each other, and keep company at meals and refreshments. Such a society did Mr. Pool find out, whereof Serjeant Wild was one, and every one of them proved eminent, and most of them are now preferred in the law, and Mr. Pool at the latter end of his life took such a pride in his company that he affected to furnish his chambers with their pictures. There are many reasons that demonstrate the use of society in the study of the law -- 1st. Regulating mistakes; oftentimes a man shall read and go away with a sense clear contrary to the book, and he shall be as confident as if he were in the right; this his companion shall observe, and sending him to the book, rectify his mistake. 2d. Confirming what he has read. For that which was confused in the memory, by rehearsing will clear up and become distinct, and so more thoroughly understood and remembered. 3d. Aptness to speak. For a man may be possessed of a book-case, and think he has it _ad unguem_ throughout, and when he offers at it shall find himself at a loss, and his words will not lie right and be proper, or perhaps too many, and his expression confused; when he has once talked his case over, and his company have tossed it a little to and fro, then he shall utter it more readily with fewer words and much more force. Lastly, the example of others, and learning from them many things which would not have been otherwise known. In fine, the advantages of a fit society are to a student superior to all others put together, and I shall not go about to make a complete catalogue of them.

I come now to another article which is reporting, that is, attending the Courts of Justice, and there observing what passes, and noting down what is thought material, for the doing which most of the law books called Reports are a pattern, for they are but the debates, arguments, and resolutions of controversial law, noted down for memory by some Counsel or Judge whose eminence gives them reputation and value. The custom of having solemn Reporters determined with the Year Books only Hetley was later, who, I think, values himself upon having been a Reporter assigned. Of later times, Reports have teemed from the press, more from the profit of the copy than any good to the law, for the opinions and resolutions begin to contradict one another so much that a selection

is fit to be made and the rest suppressed, and as they
are, they load a student's time most intolerably, for most
think they are obliged to know them and study them
accordingly, whereof the worst consequence is, that the
older and more authentic and valuable books of the law are
slighted and passed by.   But this out of place: the
business in hand is the attendance of the students upon
the Courts of Justice, there to report for themselves as
well as they can; this is done not so much to learn by
collecting of law, but to observe the course of the court
and method of practice, that they may learn the phrase and
language of the Court, and know how Counsel behave
themselves towards it, and what the Court expects from
Counsel, and in a word the expetenda and fugiendus in
practice, against they come there themselves.   And without
this introduction, it must needs be thought, how raw and
incompetent gentlemen must be that prefer themselves in
business.   I confess there is great difference in times,
and according as the Bar and Bench is supplied with men of
learning and good nature.   I have known the Court of
King's Bench sitting every day from eight till twelve, and
the Lord Chief Justice Hales managing matters of law to
all imaginable advantage to the students, and in that he
took a pleasure or rather pride; he encouraged arguing
when it was to the purpose, and used to debate with the
counsel so as the court might have been taken for an
academy of Sciences as well as the seat of justice.   And
in other times business has shrunk, the Judges not
appearing till eleven in the morning, and then being very
short and hasty in their dispatches, ruling things without
debate, and not enduring their own rules to be disputed;
and more than this, what with the many discouragements and
perverseness of times, few or no suitors will be at the
cost of upholding arguments, and the business of that
court reduced to matters of course, and when disputes
happen they are altogether about factious wrangles in
corporations upon mandamus and returns, and actions
grounded thereon, which have little or no learning
depending upon them, and the spirit of the causes moving
rather from factious spirits than doubts of law; so that
it is a more reasonable account of attending there for
news, and to hold forth in coffee-houses, than to trouble
pen and paper with noting.   Now I observe two errors in
the direction of students to this matter -- 1st. that
they go to the courts too soon; 2d. that they attend at
the wrong place. 1st. What the advantage by attending is
at court.   It is certain that more law is to be gathered
by reading than at court, and if it were not for practice
it were better not to come there, but to take the cases
resolved that are fit to be known from report of others,
and employ the morning, which is the prime of their time,
in their chamber reading and common-placing.   Now it is
usual after a year or two's residence in the Inns of
Court, for all students to crowd for places in the King's
Bench Court, when they are raw and scarce capable of
observing any thing materially, for that requires some
competent knowledge, and the bad consequence is that it
makes them pert and forward, and apt to press to the bar

when they are not half students, and that is the downfall
of more young lawyers than all other errors and neglects
whatever. For this reason I would not have any lose time
from their studies after this manner till after four or
five years' study, and two years afore they come to the
bar, which should not be before seven of study, is more
than enough, especially when to get a place they must be
very early, and idle about, or worse, till the court sits,
and then with little more profit than such may expect that
come only to hear news. Nay, it will be found that form
some years after calling to the bar their best employment
will be that of sitting there and reporting, as I know
full well, without more of refreshment than a motion or
two in a term. This length of time in the approaches to
practice must be endured, for what inconvenience is it
when a man has once firmly dedicated his whole life to the
law? If any good fortune invites to any steps forwarder,
there he is to embrace the opportunity; if not, he cannot
be secure of moderate success in the profession, but by
entering by proper means, and not per saltum, leaping over
hedge and ditch to come at it. An egg may have more than
its natural heat, but will hatch or be addle; therefore,
let the motions be rather phlegmatic than mercurial, for
it is a true saying, soon ripe soon rotten. The other
error is going to the King's Bench and not the Common
Pleas. It is said the Common Law is at home in the Common
Pleas, but a guest in the King's Bench; and it is certain
that the business of that Court is less pregnant of law
than at the Common Bench. The causes of the Crown,
Corporations, matters of the Peace and concerning the
Government, take up most of that little time they allow
there, which, as I said, are more faction and wrangle
there than law. But at the Common Pleas there is little
but merely matters of law agitated; they proceed by
originals; the processes are those of the Common law;
whatever disputes may happen in the main, there will not
want many touching the proceedings, that is, of Essoins,
Defaults, Appearances, Returns, &c. very fit for a lawyer
to know, for he may hope in time to be at the Coif, and
then he will have need enough of all his observations.
Therefore my advice is, that a student shall bestow two
years before he is called to the Bar, the first at the
Common Pleas and the last at the King's Bench, and if any
shall say the latter is not enough to learn the course of
the court where he is to practice, I answer, that will be
supplied after he is called to the bar, for his business
for some years will not so overwhelm his time but he will
have much lying on his hands for noting and observing the
course of the Court, for the law gathered is very
inconsiderable while he attends at the bar in quality of a
practiser; and there is further reason to prefer
attendance at the Common Pleas, it is not so crowded as
the King's Bench is; a gentleman may come at ten in the
morning and have a place, but there he may come at six and
fail of a tolerable post to attend in, the difference of
which, as to the well employment of your time, is
notorious enough: if it be considered what three or four
hours in a morning is in study, it will not be thought fit

to throw it away in idle attendance. Lastly, it remains
to speak of practice. But that is so far off, when the
discourse is to a student at his first entrance, as all
insinuations about it may be well spared, and when
gentlemen come so forward they will scarce think
themselves to seek what belongs to their calling; and
besides it is a large field, and admits more accurate
reflections than this dispatch will permit, and if
occasion were, I could furnish some hints from a curious
hand, as may be done in due time: therefore at present I
shall only repeat the caution I have already touched, that
the student doth not rush upon it too soon; that observed,
and the antecedent time well employed, a gentleman cannot
fail of success in his profession, such as shall amply
compensate all his pains, make him generally esteemed and
courted, and at length and so probably as may accounted in
his turn earlier or later as it may happen to be taken
into preferment and authority, and so conclude his days
with honour, and the felicity of having an estate to leave
of his own getting.
      A reporter ought to have two books, one for his notes
in the court, and the other for writing them over fair
into, and it should be the afternoon's work never to be
omitted, the transcribing from the note-book into the fair
book, and correcting from the memory then fresh, all cases
and matters of law that were thought worth the noting in
the morning, and then this fair book will ever be useful
and intelligible, whereas the note-book shall be so
disorderly wrote, that after a little time the reader
himself shall scarce know what to make of it. Some are so
careful to examine all the books cited, and many have
acquired short-hand, pretending to take every word, but
this latter I do not think so well, because, if a student
understand the point and the reasons, he will be able to
set them down short and plain to himself while others are
speaking, and so he practises to contract and to write
material and short, but taking every word makes him not
careful to distinguish between what is pertinent and what
not, and of what usually passes in the courts the former
is thin spread, and the latter not very scarce. It is a
great advantage to have access to the company of Judges or
men in eminent practice, for such are commonly very
condescending and friendly to young men who are out of all
emulation with them, and they will be pleased to instil
notions of law, and some are not better entertained than
with putting cases to them and taking their answers, which
given with judgment and modesty, is very engaging, and
sometimes has created friendships that have been
introductive into great preferments. The keeping of
Courts Leet and Baron is a most useful practice to a
student, and as it is the lowest of employments in the
law, so fittest to begin at, for no ground is so sure as
that which is gained by inches. Some have been so unhappy
by good fortune, if I may so say, to be let into business
at the upper end, for cessante causa cessat effectus. The
favour removed, they could never maintain their post; and
after that, it was more difficult to recover any ground,
than for a student that creeps in by degrees to gain it.

Court-keeping exercises a dealing with country people, and shows their humours, and which way to surround them. Besides, there is a practice of dispatch, a management of authority, and the use of forms; this latter is of more consequence than one would imagine. I knew a Lord Keeper, when first a student, kept courts, and made up all his rolls, and wrote the copies with his own hands, and having no means to keep a clerk, thought he did not foul his fingers in so doing. It is a vulgar observation, that the attornies get ground of the long robe, as it is called, the reason of which is, the gown has derelicted the practice of forms, so that all is now left to them; and such as profess only to afford a little discourse and take money, shall not be applied to, but for necessity, when their advice is wanted, and it is not one business of a thousand that comes them; the former part is nearer the client than the counsel. I have heard Serjeant Maynard say he has several times gone the western circuit on foot, and that no attorney made breviate of more than the pleadings, but that the counsel themselves perused and noted the evidences; if deeds, by perusing them in his chamber, if witnesses, by examining them there also before the trial, and so were never deceived in the expected evidence, as now the contrary happens, the evidence seldom or never comes up to the brief, and counsel are forced to ask which is the best witness. But the abatement of such industry and exactness, with a laziness also, or rather superciliousness, whereby the practice of law forms is slighted by counsel, the business, of course, falls to the attornies. I forgot to take notice of the elder compilers of the law, Bracton, Britton, and Fleta. Who would have an historico-critical account of them will find it in the dissertation of Selden at the end of Fleta. It is certain in their time they contained the body of the common law, and in fit cases they are authority, and are cited at this day, my Lord Coke says, for ornament, which is a jest. The clergy then were Judges and Serjeants, so they affected the form and model of the civil law, and compiled methodically in Latin, as appears by Bracton and Fleta. But time has so antiquated these books, that they are become useless in a regular course of study, and they are to be looked into chiefly for curiosity and accomplishment, for the more books a lawyer reads well, the more curious and inquisitive will his knowledge of the laws and history of them be. And to say truth, although it is not necessary for counsel to know what the history of a point is, but to know how it now stands resolved, yet it is a wonderful accomplishment, and without it a lawyer cannot be accounted learned in the laws. And for the history of the law, its rise is to be taken from Glanville, who was Cap. Justic. Angliae, when, after the Conquest, the law, as it was then, a compound of the Norman principally, and then, as subject to it, a little of the inferior Saxon institution, was licked into some tolerable form, since which it has received change enough.
   These books I put for the course, with aids.
   Course   Aids

Littleton.   Terms of the Law.
Perkins.   Diversity of Courts
            Old Tenures, and Doctor and Student.

            Fitzherbert's Natura Brevium.
Plowden.   Crompton's Jurisdiction of Courts.
            Staunford's Pleas of the Crown.

            Coke's Jurisdiction of Courts.
Hen. 7   ------ Pleas of the Crown.
Keilway   ------ Commentary on Magna Charta.

Leonard   Petit Book.
Coke's Reports.   Coke on Littleton.
Dyer.   Bracton.
Moor.   Britton.
Crook.   Fleta.
Palmer.   Glanville.

Here may be supplied what was too short touched about
common placing, a thing that much retards reading, and
will be thought at first very troublesome; but there is a
knack or dexterity acquired by practice that will make it
more easy. For it is very tedious to write at length as
verbatim out of the book, therefore a student is to use
himself to contract the sense of a case, point, or period,
as thus: -- be the sentence, that an executor who assents
to a specific legacy, not having assets to satisfy the
testator's debts, shall be charged of his own estate as
for a wasting, write only thus -- assent to legacy sans
assets, devastavit -- and by this, other instances may be
imagined to show the compendium necessary to be made in
common placing, and how it may be done; and a student must
be very attentive about it, and thereby he will exercise,
and at length get a habit of extracting the material part
of a business, and to develope the accoutrements, as well
as to abridge his pains in writing. He must expect to
lose his first pains as well as the paper and book he
uses, though this is not to be thrown away; and the second
undertaking will go on well, and the book be a vade-me-cum
as long as he lives. All the words and discourse in the
world will not give such an idea of this work as one
month's practice; and the use of the pen must never be
grudged, but, as a horseman's sword, it must always be
ready, if not drawn.

                    FINIS

      Section of Notes & Illustrations Omitted

– 3 –

Thomas Wood

Some Thoughts Concerning the Study of the Laws of England in the Two Universities (1708)

REVEREND SIR:

I have received my kinsman from your hands, and thank you for your care of his education; particularly for that sense of true piety and loyalty with which he is endowed. My friends assure me that the young man can give a tolerable account of the old and new philosophy, and that he is not ignorant of the finesses in the classicks.

He is designed for the priesthood, and is now of age to enter into Holy Orders. In encourage his intentions, as suitable to his genius and inclinations; and because a noble Lord has promised to take him into his house, and provide for him.

But after all my hopes that he may raise his family, I must beg your pardon if I complain that he is very ignorant of the world, and of mankind, that he seems to have a positive, self-conceited and despising way with him in every thing he says or does, for want of conversation with wiser men than himself, and an inbred contempt of two things, the knowledge whereof is almost necessary to give one a distinguishing character. I mean a general knowledge of the laws of his country and some insight into business.

As to the latter, it is indeed of so comprehensive a nature, that a discourse on that subject ought to be directed to those who have the government of a nobleman, that can bear the expense of particular tutors qualified for that purpose. For to instruct a youth in the knowledge of men and business, it will be requisite to teach him how to command his temper; to be cautious and reserved; to reason well; to speak fluently; to converse inoffensively, and not to have a mean opinion of any man; to bear insolence and rudeness, slander and reproaches with patience and decency; and then, upon all opportunities, to prompt him to make observations upon every man's calling and profession, (particularly in mechanical trades and husbandry) and to have some knowledge in the way of bartering, and the price of commodities, &c. which will take up a governor's whole

employ, and can scarce be thought a proper undertaking for
an university tutor; tho' an acquaintance with one in each
profession would much forward this knowledge of business;
and tho' this sort of learning is of more value than a
thousand systems of empty and fruitless theories.

But my kinsman is extremely ignorant even in dealing
for what he wants; has no opinion of frugality, is ashamed
to cheapen any thing, gives every man his first price when
he buys; and thinks all the world as honest as himself.
And indeed many young scholars know not the value of their
own books, or of the cloaths which they wear; upon which
account the education of a youth in the universities in
much more chargeable than is necessary. And yet <u>this</u>
mischief might be prevented by the oversight of a common
tutor, and a few instructions, without prejudice to his
other studies; and might tend to his advantage in many
respects, as well as be a means to invite parents to send
their children to those learned societies; who often
dispose of them another way, as not being able to allow of
so expensive an education. This learning (I say) of
buying necessaries wisely, might be expected to be taught
by those that have the care of the ordinary scholars; tho'
pains and expense are requisite to teach the knowledge of
<u>business</u> in a larger extent. Therefore I shall insist no
longer on that point, because there is no fault in your
government upon that score.

But for the <u>laws</u> of our country, they ought to have a
part in the education of an <u>English</u> gentleman, for they
come under the topik of learning, and ought to be rang'd
within the method of his studies, to qualify a young man
to have some insight into <u>business</u> too. Here then, I do
blaime your Constitution, that you have not yet been
convinc'd of the necessity of teaching young scholars the
<u>grounds</u> of that useful part of knowledge, which may be
done without any extraordinary trouble or charge. I do
not mean so much of our law only as is to be collected
from our <u>English</u> histories, (histories that delight and
instruct at the same time in civil prudence, and the
knowledge of the manners of our people, and yet are much
neglected) but so much of it too as may lead one into the
rules of right and wrong in relation to private property,
without meddling with the wrangling or captious part of
it.

Those that intend to make the law their <u>calling</u> must
constantly attend the highest courts, otherwise it will be
impossible to be masters of the practice, without hearing
the debates of the council, and the opinions of the
learned judges upon it. But then considering that you
have many persons amongst you of the nobility, who think
themselves above the study of the common law with the
ordinary students in the Inns of Court; and others who
care not to fetch that compass in their studies; because
of the charge or tediousness of it; and others design'd
for the priesthood, who, by custom, are in a manner barr'd
those societies; I wonder that such youths are not
instructed in their colleges at home in a <u>general</u> and
<u>compendious</u> knowledge of our laws, and the reason of them,
that they may understand what they hear or read upon that

subject; and that the publick may have the benefit of
their academical learning joined with it.

The excellent Bishop <u>Stillingfleet</u> hath shewn the way
how scholars ought to study the law, and what progress may
be made by a <u>private</u> search.   He hath written so
accurately upon some subjects of it, that none of the long
robe have hitherto pretended to correct him.   His argument
in the house of Peers (to settle peace and quietness in
our universities) upon the case of <u>Philips</u> and <u>Bury</u>,
concerning the visitational power, then an abstruse
question, was never yet answered; tho', for some reasons,
I believe, he had the assistance of an excellent argument
delivered in the <u>Queen's-Bench</u>, before he thought upon
that subject.   If that worthy prelate had had a due
respect paid to his skill in our laws, he might have
presided in our highest Courts of Justice with as much
reputation to the publick, as ever any ecclesiastic before
him.   And there are now some eminent divines living, who
have a great insight into the general parts of our common
law, from an occasional and private enquiry into our
books.

In the universities there are publick professors of
the <u>Roman</u> law, and lectures read in the schools upon some
general titles of it.   And young men think themselves
obliged to read an <u>Institute</u> of the imperial law, and a
comment upon the title <u>De Regulis Juris</u>; and then to study
<u>Grotius</u> and <u>Puffendorf</u>.   Every one who pretends to be a
scholar, ought to read thus far in the Civil law, and to
know the best books in that profession.   These two last
authors have drain'd out of many volumes of the Civil law,
the greatest part of the rational learning concerning the
natural rights of mankind, which our <u>English</u> lawyers do
not disallow of.   But if you go farther in this study,
have a care lest you take a fancy, (as too many have done)
of bringing our laws to the standard of the Civil law in
<u>every point</u>, and without enquiry what is in use, or not;
because it sets the understanding of an <u>English</u>-man upon a
wrong biass, and makes him less capable of serving at home
in many publick stations.   A Civil lawyer in the House of
Commons, in my memory, was an instance of this truth, who,
upon every debate, would be amusing the House with
authorities out of the <u>Digest</u> and <u>Code</u>, and giving them to
understand how matters have been heretofore managed in the
<u>Rota</u>, or <u>Imperial Chamber</u>; whereas some of our own lawyers
think themselves as wise as <u>Papinian</u> or <u>Ulpian</u>, having the
advantage of coming after them; and some of our senators
as good judges of reason, and of what is proper to be
done, as any foreign assemblies, or tribunals.   The
civilian might have spoke more to the purpose if he had
cited texts out of the book of <u>Numbers</u> and <u>Deuteronomy</u>,
and told them how affairs stood formerly in the Sanbedrim.
The Common law has long since borrow'd almost all that's
worth knowing from the <u>Romans</u>.   The niceties of their
<u>practice</u> is of no use.   The most learned advocates in our
<u>Arch-Bishops-Courts</u>, very seldom cite authorities in
relation to <u>that</u> part; but after a plain method of <u>process</u>
laid down, have an eye upon the <u>laws of England</u> in their
determinations, when plausible reasons plead for them.   So

that this study may be encouraged under the management of a judicious person, of one that is not a pedant, or a bigot to it.

The Canon law is also read and practised within the universities: and even divines think themselves under a necessity to read the Institutes drawn up by Lancellot or Corvinus, and to consult the Decrees and the Decretals with the chief canonists for settling of cafes of conscience, and to inform themselves in church-history. This method also is so far commendable; and if divines would inspect the registers of our ecclesiastical courts, and Clark, as to the general practice, they might be sufficiently qualified for the offices in those courts; the profits of which honorable posts are often of necessity given to the laity over the clergy, (furnishing our enemies with a specious objection against our ecclesiastical government) because the clergy are generally unfit for them. As to the common business, Lynwood, Degg, Godolphin, Watson, &c. are the oracles which our best canonists will vouchsafe to consult upon all occasions; and every student may quickly learn the skill of turning to an Index, as well as the most celebrated practisers.

Some other arts and sciences taught in the universities scarce deserve the pains and labor employ'd about them: The nut is so hard or so dry, that it is not worth while to crack it for the sake of the kernel. And certainly, that cannot be learning, which is of no use to the publick. We must do by these, (while we grow in years) as some do by their young university acquaintance, shake them off by degrees, and endeavor to forget them. For that which may be commendable in a young wit, may be impertinence in an old one. Learning which makes men wise is principally to be sought after: or if we study words at first, we ought to study things afterwards. A prudent man need not be asham'd that he has not spent many years in turning over books of logical and methaphysical disputations, in composing Greek and Latin orations, (compositions in English upon moral and political subjects, will be more useful) in sweating over the poets, or in versifying; in criticisms, or searching out the various readings on prophane authors, in chronological niceties, or in some sort of Greek and Roman antiquities, or on subjects which have been always disputable, and will be to the end of the world. 'Twas a satisfactory saying of Themistocles, -- That he knew how to raise a city from a low to a flourishing state, tho' he could not play upon a fiddle. Not but that some few may be allow'd to labour in such amusements for their own satisfaction, (and that they might not employ their parts to the disturbance of the publick) or for the diversion of thinking men, who are really scholars; or to cure the melancholly and spleen of those that would be thought so. But three or four in an university are enough to set forth such an entertainment as every town thinks it self well enough provided for, if it maintains only but one set of musick, whether good or bad.

Since then other arts and sciences are less moment are esteemed to be a part of academical learning; why must our own laws, the Common Law of England be banished thence, and young scholars in a manner debarred that study? It is infinitely of more use amongst us, even than the Civil and Canon laws; for it is twisted and interwoven almost into all manner of discourse and business, comprehending almost all that is valuable with us in those laws. And surely he was in the right, who advised, "To apply ones self more to necessary studies, than to those for which we may seldom or never have occasion."

To see men of vast study, and pretending to variety of knowledge, not able to read one of our records in the original, or the laws of their own country in its proper language, or to be ignorant of the nature of a freehold, fine, recovery, or the way how estates real or personal descend, or may be convey'd; or to talk impertinently and wide upon a common point, it must of necessity create a mean opinion of them in the standers by and render them contemptible under the smiles of a Sollicitor.

Because of this ignorance you may often hear our lawyers say, that they had rather have any other clients than clergymen or scholars; for they ask so many odd questions, and will have a reason for every thing in their own way: whereas a good reason in the schools is not always a good reason in a Court. And 'tis because of this one defect why our lawyers generally despise the clergy, and think them unfit to be employed in any publick station out of their ordinary sphere; and that thence the clergy, (being conscious of that defect) raise in themselves early prejudices against the profession of the Common Law as an enemy to their order; and very imprudently set themselves against those persons whom they will never (as yet) be able to engage with success.

But to persuade young scholars to the study of the Common Law, after three or four years spent in other arts and sciences, let them be inform'd, that if they qualifie themselves to read some reports or arguments in our law, they may learn from thence plainness of expression without affectation; perspicuity of method; solid reasoning without scholastick niceties: And what better end can they propose by their other studies? I may say of the Common Law, as an ingenious gentleman has said of the mathematicks, that it will accustom the mind to attention, give it a habit of close reasoning, and free it from prejudice and credulity. Yet with this advantage beyond the speculative part of the mathematicks, that a superficial knowledge of our law will be more useful than such a knowledge in the mathematicks; which will scarce serve any other purpose than to tie and untie a knot, or to furnish a man with uncommon discourse. One must be a master of that science, or else he will profit little by it.

It will be of great use to scholars in their colleges upon debates concerning the meaning of their statutes, and the power of their visitors; for that the Canon Law is the only rule to judge of them, or that visitors may execute their sentences with ecclesiastical censures, is an

exploded opinion.   They will be directed also how to
discourse more properly with their tenants or their
council, and to manage the college revenues with more
understanding, and to better advantage.   Their Governors
have greater need of this learning, because their chief
business is to direct in the temporal affairs belonging to
their societies.

Many young gentlemen of estates retire early from the
universities into the country, and are put into the
commission of the peace soon after.   Now if they are
taught here no more than the meaning of our law - terms
and their definitions, or to understand an act of
Parliament, they would be more serviceable to their
country in such stations, and not led into ridiculous
mistakes by ignorant clerks, as they too commonly are.

If our student enters at last into Holy Orders, and
is taken into the family of some person of quality as a
chaplain, he will have more esteem there on this account,
and be consulted in their secular concerns as well as
spiritual; whereas at present, (thro' the irreligion of
the age we live in) such men are frequently retain'd only
for fashion sake, and too often slighted as mere scholars.

If he is prefer'ed from thence, or the College, to a
country benefice: a general knowledge in our laws will
raise his character in the neighbourhood, and keep his
litigious parishioners in some awe.   For they will be glad
of occasions to invade his right, and to make their parson
truckle to them, because they see daily that clergymen are
frequently frighten'd into unreasonable compliances by the
power of a sordid patron, or threats of others, being
ignorant of the advantages on their own side; dreading to
swim far for fear of sinking.   An arrest of a poor vicar
is a sort of an execution; and the fight of a writ is
astonishing to him.   But were clergymen acquainted with
the little arts of attornies, or sensible of their ways of
raising false alarms, they would not be so full of
continual fears and distrust, and might apprehend that
they were not so near destruction and ruin, as they are
apt to imagine.

Heretofore clergymen studied the Canon law, when
their properties were subject to that law, and now since
our temporal courts have the rule almost in all cases, why
is there not the same reason to study our Common law?

Observe, that I suppose my clergyman to be upon his
Defence, and to stand upon his guard.   I would by no means
have him so confident of his skill, as to prosecute for
every trifle, under pretence of suing for the rights of
his church, and the benefit of his successors.   No,
nothing renders a minister of the gospel more odious to
his people, than a contentious and a craving temper.   And
if his parishioners should once foil him at law, (which if
swearing will do the business, is not a thing impossible)
they would despise him ever after, and make his life
uneasie.   I put the case as if he were under the necessity
of prosecuting or defending; and then I am confident that
he will see no reason to repent of having spent some time
in reading the Elements of our law and our acts of
Parliament, as to have skill enough to understand what he

reads in our common books or our statutes; or to put his
case right, and to apprehend the opinion of his council;
or the method how to proceed upon a probable or sure
bottom.

A general knowledge of the English laws will make him
very useful amongst his parishioners, not only to support
them against the oppression of others, but to determine
common controversies by way of arbitration amongst them.
The country farmers often disquiet themselves and others
upon mere fancy, and squander away their time and money
for advice upon very obvious matters relating to their
private concerns; but a little plain law-reasoning may
compose their minds and convince them. As this will be a
minister's duty, so he will gain the love and esteem of
his flock by it. But be sure, let him do all this for
God's sake, and never accept of a fee or present for his
pains; as necessary to avoid all suspicion of covetousness
or desire of thrusting his sickle into other mans corn.
However the abuse of good things can be no argument
against the true use of them.

Clergymen ought to study our law for their own sakes
too, because no men in the nation are under so many
forfeitures and temporal obligations, or tied to the
observance of more laws, Ecclesiastical and Civil, than
themselves. Passing over the laws which they are bound to
observe in common with other subjects: Let any one read
the Statutes of Uniformity, to qualifie himself for
institution and induction into a benefice, and I believe
he will be satisfied that the knowledge of some law is
necessary to apprehend their meaning. I never heard of
any man that performed all (that seems to be required)
exactly. It is to be wish'd that these acts were all
thrown into one plain statute, for as they stand they are
so intricate, that they are become mere snares upon the
clergy: The most zealous conformists to the doctrine and
discipline of our church have been ousted of their titles
for some small defects and omissions, which could never be
the intention of our legislators. Let any one also read
the Test Act; the Acts concerning First Fruits, and Tenth;
Simony; Residence; the Fifth of November; the Twenty-ninth
of May; the Act against Cursing and Swearing; the Statutes
concerning Marriages, Births and Baptisms; Burials in
Wollen; concerning Briefs, Beggars, & c. besides
Proclamations, Injunctions, Canons and Constitutions
almost innumerable, and he will be of my opinion, that
those laws ought, to be studied by the beneficed clergy;
and that they do require some industry to understand them
and avoid their penalties.

Perhaps the higher powers may think it convenient to
put a clergyman into the commission of the peace; this
gives him more credit and authority, especially if he has
equal knowledge in his duty with the rest of his
companions. However, this affords him an opportunity to
converse with the best men in the county, at the Assizes
and Sessions, and to improve his study, and thereby to be
able by his skill and interest to protect his brethren of
the clergy, and others, from any hard usage or oppression.
If he is cautious in his private conversation with the

gentry here, and of a merciful and healing temper, in all
probability he may have some influence.

The business of a country justice may be understood
without much difficulty: Dalton (to be consulted when a
case offers) will sufficiently instruct him in the law
concerning Felonies, Hue and Cry, Forcible Entries, Bail
and Mainprize, Breaches of the Peace, and Good Behaviour,
Settlements of the Poor, Bastard Children, Parish Rates
and Taxes, Cottages, Highways, Ale-Houses, Game,
Constables and Overseers, Lord's-Day, Swearing and
Cursing, Drunkenness, Vagrants, Watch and Ward, Waggons
and Carts, or the like common business. Kilburn will
furnish him with good forms for licenses, warrants,
Mittimus's, recognizances, orders, passes, &c. when the
law is to be put in execution out of the sessions; as
other common books will give him some directions for the
business to be done within it.

And now methinks it is no such disagreeable sight,
(as some imagine) to see the laity and clergy, (Moses and
Aaron) sit upon the bench together in a court of justice.
Probably it had been more for the interest of our clergy,
if the Bishop of the Diocese and the Elderman had
continued to sit together in the same court to this day,
as they did till the 21 year of William the Conqueror.

In some of the inferior clergy were return'd and
impanelled upon juries in causes that concerned the rights
of the church, (as they are upon tryals of a Jus
Patronatus in the spiritual courts) I see no absurdity in
it. They cannot be forced to it, but they may consent and
waive their privilege. Sure I am that experience shews it
to be folly to trust those causes wholly to a lay-jury;
half of which too often are dissenters to the establish'd
church, or well-wishers to them. They will be put into
better hands, if clergymen (acquainted a little with law
affairs) were mixed with them.

The country clergy will never live in credit or
esteem, till some of them are invested with more power and
interest in civil affairs, or more of them put into the
commission of the peace. Where the clergy are slighted,
religion will be slighted too. Now the rustics know no
difference betwixt parish priests. In their opinion all
are equally deserving, except where there is gross
immorality. Those that live with the greatest hospitality
sometimes fare the best. But as for retired sobriety,
deep learning, solid preaching, private instruction, &c.
without authority; these are vertues which seldom create
any real respect amongst the generality of them, but are
often misconstrued into covetousness, hypocrisie, ill
nature, and a troublesome behavior. They will judge only
by external appearances in their families, and the
interest they have in the country. So that if some
clergymen were armed with a little power to punish
extraordinary extravagancies, the clowns would value them
and be sooner brought to live regularly, than by good
example, or religious advice only. These will not fill
their bellies, or empty their pockets. They love where
they can get, and fear where a little of their money may
be in danger.

If a clergyman is preferr'd to a higher post, let him be assured, that there is no understanding our constitution without some knowledge in our common and statute laws. He must have studied the Prerogative, as well as the liberties of the people, and their rules concerning property; for after all the schemes that are laid down to make us a happy nation, the clergy in a more particular manner are concerned to support the monarchy in its just rights, as their truest friend. In a word, no man must pretend to govern well here in England, unless he takes our laws for his guide: And particularly my Lords the Bishops will find the advantage of this knowledge in governing Diocesses at home, by being informed in the true extent of their own power in their palaces and in their courts, and how to defend their jurisdictions; whereas for want of this learning some of them heretofore have frequently fell into great mistakes, making themselves liable to actions, or else have been often defied by most notorious offenders, who escaped punishment by discouraging them with processes out of the temporal courts; topping upon those about them, who wanted skill and ability in our laws to advise and manage the proceedings against them.

Upon these accounts the study of our laws is to be recommended to the universities for the education of your youth; especially for those who design for Holy Orders, that they may be put in a way to make farther improvements to claim their rights, and to defend themselves in the several stations which they may be afterwards called to.

But if temporal considerations will not have any influence, let it be enquired whether this study will not very much contribute to their knowledge in divinity; I mean as to the casuistical part, and the resolutions of cases of conscience: For oftentimes our duty towards God is to be regulated by the determinations of humane laws; which will make that to be reason now, which was not so before the determination. For example, the eldest son shall inherit his father's lands at the Common law; and if no sons, all the daughters equally; in Burrough English, the younger son shall be heir; and in Gavelkind, all the sons together shall inherit the land, as daughters at the Common law. Now if the question is asked, how ought lands to descend according to conscience? The law gives directions. Conscience gives it to the eldest son in one county; conscience gives it to the youngest in another; and conscience gives it to sons or daughters share and share alike in a third. And so conscience ought to follow the determination of law upon this following question, viz. A man seised in fee hath a son, and makes his will, and devises the estate to his own father: The will is written with the testator's own hand, subscribed with his name, sealed with his own coat of arms, and published in the presence of two witnesses. The son notwithstanding enters upon the land as heir, and insists, that by the Act of Parliament, 29 Car. 2 there ought to be three witnesses at the least to every devise of a freehold. I take it to be very clear, that the son is not bound to submit to his father's intention: For as the will is void in law, so it lays no obligation upon him in conscience to submit to it. And therefore I have often reflected upon the mistakes of some good men, who have perplexed others with doubts and scruples about their title to their estates; urging the design and intention of testators; and calling upon equity and conscience in opposition to the decisions of law, as if conscience and reason were never to be ruled by it.

But as an answer to all this which is advanced on behalf of the clergy, upon a supposal, that they may be now and then a little more concerned in a share of the Civil affairs: Some overrighteous men, (who think it convenient to keep the clergy low) will tell you with great demureness, "That clergymen have business enough to do if they mind their cures only; that he who has the care of souls, may spend all his time in reading, meditation, prayer, preaching, catechising, and visiting the sick: Upon which account the apostles declared, they would not leave the word of God and serve tables; tho' that employment was an office in the church."   To this effect an author, who speaks the sense of a party.   The former part of this argument may as easily be turned against lawyers, soldiers, and tradesmen; they have business enough in their own callings.   But to give a plain answer: To leave the word of God and serve tables, would be to desert their cures.   For those who served in that office were the treasurers of the church, and kept the common stock, and those estates which were laid at the apostles feet, to distribute them to the poor, as they saw occasion; which office the twelve apostles could not discharge without other assistances.   But cannot we spare a few clergymen out of fifteen thousand, to look now and then into a law book; or some few in a county to go sometimes for two or three days to the next market town, to consult with their lay friends, for the good government of the neighbourhood, without forsaking their callings? The clergy need not forsake their cures or spiritual affairs, or do any thing inconsistent with their function by such a study, or by some sort of secular employments; for at such times they are promoting the interest of religion, by studying how to defend it, and serving God in regulating mens manners thro' justice or mercy.

The apostles lived under heathen princes, and could not be employed in temporal offices under them without scandal to christianity; but now when kings themselves are Christians; the clergy invested with civil authority, have great opportunities to advance the gospel, and maintain the government of the church.   And if some of the fathers have shew'd their dislike of employing clergymen in secular affairs, their notions seem to have been calculated for a monastick life, which can have no force in a Protestant country.   Ecclesiastical persons may as well be debarr'd to have any temporal estate, or to be executors or administrators, guardians or trustees.   But to look higher: suppose one of the blood royal was a clergyman, and the crown should descend to him, he may execute both those offices, and be God's anointed in both. Before the law Melchisedeck was king and priest.   And it was never thought a crime in the Jews to give commission to their priests to be even generals in war, and governors of provinces.   Under the law controversies were to be decided by the priests and judges, Deut. 17 and 19.   Eli was both a priest and a temporal judge; and Esdras, after the captivity, was both a priest and chief governor in secular affairs.   Our Savior indeed refused to give judgment in a criminal cause of adultery, and in a civil cause, about dividing an inheritance; but he did this to convince the Jews, that to be a king was no part of the Messiah, and because he was a private person, and had no such authority in that common-wealth.   But St. Austin is so far from thinking it unlawful for a bishop to judge in civil causes, that he infers from 1 Cor. 6 a necessity for him to undertake that duty.   Truly, where a Christian society is planted amongst hereticks or Schismaticks, it is of necessity that the clergy should accept of a share with the laity; and then if the civil affairs are such wherein civil and ecclesiastical offices may be united in the same person, without prejudice to either of those employments, I cannot find any reason why clergymen should be totally excluded.

The same author intimates,

> That several laws have been made to restrain the clergy from exercising secular employments.   The emperors Honorius, Theodosius, and Justinian have prohibited the same by the Civil law; and the Common law of England too seems to discourage it, as appears by a special writ in the Register, providing that a master of a hospital, being a clergyman, should not be chosen an officer in a mannor, to which that hospital did belong, as contra legem & consuetudinem regni & non consonum.

I'll agree that clergymen ought not to be shopkeepers or farmers, or to interpose in any such secular affairs; nor to be Bailiffs or constables, nor to serve in any mean offices; and that a rescript of Honorius and Theodosius and a decree of Justinian seem to be against their intermeddling in any secular affairs at all: Nay, that the Canon law speaks to the same purpose, as also a constitution of Othobon.   But this does not prove that the clergy ought not to study the law.   And if the Civil and Canon laws prohibit them to bear secular offices, positive laws are not immutable.   But what signifie these imperial laws, and these canons here in England, if they were never received, or incorporated into the body of our Common law? Or if they are contrary to the law of the land?   What will become of the whole frame of our government, and of our just rights and properties, if the producing of imperial edicts, (I say the same of canons) would be sufficient to overthrow them?   Yet Constantine, before the papal power was advanced) suffered the bishops to try all manner of causes, which concerned either clergy or laity, upon appeals from the civil magistrate.   Upon which the constitutions De Episcopals Judicie in the Theodosian, and that De Episcopali Andientia in the Justinian Code were founded.   And the gloss upon the novels of Justinian observes, that bishops, (the case is the same of other clergymen) may concern themselves with the affairs of the commonwealth when their prince calls and commands them.

As to the restraint of the clergy by the Common law, it is to be observed, that the writ in the register exempts the clergy from mean offices for the honor of the church; but does not prohibit or restrain them. Neither Common nor Statute law exempts or restrains them from secular employments of credit. Nay our laws do allow episcopal and archidiaconal jurisdiction to clergymen to punish even laymen for crimes not only of a spiritual nature, as incest, adultery, fornication, heresie, &c. but to try causes between laymen in temporal matters, touching wills, legacies, defamation, &c. and to license surgeons, midwives, and school-masters. By our fundamental constitution, bishops are members of the upper House of Parliament, who in concurrence with the lay-peers, try all causes upon writs of error out of the Queen's-Bench, and appeals from our courts of equity. And all this is very reasonable, since our church has been united and incorporated into the Civil state. For the clergy ought to have a share with the laity in the governing part, where the rights, and freeholds of the clergy as well as laity are concerned in it. And I believe there is scarce any monarchy in the world where the clergy are excluded from it. 'Tis true, "The two Houses complain'd in the 45 year of Ed. 3 again clergy officers in the government; and that such allowances might hereafter tend to the disinherison of the Crown, and great prejudice of the Realm, and therefore they pray the King that he would employ laymen." This was a very seasonable complaint, when the Pope maintain'd his usurped authority over our monarchs by this practice. But are our clergy now under oaths to support the Pope's supremacy? Is it the interest of our clergy to destroy our monarchy, or to subject it to a foreign power? When that is the case, I will concur with the enemies of the clergy to petition again to remove them, and that they may not be trusted out of the bounds of their parishes. But as the matter stands at present, an exclusion of the clergy may rather promote the Pope's business by dividing the interest of the church from that of the state, tho' the reformers in 1641 did not see into this dangerous consequence, when they prevailed upon King Charles the First to disable clergymen, by act of Parliament, from exercising any temporal authority or jurisdiction. However, the clergy have the law now on their side, and that Act of 41 was repealed upon the Restoration, by the 13 Car. 2 Chap. 2. And I believe no one will oppose their having a small share in some civil employments, but those that desire to trample on them; or that under a shew, of inveighing against the grandeur of the church of Rome, and the ambition and pride of its clergy, really hate that a Protestant clergy should live in any credit. Nay, it is manifest enough that even the clergy, (as they are called) amongst our dissenters, who are great sticklers with some of our own laity against such allowances, do themselves exercise civil authority over the respective members of their congregations with a high hand, tho' they call it spiritual power, or disguise it with another name. But if there must be a distinction in the exercise of these two powers, why must mere laymen amongst them exercise spiritual jurisdiction, and our clergy be excluded from the exercise of civil?

Did I propose any thing to gratifie ambition, or that would turn to the prejudice of the ministerial function, I should abhor the thoughts of it; but if I aim at nothing but the credit of the clergy, their spiritual and secular interests, and that they may be made capable of such employments as are allow'd by Scripture, and the practice of the church from the time of Constantine; and all this for the benefit of the state as well as of the church; I cannot be persuaded but that good and wise men of the laity will be pleas'd with such assistance in their civil affairs, and with such an union of persons and interests, which our enemies desire should be always divided.

However, submitting this question concerning the capacity of spiritual persons to act in temporal matters, to the determination of our superiors, I only beg leave to advise your youth design'd for Holy Orders, to make the laws of England part of their studies, for the many reasons which I have hinted at. And therefore to look back upon the principal subject, I shall proceed, from a persuasion to study the general knowledge of the laws of England in the universities, to give some hints how that study may be carried on amongst you, (for the present purpose) with as little pains as many others, of less use. And herein I shall only represent to you the thoughts of some considerable lawyers, whom I have discoursed with upon this subject; not presuming to trust to my own judgment in so nice a matter.

It is to be much lamented, that we have not any complete system of our laws. We are forced to learn it chiefly by tradition, and observations upon the practice of it in the highest courts. But for want of such a system, there have been several methods recommended to young beginners, who do not design to make the law their profession. Amongst others, it has been advised to read, first of all, Finch's Discourse of Law. This is the most methodical book extant that ever was wrote by one of our profession; it almost follows the method of Justinian's Institutes. For having by way of introduction treated of the law of nature and reason, and of positive laws: He discourses, 1. Of persons taken notice of in the Common law. 2. Of rights and professions. 3. Of offences. 4. Of courts of judicature, or of original and judicial process. Indeed, (say they) if this book was revised by marking what is antiquated, and by adding the new statutes with references to Coke's commentary on Littleton, &c. a youth might have a good system in his mind in a short time. However, let Wentworth's Office of an Executor, and Hales's Pleas of the Crown be read in order when the scholar reads of testaments, and of offences, and in the second and third books of Finch's Discourse of Law. That book under the name of Wentworth may be relied on, while Swinburn and Godolphin of Testaments (being mixtures of Common and Civil law) are not always to be trusted. For the farther understanding of some <u>other</u> chapters, there are many books of late published upon <u>particular</u> subjects, as in other arts and sciences, which may be cursorily consulted where the system is too short or difficult.

But after all, <u>Littleton's Tenures</u>, with <u>Coke's Commentary</u>, (at least as far as the text is directly explained) must be read and studied, if the student intends to proceed upon a sure bottom. For to those books, and the rest of <u>Coke's Institutes</u>, the scholar must be always turning, they being the best authorities in our law. <u>Coke</u> need not to be followed in his digressions and variety of cases; for it is not designed to make our student as great a lawyer as himself. But whatever is read, the student may always keep <u>Finch's</u> method in his mind, and upon a review reduce all to his order. This will enable him to improve himself by discourse and by conversation with attorneys and lawyers.

It is adviseable to get a common-place book, after two years are spent in the course of reading, to enter the abstract or substance thereof under proper alphabetical titles. <u>Rolls</u> or <u>Danvers's Abridgments</u>, &c. will be of great use to him, where with his own collections, he may ever after see at one view the general cases concerning any one subject.

All methods suppose that you have the <u>statutes</u> abridged by <u>Wingate</u> and <u>Washington</u>, &c. as also <u>Cowel's Interpreter</u>, or <u>Blunt's Dictionary</u> to explain the <u>law-terms</u>, and <u>Fitzherbert's Natura</u> Brevium to be occasionally informed in the nature of the common <u>writs,</u> which are mentioned or referred to.

Amongst our <u>statutes</u> or <u>acts</u> of Parliament, have a particular eye on the Statute of <u>Tenures</u> enacted the 12 <u>Car</u>. 2 and the Statute of Frauds and <u>Perjuries</u> made the 29 <u>Car</u>. 2. For much of the law is altered by them since <u>Littleton</u>, <u>Finch</u> or <u>Coke</u> wrote. And so regard must be had to those Act of Parliament which are of daily use. Such are the statutes, (to take them in an alphabetical order, as in the abridgment) concerning <u>administration of intestates estates, bail and mainprise</u>, the <u>crown, distresses, election, fines, habeas corpus, informers, judicial proceedings, or amendments of the law, limitation of actions</u>, the <u>enabling and disabling</u> statutes concerning <u>leases,</u> the statutes concerning the <u>dissolution of monasteries, officers</u> and <u>offices, recoveries, residence, service and</u> sacraments, tithes, uses and <u>enrollments,</u> &c.

At the first entrance on study, let the student be taught what <u>titles</u> of the law are least in use, to save him an unnecessary trouble: If this is observed, the learning will not be so difficult or tedious as is commonly imagined. <u>Sir Matthew Hales's</u> preface to <u>Roll's Abridgment</u> will inform him,

That the title of <u>Dower</u>, and its several kinds, (as <u>ad ostium ecclesiae</u>, &c.) is neglected by the common use of jointures.

That the titles of <u>Homager, Fealty, Escuage, Homage Auncestrel</u>, may be cursorily read over.

That Tenures by Knight Service, and its appendixes,

as Wardship, &c. are all become useless by the Act of Alteration of Tenures.

That Tenure in Villenage, and the several appendixes thereof are now also antiquated.

That the titles of Profession and Deraignment are wholly taken away.

The learning touching the title of Rents now depends much upon the statutes of Distresses, particularly upon the 2 W.&M. Chap. 5 which is an alteration but of late.

That preface will acquaint him that the title of Descents, to take away Entries, and continual claim, is very much abridged by the 32 H. 8. ch. 33.

That the title of Atturnment was a difficult title with its appendixes, Quid Juris clamat, quem redditum reddit, per quae servitia, &c. But it grew almost obsolete by the invention of fines to uses, by bargain and sale, by lease and release, and by deeds enrolled, according to the Statute 27 H. 8 ch. 16 which also supplies the difficulties of execution of estates by Livery and Seisin. And indeed the learning of Atturnments is now wholly rendered useless by the 4 & 5 of Q. Anne, entitled, An Act for the Amendment of the Law.

Some kind of releases and confirmations are also supplied by the aforesaid new inventions.

The titles of discontinuance and remitter are mightily abridged by several acts of Parliament.

And thus the title of warranty need not take up much study of our young scholar. Warranties of tenant for life and collateral warranties are made void by the 4th and 5th of Queen Anne.

By this time you may see that Coke's Commentary on Littleton is shrunk up to one third.

It will save the young scholar a great deal of pains and make his study easier and shorter yet, if he is acquainted betimes, that the remedy of assizes, and their several forms and proceedings, are out of use in recovering possessions; and that ejectments are come into their place. Assizes are seldom brought, unless for recovering possession of offices. Real actions, as writs of right, writs of entry, &c. and their several appendixes, are now also out of use. It is a shorter way to recover possessions by ejectment. Only in common recoveries, the form of such real actions is preserved.

The usual methods of tryal at this day are by ejectments for possession of lands, quare impedit for a disturbance in a title to a rectory, &c. And for recompence in money we make use of actions upon the case, (in trespass, assumpsit, trover and conversion) action of covenant, debt, trespass, vi & armis. See farther of the alterations in the Common Law Hales's Preface beforementioned, where you may also find a reflection upon university-learning, and what improper judges such scholars are of the reasonableness and study of the Common law. But, sir, I am endeavouring now to prevent these reflections for the future.

As for the forms of pleadings in our courts at Westminster, there are several modern books which will shew the student precedents from the original writ and

declaration, to the writs of execution, and writs of
error, with which he need not trouble himself any more
than with a bare perusal to compare these entries with the
subject he reads on; perhaps they are not exact, but they
will serve his turn.

But as to practice, the statutes of jeofails,
judicial proceedings, and amendments of the law, will shew
how much the old niceties in form are taken away, to
prevent any laborious enquiries on that heavy subject, 8
H.6. 12 & 15.   32 H.8.30.   37 H.8.8.   18 Eliz. 14.   27
Eliz. 5.   21 Jac. 13. 16 & 17 Car. 2.8.   4 & 5 W. & M. 18.
10 & 11. W. 3.14.   4 & 5. Anne.

Sir Orlando Bridgman's Conveyancer; Billinghurst's
Arcana Clericalia, &c. will acquaint you with the order
and formal parts of a deed, and the several forms of
conveyances.

And thus for the practice of the high-court of
chancery, there are several modern books drawn up for the
use of young clerks, whichwill instruct the scholar in the
form of a subpoena, attachment, proclamation, commission
of rebellion, bill and answer, plea, demurrer,
replication, the form of an order, affidavit,
interrogatory, commission to examine witnesses, &c.
deposition, decree, and sequestration.   There are also
reports of chancery cases, lately published, which may be
of use.

With these instructions, furniture and expence, a
young scholar in the university may gain a tolerable
insight into our laws, and a general notion of our way of
practice, and be able hereafter to understand our reports
which are most reasoning, when he desires to be satisfied
in the judgment or decision upon any case occurring in the
course of his enquiries.   Heretofore it it was thought
most adviseable to begin with the year books, and the
oldest reports; but now because of the great alterations
of our laws, it is thought most proper for a student to
begin with the latest; or if he cares not to go any
farther, he may depend upon the great Abridgments
before-mention'd, and follow their references to a report,
when he has a mind to read upon his case at large.   A
method which no wise man would propose to one that designs
for the bar, because it is too superficial.   It is offered
as a method to a private tutor only, or a young scholar in
our universities, who designs for another profession, or
no profession at all, that he may be something inform'd in
the nature of the laws, under which he lives.

The Chancellor's Court in your university might be so
regulated as to conduce very much to improve this study.
Your fondness for the Civil law upon all occasions is very
unaccountable, and of very pernicious consequence.   The
oath of your judges is, to determine according to the
laws, statutes, privileges, liberties and customs of the
university, without any special direction to observe the
Roman law in their sentences and decrees.   The charters
mention nothing of the Civil law, but give the judges
leave to try causes either according to the statutes,
privileges and customs of the university, or pursuant to
the law of the land, at discretion.   Now does not your

constitution give liberty to take in the Common law with
your statutes and customs? The present strictness of a
Civil law practice is to no rational purpose, and of very
little use elsewhere. And tho' the process ought to be by
libel, (as your statutes require) yet the further
proceedings must be summariè, simpliciter, & depl'ano,
abfq, strepita & figura jadicii and sola rei veritate
inspecta, &c. In criminal causes 'tis sufficient if the
register sets down the accusation in an act of court. If
this is so, what a deal of formal trifling and expence has
there been upon the admission of libels and articles, and
upon the doctrine of nullities!

     Your statutes are plain and certain rules of
government, and easie to be understood by an honest mind;
but if you give ear to unnatural distinctions, fetches and
shifts, and to the variety of opinions from every writer
in the Civil law, there is nothing to be expected, but an
overthrow of your discipline; nothing but uncertainty and
inconsistency. But this may be prevented hereafter, if
you have more regard to upright and manly reasoning, and
to matter of substance in all debates and tryals, and to
the laws of England in your decrees, when your statutes
are silent. Those are particular, certain, and uniform.
'Tis true, a regard ought to be had to the laws in the
Digest and Code, (the Civil law is wholesome, if taken
with moderation) or to the opinions of Bartolus and
Baldus, and the learned commentators upon those laws. The
decisions of the chamber and the rota shall be always
thought on with great esteem, for their reasons are
oftentimes very admirable; but what is their bare
authority without a reason, or their way of practice to
us? As for their reasons too, and force of argument, we
see the Roman law is much alter'd in all countries since
it was first collected by Justinian; and that there is a
learned war amongst the interpreters, about the equity of
those laws, as any one that consults the books De LL.
Abrogatis, or DeJure Novissimo, De Opinionibus Communibus
contra Commanes, De Moribus Hodiernis, &c. may be fully
convinc'd. Besides, the common lawyers as much magnifie
the wisdom of our own law, where it differs from the Civil
law, and are ready to maintain, that nothing can be the
Common law of England, but what is consistent with right
reason, and the law of God. They are willing to be tried
by those tests, and to enter into a comparison. However,
the laws of England must prevail here, and old Littleton
and Coke, (tho'despised by those that do not understand
them) will keep up their characters; because by their
reasons property must at last be decided. Why then all
this dotage upon every part of the Roman law?

     By the Civil law a judge may be refused if you do not
like him, for one and forty reasons. But the law of
England, and your own constitution cannot bear this law.
Your discipline will be overturn'd by such an allowance;
for who shall control or act in the stead of your
chancellor or vicechancellor; or correct or imprison him,
if he will not be refused.

     By the Civil law a man's servant cannot be a witness
for him, nor a son for a father, or vice versa; nor any

one that is near of kin to him; no one is of full age till
five and twenty; men may be forced to be guardians; women
cannot be witnesses in criminal causes. All words against
good manners, (tho' not injurious) are actionable or
punishable, &c. And these laws may be defended with
plausible reasons. But our lawyers have as good reasons
on the contrary; and our superiors will never endure that
you should set up unknown rules to govern the property of
Englishmen, or that our rights should be determin'd by any
other laws than our own. Your chancellor's court subsists
in subordination to Her Majesty's Court of Chancery, by
the express words of your statutes. That is governed by
the jus acqui & boni, with regard to the maxims of our
Common law, and cannot be presum'd to favour any strange
laws amongst you, especially where they do not immediately
tend to the advancement of religion and learning.

I must therefore conclude, that (when your statutes
are silent) a mixture at least of both laws must be
admitted into your court, viz. the summary way of
proceeding by the Civil law in point of practice, and the
equity and reason of the Civil law against strict Common
law; as in the case of forfeitures and accidents, or in
points undetermined at the Common law; as such equity
governs in our Chancery. But, methinks you should prefer
the Common law, where the Civil law is out of use, or when
those two laws thwart each other, particularly in trade,
or in their fundamental maxims. Nolumus leges Angliae
mutari que bucusq; usitatae sunt & approbatae, 20 H. 3.
The civilians beyond sea think it as scandalous to be
ignorant of the laws and customs of their own country as
of the Roman law, and observe their own customs in the
first place; and your statutes suppose that the civilians
bred amongst you should be learned in our laws too, and in
all probability for the same end and purpose. Dr. Ridley,
Cowel and Cosens, & c. those famous civilians, had become
as if they had never been born, (which will be the fate of
some of their children after them) if they had not
distinguished themselves by their skill in the laws of
England.

Such a regulation of your court tends only to reduce
it to its true constitution, whereby the Civil law might
be made more useful to the publick, and the knowledge of
our own laws advanc'd with it, to the benefit of the young
scholars that attend the court, and of all others that are
concerned in it.

Having now given some reasons why the general
knowledge of the laws of England should be studied in the
universities, together with a hint of a method how you may
direct you young scholars to enter on that study, as also
a way to improve in it, I am not without hopes but that my
proposal may take effect upon some of the most industrious
and ingenious part of the young gentlemen; tho' at present
it may be subject to variety of opinion and censure of
others, especially of those who are grown old in mistaken
notions of useful learning. I sincerely profess, that I
have been long persuaded that such a knowledge may prove
hereafter for the service of the Queen, the Honour, and
interest of the clergy, and consequently for the Honour

and interest of the universities.   Excuse therefore the
presumption of sending my thoughts to you on this subject,
because this proposal is well intended, proceeding from my
hearty wishes for your prosperity.

I am, with all esteem, (for your readiness and
industry in promoting the publick good, and on many other
accounts).

REVEREND SIR, your most obliged and humble servant.

– 4 –

William Blackstone

A Discourse on the Study of the Law
(1759)

Mr. Vice-Chancellor, and Gentlemen of the University, the general expectation of so numerous and respectable an audience, the novelty, and (I may add) the importance of the duty required from this chair, must unavoidably be productive of great diffidence and apprehensions in him who has the honour to be placed in it. He must be sensible how much will depend upon his conduct, in the infancy of a study, which is now first adopted by public academical authority; which has generally been reputed (however unjustly) of a dry and unfruitful nature; and of which the theoretical, elementary parts have hitherto received a very moderate share of cultivation. He cannot but reflect that, if either his plan of instruction be crude and injudicious, or the execution of it lame and superficial, it will cast a damp upon the farther progress of this most useful and most rational branch of learning; and may defeat for a time the public-spirited design of our wise and munificent benefactor. And this he must more especially dread, when he feels by experience how unequal his abilities are (unassisted by preceding examples) to complete, in the manner he could wish, so extensive and arduous a talk, since he freely confesses, that his former more private attempts have fallen very short of his own ideas of perfection. And yet the candour he has already experienced, and this last transcendent mark of regard, his present nomination by the free and unanimous suffrage of a great and learned university, (an honour to be ever remembered with the deepest and most affectionate gratitude) these testimonies of your public judgment must entirely supersede his own, and forbid him to believe himself totally insufficient for the labour at least of this employment. One thing he will venture to hope for, and it certainly shall be his constant aim, by diligence and attention to atone for his other defects; esteeming, that the best return, which he can possibly make for your favourable opinion of his capacity, will be his unwearied endeavours in some little degree to deserve it.

The science thus committed to his charge, to be cultivated, methodized, and explained in a course of academical lectures, is that of the laws and constitution of our own country: a species of knowledge, in which the gentlemen of England have been more remarklably deficient that those of all Europe besides. In most of the nations on the continent, where the civil or imperial law, under different modifications, is closely interwoven with the municipal laws of the land, no gentleman, or at least no scholar, thinks his education is completed, till he has attended a course or two of lectures, both upon the institutes of Justinian and the local constitutions of his native soil, under the very eminent professors that abound in their several universities. And in the northern parts of our own island, where also the municipal laws are frequently connected with the civil, it is difficult to meet with a person of liberal education, who is destitute of a competent knowledge in that science, which is to be the guardian of his natural rights, and the rule of his civil conduct.

Nor have the imperial laws been totally neglected even in the english nation. A general acquaintance with their decisions, has ever been deservedly considered as no small accomplishment of a gentleman; and a fashion has prevailed, especially of late, to transport the growing hopes of this island to foreign universities, in Switzerland, Germany and Holland; which, though infinitely inferior to our own in every other consideration, have been looked upon as better nurseries of the civil, or (which is nearly the same) of their own municipal law. In the mean time it has been the peculiar lot of our admirable system of laws, to be neglected, and even unknown, by all but one practical profession; though built upon the soundest foundations, and approved by the experiences of ages.

Far be it from me to derogate from the study of the civil law, considered (apart from any binding authority) as a collection of written reason. No man is more thoroughly persuaded of the general excellence of it's rules, and the usual equity of it's decisions; nor is better convinced of it's use as well as ornament to the scholar, the divine, the statesman, and even the common lawyer. But we must not carry our veneration so far as to sacrifice our Alfred and Edward to the manes of Theodosius and Justinian: we must not prefer the edict of the praetor, or the rescript of the roman emperor, to our own immemorial customs, or the sanctions of an english parliament; unless we can also prefer the despotic monarchy of Rome and Byzantium, for whose meridians the former were calculated, to the free constitution of Britain, which the latter are adapted to perpetuate.

Without detracting therefore from the real merit which abounds in the imperial law, I hope I may have leave to assert, that if an englishman must be ignorant of either the one or the other, he had better be a stranger to the roman than the english institutions. For I think it an undeniable position, that a competent knowledge of the laws of that society, in which we live, is the proper accomplishment of every gentleman and scholar; an highly useful, I had almost said essential, part of liberal and

polite education: and in this I am warranted by the
example of ancient Rome; where, as Cicero informs us, the
very boys were obliged to learn the twelve tables by
heart, as a carmen necessarium or indispensable lesson, to
imprint on their tender minds an early knowledge of the
laws and constitutions of their country.

But as the long and universal neglect of this study,
with us in England, seems in some degree to call in
question the truth of this evident position, it shall
therefore be the business of this introductory lecture, in
the first place to demonstrate the utility of some general
acquaintance with the municipal law of the land, by
pointing out its particular uses in all considerable
situations of life.   Some conjectures will then be offered
with regard to the causes of neglecting this useful study:
to which will be subjoined a few reflections on the
peculiar propriety of reviving it in our universities.

And, first, to demonstrate the utility of some
acquaintance with the laws of the land, let us only
reflect a moment on the singular frame and polity of that
land, which is governed by this system of laws.   A land,
perhaps the only one in the universe, in which political
or civil liberty is the very end and scope of the
constitution.   This liberty, rightly understood, consists
in the power of doing whatever the laws permit; which is
only to be effected by a general conformity of all orders
and degrees to those equitable rules of action, by which
the meanest individual is protected from the insults and
oppression of the greatest.   As therefore every subject is
interested in the preservation of the laws, it is
incumbent upon every man to be acquainted with those at
least, with which he is immediately concerned; lest he
incur the censure, as well as inconvenience, of living in
society without knowing the obligations which it lays him
under.   And thus much may suffice for persons of inferior
condition, who have neither time nor capacity to enlarge
their views, beyond that contracted sphere in which they
are appointed to move.   But those, on whom nature and
fortune have bestowed more abilities and greater leisure,
cannot be so easily excused.   These advantages are given
them, not for the benefit of themselves only, but also of
the public: and yet they cannot, in any scene of life,
discharge properly their duty either to the public or
themselves, without some degree of knowledge in the laws.
To evince this the more clearly, it may not be amiss to
descend to a few particulars.

Let us therefore begin with our gentlemen of
independent estates and fortune, the most useful as well
as considerable body of men in the nation: whom even to
suppose ignorant in this branch of learning is treated by
Mr. Locke as a strange absurdity.   It is their landed
property, with its long and voluminous train of descents
and conveyances, settlements, entails, and incumbrances,
that forms the most intricate and most extensive object of
legal knowledge.   The thorough comprehension of these, in
all their minute distinctions, is perhaps too laborious a
task for any but a lawyer by profession: yet still the
understanding of a few leading principles, relating to

estates and conveyancing, may form some check and guard upon a gentleman's inferior agents, and preserve him at least from very gross and notorious imposition.

Again, the policy of all laws has made some forms necessary in the wording of last wills and testaments, and more with regard to their attestation. An ignorance in these must always be of dangerous consequence, to such as by choice or necessity compile their own testaments, without any technical assistance. Those who have attended the courts of justice are the best witnesses of the confusion and distresses that are hereby occasioned in families; and of the difficulties that arise in discerning the true meaning of the testator, or sometimes in discovering any meaning at all: so that in the end his estate may often be vested quite contrary to these his enigmatical intentions, because perhaps he has omitted one or two formal words, which are necessary to ascertain the sense with indisputable legal precision, or has executed his will in the presence of fewer witnesses than the law requires.

But to proceed from private concerns to those of a more public consideration. All gentlemen of fortune are, in consequence of their property, liable to be called upon to establish the rights, to estimate the injuries, to weigh the accusations, and sometimes to dispose of the lives of their fellow-subjects, by serving upon juries. In this situation they are frequently to decide, and that upon their oaths, questions of nice importance, in the solution of which some legal skill is requisite; especially where the law and the fact, as it often happens, are intimately blended together. And the general incapacity, even of our best juries, to do this with any tolerable propriety, has greatly debased their authority; and has unavoidably thrown more power into the hands of the judges, to direct, control, and even reverse their verdicts, than perhaps the constitution intended.

But it is not as a juror only that the english gentleman is called upon to determine questions of right, and distribute justice to his fellow-subjects: it is principally with this order of men that the commission of the peace is filled. And here a very ample field is opened for a gentleman to exert his talents, by maintaining good order in his neighbourhood; by punishing the dissolute and idle; by protecting the peaceable and industrious; and, above all, by healing petty differences and preventing vexatious prosecutions. But, in order to attain these desirable ends, it is necessary that the magistrate should understand his business; and have not only the will but the power also, (under which must be included the knowledge) of administering legal and effectual justice. Else, when he has mistaken his authority, through passion, through ignorance, or absurdity, he will be the object of contempt from his inferiors, and of censure from those to whom he is accountable for his conduct.

Yet further; most gentlemen of considerable property, at some period or other in their lives, are ambitious of representing their country in parliament: and those who

are ambitious of receiving so high a trust, would also do
well to remember its nature and importance. They are not
thus honourably distinguished from the rest of their
fellow-subjects, merely that they may privilege their
persons, their estates, or their domestics; that they may
list under party banners; may grant or with-hold [sic]
supplies; may vote with or vote against a popular or
unpopular administration; but upon considerations far more
interesting and important. They are the guardians of the
English constitution; the makers, repealers, and
interpreters of the English laws; delegated to watch, to
check, and to avert every dangerous innovation, to
propose, to adopt, and to cherish any solid and
well-weighed improvement; bound by every tie of nature, of
honour, and of religion, to transmit that constitution and
those laws to their posterity, amended if possible, at
least without any derogation. And how unbecoming must it
appear in a member of the legislature to vote for a new
law, who is utterly ignorant of the old! what kind of
interpretation can he be enabled to give, who is a
stranger to the text upon which he comments!

Indeed it is really amazing, that there should be no
other state of life, no other occupation, art, or science,
in which some method of instruction is not looked upon as
requisite, except only the science of legislation, the
noblest and most difficult of any. Apprenticeships are
held necessary to almost every art, commercial or
mechanical: a long course of reading and study must form
the divine, the physician, and the practical professor of
the laws: but every man of superior fortune thinks
himself born a legislator. Yet Tully was of a different
opinion: "It is necessary, says he, for a senator to be
thoroughly acquainted with the constitution; and this, he
declares, is a knowledge of the most extensive nature; a
matter of science, of diligence, of reflexion [sic],
without which no senator can possibly be fit for his
office."

The mischiefs that have arisen to the public from
inconsiderate alterations in our laws, are too obvious to
be called in question; and how far they have been owing to
the defective education of our senators, is a point well
worthy the public attention. The common law of England
has fared like other venerable edifices of antiquity,
which rash and unexperienced workmen have ventured to new
dress and refine, with all the rage of modern improvement.
Hence frequently its symmetry has been destroyed, it's
proportions distorted, and it's majestic simplicity
exchanged for specious embellishments and fantastic
novelties. For, to say the truth, almost all the
perplexed questions, almost all the niceties, intricacies,
and delays (which have sometimes disgraced the english, as
well as other, courts of justice) owe their original not
to the common law itself, but to innovations that have
been made in it by acts of parliament; "overladen (as lord
Coke expresses it) with provisoes and additions, and many
times on a sudden penned or corrected by men of none or
very little judgment in law." This great and
well-experienced judge declares that in all his time he

never knew two questions made upon rights merely depending upon the common law; and warmly laments the confusion introduced by ill-judging and unlearned legislators. But if, he subjoins, acts of parliament were after the old fashion penned, by such only as perfectly knew what the common law was before the making of any act of parliament concerning that matter, as also how far forth former statutes has provided remedy for former mischiefs and defects discovered by experience; then should very few questions in law arise, and the learned should not so often and so much perplex their heads to make atonement and peace, by construction of law, between insensible and disagreeing words, sentences, and provisoes, as they now do. And if this inconvenience was so heavily felt in the reign of queen Elizabeth, you may judge how the evil is increased in later times, when the statute book is swelled to ten times a larger bulk; unless it should be found, that the penners of our modern statutes have proportionably better informed themselves in the knowledge of the common law.

What is said of our gentlemen in general, and the propriety of their application to the study of the laws of their country, will hold equally strong or still stronger with regard to the nobility of this realm, except only in the article of serving upon juries. But, instead of this, they have several peculiar provinces of far greater consequence and concern; being not only by birth hereditary counsellors of the crown, and judges upon their honour of the lives of their brother-peers, but also arbiters of the property of all their fellow-subjects, and that in the last resort. In this their judicial capacity they are bound to decide the nicest and most critical points of law; to examine and correct such errors as have escaped the most experienced sages of the profession, the lord keeper and the judges of the courts at Westminster. Their sentence is final, decisive, irrevocable: no appeal, no correction, not even a review can be had: and to their determination, whatever it be, the inferior courts of justice must conform; otherwise the rule of property would no longer be uniform and steady.

Should a judge in the most subordinate jurisdiction be deficient in the knowledge of the law, it would reflect infinite contempt upon himself and disgrace upon those who employ him. And yet the consequence of his ignorance is comparatively very trifling and small: his judgment may be examined, and his errors rectified by other courts. But how much more serious and affecting is the case of a superior judge, if without any skill in the laws he will boldly venture to decide a question, upon which the welfare and subsistence of whole families may depend! where the chance of his judging right, or wrong, is barely equal; and where, if he chances to judge wrong, he does an injury of the most alarming nature, an injury without possibility of redress!

Yet, vast as this trust is, it can no where be so properly reposed, as in the noble hands where our excellent constitution has placed it: and therefore placed it, because, from the independence of their fortune and the dignity of their station, they are presumed to employ that leisure which is the consequence of both, in attaining a more extensive knowledge of the laws than persons of inferior rank: and because the founders of our polity relied upon that delicacy of sentiment, so peculiar to noble birth; which, as on the one hand it will prevent either interest or affection from interfering in questions of right, so on the other it will bind a peer in honour, an obligation which the law esteems equal to another's oath, to be master of those points upon which it is his birthright to decide.

The roman pandects will furnish us with a piece of history not unapplicable to our present purpose. Servius Sulpicius, a gentleman of the patrician order, and a celebrated orator, had occasion to take the opinion of Quintus Mutius Scaevola, the oracle of the roman law; but for want of being conversant in that science, could not so much as understand even the technical terms, which his counsel was obliged to make use of. Upon which Mutius Scaevola could not forbear to upbraid him with this memorable reproof, "that it was a shame for a patrician, a nobleman, and an orator to be ignorant of the law under which he lived." Which reproach made so deep an impression on Sulpicius, that he immediately applied himself to the study of the law; wherein he arrived to that proficiency, that he left behind him about a hundred and fourscore volumes of his own compiling upon the subject; and became, in the opinion of Cicero, a much more complete lawyer than even Mutius Scaevola himself.

I would not be thought to recommend to our english nobility and gentry to become as great lawyers as Sulpicius; though he, together with this character, sustained likewise that of an excellent orator, a firm patriot, and a wise indefatigable senator; but the inference which arises from the story is this, that ignorance of the laws of the land hath ever been esteemed dishonourable, in those who are entrusted by their country to maintain, to administer, and to amend them.

But surely there is little occasion to enforce this argument any farther to persons of rank and distinction, if we of this place may be allowed to form a general judgment from those who are under our inspection: happy, that while we lay down the rule, we can also produce the example. You will therefore permit your professor to indulge both a public and private satisfaction by bearing this open testimony, that in the very infancy of these studies among us, they were favoured with the most diligent attendance, and pursued with the most unwearied application, by those of the noblest birth and most ample patrimony: some of whom are still the ornaments of this seat of learning; and others at a greater distance continue doing honour to it's institutions, by comparing our polity and laws with those of other kingdoms abroad, or exerting their senatorial abilities in the councils of the nation at home.

Nor will some degree of legal knowledge be found in the least superfluous to persons of inferior rank; especially those of the learned professions. The clergy

in particular, besides the common obligations they are
under in proportion to their rank and fortune, have also
abundant reason, considered merely as clergymen, to be
acquainted with many branches of the law, which are almost
peculiar and appropriated to themselves alone.   Such are
the laws relating to advowson, institutions, and
inductions; to simony, and simoniacal contracts; to
uniformity, residence, and pluralities; to tithes and
other ecclesiastical dues; to marriages (more especially
of late) and to a variety of other subjects, which are
consigned to the care of their order by the provisions of
particular statutes.   To understand these aright, to
discern what is warranted or enjoined, and what is
forbidden by law, demands a sort of legal apprehension;
which is no otherwise to be acquired than by use and a
familiar acquaintance with legal writers.

For the gentlemen of the faculty of physic, I must
frankly own that I see no special reason, why they in
particular should apply themselves to the study of the
law; unless in common with other gentlemen, and to
complete the character of general and extensive knowledge;
a character which their profession, beyond others, has
remarkably deserved.   They will give me leave however to
suggest, and that not ludicrously, that it might
frequently be of use to families upon sudden emergencies,
if the physician were acquainted with the doctrine of last
wills and testaments, at least so far as related to the
formal part of their execution.

But those gentlemen who intend to profess the civil
and ecclesiastical laws in the spiritual and maritime
courts of this kingdom, are of all men (next to common
lawyers) the most indispensibly obliged to apply
themselves seriously to the study of our municipal laws.
For the civil and canon laws, considered with respect to
any intrinsic obligation, have no force or authority in
this kingdom; they are no more binding in England than our
laws are binding at Rome.   But as far as these foreign
laws, on account of some peculiar propriety, have in some
particular cases, and in some particular courts, been
introduced and allowed by our laws, so far they oblige,
and no farther; their authority being wholly founded upon
that permission and adoption.   In which we are not
singular in our notions; for even in Holland, where the
imperial law is much cultivated and its decisions pretty
generally followed, we are informed by Van Leeuwen, that
"it receives it's force from custom and the consent of the
people, either tacitly or expresly given: for otherwise,
he adds, we should no more be bound by the law, than by
that of the Almains, the Franks, the Saxons, the Goths,
the Vandals, and other of the ancient nations."   Wherefore
in all points in which the different systems depart from
each other, the law of the land takes place of the law of
Rome, whether ancient or modern, imperial or pontifical.
And in those of our english courts wherein a reception has
been allowed to the civil and canon laws, if either they
exceed the bounds of that reception, by extending
themselves to other matters, than are permitted to them;
or if such courts proceed according to the decisions of

those laws, in cases wherein it is controlled by the law
of the land, the common law in either instance both may,
and frequently does, prohibit and annul their proceedings:
and it will not be a sufficient excuse for them to tell
the king's courts at Westminster, that their practice is
warranted by the laws of Justinian or Gregory, or is
conformable to the decrees of the Rota or imperial
chamber. For which reason it becomes highly necessary for
every civilian and canonist that would act with safety as
a judge, or with prudence and reputation as an advocate,
to know in what cases and how far the english laws have
given sanction to the roman; in what points the latter are
rejected; and where they are both so intermixed and
blended together, as to form certain supplemental parts of
the common law of England, distinguished by the titles of
the king's maritime, the king's military, and the king's
ecclesiastical law. The propriety of which enquiry the
university of Oxford has for more than a century so
thoroughly seen, that in her statutes she appoints, that
one of the three questions to be annually discussed at the
act by the jurist-inceptors shall relate to the common
law; subjoining this reason, "quia juris civilis studiosos
decet haud imperitos esse juris municipalis, &
differentias exteri patriique juris notas habere." And
the university of Cambridge, in her statutes, has declared
herself to the same effect.
      From the general use and necessity of some
acquaintance with the common law, the inference were
extremely easy, with regard to the propriety of the
present institution, in a place to which gentlemen of all
ranks and degrees resort, as the fountain of all useful
knowledge. But how it has come to pass that a design of
this sort has never before taken place in the university,
and the reason why the study of our laws has in general
fallen into disuse, I shall previously proceed to enquire.
      Sir John Fortescue, in his panegyric on the laws of
England, (which was written in the reign of Henry the
sixth) puts a very obvious question in the mouth of the
young prince, whom he is exhorting to apply himself to
that branch of learning; "why the laws of England, being
so good, so fruitful, and so commodious, are not taught in
the universities, as the civil and canon laws are?" In
answer to which he gives what seems, with due deference be
it spoken, a very jejune and unsatisfactory reason; being
in short, that "as the proceedings at common law were in
his time carried on in three different tongues, the
english, the latin, and the french, that science must be
necessarily taught in those three several languages; but
that in the universities all sciences were taught in the
latin tongue only; and therefore he concludes, that they
could not be conveniently taught or studies in our
universities." But without attempting to examine
seriously the validity of this reason, (the very shadow of
which by the wisdom of your late constitutions is entirely
taken away) we perhaps may find out a better, or at least
a more plausible account, why the study of the municipal
laws has been banished from these seats of science, than

what the learned chancellor thought it prudent to give to
his royal pupil.

That ancient collection of unwritten maxims and
customs, which is called the common law, however
compounded or from whatever fountains derived, had
subsisted immemorially in this kingdom; and, though
somewhat altered and impaired by the violence of the
times, had in great measure weathered the rude shock of
the norman conquest. This had endeared it to the people
in general, as well because its decisions were universally
known, as because it was found to be excellently adapted
to the genius of the english nation. In the knowledge of
this law consisted great part of the learning of those
dark ages; it was then taught, says Mr. Selden, in the
monasteries, in the universities, and in the families of
the principal nobility. The clergy in particular, as they
then engrossed almost every other branch of learning, so
(like their predecessors the british druids) they were
peculiarly remarkable for their proficiency in the study
of the law. Nullus clericus nisi causidicus, is the
character given of them soon after the conquest by William
of Malmsbury. The judges therefore were usually created
out of the sacred order, as was likewise the case among
thenormans, and all the inferior offices were supplied by
the lower clergy, which has occasioned their successors to
be denominated clerks to this day.

But the common law of England, being not committed to
writing, but only handed down by tradition, use and
experience, was not so heartily relished by the foreign
clergy; who came over hither in shoals during the reign of
the conqueror and his two sons, and were utter strangers
to our constitution as well as our language. And an
accident, which soon after happened, had nearly completed
its ruin. A copy of Justinian's pandects, being newly
discovered at Amafsi, soon brought the civil law into
vogue all over the west of Europe, where before it was
quite laid aside and in a manner forgotten; though some
traces of it's authority remained in Italy and the eastern
provinces of the empire. This now became in a particular
manner the favourite of the popish clergy, who borrowed
the method and many of the maxims of their canon law from
this original. The study of it was introduced into
several universities abroad, particularly that of Bologna;
where exercises were performed, lectures read, and degrees
conferred in this faculty, as in other branches of
science: and many nations on the continent, just then
beginning to recover from the convulsions consequent upon
the overthrow of the roman empire, and settling by degrees
into peaceable forms of government, adopted the civil law,
(being the best written system then extant) as the basis
of their several constitutions; blending and interweaving
it among their own feodal customs, in some places with a
more extensive, in others a more confined authority.

Nor was it long before the prevailing mode of the
times reached England. For Theobald, a norman abbot,
being elected to the see of Canterbury, and extremely
addicted to this new study, brought over with him in his
retinue many learned proficients therein; and among the

rest Roger sirnamed Vacarius, whom he placed in the
university of Oxford, to teach it to the people of this
country. But it did not meet with the same easy reception
in England, where a mild and rational system of laws had
been long established, as it did upon the continent; and,
though the monkish clergy (devoted to the will of a
foreign primate) received it with eagerness and zeal, yet
the laity, who were more interested to preserve the old
constitution, and had already severely felt the effect of
many norman innovations, continued wedded to the use of
the common law.   King Stephen immediately published a
proclamation, forbidding the study of the laws, then newly
imported from Italy; which was treated by the monks as a
piece of impiety, and, though it might prevent the
introduction of the civil law process into our courts of
justice, yet did not hinder the clergy from reading and
teaching it in their own schools and monasteries.

From this time the nation seems to have been divided
into two parties; the bishops and clergy, many of them
foreigners, who applied themselves wholly to the study of
the civil and canon laws, which now came to be inseparably
interwoven with each other; and the nobility and laity,
who adhered with equal pertinacity to the old common law:
both of them reciprocally jealous of what they were
unacquainted with, and neither of them perhaps allowing
the opposite system that real merit which is abundantly to
be found in each.   This appears on the one hand from the
spleen with which the monastic writers speak of our
municipal laws upon all occasions; and, on the other, from
the firm temper which the nobility shewed at the famous
parliament of Merton; when the prelates endeavoured to
procure an act, to declare all bastards legitimate in case
the parents intermarried at any time afterwards; alledging
this only reason, because holy church (that is, the canon
law) declared such children legitimate: but "all the
earls and barons (says the parliament roll) with one voice
answered, that they would not change the laws of England,
which have hitherto been used and approved." And we find
the same jealousy prevailing above a century afterwards,
when the nobility declared with a kind of prophetic
spirit, "that the realm of England hath never been unto
this hour, neither by the consent of our lord the king and
the lords of parliament shall it ever be, ruled or
governed by the civil law."   And of this temper between
the clergy and laity many more instances might be given.

While things were in this situation, the clergy,
finding it impossible to root out the municipal law, began
to withdraw themselves by degrees from the temporal
courts; and to that end, very early in the reign of king
Henry the third, episcopal constitutions were published,
forbidding all ecclesiastics to appear as advocates in
foro saeculari; nor did they long continue to act as
judges there, not caring to take the oath of office which
was then found necessary to be administered, that they
should in all things determine according to the law and
custom of this realm; though they still kept possession of
the high office of chancellor, an office then of little
juridical power; and afterwards, as it's business

increased by degrees, they modelled the process of the court at their own discretion.

But wherever they retired, and wherever their authority extended, they carried with them the same zeal to introduce the rules of the civil, in exclusion of the municipal law. This appears in a particular manner from the spiritual courts of all denominations, from the chancellor's courts in both our universities, and from the high court of chancery beforementioned; in all of which the proceedings are to this day in a course much conformed to the civil law: for which no tolerable reason can be assigned, unless that these courts were all under the immediate direction of the popish ecclesiastics, among whom it was a point of religion to exclude the municipal law; pope Innocent the fourth having forbidden the very reading of it by the clergy, because its decisions were not founded on the imperial constitutions, but merely on the customs of the laity. And if it be considered, that our universities began about that period to receive their present form of scholastic discipline; that they were then, and continued to be till the time of the reformation, entirely under the influence of the popish clergy; (sir John Mason the first protestant, being also the first lay chancellor of Oxford) this will lead us to perceive the reason, why the study of the roman laws was in those days of bigotry pursued with such alacrity in these seats of learning; and why the common law was entirely despised, and esteemed little better than heretical.

And, since the reformation, many causes have conspired to prevent its becoming a part of academical education. As, first, long usage and established custom; which, as in every thing else, so especially in the forms of scholastic exercise, have justly great weight and authority. Secondly, the real intrinsic merit of the civil law, considered upon the footing of reason and not of obligation, which was well known to the instructors of our youth; and their total ignorance of the merit of the common law, though its equal at least, and perhaps an improvement on the other. But the principal reason of all, that has hindered the introduction of this branch of learning, is, that the study of the common law, being banished from hence in the times of popery, has fallen into a quite different chanel, and has hitherto been wholly cultivated in another place. But as this long usage and established custom, of ignorance in the laws of the land, begin now to be thought unreasonable; and as by this means the merit of those laws will probably be more generally known; we may hope that the method of studying them will soon revert to its ancient course, and the foundations at least of that science will be laid in the two universities; without being exclusively confined to the chanel which it fell into at the times I have been just describing.

For, being then entirely abandoned by the clergy, a few stragglers excepted, the study and practice of it devolved of course into the hands of laymen; who entertained upon their parts a most hearty aversion to the civil law, and made no scruple to profess their contempt, nay even their ignorance of it, in the most public manner. But still, as the ballance of learning was greatly on the side of the clergy, and as the common law was no longer taught, as formerly, in any part of the kingdom, it must have been subjected to many inconveniences, and perhaps would have been gradually lost and overrun by the civil, (a suspicion well justified from the frequent transcripts of Justinian to be met with in Bracton and Fleta) had it not been for a peculiar incident, which happened at a very critical time, and contributed greatly to its support.

The incident I mean was the fixing the court of common pleas, the grand tribunal for disputes of property, to be held in one certain spot; that the seat of ordinary justice might be permanent and notorious to all the nation. Formerly that, in conjunction with all the other superior courts, was held before the king's capital justiciary of England, in the aula regis, or such of his palaces wherein his royal person resided, and removed with his houshold from one end of the kingdom to the other. This was found to occasion great inconvenience to the suitors; to remedy which it was made an article of the great charter of liberties, both that of king John and king Henry the third, that "common pleas should no longer follow the king's court, but be held in some certain place:" in consequence of which they have ever since been held (a few necessary removals in times of the plague excepted) in the palace of Westminster only. This brought together the professors of the municipal law, who before were dispersed about the kingdom, and formed them into an aggregate body; whereby a society was established of persons, who (as Spelman observes) addicting themselves wholly to the study of the laws of the land, and no longer considering it as a mere subordinate science for the amusement of leisure hours, soon raised those laws to that pitch of perfection, which they suddenly attained under the auspices of our english Justinian, king Edward the first.

In consequence of this lucky assemblage, they naturally fell into a kind of collegiate order; and, being excluded from Oxford and Cambridge, found it necessary to establish a new university of their own. This they did by purchasing at various times certain houses (now called the inns of court and of chancery) between the city of Westminster, the place of holding the king's courts, and the city of London; for advantage of ready access to the one, and plenty of provisions in the other. Here exercises were performed, lectures read, and degrees were at length conferred in the common law, as at other universities in the canon and civil. The degrees were those of barristers (first stiled apprentices from apprendre, to learn) who answered to our bachelors; as the state and degree of a serjeant, servientis ad legem, did to that of doctor.

The crown seems to have soon taken under it's protection this infant seminary of common law; and, the more effectually to foster and cherish it, king Henry the third in the nineteenth year of his reign, issued out an

order directed to the mayor and sheriffs of London,
commanding that no regent of any law schools <u>within</u> that
city should for the future teach law therein. The word,
law, or <u>leges</u>, being a general term, may create some doubt
at this distance of time whether the teaching of the civil
law, or the common, or both, is hereby restrained. But in
either case it tends to the same end. If the civil law
only is prohibited, (which is Mr. Selden's opinion) it is
then a retaliation upon the clergy, who had excluded the
common law from <u>their</u> seats of learning. If the municipal
law be also included in the restriction, (as sir Edward
Coke understands it, and which the words seem to import)
then the intention is evidently this; by preventing
private teachers within the walls of the city, to collect
all the common lawyers into the one public university,
which was newly instituted in the suburbs.

In this juridical university (for such it is insisted
to have been by Fortescue and sir Edward Coke) there are
two sorts of collegiate houses; one called inns of
chancery, in which the younger students of the law used to
be placed, "learning and studying, says Fortescue, the
originals and as it were the elements of the law; who
profiting therein, as they grow to ripeness, so are they
admitted into the greater inns of the same study, called
the inns of court." And in these inns of both kinds, he
goes on to tell us, the knights and barons, with other
grandees and noblemen of the realm, did use to place their
children, though they did not desire to have them
thoroughly learned in the law, or to get their living by
it's practice: and that in his time there were about two
thousand students at these several inns, all of whom he
informs us were <u>filii nobilium</u>, or gentlemen born.

Hence it is evident that (though under the influence
of the monks our universities neglected this study, yet)
in the time of Henry the sixth it was thought highly
necessary and was the universal practice, for the young
nobility and gentry to be instructed in the originals and
elements of the laws. But by degrees this custom has
fallen into disuse; so that in the reign of queen
Elizabeth sir Edward Coke does not reckon above a thousand
students, and the number at present is very considerably
less. Which seems principally owing to these reasons:
first, because the inns of chancery being now almost
totally filled by the inferior branch of the profession,
they are neither commodious nor proper for the resort of
gentlemen of any rank or figure; so that there are now
very rarely any young students entered at the inns of
chancery: secondly, because in the inns of court all
sorts of regimen and academical superintendance, either
with regard to morals or studies, are found impracticable
and therefore entirely neglected: lastly, because persons
of birth and fortune, after having finished their usual
courses at the universities, have seldom leisure or
resolution sufficient to enter upon a new scheme of study
at a new place of instruction. Wherefore few gentlemen
now resort to the inns of court, but such for whom the
knowledge of practice is absolutely necessary; such, I
mean, as are intended for the profession: the rest of our

gentry, (not to say our nobility also) having usually
retired to their estates, or visited foreign kingdoms, or
entered upon public life, without any instruction in the
laws of the land; and indeed with hardly any opportunity
of gaining instruction, unless it can be afforded them in
these seats of learning.

And that these are the proper places, for affording
assistances of this kind to gentlemen of all stations and
degrees, cannot (I think) with any colour of reason be
denied. For not one of the objections, which are made to
the inns of court and chancery, and which I have just
enumerated, will hold with regard to the universities.
Gentlemen may here associate with gentlemen of their own
rank and degree. Nor are their conduct and studies left
entirely to their own discretion; but regulated by a
discipline so wise and exact, yet so liberal, so sensible
and manly, that their conformity to its rules (which does
at present so much honour to our youth) is not more the
effect of constraint, than of their own inclinations and
choice. Neither need they apprehend too long an avocation
hereby from their private concerns and amusements, or
(what is a more noble object) the service of their friends
and their country. This study will go hand in hand with
their other pursuits: it will obstruct none of them; it
will ornament and assist them all.

But if, upon the whole, there are any, still wedded
to monastic prejudice, that can entertain a doubt how far
this study is properly and regularly academical, such
persons I am afraid either have not considered the
constitution and design of an university, or else think
very meanly of it. It must be a deplorable narrowness of
mind, that would confine these seats of instruction to the
limited views of one or two learned professions. To the
praise of this age be it spoken, a more open and generous
way of thinking begins now universally to prevail. The
attainment of liberal and genteel accomplishments, though
not of the intellectual sort, has been thought by our
wisest and most affectionate patrons, and very lately by
the whole university, no small improvement of our ancient
plan of education; and therefore I may safely affirm that
nothing (how unusual soever) is, under due regulations,
improper to be taught in this place, which is proper for a
gentleman to learn. But that a science, which
distinguishes the criterions of right and wrong; which
teaches to establish the one, and prevent, punish, or
redress the other; which employs in it's theory the
noblest faculties of the soul, and exerts in it's practice
the cardinal virtues of the heart; a science, which is
universal in it's use and extent, accommodated to each
individual, yet comprehending the whole community; that a
science like this should have ever been deemed unnecessary
to be studied in a university, is matter of astonishment
and concern. Surely, if it were not before an object of
academical knowledge, it was high time to make it one; and
to those who can doubt the propriety of it's reception
among us (if any such there be) we may return an answer in
their own way; that ethics are confessedly a branch of
academical learning, and Aristotle himself has said,

speaking of the laws of his own country, that jurisprudence or the knowledge of those laws is the principal and most perfect branch of ethics.

From a thorough conviction of this truth, our munificent benefactor Mr. Viner, having employed above half a century in amassing materials for new modelling and rendering more commodious the rude study of the laws of the land, consigned both the plan and execution of these his public spirited designs to the wisdom of his parent university. Resolving to dedicate his learned labours, "to the benefit of posterity and the perpetual service of his country," he was sensible he could not perform his resolutions in a better and more effecutal manner, than by extending to the youth of this place those assistances, of which he so well remembered and so heartility regretted the want. And the sense, which the university has entertained of this ample and most useful benefaction, must appear beyond a doubt from their gratitude in receiving it with all possible marks of esteem; from their alacrity and unexampled dispatch in carrying it into execution; and, above all, for the laws and constitutions by which they have effectually guarded it from the neglect and abuse to which such institutions are liable. We have seen an universal emulation, who best should understand, or most faithfully pursue, the designs of our generous patron: and with pleasure we recollect, that those who are most distinguished by their quality, their fortune, their station, their learning, or their experience, have appeared the most zealous to promote the success of Mr. Viner's establishment.

The advantages that might result to the science of the law itself, when a little more attended to in these seats of knowledge, perhaps would be very considerable. The leisure and abilities of the learned in these retirements might either suggest expedients, or execute those dictated by wiser heads, for improving it's method, retrenching its superfluities, and reconciling the little contrarieties, which the practice of many centuries will necessarily create in any human system: a task, which those who are deeply employed in business, and the more active scenes of profession, can hardly condescend to engage in. And as to interest, or (which is the same) the reputation of the universities themselves, I may venture to pronounce, that if ever this study should arrive to any tolerable perfection, either here or at Cambridge, the nobility and gentry of this kingdom would not shorten their residence upon this account, nor perhaps entertain a worse opinion of the benefits of academical education. Neither should it be considered as a matter of light importance, that while we thus extend the pomoeria of university learning, and adopt a new tribe of citizens within these philosophical walls, we interest a very numerous and very powerful profession in the preservation of our rights and revenues.

For I think it is past dispute, that those gentlemen, who resort to the inns of court with a view to pursue the profession, will find it expedient (whenever it is practicable) to lay the previous foundations of this, as

well as every other science, in one of our learned
universities. We may appeal to the experience of every
sensible lawyer, whether any thing can be more hazardous
of discouraging than the usual entrance on the study of
the law. A raw and unexperienced youth, in the most
dangerous season of life, is transplanted on a sudden into
the midst of allurements to pleasure, without any
restraint or check, but what his own prudence can suggest;
with no public direction in what course to pursue his
enquiries; no private assistance to remove the distresses
and difficulties, which will always embarass a beginner.
In this situation he is expected to sequester himself from
the world, and by a tedious lonely process to extract the
theory of law from a mass of undigested learning; or else
by an assiduous attendance on the courts to pick up theory
and practice together, sufficient to qualify him for the
ordinary run of business. How little therefore is it to
be wondered at, that we hear of so frequent miscarriages;
that so many gentlemen of bright imaginations grown weary
of so unpromising a search, and addict themselves wholly
to amusements, or other less innocent pursuits; and that
so many persons of moderate capacity confuse themselves as
first setting out, and continue every dark and puzzled
during the remainder of their lives!

The evident want of some assistance in the rudiments
of legal knowledge, has given birth to a practice, which,
if every it had grown to be general, must have proved of
extremely pernicious consequence: I mean the custom, by
some so very warmly recommended, to drop all liberal
education, as of no use to lawyers; and to place them, in
its stead, at the desk of some skillful attorney; in order
to initiate them early in all the depths of practice, and
render them more dextrous in the mechanical part of
business. A few instances of particular persons, (men of
excellent learning, and umblemished integrity) who, in
spight of this method of education, have shone in the
foremost ranks of the bar, have afforded some kind of
sanction to this illiberal path to the profession, and
biased many parents, of shortsighted judgment, in its
favour: not considering, that there are some geniuses
formed to overcome all disadvantages, and that from such
particular instances no general rules can be formed; nor
observing, that those very persons have frequently
recommended, by the most forcible of all examples, the
disposal of their own offspring, a very different
foundation of legal studies, a regular academical
education. Perhaps too, in return, I could now direct
their eyes to our principal seats of justice, and suggest
a few hints, in favour of university learning: - but in
these all who hear me, I know, have already prevented me.

Making therefore due allowance for one or two shining
exceptions, experience may teach us to foretell, that a
lawyer thus educated to the bar, in subservience to
attorneys and solicitors, will find he has begun at the
wrong end. If practice be the whole he is taught,
practice must also be the whole he will ever know: if he
be uninstructed in the elements and first principles upon
which the rule of practice is founded, the least variation

from established precedents will totally distract and bewilder him: *ita lex scripta est* is the utmost his knowledge will arrive at; he must never aspire to form, and seldom expect to comprehend, any arguments drawn a priori, from the spirit of the laws and the natural foundations of justice.

Nor is that all; for (as few persons of birth, or fortune, or even of scholastic education, will submit to the drudgery of servitude and the manual labour of copying the trash of an office) should this infatuation prevail to any considerable degree, we must rarely expect to see a gentleman of distinction or learning at the bar. And what the consequence may be, to have the interpretation and enforcement of the laws (which include the entire disposal of our properties, liberties, and lives) fall wholly into the hands of obscure or illiterate men, is matter of very public concern.

The inconveniences here pointed out can never be effectually prevented, but by making academical education a previous step to the profession of the common law, and at the same time making the rudiments of the law a part of academical education. For sciences are of a sociable disposition, and flourish best in the neighbourhood of each other: nor is there any branch of learning, but may be helped and improved by assistances drawn from other arts. If therefore the student in our laws hath formed both his sentiments and style, by perusal and imitation of the purest classical writers, among whom the historians and orators will best deserve his regard; if he can reason with precision, and separate argument from fallacy, by the clear simple rules of pure unsophisticated logic; if he can fix his attention, and steadily pursue truth through any the most intricate deduction, by the use of mathematical demonstrations; if he has enlarged his conceptions of nature and art, by a view of the several branches of genuine, experimental philosophy; if he has impressed on his mind the sound maxims of the law of nature, the best and most authentic foundation of human laws; if, lastly, he has contemplated those maxims reduced to a practical system in the laws of imperial Rome; if he has done this or any part of it, (though all may be easily done under as able instructors as ever graced any seats of learning) a student thus qualified may enter upon the study of the laws with incredible advantage and reputation. And if, at the conclusion, or during the acquisition of these accomplishments, he will afford himself here a year or two's farther leisure, to lay the foundation of his future labours in a solid scientifical method, without thirsting too early to attend that practice which it is impossible he should rightly comprehend, he will afterwards proceed with the greatest ease, and will unfold the most intricate points with an intuitive rapidity and clearness.

I shall not insist upon such motives as might be drawn from principles of oeconomy, and are applicable to particulars only: I reason upon more general topis. And therefore to the qualities of the head, which I have just enumerated, I cannot but add those of the heart;

affectionate loyalty to the king, a zeal for liberty and
the constitution, a sense of real honour, and well
grounded principles of religion; as necessary to form a
truly valuable english lawyer, a Hyde, a Hale, or a
Talbot. And, whatever the ignorance of some, or
unkindness of others, may have hertofore untruly
suggested, experience will warrant us to affirm that these
endowments of loyalty and public spirit, of honour and
religion, are no where to be found in more high perfection
than in the two universities of this kingdom.

Before I conclude, it may perhaps be expected that I
lay before you a short and general account, of the method
I propose to follow in endeavouring to execute the trust
you have been pleased to repose in my hands. And in these
solemn lectures, which are ordained to be read at the
entrance of every term, (more perhaps to do public honour
to this laudable institution, than for the private
instruction of individuals) I presume it will best answer
the intent of our benefactor and the expectation of this
learned body, if I attempt to illustrate at times such
detached titles of the law, as are the most easy to be
understood, and most capable of historical or critical
ornament. But in reading the complete course, which is
annually consigned to my care, a more regular method will
be necessary; and, till a better is proposed, I shall take
the liberty to follow the same that I have already
submitted to the public. To fill up and finish that
outline with propriety and correctness, and to render the
whole intelligible to the uninformed minds of beginners,
(whom we are too apt to suppose acquainted with terms and
ideas, which they never had opportunity to learn) this
must be my ardent endeavour, tho'by no means my promise to
accomplish. You will permit me however very briefly to
describe, rather what I conceive an academical expounder
of the laws should do, than what I have ever known to be
done.

He should consider his course as a general map of the
law, marking out the shape of the country, its connections
and boundaries, it's greater divisions and principal
cities: it is not his business to describe minutely the
subordinate limits, or to fix the longitude and latitude
of every inconsiderable Hamlet. His attention should be
engaged, like that of the readers in Fortescue's inns of
chancery, "in tracing out the originals and asit were the
elements of the law." For if, as Justinian has observed,
the tender understanding of the student be loaded at the
first with a multitude and variety of matter, it will
either occasion him to desert his studies, or will carry
him heavily through them, with much labour, delay, and
despondence. These originals should be traced to their
fountains, as well as our distance will permit; to the
customs of the Britons and Germans, as recorded by Caesar
and Tactitus; to the codes of the northern nations on the
continent, and more especially to those of our own saxon
princes; to the rules of the roman law, either left here
in the days of Papinian, or imported by Vacarius and his
followers; but, above all, to that inexhaustible reservoir
of legal antiquities and learning, the feodal law, or, as

Spelman has entitled it, the law of nations in our western orb. These primary rules and fundamental principles should be weighed and compared with the precepts of the law of nature, and the practice of other countries; should be explained by reasons, illustrated by examples, and confirmed by undoubted authorities; their history should be deduced, their changes and revolutions observed, and it should be shewn how far they are connected with, or have at any time been affected by, the civil transactions of the kingdom.

A plan of his nature, if executed with care and ability, cannot fail of administering a most useful and rational entertainment to students of all ranks and professions; and yet it must be confessed that the study of the laws is not merely a matter of amusement: for as a very judicious writer has observed upon a similar occasion, the learner "will be considerably disappointed, if he looks for entertainment without the expence of attention." An attention, however, not greater than is usually bestowed in mastering the rudiments of other sciences or sometimes in pursuing a favorite recreation or exercise. And this attention is not equally necessary to be exerted by every student upon every occasion. Some branches of the law, as the formal process of civil suits, and the subtile distinctions incident to landed property, which are the most difficult to be thoroughly understood, are the least worth the pains of understanding, except to such gentlemen as intend to pursue the profession. To others I may venture to apply, with a slight alteration, the words of sir John Fortescue when first his royal pupil determines to engage in this study. "It will not be necessary for a gentleman, as such, to examine with a close application the critical niceties of the law. It will fully be sufficient, and he may well enough be denominated a lawyer, if under the instruction of a master he traces up the principles and grounds of the law, even to their original elements. Therefore in a very short period, and with very little labour, he may be sufficiently informed in the laws of his country, if he will but apply his mind in good earnest to receive and apprehend them. For, though such knowledge as is necessary for a judge is hardly to be acquired by the lucubrations of twenty years, yet with a genius of tolerable perspicacity, that knowledge which is fit for a person of birth or condition may be learned in a single year, without neglecting his other improvements."

To the few therefore (the very few, I am persuaded,) that entertain such unworthy notions of an university, as to suppose it intended for mere dissipation of thought; to such as mean only to while away the awkward interval from childhood to twenty one, between the restraints of the school and the licentiousness of politer life, in a calm middle state of mental and of moral inactivity; to these Mr. Viner gives no invitation to an entertainment which they never can relish. But to the long and illustrious train of noble and ingenuous youth, who are not more distinguished among us by their birth and possessions, than by the regularity of their conduct, and their thirst

after useful knowledge, to these our benefactor has
consecrated the fruits of a long and laborious life, worn
out in the duties of his calling; and will joyfully
reflect (if such reflections can be now the employment of
his thoughts) that he could not more effectually have
benefited posterity, or contributed to the service of the
public, than by founding an institution which may instruct
the rising generation in the wisdom of our civil polity,
and inform them with a desire to be still better
acquainted with the laws and constitution of their
country.

– 5 –

Frederick Ritso

Introduction to the Science of the Law
(1815)

Upon questions of difficulty, in which others are equally involved with us, we naturally direct our first attention to the practice of "the many," and are generally much more disposed to assent to its propriety, than to be at the pains of convincing ourselves of its merits. From the influence of this popular way of thinking, a man will conform himself to the grossest errors, or incur the most unnecessary and often fatal embarrassments with unenquiring indolence and inconsideration. He will be apt to disregard the silent testimony of his proper reason and judgment, and seeing the resignation, which is shown by others, under the same circumstances, he will consider it as a sort of excuse, at least in his own eyes, for his particular folly or supineness.

It is more particularly in the prosecution of that professional science, of which we are now treating, that we see the inconvenience, and extreme danger of thus blindly falling into the common practice. There hardly indeed passes a day, which does not produce the repetition of the same question; -- what plan, what course of reading would you recommend to us, in order that we may be competently instructed in the laws, and local constitutions of our native land? A question upon which depends the most important and valuable branch of liberal and polite learning, and which is personally interesting, not to every professional reader alone, but to every gentleman and scholar in the kingdom.

I presume then, with all due deference, from a knowledge of the inconveniences, which, in common with every unassisted beginner, I have had to contend with, in the prosecution of this course of study, that the discussion of the proposed plan of education, recommended to us by one of our ablest and most eminent judges, will be not unacceptable to those who are desirous of attaining to this branch of instruction. Such is, in few words, the object of the following publication; and, I trust, that the more candid reader will impute it less to the vanity of being an author, that I give it under my own name, than to a wish to evince the sincerity with which I offer it, and to shew myself responsible for its accuracy.

to a wish to evince the sincerity with which I offer it, and to shew myself responsible for its accuracy.

The profession, which of all others is more peculiarly the province of reason and of intellect, and affords the most extensive field for the exercise of the energetic powers of "the mind," is unquestionably that which we understand, in one word, by "the bar." In many other paths of life, (for it is not necessary that we should speak of any one in particular,) a man may be advanced by other talents than his own: he may have many a better recommendation in his favour than that for which he would be indebted to his own exertions, and an acquired patronage may supersede the necessity of deserving it. The profession of the law, on the contrary, yields no tributary honours to the canvassings of affection, nor affords its unsullied laurels to be prostituted to the fugitive and accidental pretensions of adventitious patronage. The reliance of the law student must be on his own strength; he must rise by his own single proficiency; he must be the artificer of his own fortune; -- neither, indeed, is there any other profession in which more diligent and persevering application is required, or which, in the exercise of its higher functions, demands more extraordinary efforts of quickness and subtilty of apprehension, of vigour and versatility of intellect, of solidity of judgment, of accurate and profound reasoning, and of delicacy and precision of expression. It is not to be minutely conversant in the letter and the practice of the law alone, in which the advantage of a law education principally consists, but rather in the attainment, by long study and meditation, of those superior qualifications of an enlarged and enlightened understanding, which are necessary to fulfill with dignity the functions of a lawyer, whether to aid, by the wisdom of his counsels, the dispensations of administrative justice, or to defend the life, the honour, and the fortune of his clients, and to render the cause of truth and innocence triumphant.

But let us here pause a moment, to consider of the means by which we may, ultimately, attain to this high professional merit and desired improvement of education. What scheme, -- what plan of study shall we adopt, in order to arrive at it? We little think of the extent of the inconvenience we incur when we embark upon this new element, to launch as it were into a new sphere of science, with no public directions in what course to pursue our studies, and with no private assistance to remove the distresses and difficulties which always embarrass the beginner!

Indeed, when we reflect upon this single circumstance, we shall find it to be easily accounted for, that we are exposed to more frequent disappointments and miscarriages in this particular line of life than in any other. We all set out with the same land of promise before us, and not unfrequently, (I apprehend,) with the same degree of personal vanity and confidence in the expectation of reaching it. But the scene changes as we advance: increasing doubts insensibly overcloud the prospect which was at first so inspiring, till meeting with an incessant train of unforeseen obstacles, we are kept in a constant state of the most discouraging uncertainty and conjecture; we cannot choose, but guess, at what we have not experience enough to see in a clearer point of view, and at every successive question that arises, we find new subject for surprise and perplexity.

It is this inconvenience of having neither fixed directions to pursue, nor particular assistance to recur to, under encreasing difficulties and embarrassments, that gives occasion to the immense disproportion there is between "the many" who enrol themselves in this learned and honourable profession, and "the few" who have the good fortune to succeed in it. The eventual disappointments we complain of, have no other than this foundation; inde mali labes, there lies the root of the disease; but, like the inexpert physician, who loses his labour upon the symptomatic, while he overlooks the principal disorder, we lament the difficulties we are exposed to, and yet persist to follow a plan of education in which they are radically inherent. For such in fact I take to be the prevailing system (as I shall endeavour more fully to demonstrate in the course of the succeeding pages) of reading and common-placing Blackstone's Commentaries, and of attending a special pleader's or attorney's office for some two or three years, to copy precedents. When we afterwards emerge into the profession from this officinal purgatory, how few of our number reach the happy plains: --

> Exinde per amplum
> Mittimur elysium, et pauci laeta arva tenemus!

It is, indeed, far from my intention to presume to insinuate that those professional gentlemen who have pupils under their care, do not do them ample justice; but, independently of the avocations of actual business, by which they are principally occupied, it is not expected of them, according to the prevailing system, that they should give lectures. We must take the general usage as it is, and not build upon those rare instances which are but exceptions to it. Men will not read with their pupils, when they can set them down quietly at the desk to copy precedents; -- they will not, unsolicited, volunteer the arduous undertaking of developing the science of the law, of explaining the theory of its principles, of demonstrating the results, elucidating the analogies, and in short, of clearing away each technical difficulty by discussion. How much easier is it to leave the student to the exercise of his own industry, to copy precedents of which no discussion is required, and to read and common-place Blackstone's Commentaries, which, as far as they go, have need of no explanation! An inexperienced beginner in the profession commences his education under these auspices. Like the good monk who reads his breviary as he finds it, he believes that this is the best of all possible plans to be adopted, and the ne plus ultra of professional learning: --

Beyond this flood a frozen continent
Lies dark and wild, beat with perpetual storms
Of tempest and dire hail!

But this contracted and illiberal notion of the
nature of an introduction to the science of the law, has a
tendency, among its many other ill consequences, to bring
this branch of instruction into discredit and disesteem.
It tends to confound the lawyer with the practitioner, the
liberal scholar with the mechanic, and consequently to
render an application to this course of study both an
irksome and an endless labour, distasteful to the man of
science, and fit for those only whose intention it is to
follow the law as a profession.

That men, who in all other respects possess an
acknowledged superiority in point of education, should be
thus precluded, as it were, from this most interesting and
important species of information, -- that they should be
shut out from the knowledge of the local constitutions of
their native land, through a prejudiced misapprehension of
the means of attaining it, is at once a most humiliating
and disgraceful spectacle, dishonourable and injurious to
the individual, and inconvenient, and mischievous to the
community. The former, indeed, will in many instances be
found to be wanting to himself, both as a British
gentleman and a British subject; he will frequently be
unequal to those ordinary practical duties, in the
conscientious discharge of which consists the essential
difference between the good member of society and the bad;
he is no fit person to be referred to in the character of
an arbitrator; he is unworthy to be confided in as the
appointed guardian or trustee of a common family
settlement! The same humiliating incapacity which unfits
him for the discharge of these private duties, renders him
an equally insignificant and useless member of society
upon occasions of a more public nature. The juror, upon
whose solemn verdict depends the adjudication of the
property or the disposal of the lives of his fellow
subjects, has not unfrequently to decide complicated
questions both of <u>law</u> and <u>fact</u>, of which a more than
ordinary degree of legal skill and judgment is necessarily
required in the solution. In gentlemen appointed to fill
the commission of the peace, (a situation in which they
have such ample power to maintain the good order of their
neighbourhood,) a want of instruction in this species of
learning, is confessedly still more inconsistent and
inexcusable. Will the magistrate who misunderstands his
business or misconceives his authority, administer legal
and effectual justice; or will he not rather be the object
of the contempt of his inferiors, and expose himself to
the censure of those to whom he is accountable for his
conduct? The inconvenience increases in proportion as the
sphere of action is enlarged. The man who has not legal
skill and judgment enough to serve with ability upon a
jury, or to act as a justice of the peace, of how much
less ability is he to represent his country in parliament,
and to fulfil the more arduous and comprehensive duties of
statesman and legislator! -- So necessary is it that every

man of rank and fortune in the kingdom should apply
himself by a regular and methodical course of study, to
acquire at least a competent knowledge of the nature and
principles of the laws and the constitution of his
country!

But there is likewise another point of view in which
the proposed lucubrations have a much more extensive
influence than we are apt at first sight to be aware of,
and may be attended with the happiest advantages. -- They
eminently invigorate and fortify the mind's noblest
faculty -- the power of attention; they disciplines the
understanding, excite discrimination, give activity and
acuteness to the apprehension, and correct and mature the
judgment.   They teach us to think and to reason in our
youth, and will serve to employ us, and to render us
useful to others in old age.   In prosperity they grace and
embellish, in adversity they afford us comfort and
support.   There is no profession, no situation in life, in
which they do not at some time or other come into use:
they proceed with us through every vicissitude, attend us
in every walk, and imperceptibly nourish in our minds that
virtuous self-dependence which is the foundation of
whatever is dignified in character, and the parent of all
great and noble resolutions.

Neither is it in the improvement of the understanding
alone that we experience the advantages to be derived from
this course of study; it tends to improve the heart
equally, and has a visible influence in meliorating and
determining the moral character.   We insensibly awaken to
better feelings, and conceive a livelier and higher sense
of all our social and civil duties, from being impressed
with the evidences of truth and reason, upon which the
knowledge of the science of the law depends.   Perhaps the
truth of this remark, in which there is neither prejudice
nor enthusiasm, may be thus accounted for: in the study
of the mathematics, for example, if we take any primary
maxim or received truism, as "that two things which are
equal to a third, are equal to each other, or that equals
being taken from equals, equals will remain," the
conviction which it produces operates merely upon the
intellect, and has no immediate influence upon us in our
views of men and things as members of society.   But the
principles upon which the science of the law depends, are
in this respect widely different: the perception for
instance, of the degree of civil obligation we are under,
"to live honourably, to do wrong to none, and to render to
every man what is due to him," (which are three
fundamental maxims in the theory of judicial or legal
reasoning,) not only enlarges and informs the mind, but
tends, at the same time, to meliorate and determine the
moral character.   In the progress of this interesting
investigation, and the resulting conviction to which it
leads, of the equitable policy of each decision or rule of
law, the student will, therefore, not only have his
understanding enlightened and his mind improved, but will
infallibly become, at the same time, both a better man and
better citizen.   I conclude, that the course of study
which possesses these peculiar advantages, is rather to be

esteemed and attended to, for the purposes of education in
general, than all the learning in the world besides. For
I regard not the most exalted faculties of the human mind
as a gift worthy the Divinity, nor any assistance in the
improvement of them as a subject of gratitude to my
fellow-creatures, but from a conviction that to inform the
understanding corrects and enlarges the heart.

     To the student who intends to follow the practice of
the law, there are likewise further considerations to be
offered, and such as none ever neglected with impunity.
The obligations which are incurred at our own discretion,
are those of all others of which we are to be the least
excused for failing in the observance; and that which was
before incumbent upon us, becomes doubly so from being
identified with the discharge of a professional duty.   I
would ask then, have we taken any and what steps, in order
to prepare ourselves to fulfil the duties of this
self-created responsibility?   Shall we set out, for
instance, independently of all systems, and without having
any fixed plan before us, relying with the unprofessional
and unlearned reader upon the elements of the law, as we
find them recapitulated in Blackstone?   Or it is the
better way, do we imagine, to enter at once upon the
technical part, or, as it is sometimes called, the
business of the law, expecting to emerge forsooth from the
desk to science, and deferring in the meantime the
investigation of each difficult or doubtful doctrine, to
be ascertained at any future period when we may happen to
have occasion for it in practice?   This, indeed, would be
to plunge into the very error which has been constantly
deprecated by all our best and most approved lawyers, and
especially by Lord Coke himself, who ceases not to warn
and to conjure the student (in those pithy and quaint
words which are therefore more likely to impress
themselves upon the memory) against the "praepropera
praxis," and the "praepostera lectio."   From the
expectations we are apt to form of our infant talents,
and, perhaps, from an eagerness (which is still more
natural to us) to meet the expectations of others, we
almost insensibly fall into this fatal error; hurrying
into the profession as if the practitioner must be of
course the lawyer, when, alas! we have hardly yet science
enough to discuss an ordinary marriage settlement, or to
analyze a common report with accuracy. Modus mihi quidam
videtur tenendus, ne quae praepropere distringatur
immatura frons, et quicquid est illud adhuc acerbum
proferatur. Nam inde et contemptus operis innascitur, et
fundamenta jaciuntur impudentiae, et (quod est ubique
perniciosissimum) praevenit vires fiducia.

     It is true, that experience does not always come with
years, neither are grey hairs and a furrowed countenance
infallible marks of superior discernment and learning.
But there is something so preposterous in the premature
confidence of the beardless lawyer, that the very name of
the thing alone seems to carry with it an apparent
insinuation of ridicule. Do not let us deceive ourselves.
Professional instruction is no more to be forestalled,
than it is to be dispensed with. It is not the desultory

superficial smattering which a man may pick up any where
or every where, but the slow-paced erudition which grows
out of much patient reading and reflection.   It implies
the "viginti annorum lucubrationes," -- the results of the
study and meditation of a long series of years.   To affect
to hurry over, with slovenly inconsideration, this vast
and profound learning, betrays an entire ignorance both of
the nature and principles of it, and is one of the last
efforts of indiscretion and puerile vanity.   They were
lawyers such as these (I ween) that Cicero alludes to in
his Oration for Muraena, when he says "if you provoke me I
will make myself a lawyer in three days."   Si mihi
stomachum moveritis, triduo me jurisconsultum esse
profitebor.
     With respect, indeed, to the system of copying
precedents and filling up the marginal references in
Blackstone's Commentaries, there is no such apparent
defect (it must be allowed) in the quantity of either time
or labour which is usually bostowed upon it.   The only
objection to be found, is in the resulting inconvenience,
"that after having regularly gone through the prescribed
probation, the student has still the same irksome and
endless prospect before him -- the same doubts to perplex
-- the same difficulties to embarrass."   And here,
perhaps, it may be necessary to explain, that Blackstone's
Commentaries were never intended to be an institute for
educating and forming lawyers.   On the contrary, if we
examine them in this point of view, there can be nothing
more circumscribed and incomplete, than the information
they contain, nor more superficial and uninstitutional
than their manner of treating it; and, which is still more
distressing to the student, they abound with
contradictions and professional errors.   Of these, indeed,
I am aware that a very large proportion has been already
pointed out or corrected in the later editions, and much
useful learning has been supplied by the labour of
annotation.   This, however, is by no means the principal
ground upon which I contend against the propriety of
recommending the study of Blackstone's Commentaries as the
most advisable method of educating and forming men to be
lawyers.   They are not the supervenient inaccuracies which
are to be remarked in them, that I principally object to,
but their total misapplication in opposition to what the
learned commentator himself designed, to a purpose to
which they are in every point of view wholly inadequate.
In proceeding to show that this opinion has not been
unwarrantably concluded, I shall also expose, as far as I
am able, the truly absurd system (by which it has usually
been accompanied) of copy-precedents in an office; -- a
drudgery at which common sense revolts, and which is
equally unscientific and unlawyer-like.   But I shall beg
leave to preface the observations I may have to offer upon
this part of my subject by a few introductory remarks upon
the nature of the reasoning theory, or common sense of the
law; for if it were not from some strange misunderstanding
in this particular, there would not, I apprehend, be the
occasion which there now is, to say any thing in its
vindication.   That the means of acquiring may be fairly

estimated, let us first understand each other with respect
to the quality of the thing to be acquired.

In the first place, then, it is to be premised, that
the ground-work of our whole system of civil or municipal
jurisprudence, is that which we usually call, in one word,
"the common law," and which implies both the written
statutes of the realm, and the unwritten received customs
and usages together, the lex scripta et non scripta: and
it is, therefore, indifferently called "common law," or
"common right," being common to every one without any
particular act or reservation of his own.

The student who proposes to enter upon this course of
study, will, therefore, in the first place, have to direct
his principal attention to that most instructive and most
useful part of the history of our own country which
relates to the progress of improvement in the civil state.

Institutions which originated in the necessities of
our ancestors, must be necessarily traced back to the same
ancient source for their construction.   The only sure
guide that can be had in the investigation of the theory
of their principles, is the knowledge of the circumstances
to which they were accommodated, of the occasional or
local demand for them, of the original mischief to be
provided against, or the particular inconvenience that was
intended to be prevented by them.   And although it might
seem, perhaps, that every gentleman, or at least every
scholar, in the kingdom, should be already acquainted with
the branch of instruction, as far as it stands connected
with our general history, yet how seldom is it that our
general history has been presented to us, in this point of
view, as the object of our earlier attention and study.

It demands the exercise of our riper judgment to
apprehend through what vicissitudes the prosperity of a
state is made to depend upon the wisdom of its
legislature; to examine the boundary of those restrictions
upon natural liberty, which are necessary to be imposed
for the common good; to appreciate the causes of the
improved condition of the people in the progressive
improvement of their municipal institutions and civil
usages; and to trace the reverses that lead to anarchy and
the dissolution of empire, -- to the dereliction of those
fundamental maxims of common equity and common right,
which give to society the basis of its political
constitution, and dispose it to lasting harmony.

This inseperable affinity between the sources of
historical and of legal learning, may be said to
constitute one of the brightest images in the theory of
professional education; for as, on the one hand, our
history throws light upon our laws, so, in proportion to
the erudition we acquire as lawyers, we equally ensure our
proficiency as historians: they are sister Sciences,
which go hand in hand together, and mutually elucidate and
assist each other.

But the still more distinguishing characteristic of
professional learning in general, and which at the same
time fully evinces how much better adapted it is to the
researches of the more enlightened and liberal scholar
than to the labours of the plodding copyist, is the

inexhaustible variety, together with the fund of materials it affords for the exercise of "intellect," and the application of "the powers of reasoning."

A man may have as clear, certain, and demonstrative a knowledge of propositions in law, as of propositions in geometry or the mathematics; "for it suffices to the demonstration of any proposition, that the agreement or disagreement of the ideas of which it consists, can be so plainly and clearly perceived, that when it comes to be reflected upon, at any other period, the mind assents to it without doubt, and is certain of the truth of it." In the Essay on the human Understanding, the philosophic writer, having asserted this universal proposition, proceeds to remark, that "a man may be certainly said to know all those truths which are lodged in his memory, by such foregoing, full, and clear perception;" "and thus," he concludes, "the measure of right and wrong is to be made out by necessary consequences, from principles as incontestible as those of the mathematics, to any one who will apply himself with the same indifferency and attention to the one as he does to the other of these sciences."

There is no doubt, that the knowledge of the theory of the law must be afterwards perfected by practice; for the law is not a speculative but a practical science. But, even in this point of view, it becomes us, in the first instance, to apply ourselves to learn the arguments and the reasons of the law, in order to be prepared by it to understand the principles upon which practice is grounded. Lord Coke distinctly and repeatedly tells us, that "the law, nay the common law itself, is nothing else but reason;" that "it implies that perfection of reason whereunto a man attains by long study, often conference, long experience, and continual observation;" and, lastly, that "we must, therefore, diligently apply ourselves (avoiding those enemies to learning, the praepropera praxis et praepostera lectio,) to a timely and orderly course of reading, that, by searching into the arguments and reasons of the law we may so bring them home to our natural reason, that we may perfectly understand them as our own." This is in substance the uniform tenor of Lord Coke's advice and injunction to students; and what more useful branch of human instruction is there, or at once more interesting, more edifying, or more delightful to a man of liberal and improved mind, than thus scientifically to investigate the local constitutions of his native land, by deducing them, by necessary consequences, from those incontestible principles of plain reason and common intendment upon which they were originally framed or adopted! Non enim à Praetoris edicto neque ex duodecim tabulis, sed penitùs ex intimâ philosophiâ hauriendam juris disciplinam puto. Qui aliter jus tradunt, non tam justitiae quam litigandi vias tradunt.

But there are some who have imagined a sort of distinction, in the exposition of the theory of the law, between artificial reasoning and that of common sense; as if every proposition which partakes of a more artificial construction, and which consequently requires a more

elaborate method of proof in the illustration of it, can
therefore no longer be said, with propriety, to be common
sense; or, in other words, as if the idea of common sense
were in this instance necessarily to be confined to those
objects of science alone which are self-evident. The
philosophy of the reason, or common sense of the law, for
which we are here contending, is not always, (as Lord Coke
expresses it,) to be understood of every unlearned man's
reason, but of that which is warranted by authority of
law; or, as he describes it in another place, it is to be
understood of an artificial perfection of reason, acquired
by long study, observation, and experience; but which,
after all, amounts to no more than the same kind of
general preparation, which is necessarily required from us
in the pursuit of every other equally scientific object or
investigation whatever? The advancement of knowledge has
this condition inseparably attached to it, --

> "The man who reads, and to his reading brings not
> A spirit and judgment equal or superior,
> Uncertain and unsettled still remains."

Perhaps an example or two may serve to place this
matter in a clearer light: "Every proposition is said to
be demonstrable in its nature, when the mind can certainly
perceive the agreement or disagreement of the ideas of
which it consists, whether immediately, as in the case of
intuitive perception, or through the medium of those
intervening ideas which are called proofs." Now there is,
generally speaking, this perceivable agreement or
disagreement to be found in all our common-law doctrines;
that is to say, so far as they are capable of being put
into general propositions, however difficult those
propositions may be to the unprepared reader, or how
artificial soever in their construction. Let us take, for
example, the three following rules or maxims: 1st. "that
the father shall not be heir to the son;" 2nd. "that lands
descended or devised, shall not be charged with the simple
contract debts of the ancestor or devisor, although the
money may have been laid out in the purchase of those very
lands;" and 3d. "that lands shall rather descend to a
remote relation of the whole blood, or even escheat to the
lord, in preference to the owner's half brother." We have
here then, three distinct propositions, in which, upon the
first view of them, there is nothing like plain reason and
common sense to be discovered, without the help of those
intervening ideas from which we learn, first, that, under
the feudal system, (as it formerly subsisted in this
kingdom, till about the middle of the 17th century,) there
were certain personal military services to be performed,
as the price or condition upon which all lands were held,
and to which, therefore, the father, from his more
advanced age, was reasonably supposed to be less
competent; and, secondly, that it was equally matter of
policy, during the same period, that the freeholder, by
whom the feudal services were to be performed, should not
be distracted, by civil suits, from the discharge of so
important a duty; and, thirdly, that the right of

succession of the whole blood was only admitted upon
questions of adjudication of title, as a mere rule of
evidence to supply the frequent impossibility of proving a
descent from the first purchaser, without which (according
to a fundamental maxim of our law) no inheritance was ever
allowed, and, consequently, that this was an indulgence to
which the demi-kindred could have no reasonable
pretension; the descendants of one ancestor being much
less likely to be in the direct line of the purchasing
ancestor, than those who are descended from the same
couple of ancestors.

And what, then, do I mean to conclude from hence? I
answer, that the occasion of the difficulty (if any) which
occurs in the foregoing propositions, arises from a want
of due knowledge in ourselves, of the extent to which the
principles of the feudal polity have been engrafted into
our established system of remedial jurisprudence, and the
consequent distinction which the common law has taken
between feudal and commercial, with respect to the descent
or alienation of real or landed property.

From the period of the establishment of the feudal
polity in England, in the reign of William the Norman,
there seems to have been kept up a sort of constant
struggle between the spirit of commercialism, on the one
hand, and that of feudality on the other; and the
consequent operation of these two grand principles is to
be traced in every part of our law of landed property.
The construction of testamentary alienation, for example,
was originally adopted upon a purely commercial principle,
and in relaxation of the rigour of the feudal system,
which had a direct tendency to take lands out of
commerce, and to render them inalienable. But here,
again, the operation of a feudal principle interferes, and
requires a seisin in the devisor, analogous to that of the
feoffor or grantor in the case of alienation by deed; so
that, by the law of England, a will or devise of lands
does not operate by way of appointment of an heir
generally, as in the Roman law, but by way of legal
conveyance of the lands themselves; and, consequently,
cannot operate on any freehold lands, of which, at the
time of making the will, the party had not this species of
seisin. It is the same in the proposition, secondly above
mentioned, respecting the heir; when lands were allowed to
be freely aliened, for the sake of commerce, (for which
property is chiefly valuable,) it seemed to follow, as a
necessary consequence, that they should also be attached
for the debts and other incumbrances of the ancestor, upon
the same principle; but here, again, the operation of the
feudal law interfered, and, upon the principle "that the
heir claimed nothing from the ancestor, but came in under
the original feudal grant," it was held that he should not
be generally liable, like the executor, to the ancestor's
debts of every kind, but only to debts of record, and
debts by specialty, in which the heir was named; and the
same distinction continues, under certain qualifications,
to prevail even to this day. And so in the two other
examples which have been mentioned. The feud was made
"generally" heritable in relaxation of the rigour of the

feudal system; but the restriction that the father should not succeed otherwise than collaterally, and the total exclusion of the half-blood, were the consequences of purely feudal principles.

If it is necessary that this demonstrable quality of the doctrines of our common law should be elucidated by any further examples, I would ask, upon what principle is it, -- that a release, which is a discharge of a bond before the day of payment, is no discharge of a rent? -- That a lease to commence at any after-period, if made for years, shall be good, but if made for life shall be void? -- That the enlargement of a rent by release or confirmation, is to be understood only of rents in esse, and not of newly created rents? -- Or, lastly, that a condition, "that if the donee die without issue, the donor and his heirs may enter," shall be void and of no effect; but if the condition be, "that if the donee discontinue and die without issue, that then the donor and his heirs may enter," this shall be a good condition and binding upon the parties?

In the first place, let us take the release, which is a discharge of a bond, but not of a rent, before the day of payment; and yet the obligee can no more bring an action for the debt on bond, than the lessor can for the recovery of the rent, before the day of payment; and, consequently, there is an apparent difficulty in this instance, which is not to be cleared up but by explanation, and the help of reasoning discussion. As for example: a bond imports an actual or present debt; in the language of the law, it is debitum in praesenti quamvis solvendum in futuro. There is here then a right, although a dormant or suspended right in the obligee to a thing certain, and of which his release is, therefore, a sufficient discharge. And so it is in all similar cases; as in that, for instance, of the release of an action by an executor before probate, which is a good release; and yet, before probate, the executor can bring no action. But otherwise it is in the case of a rent. Why? Because a rent, before the day of payment, is only a debt accruing, and not a debt accrued. There is here no dormant or suspended right of action in the lessor to a thing certain, but, on the contrary, the thing itself is uncertain, future, and contingent. For, since the rent is to be paid out of the profits of the land, if the tenant be evicted before the day of payment, the rent will be avoided altogether. It is clear, then, that a release of all actions can be of no effect to extinguish a rent before the day of payment; because, at the time of the release, the consideration for which the rent was to be given, viz. the future enjoyment of the land, was not executed. And so it is in the case of a breach of covenant, upon the same principle. The covenantee may release all actions, &c. without discharging the covenant. And so, again, in the case of an annuity.

The second proposition turns upon the distinction, which has been already noticed, between the feudal and commercial nature of real or landed property. Under the feudal system, the proper feudatory or freeholder had

always his estate for life, at least, and was regularly
invested with it by the public and solemn act of livery of
seisin, for notoriety-sake; as well that the rightful
claimant might know against whom to bring his action, in
the case of a disputed title, as also that the lord might
run no risk of being defrauded of his feudal fines and
services. It became then impossible, from the very nature
and constitution of these estates of freehold, at the
common law, that they should be allowed to take effect at
any after-period; for that would be to suppose a man to
retain the possession in himself, after having delivered
that same possession to another; quod esset absurdum. But
on the other hand, the ceremony of investiture, by livery
of seisin, was held to be unnecessary, under the feudal
system, to the creation of estates for years; for the
tenant for years, or, as he is sometimes called, the
termor or tenant of the term, was considered as no other
than the bailiff or locum tenens of the freeholder; and,
therefore, estates for years being suffered to enure as
matters of mere contract, there could be no objection to
their taking effect either immediately or at any
after-period, as might happen to be agreed upon between
the parties.

     Thirdly, let us suppose A. having a rent-charge in
fee out of B.'s lands, grants it to C. for a year; he may
afterwards enlarge it, by release or confirmation, to C.
for any number of years, or for life, or otherwise. For
every subsequent augmentation which is so made of C.'s
estate in the rent, is derived out of the reversion which
is in the grantor of that same rent. But, if A. grants a
rent-charge to C. out of his own land, there is evidently
no remainder over, or reversion of this rent, out of which
any further augmentation can be derived.   In the former
case, there was a rent in esse, the reversion of which was
in the grantor; but, in the latter, the grant from A. to
C. was not of a part of what A. himself had, but of a
newly created rent; and, consequently, though A. by a new
deed of grant may create a new rent-charge, to take effect
upon the surrender or determination of the old, yet of the
old rent-charge he can make no further enlargement.   For
out of what is he to enlarge it? There is no reversion or
remainder over, upon which a release or confirmation can
operate pro incremento.

     Lastly, suppose an estate-tail to be created with a
condition, that if the donee die without issue, the donor
and his heirs may enter; the condition is void.   Why?
Because the donor in such case might have entered at any
rate; and words which provide for no more than must
necessarily take place without their intervention, are
nugatory and of no effect.   Hence the legal maxim,
expressio eorum quae tacitè insunt nihil operatur.   "And,
therefore," says Lord Coke, "the widow whom it was
intended to defraud by these words, shall have her dower."
But where the condition was, that if the donee
discontinued, and died without issue, the donor and his
heirs might enter, the condition was good in law, because
the donor in that case could not have entered otherwise
than by force of the condition, but would have been driven

to the expensive and dilatory process of a <u>formedon in the reverter</u>.

Having thus exemplified that the theory of our common-law learning is capable of demonstration and knowledge, (and of which there will necessarily occur many further specimens in the sequel of this inquiry,) it becomes us, in the next place, to consider to what course of reading we ought to apply ourselves, or what system of education to follow, in order to be duly instructed in it. It is, confessedly, of the greatest importance, that the law-students should be well versed in classical learning, and especially in logic; as appears from the very nature of the sources from which the arguments and proofs of the common law are principally drawn, and which, for the satisfaction of the reader, I will endeavour briefly to recapitulate in another place. But, how humiliating must it be to a man, who has been thus liberally educated, according to the usage of our Universities, to have to sit down afterwards, for two or three years, at the desk in an office, to copy precedents, in subservience (as Blackstone calls it) to attorneys and special pleaders! Or, supposing the drudgery of the thing to be left quite out of the question, I would ask what in the name of fortune is he likely to gain by it? The knowledge of the minutiae of practice? —— It may be so; but these are secondary considerations, and of no further use or consequence, even to the student who intends to follow the law as a profession, than so far only as they have their foundation in particular principles or rules of law, which demand from us the application of an intelligent mind, and not the labour of our hands in copying precedents. Neither will he have the consolation, in the mean time, of becoming even a tolerable pleader. For pleading too is matter of science and of liberal study, and, like the law itself, (of which it has not unaptly been called the handmaid,) is demonstrable, through all its branches, by the same unsophisticated conclusions of plain reason and common intendment.

J.H. Dawson

Suggestions as to the Course of Study to be Adopted, and the Selection of Books, by Parties designed for Attorneys and Solicitors (1830)

The object of the Author, in the following pages, is, to endeavour to point out, how gentlemen intended for attorneys or Solicitors, ought to be educated in their early years; the mode that should be adopted, wheN they have finished their general education; and the most eligible manner in which they should direct their studies during their professional schoolship; -- what books they ought to peruse; and the most profitable way of amassing knowledge, and conducing to their ultimate success.

Law, it has been said, by one alike eminent for his professional attainments, and his general erudition, is a science, which distinguishes the criterions of right and wrong; which teaches to establish the one, and prevent, punish, or redress the other; which is universal in its use and extent -- accommodated to each individual, yet comprehending the whole community. It has been accordingly designated as the most honourable occupation of the understanding, being the most immediately subservient to the general safety and comfort. "There is not," says Sir James Mackintosh, "in my opinion, in the whole compass of human affairs, so noble a spectacle as that which is displayed in the progress of jurisprudence; where we may contemplate the cautious and unwearied exertions of a succession of wise men through a long course of ages, withdrawing every case as it arises from the dangerous power of discretion, and subjecting it to inflexible rules; extending the dominion of justice and reason, and gradually contracting within the narrowest possible limits the domain of brutal force and arbitrary will. This subject has been treated with such dignity by a writer who is admired by all mankind for his eloquence, but who is, if possible, still more admired by all competent judges for his philosophy; a writer, of whom I may justly say, that he was 'gravissimus et dicendi et intelligendi auctor et magister,' that I cannot refuse myself the gratification of quoting his words: 'The science of jurisprudence, the pride of human intellect, with all its defects, redundancies, and errors, is the collected reason of ages, combining the principles of original justice with the infinite variety of human concerns.'"

These remarks are only made to exhibit to the reader, what an extensive field opens before him, for the exercise of those qualifications that adorn and dignify human nature, and thereby to convince him of the arduous nature of the profession, to which he is emulous of belonging. I may be, however, taunted with the hackneyed topic, that the occupations of an Attorney are not those which call for such information as is so essential in the higher grades of the profession. I may be told, that it suffices, if the Attorney knows at what office to direct his clerk to make application for a writ -- where to file a particular paper, and such like mechanical knowledge; and that it is in his power to consult his Pleader, Conveyancer, or Barrister, and thus avoid any dilemma he may have a chance of falling into. In answer to this, I will allow that, in many cases, great extent of knowledge may not be actually requisite; -- but, in the course of an extensive practice, would it be possible for an Attorney to escape the quicksands that would beset him, were he supported by no other aid than an acquaintance with the mere routine of business? Could he consult and advise his clients to adopt or refuse a particular line of conduct -- whether his advice were to be founded, either on legal or moral grounds? In the midst of the important questions submitted to him, would he not rather be continually misleading his employer? His legal adviser could not be always found at his elbow. It might be essentially necessary he should be enabled to give decisive answers, at a moment when he could have no means of referring to any quarter, and must solely depend on what information he himself possessed. All that can be said, is, that the advice of a Barrister or Chamber Counsel is salutary in a high degree when viewed as a dernier resort, in cases of difficulty, but ought never to justify an Attorney's want of a knowledge of the principles of the science. The details of business and general routine of an Attorney's office, are such as, in many cases, preclude his trusting his client's interest to his own observation. The multiplicity of pursuits in which he is engaged renders it imprudent. It would argue but little foresight or precaution to direct an important cause through its various stages, without taking advantage of every aid that presents itself. And what is one of those aids, in the case under consideration? Why, simply this: that a man combining in himself the complex characters of a person practising in different courts, in courts of Common Law and Equity, should have recourse to, and place implicit reliance upon, the opinion of an individual, who has made a particular branch of the profession, or the practice of one court, his distinct and peculiar study.

It is, therefore, evident, that the mind of an Attorney should, if possible, be stored with as much information, both of a general nature and legal character, as can be attained by him.

The consideration of our subject may be classed into three different periods:

1st.   Previous to the Clerkship
2d.   During the Clerkship.
3d.   After the expiration of the period of service.
But, before proceeding to the immediate development
of our views, it may be premised, that the Law is of all
professions one which parents should abstain from forcing
their children to embrace -- nay, it is of all others, one
to which, if the mind is not prone, it will never be
reconciled. The bent of the genius of the intended pupil
should be marked, and a careful examination should be made
as to his qualifications. For instance, the Law Student
should be possessed of a tolerable degree of perception.
This faculty is allowed to be necessary in the pursuit of
every science. In the profession of the Law it is
indispensable: -- a good memory, and intense application,
will not qualify a man to do complete justice to his
client, unless he be endowed with a sufficient share of
natural sagacity.
Again, a retentive memory is, in the profession of
the Law, a most valuable faculty. It cannot be supplied
by any succedaneum -- the common-place book, and memoria
technica may be of service; but can never be used as
actual substitutes. The acquisition and retention of
legal knowledge must be co-existent.
Besides perception and memory, that power of the
human mind must not be however wanting, which enables us
to examine the relative bearing of ideas; their extensive
and varied adaptations; their substantial meaning and
tendency; the use that is made of them by others; and
their approximation to correctness and solidity. Judgment
it is, that steadies our conceptions. Vivid perhaps at
first, impressed upon the mind by a casualty, or
entertained by chance, our first view of a subject might
be far from proper; the imagination might imbue the mind
with an erroneous notion, and induce us to form a hasty,
precipitate, and superficial conclusion. Judgment tempers
this, and avoids the evils inherent in a quickness of
apprehension.
But with all these acquirements, with all these
faculties in their full vigour, the student must be
capable of steady and unwearied application. In the
absence of unceasing industry, it is impossible to attain
any eminence: in such a case, inferior understandings
would frequently outstrip superior abilities.

1st.   Previous to the Clerkship.

It is now our duty to consider the conduct of the
pupil previous to the Clerkship.
After the age of six or seven, it is the advice of
the writer, that any person intended for the profession of
an Attorney should be sent to a public seminary. The
advantages to be derived from association with
competitors, are so great, and have been so frequently
eulogized, that it is unnecessary to dilate upon them.
Such seminary should also be, what is generally
distinguished by the denomination of a Commercial Academy.

Too much time should not be spent on an acquirement of a thorough knowledge of the Latin or other dead languages; although this seems by some to be considered indispensable.   Mr. Wright, who conveys, in his work addressed to Attorneys, many useful and salutary remarks, views this as absolutely essential.   All the author would, however, recommend, would be, to learn the rudiments of the language, and not go through a regular course of classical erudition.   So much more valuable information is requisite, that the pupil will find ample to fill up his time: -- let him be thoroughly grounded in the English language -- let him become a good arithmetician, and go through a course or two of mathematics -- let him study history: ("An acquaintance with history, and particularly that of our own country, will be absolutely necessary. Without a knowledge of the history of his own country, no man can become intimately acquainted with his country's laws.   Nothing can so well illustrate our admirable constitutional regulations and legal decisions, as a knowledge of the customs and manners of our ancestors, of their establishments, and of the causes of innovations and amendments in our constitutional code"); -- and let him be made acquainted with geography.   The student should also, both at this period of his career and during his Clerkship, read some established author on logic, and also on ethics.   Such a course of study is what, with proper care and attention, a young man may finish before he is eighteen; at which period it would be desirable he should enter a Solicitor's office.

     2d.   During the Clerkship.

     The point next to engage our attention is, what is the course of study to be adopted by a clerk serving his articles?   The chief difficulty that here presents itself, is, the reconciling of practice with theory, so as to obviate objections that may be made to too great attention to either.   They are, however, so far from being incompatible, that, it is conceived, no serious difficulty will prevent a medium being pointed out.   He should not, on the one hand, in the words of Mr. Preston, "be taught by form or precedent, rather than by principle.   He should not be made to copy precedents, without knowing either their application, or those rules on which they are grounded."   But, on the other hand, he should not, it is conceived, have his attention directed to the perusal of books on general and civil law.   The object ought to be, to direct him to those works which would tend most to elucidate his actual occupations; "for, whatever may be the extent of the elementary scale on which he commences, he must bring his theory to a juncture at which it will accord with, imbibe, and explain, the actual practice in which he is engaged; otherwise, the practice will be lost upon him, because he will not understand it; and, if his outline is too large, he will not fill it up to the point of union while his clerkship continues."   To use the words adopted in an article in the Law Magazine, "The object

ought to be, not to form a finished jurist; but a
well-informed working attorney." With this view, let the
student, during his articleship, universally search out
the law appertaining to what his master has deputed him to
execute: he will thus combine theory with practice, and
avoid a too rigid adherence to either.

The systematic, and regular, course of reading, the
author would recommend, would be as follows: -- First,
read De Lolme on the British Constitution; the style is
plain and intelligible, and, although it has been termed
"a performance deep,solid, and ingenious," it is entitled
to credit of a higher cast, that the ideas never seem to
partake of abstruseness. Next peruse the 1st vol. of
Blackstone's Commentaries; after which, read the 3d vol.
of the same work, and next the 2d. Then recur to the 3d
vol., following it up with Mr. Stephens' scientific work
on Pleading. The author would next recommend a re-perusal
of the 2d vol. of the Commentaries, following that up with
Watkins' Principles of Conveyancing. The next work to be
studied seems to be Fonblanque's Treatise on Equity, or
Maddock's Chancery Practice. Then, if possible, read the
1st Institute, as arranged by Thomas, omitting those
titles, or parts of titles, altered or amended by the
forthcoming report on our law. Next study Selwyn's Law of
Nisi Prius, which book may with much advantage be read
twice or three times, along with Mr. Petersdorff's
Supplement to Blackstone's Commentaries, which forms an
admirable compendium of the law relating to actions. Then
read a work on Evidence, -- perhaps the better course
would be to read Phillipps' Treatise; after which Roscoe's
Digest on the same subject. By this time, the pupil will
be fit to read Chitty's Pleading to advantage: after
which, he should peruse Lord Redesdale's Treatise on
Equity Pleadings. Let the student now read attentively a
book on the practice of the courts: as relates to the
King's Bench and Common Pleas, Tidd or Archbold; as
relates to the Exchequer of Pleas, the work on that
subject, written by Mr. Manning; and as relates to
Chancery, Turner and Venables. Mr. Preston's Treatise on
Estates, and the 3d vol. of his Conveyancing, should now
be taken up; as also Mr. Sugden's work on Vendors and
Purchasers; Mr. Coote on Mortgages; Mr. Watkins on
Copyholds by Coote and Morley, or by Mr. Coventry; Roberts
on Wills; and Mr. Cruise's 6th volume of the Digest,
wherein he will find most of the learning contained in Mr.
Fearne's work on Executory Devises. It would be highly
useful and instructive to the student, however, to peruse
Mr. Fearne's admirable essay on the subject of Contingent
Remainders and Executory Devises. "It is generally
considered, as a most beautiful combination of logical
accuracy, and profound legal learning; and these are not
its only merits; the style of it, which is peculiar, not
to say original, has not merely perspicuity and exactness,
but much vivacity and elegance." Should the above course
of reading startle the student, all the author can say,
is, he regrets it is not in his power to see how a full
and competent knowledge of the law can be obtained without
it. The 1st Institute is certainly a work that requires

no ordinary exertions to wade through; but should its bulk deter the student, let him, in the order in which it is placed, again peruse the 2d volume of the Commentaries, with the Abridgment of the Institute, by Hawkins, edited by Mr. Rudall.

It would be advisable that the student should now peruse Mr. Serjeant Russell's work on Crimes and Misdemeanors; and let him, especially if destined for country practice, carefully read Bott's or Nolan's Poor Laws.

As a work of general reference, forming a complete substitute for the Common Law Reports, and containing many valuable titles in our law, the author cannot refrain from recommending the student to have always at his elbow, -- Mr. Petersdorff's Abridgment of the Reports, and also Mr. Paget's periodical work, the Law Journal.

The method of reading, and time to be devoted to it, may call for some remarks. All that it is necessary to observe, however, is, that the mind should never be permitted to become fatigued; and in perusing any author, it is recommended to the student to trust to his memory, and not use common-place books.

"What is committed to paper, is seldom committed to the mind: and the observations which are transcribed, are perhaps never recollected, until accidentally re-perused. Thus common-place books deceive, instead of assist us, and they steal from the mind what it would otherwise retain. For the first two or three years of clerkship, they are not to be adopted; because, in common-place books, all decisions and points of law which are important should be inserted; and as, at this period of a clerk's studies, almost every one will be so, he would be induced to insert many which he will so frequently meet with, that he cannot fail to remember them.

"What is attentively read will be better understood, and more deeply impressed on the mind, by frequently reflecting upon it, than by committing it to paper. Biographers tell us of literary men reading with pens in their hands, to make extracts and remarks; but probably their extracts were merely references to the work, accompanied by some doubt or useful observations of their own. Why should they copy what they might immediately, when required, find printed? Students should not thus consume time, which they may much more advantageously employ in reading and reflection.

"Since almost every law book has an index, why should common-place books be used? If the index is a good one, it may, when necessary, be consulted on any particular subject, with as much, and perhaps more, advantage than a common-place book. If it is defective, the reader may, with very little labour, and with great advantage to himself, as he peruses the work, easily make a good index. These are my sentiments on common-place books; but the student should not adopt my opinions before he is convinced of their propriety.

It is, however of great use to the student, to note his doubts on any subject, to be reserved for further investigation; and, on many occasions, it is by no means a waste of time, to peruse a chapter or section, shut the book, reflect for half an hour on what you have read, then endeavour to commit your ideas to paper, and afterwards compare then with your original. The author was accustomed, during the progress of his studies, to find the latter method of material benefit.

It would be advisable that the clerk should attend a course of lectures on the Laws of England. A professorship was appointed last year in the University of London, at which period Mr. Petersdorff commenced delivering a private course of Lectures in Lyon's Inn Hall. The advantages to be derived from an attendance on lectures are thus summed up by Mr. Petersdorff: --

"The student, by subscribing to lectures, opens an entire new avenue for the obtaining information in addition to his previous resources. It fixes an hour in his mind at which he would naturally feel it obligatory upon him, to devote himself to his profession. It diminishes an inclination to exercise the privilege of postponing his intention to study. It affords him an opportunity of removing any difficulty he may have encountered during the progress of his reading. It checks the influence of indolence; relieves the tediousness of private study; affords a species of pleasure and recreation; calls into requisition faculties not usually exerted in the perusal of books; abridges his labours; improves his memory; accustoms him to the taking of notes; familiarizes him with a habit of giving exclusive attention to the arguments of others; creates in his mind a laudable inclination to disquisitionize; awakens attention; removes the impression that his advancement is slow; engenders feelings of generous competition; and augments and strengthens the reasoning powers. For a lecturer ought not to rest satisfied with giving the necessary information in a plain and didactic style, in short or detached sentences. It is his primary duty to excite the zeal, and attract and stedfastly fix the attention of his hearers; to anxiously watch the effect produced by each passage; to repeat and illustrate the same doctrines, if a difficulty in comprehending them be evinced; or pass them rapidly over, according as the complex or simple nature of the topic, and quickness of perception or obtuseness of the minds of his auditory, render copiousness or brevity necessary. If he cannot make himself distinctly understood in one shape, or by one illustration, he ought to have recourse to another form of expression or mode of exemplification, until he is fully satisfied that his positions are sufficiently comprehended, and adequately impressed upon the minds of his auditors. It is this capability of varying the statements, consistently with the acuteness or slowness of perception exhibited by the hearers, which so essentially distinguishes private study from listening to an experienced public teacher. True it is, that an individual may often acquire more information, if possessed of natural talents, by private application and study, than he can ever attain by availing himself of any system of instruction derived through the medium of public

communication.   But it is at the same time to be
remembered, that though, by attending lectures
exclusively, no student can ever become a complete master
of the science, yet the path by which he may reach the
object he has in view with greater facility, may be
pointed out, and an indiscriminate course of study
avoided."

    It may not be inexpedient for the author to hint to
the law student the necessity of confining his attention
to his own profession.   The force of mind must have an
operation proportionably powerful as it is directed to one
object.   The most common error is an indulgence in what is
falsely called general knowledge.   It too frequently
arises from a vain self-conceit; an over-anxiety to
attract attention, and gain a momentary applause.   Such
pursuits should be always kept subservient to the grand
object, viz. that of establishing a superiority in the
science of the law.   The art of directing, controlling,
and concentrating the powers of the mind, is one of much
too difficult a nature ever to be lost sight of; and any
deviation from what has been just recommended, is too
often indulged in, to such an extent, that the
consequences of the error become irretrievable.

    3d.   After the Expiration of the Period of Service.

    Subsequent to the termination of the pupil's period
of service, it might be highly advantageous to him to
spend a twelvemonth in the chambers of a special pleader,
conveyancer, or barrister, so as to have the opportunity
of copying the most approved precedents, and deriving such
farther instruction as might be acquired.   This he could
do during his clerkship, according to the provisions of
the 1 and 2 Geo. 4.   At all events, he should not be over
hasty in commencing practice: frequent disappointments
occur from a premature beginning.   Let him be patient,
studious, and vigilant, in searching for the most apposite
commencement of his career.   On this subject, Mr. Tompson
has some very judicious remarks, with referring to which,
the author will close his observations, hoping that the
hints thrown out as to the course of study to be pursued,
may prove the means of benefiting some of those who may
choose to peruse the foregoing pages.

– 7 –

Thomas J. Hogg

An Introductory Lecture on the Study of the Civil Law (1831)

To The Right Honorable HENRY, BARON BROUGHAM AND VAUX, Lord High Chancellor of Great Britain.

MY LORD,

HAVING observed that the Council of the University of London had signified, by repeated advertisements, their desire to engage a Professor of Civil Law; as I took a lively interest in the success of that institution, and had some knowledge of the Civil Law, my attention having been directed towards it early in life, as well as to the Law of Nations, by my father, who had studied for some time at Trinity Hall, in Cambridge, with the intention of practising as an advocate at Doctors' Commons; and as it appeared, also, that the duties of the Law Professors in the University of London were not incompatible with attendance on the circuit and at the sessions, and with the other avocations of a barrister, I resolved to offer my services in teaching that department of legal science. I inquired, in the first instance, whether the Professorship was designed for any particular person--and I was informed that it was not, and that the Council, on the contrary, were really anxious to procure a fit instructor; and I was directed to make a formal application to your Lordship in writing, as being the most active and the most competent of those who took a share in the management of the legal department of the University. I accordingly addressed a letter to you in the summer of the year 1827. I had an interview with you soon afterwards; you spoke of the application which I had lately made with many of those obliging expressions which the partiality of a kind friend dictates; and you told me, that not only would the Council certainly accept my offer, but they wre most happy to have received it, for no other person had proposed to undertake the office, who united a practical acquaintance with the Laws of England, and this was deemed an indispensable requisite, with a knowledge of the Civil Law; and you assured me, that I should immediately be appointed Professor, with a competent salary, which was specified.

As I was in the habit of meeting you daily in the Court of King's Bench, we often conversed together on the subject, and you urged me to apply myself vigorously to the science which I was to teach, because much would be expected from my exertions.   Other sciences might be learned elsewhere: the Civil Law, a most important study, unhappily too much neglected in England, would be taught at the University of London alone; by common consent we should enjoy a monopoly of a part of professional education, which all other civilized nations so highly prized.   Being yourself well acquainted with that branch of jurisprudence, you suggested the proper manner of teaching it, and pointed out various authors whose works ought to be read with my pupils, I was urged in like manner by other persons, and I received, directly or indirectly, the like assurances from the most active and distinguished members of the Council.

I was animated by these exhortations, and I was ambitious to be useful, and to distinguish myself in a new and honorable occupation; and, as your Lordship well knows, the attractions of a liberal pursuit increase in proportion to the progress the student makes in it, I accordingly devoted myself almost entirely to Civil Law during the first year; I studied it scarcely less diligently during the second; and I did not lay it aside altogether during the third year after my application for the Professorship.

I complained, from time to time during this long period, that the appointment was delayed; but the reasons offered for the delay seemed to be satisfactory; and in proportion as I had advanced far, the inducement not to recede became more powerful.   At last, I own, notwithstanding my zeal, my expectations had considerably abated, and your Lordship informed me, that, having been repeatedly defeated in endeavoring to bring he Council into your views respecting the Civil Law appointment, and having experienced much annoyance and vexation in urging it on their notice, more times, and in more ways than you could enumerate, you did not believe that, in the distressed state of the finances of the University, they would incure more liabilities for salary.

Since I had been induced to devote so much time and trouble to the Civil Law, although I should not certainly have made such a proposal originally, in the hope of doing some little good to the University, and that I might not entirely lose the credit, which I trusted would have resulted from my exertions, I addressed a letter to the Council about a year ago, offering, if they would appoint me Professor, without a salary, as they had lately elected others, to give a short course of lectures, at a low price, or gratuitously, or on any terms, or to any persons, they might direct.   To this proposal I never received an answer; but I attribute the omission, not to intentional incivility, but to the distracted condition in which the University then unhappily was.

In the course of my long and assiduous studies I produced not only the Introductory Lecture, which I now offer to your Lordship, but many others also, a portion of

which I ay possibly hereafter select for publication. I
have stated these matters, not for the purpose of
reminding your Lordship of what you never forgot, or
failed to regret, still less for the sake of casting blame
upon any individuals, for I have carefully abstained from
speaking of the alleged causes of our failure; I have only
referred to them, with your Lordship's approbation, to
show that this is not an officious, unauthorized
composition, assigned to a fictitious occasion, but was
actually written under the conviction that it was
certainly to be delivered, as it professes. I now publish
it, chiefly to convince those friends, who kindly take an
interest in my welfare and my pursuits, that, although I
may not have been profitably employed, I have certainly
not been idle.

In devouting myself so long to the study of the Civil
Law, I undoubtedly consumed much valuable time, and
withdrew myself from more lucrative pursuits; and I have,
moreover, been entirely disappointed as to those objects,
the attainment of which was the motive for my toils and
sacrifices. So far, perhaps, I may be deemed unfortunate;
your Lordship says of me--"that nobody was ever worse
used;" but I will not repine, for my studies were not
without pleasure and profit. In the most elevated station
of our profession your Lordship has already demonstrated
the superiority of the ancient discipline; I may possibly
venture to hope, that, in a more humble capacity, I may
one day prove, that the Jurisprudence of old is an
acquisition which can never be made in vain.

The theory of the English constitution has long been
deemed beautiful, and, indeed, absolutely perfect; the
practical effects of our actual government,
notwithstanding certain considerable aberrations from the
ideal system, and divers grievous abuses and
irregularities, have been justly acknowledged to be
excellent; the prosperity, security, and happiness of the
people have been preserved and augmented, and the
enjoyment of an unequalled freedom has been reconciled
with good order, tranquility, and obedience.

It has always been our pride to boast of these
blessings; to boast of our glorious constitution, at home
and abroad. At home, we address our countrymen; and it is
not wonderful, therefore, that our praises should be
echoed back by hearers, who are not less satisfied than
ourselves with the theme of our eulogy. Whenever an
Englishman expounds to a stranger, of whatever nation, the
extent and peculiar nature of his own felicity, and of
that of his fellow citizens, and the happy organization of
the polity of his native land, he finds that his
assertions are not only accepted, but anticipated; he
tells what is already known; he affirms what is fully
believed; and however boastful he may be, the assent and
admiration of the foreigner run before, and far outstrip
the exultation of the self-satisfied freeman.

Upon the wisdom of laws and the integrity of
magistrates alone can public happiness rest; it is
accordingly conceded by every civilized nation, that our

law are wise and our judges just, and consequently wise also.   Throughout the Continent of Europe, this proposition is fully and freely admitted; and, in terms of general admiration, our jurisprudence is loudly and universally extolled.   The voluntary tribute of applause is always bestowed in language sufficiently strong and ardent to soother the apprehensions and gratify the desires of the most jealous: "Most admirable is the administration of justice in England!" all exclaim with fervent and sincere enthusiasm.

Since the merits of our system of laws are generally recognized, how happens it that not one of our lawyers has an European reputation?--That not a single name, however illustrious at home, is known on the Continent? Why are strangers totally ignorant of the existence of all those professors, who, as they willingly concede, have brought the most important, and, perhaps also, the most difficult of sciences, to the highest practical perfection? We will endeavor to find an answer to this question, which seems to involve a paradox.   It is not because they are accustomed to neglect the writings of our countrymen; the celebrity of Newton is not less in Germany, or in Italy, than at Cambridge; Locke is as highly esteemed in other lands as on his native soil; and Bacon receives all the deference we claim for him, and quite as much, therefore, as he is entitled to. Our English authors, whether grave or gay, are duly appreciated; or, rather, we may say, in consideration of the genius and talents of the superior class of compositions, a place of honor is frequently assigned to inferior productions, which they do not really deserve.   The comity of nations is extended in the most ample manner to our literature and to our scientific writers; but the numerouse and ponderous volumes which our lawyers have brought forth, are as little known as the lucubrations of Chinese jurists.   With respect to jurisprudence, we are entirely cut off from the great family of the human race.   Who are the principal authorities for the law of China, during the sixteenth century?   The most accomplished and instructed of the lawyers of the Continent would smile at the question, and would at once frankly acknowledge that he was entirely ignorant.   Tell me, then, who wrote best on the law of England during that period? He would probably listen more gravely, but he would certainly answer, that he was equally uninformed.   and so with respect to the seventeenth century, or the eighteenth.

Although we are not, like the Chinese, a people remote, and although the effects of our laws are, as all concede, beneficial and satisfactory, our jurisprudence is not less quaint, uncouth, and inaccessible, than the language of China.   "What have we here?   Who is that savage?" a foreign jurist would ask, with no small wonder, if the writings of Sir Edward COke, for example, were laid before him.   "Whence comes this wild man; naked, tattooed, painted, decked out with feathers, and beads, and whimsical trapp]ings, with rings and fantastic toys in his ears and nostrils;--from what island of the South Sea, or from what trackless forest? It cannot be that the was the

Attorney-General of the King of England in an age of
refinement--the contemporary of Cujacius--and that he
still is the very eye of English jurisprudence, and the
light of their law?" It would be difficult to persuade
even the most candid stranger, that so barbarous a writer,
who, in a learned age, knew just enough to enable him to
display, in every paragraph, a grotesque and ludicrous
ignorance of each of the liberal sciences, was not
entirely devoid of merit--That he had much practical
experience, and discovered singular industry in citing,
with greater or less accuracy, the authorities on which
the law chiefly rested in his day; that he was deeply read
in printed volumes composed in a peculiar jargon, the
words of three languages being used indiscriminately,
little attention being paid to grammar, and none to idiom;
and especially conversant with entries, with manuscripts
recording, in detestable Latin, and strange characters,
inscribed upon rolls of parchment of an unusual
appearance, the real or pretended proceedings of the
courts of justice of former times; and that, besides these
qualifications of doubtful value, he was, in truth, a
person of considerable acuteness and ingenuity. It would,
perhaps, be hard to convince him that Sir Edward Coke and
Cujacius were animals of the same species. In the
estimation of Cicero, or of Pliny, the modes of thinking
and of expression of the former would have a little in
common with those of the latter writer, as the habits of
the baboon wit those of the man.

     The barbarism of the middle ages lingered in this
country for several centuries longer than in the rest of
Europe, and clung closely to a system of law more purely
and absolutely feudal than any other; yet we have much of
the originality of the middle ages also--something
sterling and native--unless our partiality for the
teachers of our municipal law deceive us; but of this
hereafter.

     A distinguished lawyer of the Continent, who was well
acquainted with the language and literature of England,
and was an ardent admirer of our constitution, and of the
justice and wisdom of our laws in general, as manifested
by the unequalled prosperity of our country; who was,
moreover, a learned and candid man, and a patient student,
declared that he often seriously attempted to overcome his
repugnance for our law-books. He greatly desired, by
examining them carefully, to judge for himself--to see
with his own eyes and mind the details of our
jurisprudence; but in spite of his renewed resolutions, he
was always driven back by the repulsive power of a few
pages. He asserted, that most of the treatises which he
opened, and particularly the reports, where he law was
recorded as it was received from the living lips, or in
the written judgments, of our magistrates, seemed to be
the productions of persons in the extreme of dotage. Like
old men, who are in their second childhood, and at the
last and utmost verge of life, our writers repeated, again
and again, stale, flat, unmeaning, tiresome forms of
words, with an air of vague wonderment; whatever was
really important in principle being entirely omitted, or

negligently slurred over; those were admired, and extolled with excessive praises, whose assistance was worthless, or of small value; and works which would have diffused a flood of light over he subject, were as little noticed as if their authors had been still unborn. There was, besides, a distressing prolixity, a wearisome and endless tautology, and a complete absence of all elegant learning, with a puerile display of the first bulgar rudiments of classical instruction. Notwithstanding his censure, he readily and fully acknowledged the general excellence of our laws, and of the administration of them, declaring always, that it was impossible for any person who had travelled from the one end of England to the other, to have any doubts on that head; he persisted, however, in lamenting that the steps by which we had mounted to our present proud elevation were not laid with such obvious and visible solidity as would promise security to ourselves, and would furnish an opportunity of imitations to voluntary admirers.

The style of Blackstone is graceful and agreeable, and his Commentaries are replete with elegant erudition; their merits are fully recognized on the COntinent; but he was our contemporary--at least, we have all lived with those who lived with him, and were his friends and intimates. The productions of former generations, that contain the fountains of our law, if they are to be judged of as compositions, will admit of one sorry apology only--that we have nothing better. Of the modern law-books which are now in general use, many have been compiled by digesting cases with much care and industry and they are convenient in practice: but they are too often rude in design, and barbarous and unscholarlike in execution; whilst some, on the contrary, are so neat and precise as to be almost elegant, with occasional snatches of erudition; as, for example, the well-known Treatise of the Chief Justice of England on the Law of Shipping. The narrow technicality, and the barbarity, the gross vulgarity and ignorance,by which or legal oracles have so long been disfigured, will fully account for the unfortunate exclusion of our lawyers, although they have ever been acknowledges as masters of the art of right, from the great fraternity of jurists.

We will attempt briefly to trace the causes of those defects, whence flowed a consequence that is deeply to be deplored; we may, perhaps, impute to them another calamity also, which is still more injurious and lamentable--the gradual and still-continuing decay of the higher department of the legal profession. Sir John Popham, who was Chief Justice of England in the time of Queen Elizabeth, tells us in his Reports:--"And this I may truly say, to the encouragement and comfort of such as, being honest, do profess the law, that in the most parts of England there are more gentlemen's houses, and those of continuance, raised and advanced by that profession alone, than by all the other professions that can be spoken of and approved." It would be easy to cite many other passages to the like effect, which could not be heard without a smile. But there is no need to rely upon such

authorities, nor upon the argument, that it is manifest
the honorable occupation of an advocate has not kept pace
with the advancement of other professions and trades; for
instance, if we compare the attorney-general of the reign
of James the First, and the banker of the same period,
with a fixed body, as the House of Peers, and institute
the same comparison in the present day, we shall perceive
a wonderful difference in their relative bearings: and so
with many other examples. The degradation is not to be
regretted on account of the unimportant consideration of
comparative opulence, but because learning has been thrust
from her seat: the approaching detreusion of mind below
matter threatens with evils innumerable the ill-starred
common-wealth.

The frequent appointment to the magistracy of persons
who had not received a legal education, whereby they were
called upon to administer laws, of which they were of
necessity ignorant, has produced many disastrous
consequences; and one of he most fatal is, that not only
in law, but in other departments of knowledge, every one
is supposed to understand every thing spontaneously, and
to be qualified to decide upon it, and entitled to give an
opinion, that deserves as much respect, as that of a man
who has carefully studied and thoroughly understands the
subject. These inquiries however are beside the present
question. We now seek the causes of that barbarity, which
has shut us out from the commerce of our foreign brethren:
in tracing them it will be enough to refer in a brief and
cursory manner to historical events, with which all are
acquainted.

It is known to every one, that, under the popular
government of ancient Rome, the wisdom of the laws, and
the exact justice with which they were administered, were
not less celebrated, than they have been for some time in
our free and happy island; the judicial offices were
filled by able and distinguished persons, and it was the
pleasure and the pride of the first men in the state, to
execute the office of counsel and advocate with credit;
and they sought to gain thereby not an immediate pecuniary
recompense, but good will and gratitude; and they
accordingly acquired a prodigious and most beneficial
influence. The Roman jurisprudence was not only renowned
for equity and good sense, like that of England, but,
unlike the latter, it obtained, probably pretty early, the
fame of peculiar and exquisite elegance. To the stranger,
who should say, "The spirit of your laws, I believe, is
just and equal," the Englishman would cordially assent:
but even the least instructed, and the most national,
would scarcely deign to give an answer in words, if he
were asked, "and is not the language of your laws neat and
graceful?" Whereas, the citizen of ancient Rome, if he
had been requested to name the most elegant portion of his
country's literature, would have said at once, "our law."
Its eloquence moreover was purely of the Roman kind -- it
expressed much in few words, "Cato Romani generis
disertissimus," says Sallust, "Multa paucis absolvit:"
How many orators, on the contrary, convey little in
innumerable words!

Many have seen specimens of the style of the roman
lawyers; to them no illustration is necessary; many,
however, are unacquainted with it, and to these it may be
explained, in some measure at least, by referring them to
that felicitous brevity, which they have no doubt
sometimes noticed in inscriptions, and which records with
surprising precision a complicated matter in a very narrow
compass.   The style of inscriptions, and which records
with surprising precision a complicated matter in a very
narrow compass.   The style of inscriptions indeed, the
lapidary style, as it is sometimes called, was the
invention of the lawyers of ancient Rome, and it has been
handed down to us from them.   Their writings are
distinguished by a certain lucid, bewitching simplicity,
not less than by an exact and eloquent brevity.   It was
the object of the judges under a republican constitution,
and especially of the jurisconsults, who sought not fees,
but the good will of their clients, to satisfy the
understandings of suitors by making the reasons of the law
perfectly plain and intelligible; they were required to
terminate suits, not by wearing out the patience of the
parties by infinite delays, and by wasting their fortunes
with heavy and protracted expenses, but by unfolding the
principles of the law, and showing their application to
the facts of the case, a far more difficult and a delicate
task.   Their responses, therefore, were brief and
sententious, that they might be remembered, and, although
often refined and subtle, so clear and transparent, as to
be plain to an ordinary intellect: many a terse answer,
pregnant with wisdom, that seems simple at first sight,
was long elaborated and purified by painful meditation.
    · The sum of jurisprudence was augmented continually by
the well-weighed responses of learned men, by the
accumulated decisions of the judges, and by written laws,
until the mass became so large, that a Digest was deemed
desirable.   It was a favorite project of Julius Caesar, a
man who was imbued with the true spirit of the Civil law,
as the chaste style of his commentaries proves, and this
fragment of his treatise on analogy would alone
demonstrate, "ut tanquam scopulum," writes the illustrious
conqueror of our island, "sic fugias inauditum atque
insolens verbum."   It is probably, that such a work had
been compiled by private industry, although not under the
public sanction of authority.   Further and very
considerable additions were made by the emperors, who
freely exercised their power of making general laws under
the name of Constitutions, and of returning authoritative
answers to particular cases, which were called Rescripts.
    At the beginning of the sixth century Justinian
published a collection of Imperial Constitutions from the
time of Adrian, which is called the Code; the emperor
Theodosius the Second, more than a century before, had
composed a similar work, containing the laws of the
Christian emperors only which is still extant, and is
called the Theodosian Code.   Justinian published also an
abridgment of the writings of the most eminent lawyers,
and of the laws of the earlier emperors, in fifth books,
called the Digest, or Pandects; this great work, together

with his Code, a short introduction to the study of the
law, named the Institutions, and the Novels, or those new
Constitutions which appeared after the completion of the
Code, form, as is well known, the body of the Civil Law,
Corpus Juris Civilis.

Of the four parts, of which the entire body is
composed, the Pandects are incomparably the most precious
and important; in them we find the ancient jurisprudence
of the Republic, its wisdom and its elegance; they are
indeed a storehouse of archaeology; "Pandectas
antiquitatis promptuarium merito quis appellet, semper
enim observatione dignum a liquid accurata earum lectio
suppeditat." They were collected almost entirely from the
writings of the jurisconsults of the second and third
centuries, whose minds, however, had been formed after the
primitive discipline, and who doubtless, for the most
part, transcribed the language of an earlier and a purer
age. Persons well versed in this system of jurisprudence
were qualified for any station, and were fit for every
purpose of social life; accordingly, they were the most
distinguished characters of the age. To multiply
instances is needless, but it it notorious, that the more
illustrious of the Fathers of the Church had been
advocates by profession. The ordinary style of the age of
Justinian, as the Novels testify, is diffuse, ambitious,
and rhetorical, and it savours of that false eloquence in
which the Fathers abound, and of which we see striking
specimens in the pleadings of foreign advocates.

We must postpone the consideration of the cultivation
of the Civil Law under the Eastern empire; small success
attended the publication of the body of the Civil Law in
the West, where the authority of the empire was feeble and
uncertain. The emperor had himself set the example of
abridgment, and it was soon followed by others; breviary
followed breviary, each being shorter than the last, and
there was every reason to apprehend, that the entire
fabric of civil prudence would have been finally
epitomized away, and totally annihilated by successive
reductions. Nevertheless, the edicts of the Praetors of
old still continued to influence the decision of causes
amidst the ruins of governments and the irruptions of
barbarous nations; and from whatever source it was
immediately derived, the jurisprudence of Rome in some
degree mitigated the unhappy condition of the human race:
it never disappeared altogether even during the deepest
night of intellectual and political darkness; the further
we push our inquiries into the history of that period of
distraction and desolation, the more abundantly do we
discover distinct vestiges of its power and operation.

A strong impulse was given to the study of the Civil
Law from various causes at the commencement of the twelfth
century, which spread not only throughout Italy but over
the principal part of Europe; the schools of numerous
professors were crowded with pupils, the recorded amount
of whom appears almost incredible: and for many years the
chief occupation of the learned was to compose
commentaries of various kinds, and under different names,
upon the body of the law, and especially the most precious

part of it, the Pandects.   Sir Robert Wiseman, in his little volume, which bears the quaint title of "The Law of Laws, or the Excellency of the Civil Law above all other Humane Laws whatever," enumerates many of the species in these words: "What glosses, notes, lectures, repetitions, commentaries, paratitles, analyses, intellects, are there upon the very laws themselves? There is hardly any text of law that is not copiously written on, either in stating the true reading of it, or in clearing it from obscurity, or in enlarging upon the matter of it: then, as to the general subjects of the law and the particular cases and questions that fall under them, both speculative and practical, the tractates, discourses, counsels, questions, reports, common opinions, controversies, resolutions, practices, observations, and singulars, are without number." Infinite was the industry and remarkable the ingenuity of the Doctors, who consumed their ink and their oil for several centuries with such exemplary liberality in illustrating, or obscuring, the text of the law; but if their virtues were great, their faults also were numerous: many were their errors, many their puerilities; they wandered by an uncertain light, and one thing was still wanting.   When the study of the Greek language and literature revived in the West, this was supplied.

Although the form and structure of the body of the Civil Law be chiefly roman, yet the soul, which animates the mass, is Greek: when Justinian, in the preface to the Pandects, speaks of the father of poetry, he uses these remarkable words, which alone demonstrate, that much of the virtue of civil prudence was of Grecian origin, "apud Homerum, patrem omnis virtutis."   Accordingly, when the knowledge of the Greek language disappeared, the cultivation of Roman jurisprudence languished; and although the latter recovered more early, and seemed vigorous, it enjoyed only an animal life, until it was brought back to intellectual existence by the happy renewal of good letters. An initiation into the mysteries of Greek literature augmented and purified the critical comprehension of Latin, and a glorious race of expositors arose, who, embracing the sound interpretations and rejecting the mistakes of the mere Latinists, "Graeca et Latina eruditione abditor vulgo recusére sensus."

If a man of respectable accomplishments, and of moderate proficiency in various learning, should desire to discover how much still remains to be learned, and to compare his own attainments with an acknowledged standard, let him repair forthwith to the voluminous writings of this school of civilians. 'At the head of the most illustrious of them stands the great Cujacius, whom the praises of scholars have celebrated as a man almost divine; and it is impossible for the most sober critic to examine his numerous works, without being astonished at his marvelous acuteness, his vast industry, and his multifarious and profound erudition. Certain of his most ardent panegyrists do not hesitate to affirm, in their extreme fondness, that the seal of true greatness was affixed upon his name by his rejection, through the ignorance, and possibly the dishonesty and unnatural

self-conceit, of the rulers of the University of
Thoulouse, when he was proposed as a candidate for the
chair of Civil Law; for such they declare has ever been
the destiny of persons of real merit. However this may
be, it is certain that strangers have made ample amends to
his memory, for the dishonorable neglect of his own
countrymen. We may be permitted to smile at the honest
enthusiasm of the Germans, being quite innocent ourselves
of every excess of admiration for men of eminent learning
and genius -- whenever the honored name of Cujacius, we
are told, was mentioned in a school of law in Germany, all
present, so profound was the reverence of these patient
and ardent students for the prince of teachers, took off
their caps in token of respect. "Tanta ubique exceptus
reverentia, ut in publicis Germaniae gymnasiis si quis
Cujacium nominaret, statim omnes, honor is causa, caput
aperirent, ac pileum deponerent." Surely, that professor
may be accounted happy, whose lot it is to address such an
audience.

     Under the latin doctors, the Civil Law was studied
with zeal and diligence in every region of the civilized
world; the revival of Greek literature, and the consequent
refinement of the science, fanned the sacred flame, and
increased the number and activity of students, and added
greatly to the estimation of the ancient art of right, and
to the favor that the wise have ever shown towards the
jurisprudence of Rome. The power of beauty prevailed
everywhere, save only in a fertile island of the remote
West; there, possibly, through the proverbial and
unaccountable perversity of islanders, for men cannot love
deformity, it was uniformly resisted; and that elegant
system, which was the delight of the scholar in less
obdurate regions, was almost entirely rejected here.

     So early as the reign of Stephen, an attempt was made
to teach the Civil Law in England, which met with violent
opposition; and although schools were established at
Oxford, and lectures delivered, they were principally
attended by churchmen; and this science has been
cultivated at our Universities, and imperfectly and
partially, by the very limited number of advocates, who
designed to practice in the Ecclesiastical Courts; and it
has invariably received the smallest share of attention
from those persons to whom it would have been most
beneficial, the depositaries of our municipal law. It has
been alleged, in apology, that our proud and free
ancestors refused to extend the English hospitality to
this branch of literature, because they conceived, that
certain maxims of imperial jurisprudence were inconsistent
with their darling liberty -- their blessed liberty, their
grateful descendants may piously designate it. But this
assertion is at least doubtful, the Dutch republicans were
able to reconcile the laws of Rome with their commercial
commonwealth; and we cannot believe that our freedom has
not a more worthy foundation, than the barbarisms of the
yearbooks and of the records of our courts, or that our
happy constitution could be readily created under any sky,
by dissolving the rules of grammar and removing the
restraints of syntax. It has been alleged also, that the

Civil Law was unwelcome to our forefathers, because they were jealous of papal domination, and were resolved to withstand the usurpations of the holy see; but, unfortunately for this excuse, the Civil Law, by upholding the claims of the emperors, was favorable to the Popes; and so far were the founders of our liberties from being anti-catholics, as this would imply, that they bestowed at least their full share of their possessions upon the teachers of the dominant religion; and if we turn over the pages of the body of the Canon Law, which is the proper papal jurisprudence, we shall perceive that a large proportion of the rescripts, or decretal epistles, were sent back in answer to cases transmitted to Rome by English prelates. Truth will not permit us to assign a creditable motive for the inhospitality of our ancestors towards the civilians of their days: a vulgar narrow jealousy, the strongest of the many violent passions that inflame the unhappy ignorant, was, we fear, the real cause of their unwillingness to accept the proferred instruction and refinement. It is unnecessary, however, to inquire into the origin of former errors, when the source of them is dried up. That we are assembled here this evening, is a complete proof that the triumph of ignorance is at an end; it is our agreeable duty to consider in what manner we should endeavor to profit by the occasion that is offered to us, and how we ought to attempt, with the utmost diligence, according to the measure of our abilities, and being animated by a zeal not unworthy of the inestimable opportunity, to atone for past deficiencies by future excellence.

Having answered, in a satisfactory manner, the question that was originally proposed -- "Since the merits of our system of laws are generally recognized, why are our lawyers, however illustrious they may be at home, totally unknown to strangers?" Having found that the excessive barbarism of their writings affords the true solution of the difficulty, and having clearly traced this barbarism to their neglect of the one elegant system of jurisprudence, the remedy suggests itself; and the next question, and it is indeed a most important one, that arises, is this -- What is the best mode of teaching the Civil Law? In this age the love of innovation is conspicuous, and a greedy appetite for novelties is almost universal: the old methods, notwithstanding, are sometimes the best; with respect to legal education, they are certainly very superior to any that modern professors have suggested.

The ancient course of instruction is simple and intelligible, and wants every feature and token of quackery: it is easily stated, and as easily remembered. to read the Institutions of Justinian twice; first, for the words, attending carefully to their signification and grammatical construction, in order to seize the full and true meaning of every passage: secondly, for the sense, and with reference to the plan of the work, as a whole; the labor being diversified and enlivened by very brief references to the history and antiquities of Rome, and to the main outlines of similarity or dissimilarity between

the principles unfolded in the text and the rules of the
English law. To read slowly and attentively the titles of
the Digest of the Code, and of the Novels, and to obtain
thereby a bird's-eye view of the whole country, and to
seize the method and principal divisions of the subject,
and thus to comprehend the general nature and contents of
the body of the Civil Law. During this preliminary
exercise, the assistance of an experienced guide is
peculiarly useful, the meaning and dependence of many
titles being obvious, but of others it is exceedingly
difficult for a novice to apprehend the true bearing and
signification. Many questions commonly suggest themselves
at this period to the inquisitive and diligent student,
and it is very advantageous to receive immediate and
satisfactory answers.

The next step is to read the Pandects themselves, and
this is in truth the only method of really learning the
Civil Law; he who is well versed in them is a good
civilian, and to read and understand them is the business
of the student. To pretend that this salutary duty can be
dispensed with, would be vainly to flatter indolence; and
to offer any substitute for a necessary labor would be to
deceive. It is not expected, however, that the student
should peruse the ponderous volumes; it is not his object
to qualify himself to discharge with credit the office of
Praetor, to plead in the Roman Forum, or to give his
opinion to the citizens of Rome respecting their civil
rights. It concerns not a subject of the King of England
to know, except as a matter of history and of liberal
curiosity, that by such an act he will transgress a law of
the senate, or of the people, or will violate an imperial
constitution; his rights cannot be affected by the
perpetual edict, or by the opinions of Papinian, or of
Paulus: it is not expedient, therefore, that he should
fill his head with decisions and with the conclusions of
the law. But it is highly expedient for every person, who
means to undertake the very serious trust of an advocate,
or of a jurisconsult, who expects that he will be called
upon to administer the laws of his country, or to assume
the difficult and delicate duty of legislation, to know
how philosophically, with how much grace, simplicity, and
precision, a head of law may be treated. It should seem,
that, in a civilized country, the acquisition of this
valuable portion of knowledge ought to be deemed essential
to the accomplishment of a gentleman. The attainment
fortunately is as easy as it is becoming; it is not
necessary to wade through a sea of text, and to devour a
mountain of commentary, or to fix in the memory a huge
index of decisions; it is not essential indeed to remember
any: they were deeply interesting to the Romans of old,
but they touch not us; our business is with the method;
the method of antique jurisprudence alone will be
profitable to us. A moderate number of well chosen
specimens will be sufficient, so that they be explained
with care and fully comprehended, to unfold and illustrate
the principles, and to exhibit the method pursued by the
lawyers, magistrates, and legislators of a people
distinguished above all others for civil prudence. The

discretion of the teacher will be shown in making the
selection judiciously, for many titles have become obscure
through the lapse of time, and by reason of the difference
of manners, customs, and institutions, and from other
causes; others relate to matters that are in themselves
abstruse and of difficult comprehension: it will be
proper to choose those heads of the law, that are
generally intelligible, and where a lucid and beautiful
exposition seems only to have given expression to the
conclusions of nature and common sense.

In several countries of Europe the Civil Law was
accepted as an authority, and was considered in many cases
as obligatory, having been adopted "non ratione imperii,
sed imperio ration is."   Wherever a system of law is
binding, the last statute and the last decision will of
course often be esteemed the most important; in these
countries, therefore, the Code, and especially the Novels,
have received much attention; but we seek not positive
rules, whereby to shape our conduct, or to ascertain our
rights; our views are consequently directed principally to
the Pandects, as being the storehouse of ancient
jurisprudence, and the fountain, whence we would draw
speciments of that style, which has been so happily
described by Gravina, no mean critic nor unsuccessful
imitator of the diction he commends --

Nec minorem illi justitiam in verbis, quam in rebus
adhibuerunt, apte ovicbus utentes, nativasque sedes
illis attribuentes, Diisque ipsis dignum oration is
genus usurpantes.   Quo solo scribendi genere, non
modo jurisconsulti praestant Latinis ceteris, verum
et Latini antecellent Graecis: qui ut omnis
eloquentiae genera et invenerint, et ad summum
perduxering, Jurisconsultorum tamen Romanorum sicuti
scientia, ita et stylo caruerunt.   Habuerunt enimqq
nostri majestatem sine luxuqq, fastum sine pompa,
supercilium sine rusticitate, splendorem sine fuco,
sine horrore vetustatem, parsimoniam sine macie, sine
caligine brevitatem: ac prae ceteris melius
elegantiam cum simplicitate, cum decore proprietatem,
et oraculorum sanctimoniam blanda cum perspicuitate
conjunxerunt.

The eulogy is warm but merited, and a parody upon this
passage, in which the opposite qualities were enumerated,
would not express too strong the vices of some authors,
who have written concerning the laws of England.

But, cannot the student, some will ask, attain to
this moderate proficiency in the Civil Law, without the
aid of a professor, through solitary, unassisted study?
It is certain that he may; the diligent reader, by
perusing the text and the best commentaries attentively,
will reach not merely to the competent understanding of
the science, that is now recommended; but, should he
prosecute his inquiries for several years, he will
probably know all that can be known by the most
accomplished legal antiquary.   Those difficulties, which,
after much fruitless toil, we have at last solved by our

own efforts, are forever fixed in our memories. Where
every part of a science is valuable, and it is necessary
to acquire and to retain the whole, private, unaided study
may offer some advantages to a resolute student; but it is
otherwise when certain small portions of an extensive
plain are to be taken in and cultivated. If every object
in the city be equally interesting, and the traveller have
abundant leisure, he may walk forth alone and gaze eagerly
at all that he finds; he cannot stray: but if the
rarities be few and scattered, and his time limited, an
intelligent, or even a practices, guide will be a valuable
acquisition.   If we reject, as of light weight, the
emulation that is kindled by the intercourse of many young
men engaged in the same liberal pursuit, the benefits of
mutual suggestions, the motive to regular exertion, which
the duty of presenting to another, in company with others,
the results of prescribed inquiries creates, the complete
excision of procrastination, and the animation arising
from the living voice, the presence and the encouragement
of a zealous teacher; if, with excessive, and perhaps
undue candor, we allow that these incitements are
unnecessary to the industrious, and they alone enter upon
the study of the law, it cannot be denied, that the
difficulty of selecting the proper portions of the text of
the Pandects, and of choosing amongst an almost infinite
number of guides, of very various merit, the best, the
most plain and easy expositor of the passage selected, is
so considerable, and the inconvenience of error is so
certain, as to compel the student who refuses the help of
one who has already travelled the same intricate road, to
undergo full five times the toil, that would bring his
more diffident competitor to the same point.
     But, consider the prodigious extent of the law of
England, an objector will perhaps exclaim, look at the
hundreds of volumes that darken the walls, and they are
daily and hourly increased; how will it end, what will be
the bulk of the mass in a few more years? An intellectual
Atlas is now required to stand under the intolerable load;
the horse sinks beneath his burthen, and would you attempt
to add to it? When such an objection is raised, we seem
to hear a younger and a shriller voice, urging with
wearisome importunity this prayer -- O pity the porr
school boy; pity him; is not his lot sufficiently hard, is
he not constrained to learn every word in Ovid and in
Virgil, in Cicero and in Livy; is he not obliged to
remember all the words in all those books that are called
the classics; what time then can he have for his meals,
for sleep, for the most necessary of all his necessities,
for play; why will you compel him to learn, and with a
more painful exactness, another volume, that certainly is
not classical, and apparently has little in common with
the classics? In mercy to the youthful appellant, that he
may arrive at that proficiency in learning which his
forefathers reached, and deemed indispensable, and
especially that he may continue to enjoy whatever
relaxation is conceded to him, a judicious teacher would
at once disallow his appeal. For what would be the
condition of a scholar, who was required to learn the

Latin language without the help of the grammar. How could
he retain the sense of innumerable words, without the aids
of classification and analogy?   How could he interpret
sentences without the rules of syntax and construction?
How could he arrive at the slightest tincture of the
knowledge he sought? He would possibly at last, for the
ingenuity of man is boundless, and his patience is not to
be broken, with pain and peril, and after a lamentable
waste of time and toil, rache to a scanty, imperfect,
ill-digested, ill-founded comprehension of the more
accessible approaches of the language; precisely as we
have hitherto learned the laws of England. We do not seek
to add to labors that are already overpowering; we desire
to lighten them, to present to the student a grammar; and
it would be an insult to the understanding of everyone,
who has tasted the sweetness of even a single general
rule, of one sound principle, to enlarge upon the value of
the acquisition.
     The course of study that was formerly followed in
France, was entirely different from that which prevails
with us. During a residence of six years at a University,
the students applied themselves to the Civil Law, and then
afterwards attended the Courts, and the practitioners, to
learn the laws of their country.   The ingenious Francis
Hotman, in his work, entitled Anti Tribonian, which he
says was composed by the desire of the celebrated Michael
de l'Hopital, although it was not published until after
the Chancellor's decease, inveighs with great vehemence
against the prevailing course of study: it is not easy to
determine whether he is in jest or in earnest; if it be a
serious attack, the author was ill advised, and was
perhaps misled by that love of paradox which occasionally
betrays men of talent. The practical effects of the
French institution were admirable; being familiar with the
principles of jurisprudence the students afterwards
acquired, perfectly, and with the utmost facility, the
municipal law: the reputation of their distinguished men
was not confined within the limits of their own country,
but their works long have been, and still are, the
admiration and delight of the learned throughout Europe.
An acquaintance with the rudiments of Civil Law, and the
previous acquirements which it implies, should they ever
be deemed indispensable qualifications in the candidate
for admission to a most honorable degree, would exclude
from the bar unfit and illiberal persons; and if we could
anticipate that such would ever offer themselves, it might
be prudent to adopt an effectual and irreproachable
safeguard. Nor ought the objection have any weight with
us; if that impediment had existed formerly, the public
would have lost the benefit of the services of such an
individual, who, by his abilities alone, unassisted by
friends, elevated himself from a humble station to the
judicial office, which he executed creditably. It is
certain that real talent was never shut out for the want
of erudition; the person in question would not have been
lost to the profession, those abilities, which secured his
advancement, would have presented him to the world adorned
in a conspicuous manner with all the ornaments of

learning, that the most fastidious could ask for; and he would have been more illustrious, for the lineaments of a less noble animal would not have peeped forth to discredit the lion's skin.   Although absolute perfection be unattainable, it has always been deemed prudent to propose a high standard of morality, and so is it with professional character.

If it be conceded, that it is, without doubt, expedient to teach jurisprudence upon principle, and suggested that it would be more beneficial to take the laws of England, than of Rome, for the purpose proposed, we must answer, that we really know not how that could be done, and we doubt whether it be practicable.   The people of the North borrowed the philosophy of jurisprudence, so far indeed as they supposed that they needed it, as they derived their grammar, from Rome.   Although the rules of the Latin syntax are often inapplicable to the Teutonic languages, we have no other standard, by which we can estimate the correctness of a composition in English, than those rules; and we know by experience, that, in proportion as our countrymen are well skilled in the learned languages, they usually write their own grammatically; and it is difficult to name any person ignorant of Latin, who writes English correctly.   When we shall have discovered versions in a dialect, with which we are acquainted, of the native grammars of the saxones and teutoni, if such books ever existed, or when some powerful mind shall have extracted from our tongue an independent scheme of syntax, we will attempt to construct sentences without the guidance of the Romans; and so is it with jurisprudence, and with many other sciences.

It has been proved, that a moderate proficiency in the Civil Law would probably unite our lawyers with those of other countries, and would greatly increase their reputation by improving the style and method of our law books: as the Legislators of old were accustomed to travel for the purpose of comparing their institutions with foreign politics, we may believe, that the collation of different systems of jurisprudence in the most approved works would, in like manner, tend to the amelioration of the administration of justice throughout the world.   It is certain, that this study, by laying a solid foundation of principles, would greatly facilitate the acquisition of the knowledge of the laws of England.   So numerous are the advantages, which it promises, that it is difficult to select, and still ore difficult to arrange them.   The great masters of the Civil Law are not more remarkable for their elegance, than their brevity; the adoption of the latter excellence would be an eminent public benefit.   Our law books are commonly disfigured by an odious prolixity: this barbarous vice is still more conspicuous in the proceedings of our Courts of law, and especially of Courts of equity, and it adds largely to the expense and obscurity of our conveyances.   Mr. Butler and Sir Edward sugden, men of infinite experience, who are above all praise for practical ability in their peculiar department, extol, with unwearied hymns, "the machinery of a marriage settlement;" such is their phrase, and they declare, that it attains, with admirable certainty, the ends proposed, which are precisely those that consiste best with sound policy.   It is impossible, however, not to feel some surprise that it never occurred to these very acute persons, that the same happy results might be procured, with at least equal certainty, by fewer words, by five or six pages, instead of five or six hundred; and that there are other valuable maxims in the Civil Law besides this, "non solent quae abundant vitiare scripturas."   The same inconvenient and unbecoming prolixity is one of the most mischievous of the many imperfections of our statutes.

If it were deemed indispensable, that the mind of the student, at the commencement of his legal studies, should be tinged, however slightly, with the Civil Law, a sufficient motive would exist to retain and to cultivate that acquaintance with the learned languages, which is obtained with difficulty and easily lost:
, although it is not more difficult to hold this blessing than to win it, like those of which Demosthenes speaks, it is certainly far more rare.   The knowledge of Greek is valuable, not because it is an accession of new and strange words, not for the sake of the admirable authors who have written in that tongue, but because practical good sense is precious.   As soon as the Civil Law was explained by proficients in Greek, at the restoration of letters, interpretation became sensible, plain, and rational; and the monstrous errors and absurdities of the commentators of the middle ages gradually disappeared.   The literature of Greece has been called the medicine of the mind, and has been compared to the cathartic virtues of the Platonists, which were to be acquired in order to remove from the soul those obstacles and impediments that obstructed its progress towards wisdom and virtue.

It would be unhandsome and unjust to attempt to disparage the studies that have obtained in other places; but it is impossible not to remark, that it has been often asserted, and is generally believed, (for, what will not be credited at last, that is frequently and confidently affirmed?) that mathematics, and especially the analysis by algebraical symbols, which has been greatly extended by the French, and was brought into fashion by them, because such pursuits could not possibly suggest sentiments hostile to absolute despotism and the uncontrolled dominion of one man, that man being, moreover, a soldier, are peculiarly adapted to prepare the mind for the reception of jurisprudence.   The startling and ludicrous paradox has been erected on no more solid foundation than the naked fact, that, of the persons who labored hard to get possession, by means of algebra, of the eleemosynary foundations at one of our Universities, some have succeeded, through the same industry, and being pushed on from below by powerful assistance, in obtaining the prizes in the legal profession.   Before we can consent to sacrifice to a science that is comparatively mechanical, and rests mainly on the strength of the memory, liberal, graceful, and humanizing studies, that awaken an honest zeal for the just rights of the people, but are, at the

same time, eminently conservative of the true order and
due subordination of society, we must be satisfied that it
is impossible that equal success should attend persons
totally ignorant of mathematics, but of moderate
acuteness, of great diligence and confidence, and borne
forward upon the shoulders of a large, bold, and active
connection, who have consumed the morning of life, and the
hours natural to study, in posting a merchant's leger, or,
in the language of Blackstone, "submitted to the drudgery
of servitude, and the manual labor of copying the trash of
an attorney's office."

A competent knowledge of the Civil Law brings with it
many minor and miscellaneous benefits, which form, as it
were, the prerequisites of the scholar. It explains
various niceties in the Latin tongue, and innumerable
passages of the Latin classics; the Comedies of Plautus
teem with law -- with the venerable law of the Republic;
the orations of Cicero are fully intelligible to the
civilian alone. Jurisprudence is the light of history,
and a landmark to the vast ocean of the past. How many
curious and important questions does it involve! -- the
application of the torture, a subject of deep and painful
interest -- the consideration of slavery, an institution
of the earliest ages, that still subsists in the British
empire, which strongly arrests the attention of all, but
especially of those whose thoughts are turned towards our
colonies, and by whom the Civil Law can never be neglected
with impunity. The body of the Roman Law raises, and,
perhaps, solves the momentous inquiry -- Whether it be
expedient and practicable to reduce the whole of the Law
of England to the form of a Code. If, upon the whole, it
discourages the bold attempt, it demonstrates, that it
would be not less feasible than beneficial to repeal the
whole of our Statute Law, and, having consolidated so much
as is actually and usefully in force, to re-enact it in a
systematic and intelligible shape, and to remove the
greatest blot upon our jurisprudence, by reducing
confusion to order, and forty or fifty volumes to four or
five. The experience of Rome, the reformer is unwise who
would reject it, emboldens us to undertake temperate and
considerate changes, but it gravely represses rash and
incautious innovation: -- "Quod medicamenta morbis, hoc
exhibent jura negotiis: unde consequitur, ut non-nonquam
a judicio discordet effectus, et quod credebat conjectura
prodesse, experimento inveniatur inutile." -- Nov. 111,
in Praefat.

The history of the fortunes of the Civil Law, under
the Byzantine empire, is a subject of much curiosity, and
possesses many attractions. The Law of Nations is replete
with an engrossing interest, but it is, perhaps, doubtful,
how far it falls within the legitimate province of a
Professor of Civil Law, except so far as the jus feciale
forms a part of the Roman jurisprudence. It is due
nevertheless to the importance of this department of Law
to suggest, that, although some have rashly affirmed, that
since its decrees cannot be enforced, like those of the
municipal Law, by the sheriff and his officers, it is a
vain pursuit; it cannot, nevertheless, be too much

ventilated and insisted upon, for, the chief sanction
being public opinion; it is essential that opinion should
be distinct, universal, and firmly rooted. If we reflect
how many cruel practices in war were formerly prevalent,
that have been laid aside in modern times, and remember
that there is no other process by which a recurrence to
them can be prevented, except the expression of the
general indignation of civilized nations, retaliation
being more apt to exasperate, than to mitigate, ferocity,
we shall be sensible of the high value of the science and
of the sanction, and that they ought, for the sake of
humanity, to be enlarged and cultivated. Publicists have
been accused, and sometimes justly, of pedantry in
accumulating examples drawn from the historians of
antiquity; it is impossible to deny, notwithstanding, that
these are instructive. To support a principle, it is
always useful to give a well-authenticated instance; to
show that a nation once sacrificed, a great rule of
justice to apparent utility, not foreseeing, or not
regarding the consequences, as being remote, and that such
inconveniences followed, as compelled them bitterly to
Lament their departure from a principle, that ought never
to be violated. Such instances cannot surely be less
convincing, because the Athenians, the Peloponnesians, or
the Romans, furnish the lesson, or because it is read to
us by Thucydides or Polybius, by Livy or Tacitus.
     The words Jus Gentium formerly denoted that law, "quo
gentes humanae utuntur," and they are used in that sense
in the Pandects, and are distinguished from the Jus
Civile, the law which was in force only amongst the
citizens of a particular state: quod quisque populus ipse
sibi jus constituit, id ipsius proprium civitatis est,
vocaturque Jus Civile. Afterwards, the term, "the Law of
Nations," was used to express the intercourse of nations
or states with other nations in their public capacity,
whether in peace or war; as the Civil Law relates to the
private dealings of citizen with citizen. For this
innocuous appellation "the Law of Nations," in the more
modern sense, certain innovators have sought to substitute
the frightfully barbarous title, "International Law." It
behooves us to case out the vile pollution, lest per
adventure another generation, still further advanced in
incivility, should, with the like ignorant affection of
unnecessary precision, assail our ears with their
"Inter-civil Law." Nor is the name of our most honorable
faculty secure; the citizens of Rome styled themselves the
citizens, and their system of law, the Civil Law _____
as Homer has been named the Poet. Those who know its
worth, feel, that it well deserves the honorable
distinction; but some, who strive after a certain most
inaccurate accuracy, choose to call it "the Roman Law";
they would probably strip the father of poetry of his
simple garland, because Bavius and Maevius wrote verses
also.
     For the reasons that have been adduced, with a
diffident, and possibly an inconvenient brevity, and for
many others, that are not esteemed of less weight, but
have been suppressed through a regard for the valuable

time of an enlightened and respectable audience, it has been judged expedient to deliver a course of lectures on the Civil Law. The object to be attempted will be, <u>first</u>, to give a general notion of the system of Roman jurisprudence, of its merits, and, notwithstanding a dutiful reverence for our teachers, of its defects, and to show wherein it agrees with, and how it differs from the laws of England; its superiority and its inferiority. <u>Secondly</u>, to lay before the student select portions of the Pandects, and to introduce him to the inmost sanctuary of justice, where the venerable jurisprudence of the masters of the world still shines brightly in its pristine simplicity and chaste elegance, after a long night of darkness, and comes upon us, in its first purity, with the freshness of the morning.

It will be prudent to break the regular routine of instruction, in order to facilitate the comprehension of matters, to which a certain obscurity adheres, and to stimulate the attention by variety, by interspersing, occasionally, miscellaneous lectures, explaining the structure of the Roman constitution at different periods, the offices of the several magistrates, the formation and practice of the courts, the manner of introducing and passing laws, of executing and construing them, and on other topics, to enumerate which would be tedious. The great Roman epic, the Aeneid of Virgil, will by itself demonstrate that religion formed no inconsiderable ingredient in the polity of ancient Rome; it will be necessary, therefore, to take a survey of the priesthood, and to investigate the connection between church and state in the Pagan world. On the conversion of Constantine, the same pious zeal was transferred to Christianity; and the Code and the Novels prove the wonderful activity of imperial legislation in fortifying and regulating the new religion: so intimately indeed is the history of the Church interwoven with the Roman jurisprudence, that he must be incautions, if not profane, who would attempt to relate the former without considerable experience in the latter.

In explaining the Civil Law, and the various matters connected with it, it will be a duty of perfect obligation to avoid all vain pedantry, every display of unnecessary citation, the ostentation of erudition, and that empty and selfish vanity, which delights in an unprofitable parade of the learned languages and of strange tongues, and to endeavor, on the contrary, to unfold the doctrines and practices of antiquity with all plainness and simplicity, and in a candid and artless style; and, when it shall be necessary to derive illustrations from Grecian fountains, rather to state in our own tongue the results of reading, than to incur the risk of impeding the vision by the grammatical and rhetorical obliquities, which the original may often present. With respect to the knowledge that will be conveyed, it will be designed not for show, but for use; not to scare the unlearned and to shock the learned by ill-timed and unusual quotations in legal writings and arguments, but so to form and fashion the intellect by the best precepts and examples, that it shall appear, when exercised in conducting the more important affairs of life, to be naturally of a larger growth, and to have been further developed by a powerful but unknown and mysterious culture.

Our laws are wise and beneficent, the administration of them pure and efficient; they were generally conceived in the true spirit of Northern liberty; and they display many traces of the invention and originality of the middle ages, of the infancy of a new state of society. Truth compels us to add, that they exhibit also much of the barbarity of that period. He is wise, who is able, with a temperate and judicious hand, to remove their enormous defects; nor is it a mean attempt to essay to divest them of their rudeness, and, by the help of the Roman jurisprudence, to bring them back to the comely and perspicuous simplicity and antiquity. He who forms a right estimate of human happiness will consider a moderate success in this important project an ample compensation for much labor, misfortune, and disappointment.

THE END

– 8 –

Beverly Tucker

Lecture on the Study of the Law (1834)

YOUNG GENTLEMEN:

I gladly avail myself of an established custom, to offer some remarks on the mutual relation into which we have just entered, and the studies which will occupy our attention during the ensuing course.

This day is to you the commencement of the most important area of life. You have heretofore been engaged in studies, for the most part useful, but sometimes merely ornamental or amusing. The mind, it is true, can hardly fail to improve, by the exertion necessary to the acquisition of knowledge of any kind, even as the athletic sports of the boy harden and prepare the body for the labors of the man. But, in many particulars, what you have heretofore learned may be of little practical value in the business of life; and your past neglects may perhaps be attended with no loss of prosperity or respectability in future. Some of you are probably acquainted with sciences of which others are ignorant; but are not for that reason any better prepared for the new course of studies on which you are about to enter. Nor will such knowledge necessarily afford its possessors any advantage at the bar, or in the senate, or on any of the arenas, where the interests of individuals and nations are discussed, and the strifes of men decided. But the time is now past with you, young gentlemen, when you can lose a moment, or neglect an opportunity of improvement, without a lasting and irreparable detriment to yourselves. You this day put on the <u>toga virilis</u>, and enter on the <u>business of life</u>. This day you commence those studies on which independence, prosperity, respectability, and the comfort and happiness of those who will be dearest to you, must depend. For, trust me, these things mainly depend on excellence in the profession or occupation, whatever it may be, which a man chooses as the business of his life. The humblest mechanic will derive more of all these good things from diligence and proficiency in his trade, than he possibly can from any knowledge unconnected with it.

This, which is true of all occupations, is most emphatically true of that which you have chosen. To be eminent in our profession is to hold a place among the great ones of the earth; and they, who devote themselves to it, have the rare advantage of treading the path which leads to the highest objects of honorable ambition, even while walking the round of daily duties, and providing for the daily wants of private life. The history of our country is full of proof that the bar is the road to eminence; and I beg you to remark how few of its members have attained to this eminence in public life, without having been first distinguished in the profession. To win its honors, and to wear them worthily, is to attain an elevation from which all other honors are accessible: but to turn aside disgusted with its labors, is to lose this vantage ground, and to sink again to the dead level of the common mass. You should therefore learn to look on the profession of your choice, as the source from whence are to flow all the comforts, the honors, and the happiness of life. Let it be as a talisman, in which, under God, you put your trust, assuring yourselves that whatever you seek by means of its you will receive.

I have the more naturally fallen into these remarks, as they are in some sort suggested, and are certainly justified by the history of this institution. If you trace back the lives of the men, who at this moment occupy the most enviable pre-eminence in your native state, you will find that they received the rudiments of their professional and political education at this venerable but decayed seminary. There are certainly distinguished members of the profession, and illustrious men out of he profession, to whom this remark does not apply. But when Virginia (Magna Parens Virum), is called on to show her jewels, to whom does she more proudly point than to men who once occupied those very seats; who here received the first impulse in their career; who here commenced that generous strife for superiority which has placed them all so high.

The subject of our researches, young gentlemen, will be the municipal law of Virginia. The textbook which will be placed in your hands is the American edition of Blackstone's Commentaries, published thirty years ago by one of my predecessors in this chair. You will readily believe that it would be my pride to walk, with filial reverence by the rights which he has given us, and that, in doing so, I should feel secure of escaping any harsh animadversion from those to whom I am responsible, and who still cherish so favorable a recollection of his services. I shall certainly endeavor to avail myself of this privilege; though it may be occasionally necessary to assume a more perilous responsibility. A brief sketch of the plan which I propose to myself, will show you how far I shall follow, and wherein, and why, I shall deviate from the path which he has traced.

Municipal law is defined by Mr. Blackstone, "to be a rule of civil conduct prescribed by the supreme power of the state." By Justinian it is said, "Id quod quisque populus sibi jus constituit, vocatur jus civile:" which has been well rendered thus: "It is the system of rules of civil conduct which any state has ordained for itself."

Whatever definition we adopt, we shall find that municipal law is distinguishable into four grand divisions, which may be properly designated by the following description:

1.   That which regulates the nature and form of the body politic; which establishes the relation that each individual bears to it, and the rights and duties growing out of that relation, which determines the principles on which it exercises authority over him; and settles a system of jurisprudence by which it operates to protect and enforce right, and to redress and punish wrong.

2.   That which determines the relations of individual members of society to each other; which defines the rights growing out of that relation; and regulates the right of property, and such personal rights as must subsist even in a state of nature.

3.   That which defines the wrongs that may be done by one individual member of society to another, in prejudice of his rights, whether of person or property, and provdes means for preventing or redressing such wrongs.

4.   That which defines and denounces the wrongs which may be done by any individual member of society, in violation of the duties growing out of his relation to the body politic, and provides means for preventing and punishing such violation.

The first of these divisions is treated by Mr. Blackstone in his first book, under the comprehensive head of "The Rights of Persons."   Under the same head he includes so much of the second division as relates to such personal rights as must have belonged to man in a state of nature, and such as grow out of his relation to other individual members of society.   Such are the relative rights of husband and wife, parent and child, guardian and ward, and master and servant -- and the absolute rights, of personal liberty, and of security to life, limb and reputation.   These rights are obviously not the creatures of civil society, however they may be regulated and modified by municipal law.   They in no way depend on "the nature or form of the body politic;" nor on "the relations which individuals bear to it;" nor on "the rights and duties growing out of that relation;" nor on "the principles on which it exercises authority over individuals;" nor on "the system of jurisprudence."

As little indeed do they depend on "the rights of property," but they have much in common with them. Together with them, they collectively form the mass of "individual rights," as contra-distinguished from "political rights."   Neither class derives its existence from civil society, although both are liable to be regulated by it, and the two together form the subject of almost all controversies between man and man.   Now with rights in actual and peaceable enjoyment, law has nothing to do.   It is controversy which calls it into action; and as both this class of personal rights, and the rights of property, have the same common origin -- both subsisting by titles paramount to the constitutions of civil society;

as both are the ordinary subjects of controversy between individuals; and as these controversies are all conducted according to similar forms, decided by the same tribunals, and adjusted by the like means, -- it is found convenient to arrange them together in a course of instruction. Such I believe has always been the practice in this institution. Proposing to conform to it, I have thought it best, in the outset, to intimate this slight difference between this practice and Mr. Blackstone's arrangement.

There is another particular in which Mr. Blackstone's order of instruction has been advantageously changed at this place. His is certainly the true philosophical arrangement of the subject. When we are told that "municipal law is a rule of civil conduct prescribed by the supreme power in the state," it is obvious to ask, "what is that supreme power, and whence comes its supremacy?" When we are told that it is "the system of rules of civil conduct, which the state has ordained for itself," the first inquiry is, "what is the state?" Thus whatever definition of municipal law we adopt, the subject of inquiry that meets us at the threshold is the Lex Legum; the law which endues the municipal law itself with authority.

If the individual to be instructed were one who had heretofore lived apart from law and government, yet capable (if such a thing were possible) of understanding the subject, it is here we ought to commence. To him it would be indispensable to explain, in the first instance, the structure of the body politic; to specify the rights surrendered by individuals; and to set before him the equivalent privileges received in exchange. We too might be supposed to require a like exposition before we would be prepared to submit to the severe restraints and harsh penalties of criminal law. But in regard to controversies between individuals we feel no such jealousies. In these, the law, acting but as an arbiter, indifferent between the parties, no question concerning its authority occurs to the mind. The readiness with which we acquiesce in its decisions, is strikingly manifested in the fact, that the whole of England, Ireland and the United States are, for the most part, governed by a law which has no voucher for its authority but this acquiescence. The same thing may be said of the authority of the civil law on the continent of Europe. It thus appears that the mind does not always require to be informed of the origin of the law which regulates and enforces, or protects individual rights, before it will condescend to inquire what are its behests. Prima facie it should be so; but being, in point of fact, born in the midst of law, habituated to it from our infancy, and accustomed to witness uniform obedience to its authority on the part of those whom we were taught to obey, we learn to regard it as a thing in rerum natura, rather than of human invention; a sort of moral atmosphere, which, like that we breathe, seems a very condition of our existence.

There is therefore no inconvenience to be apprehended from taking up the subject in an inverted order, treating first of individual rights, and reserving those that grow out of the relation of the citizen to the body politic, and the correlative duties of that relation, for future inquiry.

While there is nothing to be objected to this arrangement, there is much in favor of it. It is important that they who engage in the study of political law, should come to the task with minds prepared for it; well stored with analogous information, and sobered and subdued by the discipline of severe investigation. There is a simplicity in some views of government which is apt to betray the student into a premature belief that he understands it thoroughly; and then, measuring the value of his imagined acquirements, not by the labor that they have cost him, but by the dignity and importance of the subject, he becomes inflated, self-satisfied and unteachable; resting in undoubting assurance on the accuracy and sufficiency of such bare outline as his instructor may have thought proper to place before him. But in those countries where the authority of government rests on a questionable title, they who are entrusted with the education of youth, may naturally wish to keep them from looking into it too narrowly. Hence it may be a measure of policy with them, to introduce the student, in the first place, to the study of political law, in the hope of making on his raw and unpractised mind, such an impression, as may secure his approbation of the existing order of things. The faculty of investigating legal questions, and forming legal opinions, may almost be regarded as an acquired faculty; so that, in the earlier part of his researches, the student necessarily acquiesces in the doctrines which are pronounced ex cathedra by his teacher. At this time he readily receives opinions on trust; and if it be his interest to cherish them, or if he is never called on in after life to re-examine them, he is apt to carry them with him to the grave. This is perhaps as it should be in England and other countries of Europe. Having no part in the government, it may be well enough that he should learn to sit down contented with this sort of enlightened ignorance.

But with us the case is different. The authority of our governments is derived by a title that fears no investigation. We feel sure, that, the better it is understood, the more it will be approved. It rests too on a charter conferring regulated and limited powers; and the well being of the country requires that the limitations and regulations be strictly observed. Now every man among us has his "place in the commonwealth." It is on the one hand, the duty of every man to aid in giving full effect to all legitimate acts of government; and on the other, to bear his part in restraining the exercise of all powers forbidden or not granted. Every man therefore owes it to his country to acquire a certain proficiency in constitutional law, so as to act understandingly, when called on to decide between an alleged violation of the constitution, and an imputed opposition to lawful authority. Such occasions are of daily occurrence. Scarcely a day has passed, since the adoption of the federal constitution, when some question of this sort has

not been before the public.   Such is the effect of that
impatience of restraint natural to man.   So prompt are the
people to become restive under laws of questionable
authority, and so apt are rulers to strain at the curb of
constitutional limitations, that one or the other, or both
of the spectacles, is almost always before us.
    When you come then, young gentlemen, to the study of
political and constitutional law, you will find it no
small advantage to have been engaged for some months
before in studies of a similar character.   The opinions
you will then form will be properly your own.   I may not
be so successful as I might wish, in impressing you with
those I entertain; but I shall be more gratified to find
you prepared to "give a reason for the faith that is in
you," whatever that faith may be, than to hear you
rehearse, by rote, any political catechism that I could
devise.   I shall accordingly postpone any remarks on
constitutional and political law, until your minds have
been exercised and hardened by the severe training they
will undergo in the study of the private rights of
individuals, of wrongs done in prejudice of such rights,
and of the remedies for such wrongs.   All these topics are
embraced in the second and third division of municipal
law, that I have laid before you.
    To these belong the most intricate and difficult
questions in the science of law.   In introducing you to
the study of these, let me say, in the language of one
from whom I am proud to quote, that, "I cannot flatter you
with the assurance that 'your yoke is easy and your burden
light.'   I will not tell you that your path leads over
gentle ascents and through flowery meads, where every new
object entices us forward, and stimulates to perseverance.
By no means!   The task you have undertaken is one of the
most arduous; the profession you have chosen one of the
most laborious; the study you are about to pursue, one of
the most difficult that can be conceived.   But you have
made your election.   You have severed yourselves from the
common herd of youth, who shrink from every thing that
demands exertion and perseverance.   You have chosen
between the allurements of pleasure and the honors which
await the disciples of wisdom.   You yield to others to
keep the noiseless tenor of their way in inglorious ease.
You have elected for yourselves the path that philosophers
and moralists represent as leading, up a rugged ascent, to
the temple of fame.   It may be the lot of some of you to
elevate yourselves by talents and unabating zeal, in the
pursuit you have selected.   But these distinguished honors
are not to be borne away by the slothful and inert.   Nulla
palma sine pulvere.   He who would win the laurel, must
encounter the sweat and toil of the arena.   Nor will it
suffice that he occasionally presses on to the goal.   If
he slackens in his efforts he must lose ground.   We roll a
Sysiphean stone to an exalted eminence.   He who gives back
loses what his strength had gained; and sinking under the
toil his own indolence increases, will at length give up
his unsteady efforts in despair." -- 1 T.C. Introduction,
p. vi.

I can add nothing to these striking remarks but my testimony to their truth.   There is, perhaps, no study that tasks the powers of the mind more severely than that of law.   In it, as in the study of mathematics, nothing is learned at all that is not learned perfectly; and a careless perusal of Euclid's elements would not be more unprofitable, than that of a treatise on the laws of property.   Nor will a mere effort of memory be of more avail in the one case than in the other.   Both must be remembered by being understood; by being through the exercise of intense thought, incorporated as it were into the very texture of the mind.   To this end its powers must be fully and faithfully exerted.   As, in lifting at a weight, you do but throw away your labor, until you man yourself to the exertion of the full measure of strength necessary to raise it; so, in this study, you may assure yourselves that all you have done is of no avail, if you pass from any topic without thoroughly understanding it. And let no man persuade you that genius can supply the place of this exertion.   Genius does not so manifest itself.   The secret of its wonderful achievements is in the energy which it inspires.   It is because its prompting sting, like the sharp goad of necessity, urges to herculean effort, that it is seen to accomplish herculean tasks.   He is deceived who fancies himself a favored child of genius, unless he finds his highest enjoyment in intellectual exercise.   He should go to the toil of thought like the champion to the lists, seeking in the very certaminis gaudia the rich reward of all his labors.
There may be something startling, I fear, in this exhibition of the difficulties that lie before you, and it is proper to encourage you by the assurance that by strenuous effort they may be certainly overcome.   Remember too that this effort will be painful only in the outset. The mind, like the body, soon inures itself to toil; and wears off the soreness consequent on its first labors. When this is done, the task becomes interesting in proportion to its difficulty, and subjects which are understood without effort, and which do not excite the mind to thought, seem flat and insipid.
But lest the student should falter and give back in his earlier struggles, it is the duty of the teacher to afford him such aids as he can.   This is mainly to be done by means of such an analysis and arrangement of the subject as may prevent confusion, and consequent perplexity and discouragement.
There are two sorts of analysis, each proper in its place.   The one philosophical, by which the different parts of a subject are so arranged, as to exhibit in distinct groups those things that depend on the same or like principles, and such as are marked by characteristic points of resemblance; giving a sort of honorary precedence to the most important.   The other sort of analysis may be termed logical.   It is that method by which different propositions are so arranged, as that no one of them shall ever be brought under consideration, until all others which may be necessary to the right understanding of that one, have been established and

explained.   Of this last description are Euclid's
elements, in which it is interesting to observe that no
one proposition could with propriety be made to change its
place; each one depending for its demonstration, directly
or indirectly, upon all that have gone before.
   Blackstone's Commentaries may be cited as an example
of philosophical analysis. He has indeed been careful to
avoid perplexing his reader, through the want of a
strictly logical arrangement, by dealing chiefly in
generalities, and never descending to such particulars as
might be unintelligible for want of a knowledge of matters
not yet treated of.   This I take to be the reason why his
work has been characterized as being "less an institute of
law, than a methodical guide or elementary work adapted to
the commencement of a course of study. He treats most
subjects in a manner too general and cursory to give the
student an adequate knowledge of them.   After having
pursued his beautiful arrangement, he is obliged to seek
elsewhere for farther details.   After having learnt the
advantage of system, he is almost at the threshold of the
science, turned back without a guide, to grope among the
many volumes of our crowded libraries. This cannot be
right. If system is of advantage at all, it is of
advantage throughout.   Were it practicable, it would be
better for the student to have a single work, which
embracing the whole subject, should properly arrange every
principle and every case essential to be known preparatory
to his stepping on the arena.   Much, very much indeed,
would still be left to be explored in the course of his
professional career, independent of the apices juris,
which the most vigorous and persevering alone can hope to
attain." -- Tucker's Commentary, Introduction, p. 4.
   The justice of these remarks none can deny. It might
be thought unbecoming in me to say how much the writer
from whom I quote them has done to supply such a work as
he describes. Yet I cannot suffer any feeling of delicacy
to restrain me from the duty of recommending that work to
your attentive perusal.   I shall eagerly, too, avail
myself of his permission to make frequent use of it, as I
know of no book which so well supplies the necessary
details to parts of the subject of which Mr. Blackstone
has given only loose and unprofitable sketches.   It is to
be lamented that in doing this he has so strictly bound
himself to the arrangement of that writer.   That
arrangement, as I have remarked, imposed on Mr. Blackstone
the necessity of being occasionally losse and superficial.
For want of one more strictly logical, the Virginia
Commentator often finds it impossible to go into the
necessary detail, without anticipating matters which
properly belong to subsequent parts of his treatise; and
too often, where this is impracticable, topics and terms
are introduced, the explanation of which is, perhaps,
deferred to the next volume.
   An instance will illustrate my meaning: -- Mr.
Blackstone classes remedies for private wrongs, thus:
"first, that which is obtained by the mere act of the
parties themselves; secondly, that which is effected by
the mere act and operation of law; and thirdly, that which

arises from <u>suit</u> or <u>action</u> in courts."   Now, it probably
occurred to him, that he could not go into details on the
two first of these three heads, without presenting ideas
which would be unintelligible to any who had not already
studied the third.   In striving to avoid this, he has
touched so lightly upon the other two, that his remarks on
the important subjects of distress and accords, which come
under the first head, leave the student nearly as ignorant
as they found him.   For this there was no real necessity,
as a knowledge of the two first heads is by no means
necessary, or indeed at all conducive to the right
understanding of the third.   Had the pride of
philosophical analysis, and symmetry of arrangement, been
sacrificed to the laws of logic and reason, there was
nothing to forbid the introduction of treatises on these
important topics, as copious and elaborate as those
supplied by the diligence and research of the Virginia
Commentator.   The manner in which this has been done, has
made it manifest how unfavorable the arrangement of Mr.
Blackstone sometimes is to amplification and minuteness.
The essays of the President of the Court of Appeals on
distresses and accords, leave nothing to be desired.   Yet
no one can read them profitably without having first
studied the law of remedies by suit or action.

     These, and some other instances of the same sort,
have led me to this determination.   Wishing to avail
myself of the labors of the Virginia Commentator, without
losing the benefit of Mr. Blackstone's analysis, I propose
to preserve the latter, but to make occasional changes in
his arrangement, substituting one more logical, though
perhaps less philosophical.   This, and the postponement of
the study of political law, are the only liberties I
propose to take.   The fourth division, which relates to
crimes and punishments, will be the last considered.   This
will be done not only in a spirit of conformity to Mr.
Blackstone's plan, but also because one of the most
important branches of criminal law has reference to an
offense of which no just idea can be formed without a
previous and diligent study of the Constitution and of the
science of government.

     This last mentioned subject, young gentlemen, I
should perhaps pass over but lightly, were I free to do
so, contenting myself with a passing allusion to its
connexion with the study of the law,and the encouragement
you should derive from the honorable rewards that await
distinguished merit in our profession.   But this is not a
mere school of professional education, and it is made my
duty, by the statutes of the College, to lecture
especially on the constitution of this state and of the
United States.   In the discharge of this duty it may be
necessary to present views more important to the
statesman, than to the mere practitioner.   When I think of
the difficulty and high responsibility attending this part
of my task, I would gladly escape from it; but
considerations of its importance and of the benefit to the
best interests of our country which has heretofore
resulted from its faithful execution, come in aid of a

sense of duty, and determine me to meet it firmly and
perform it zealously.

The mind of the student of law is the ground in which
correct constitutional opinions and sound maxims of
political law should be implanted.   The study of the
common law involves the study of all the rights which
belong to man in a state of society.   The history of the
common law is a history of the occasional invasions of
these rights, of the struggles in which such invasions
have been repelled, and of the securities provided to
guard against their recurrence.   A mind thoroughly
acquainted with the nature and importance of the writ of
habeau corpus, and the trial by jury, and rightly
understanding the indestructible character of the right of
private property, will hardly fail to be awake to any
attack which may be aimed at liberty from any quarter.
Hence liberty finds in the students of the law a sort of
body guard.   Their professional apprenticeship serves as a
civil polytechnic school, where they are taught the use of
weapons to be wielded in her defence.   The history of our
country from the first dawning of the revolution is full
of proofs and examples of this.   The clear view of the
rights of the colonies which led to the Declaration of
Independence, was one which hardly any but lawyers could
have taken, and of the accuracy of which none but lawyers
could have been sure.   It was from them the ball of the
revolution received its first impulse, and under their
guidance it was conducted to the goal.   Some few others
were placed forward by circumstances; but they soon fell
back, or found their proper place of service in the field;
leaving the great cause to be managed by those whose
studies qualified them to know where to insist, and where
to concede; when to ward, and when to strike.   The state
papers emanating from the first congress will,
accordingly, be found worthy to be compared with the
ablest productions of the kind recorded in history;
displaying an ability, temper, and address, which prepares
the reader to be told that a large majority of the members
of that body were lawyers.

In Mr. Blackstone's introductory lecture are some
remarks on the importance of the study of the law to
English gentlemen, strictly applicable to this view of the
subject.   "It is," says he, "perfectly amazing, that there
should be no other state of life, no other occupation,
art, or science, in which some method of instruction is
not looked upon as necessary, except only the science of
legislation, the noblest and most difficult of any.
Apprenticeships are held necessary to almost every art,
commercial or mechanical: a long course of reading and
study must form the divine, the physician, and the
practical professor of the laws: but every man of
superior fortune thinks himself born a legislator.   Yet
Tully was of a different opinion: 'it is necessary,' says
he, 'for a senator to be thoroughly acquainted with the
constitution; and this,' he declares, 'is a knowledge of
the most extensive nature; a matter of science, of
diligence, of reflection; without which no senator can
possibly be fit for his office.'"

If the part in the government allotted to the people of England renders this admonition important to them, how much more important must it be to us, who are in theory and in fact our own rulers.   Not only is every office accessible to each one of us; but each, even in private life, as soon as he puts on manhood, assumes a "place in the commonwealth."   In practice, as in theory, the SOVEREIGNTY OF THE STATE is in us.   Born to the purple, the duties of that high destiny attach upon us at our birth; and unless we qualify ourselves to discharge them, we must cease to reproach the ignorance and folly, the passion and presumption, which so often disgrace the sovereigns of the old world, and heap wretchedness and ruin on their subjects.   The same causes will have the like effects here as there.   Power does not imply wisdom or justice, whether in the hands of the few or the many: and it is only by the diligent study of our duties in this important station that we can qualify ourselves so to administer its functions, as to save the free institutions inherited from our fathers, from the same reproach which the testimony of history fixes upon all other governments.

Not only is this true in reference to us as well as to the kings of the earth, but it is more emphatically true of us than of them.   Whatever be their theory of sovereignty, and however they may prate about divine right, they all know, and feel, that, after all, they are but kings by sufferance.   They may talk of absolute sovereignty, and claim for government that sort of omnipotence which is said to reside in the British parliament.   But, after all, they know and feel, that there is much they cannot do, because there is much they dare not do.   The course of events now passing in England is full of proof of this.   We have just seen that same omnipotent parliament, new-modelling itself to suit the wishes of the people.   This act indeed, was itself an exertion of this pretended omnipotence, but wisely and discreetly exercised, in surrendering power.   It was certainly done with a very bad grace; and at this moment we see that body anxiously watching the temper of the multitude, and adapting its measures, not to the views of its members, not even to the views of the constituent body, but to the real or supposed interests of the great unrepresented mass.   Such is the check, which in spite of all positive institutions, the physical force of numbers, however degraded, and, professedly, disregarded, must exercise over their rulers; and in this check, they find a motive to justice, forbearance, and circumspection, which, in a measure, restrains the abuse of power.

But may not we, the sovereign citizens of these states, abuse power too?   When men are numerous and "strong enough to set their duties at defiance, do they cease to be duties any longer?"   Does that which would be unjust as the act of ninety-nine, become just, as being the act of an hundred?   Is it in the power of numbers to alter the nature of things, and to justify oppression though it should fall on the head of only one victim?   It would be easy to point to instances in which we all believe that majorities have done great wrong; and that

under such wrongs we have suffered and are still suffering
we all know.   But where is the check on such abuse of
power?   Constitutional authority and physical force are
both on the same side, and if the wisdom and justice of
those who wield both does not freely afford redress, there
are no means of enforcing it.   "There is no sanction to
any contract against the will of prevalent power."

The justice of these ideas is recognized in the forms
of all our governments.   The limitations on the powers of
congress and the state legislatures, are all predicated on
the certain truth "that majorities may find or imagine an
interest in doing wrong."   Hence there are many things
which cannot be lawfully done by a bare majority; and many
more, which no majority, however great, is authorised to
do.   Two-thirds of the senate must concur in a sentence of
impeachment.   The life and property of an individual
cannot be taken away but by the unanimous voice of his
triers; and all the branches of all our governments
collectively cannot lawfully enact a bill of attainder, or
an ex post facto statute.

But though such acts are forbidden by the
constitution, they may nevertheless be passed, and judges
may be found to enforce them, if those holding legisltive
and judicial offices shall be so minded.   The
constituents, too, of a majority of the legislature may
approve and demand such acts.   Where then is the security
that such things will not be done?   Where can it be but in
the enlightened sense of justice and right in the
constituent body?

I am not sure that such restraints on the powers of
public functionaries are not even more necessary in a
republican government than in any other.   A king can
scarcely have a personal interest in ruining one portion
of his dominions for the benefit of the rest, and he would
not dare to run the whole, while a spark of intelligence
and spirit remained among the people.   But in a republic,
whenever the inclination and the power to do such a wrong
concur, the very nature of the case secures the rulers
from all fear of personal consequences.   The majority is
with them.   Their own constituents are with them.   To
these is their first duty; and shall they hesitate to do
that which is to benefit their constituents, out of
tenderness to those who are not their constituents?   We
know how such questions are answered, when the occasion is
one where a fixed majority have a fixed interest in the
proposed wrong.   Is not this the reason why legislative
encroachment so much disposes men to acquiesce in
executive usurpation?   Is it not this, which, when the
barriers of constitutional restraint are seen to fall,
drives minorities, as by a sort of fatal instinct, to seek
shelter under the arm of a common master, from the all
pervading tyranny of majorities exercising the power of
universal legislation?   The wrongs of America were the act
of the parliament of England, goaded on by the people.   It
was they who claimed a right to legislate in all things
for the colonies.   It was they who demanded a revenue from
America; and the colonies, eagerly looking to the crown
for protection, maintained an unshaken loyalty, until the

king was seen to take part with their oppressors.   The
wrongs of Ireland are the act of the people of England.
Ireland is the rival of England in agriculture,
manufactures and commerce; and every concession to the
former, seems to the multitude to be something taken from
the prosperity of the latter.   But the representation of
Ireland in parliament is to that of England as one to
five; and when the Irish people cry to parliament for
redress, they are answered <u>as all appeals from minorities
are answered by the representatives of majorities</u>.   But
how would they be answered if the representative and
constituent bodies were both thoroughly instructed in the
sacred character and paramount authority and importance of
the <u>duties</u> which belong to the high function of
sovereignty?   We justly deny and deride the divine right
of kings; and we assert and maintain <u>the divine right of
the people to self government</u>.   And it is a divine right.
It is a corollary from the right and duty to fulfil the
purposes of our being, which accompany each one of us into
the world.   The right and the duty both come from the
author of that being.   He imposes the one when he gives
the other, and thus fixes on us a responsibility which
clings to us through life.   We deceive ourselves if we
think to get rid of any portion of this responsibiltiy by
entering into partnership with others, each one of whom
brings into the concern the same rights, the same duties,
and the same responsibilities;--neither more nor less than
ourselves.   We do but multiply, and divide again by the
same number.   Each receives, by way of dividend, the same
amount of right, duty, and responsibility that he carried
into the common stock.   Of so high a nature are these, and
so vast are the interests with which they are connected,
that it has been truly said, that, whether we mount the
hustings or go to the polls, we may well tremble to give
or to receive the power which is there conferred.
      Gentlemen; if these ideas be just, how important is
the duty imposed on me by that statute of the college
which requires me to lecture on constitutional law!   How
desirable is it that there should be every where schools,
in which the youth of our country should be thoroughly
imbued with correct opinions and just sentiments on this
subject!   It was Agesilaus, I think, who said that "the
business of education was to prepare the boy for the
duties of the man."   How pre-eminently important, then,
must be that branch of education which is to qualify him
to perform this highest of all social duties, and to bear
worthily his part in that relation which has been
characterized as "a partnership in all science, in all
art, in every virtue, and in all perfection; a
partnership, not only between those who are living, but
between those who are dead, and
those who are yet to be born."
      These striking words, which are from the pen of the
celebrated Edmund Burke, call to mind the high testimony
which he has borne in favor of the study of the law, as a
school of political rights.   After having acted an
important part in procuring the repeal of the stamp act,
he made his last effort in favor of the rights of the

colonies, in March, 1775. On that occasion, laboring to dissuade the British parliament from pushing America to extremities, he descanted on the love of freedom, which he pronounced to be the predominating feature in the character of our fathers. The prevalence of this passion he ascribed to a variety of causes, none more powerful than the number of lawyers, and the familiarity of the people with the principles of the common law. His ideas I will give you in his own words, for it is only in his own words that his ideas ever can be fittingly expressed.

He says, "In no country perhaps in the world is the law so general a study. The profession itself is numerous and powerful; and in most provinces it takes the lead. The greater number of the deputies sent to the congress were lawyers. But all who read, and most do read, endeavor to obtain some smattering in that science. * * * * * This study renders men acute, inquisitive, dexterous, prompt in attack, ready in defence, full of resources. In other countries, the people, more simple, and of a less mercurial cast, judge of an ill principle in government only by an actual grievance; here they anticipate the evil, and judge of the pressure of the grievance by the badness of the principle. They augur misgovernment at a distance, and snuff the approach of tyranny in every tainted breeze."

Such, young gentlemen, is the important and useful influence which the study of our profession enables its members to exert. But if, instead of preparing their minds by this study, the very men to whom the people look up for light, do but provide themselves with a few set phrases contrived to flatter and cajole them, what but evil can come of it?

"The people can do no wrong." Why! this is but what all sovereigns hear from their flatters. In one sense, it is indeed true of both, for there is no human tribunal before which either king or people can be arraigned. But neither can make right and wrong change places and natures.

"Vox populi, vox Dei." "It is the voice of God." So said the Jews of the impious Herod. But the judgments of the insulted Deity showed how mere a worm he was; and his judgments are not limited to kings, nor withheld by numbers. We may preserve all the outward forms of freedom, the checks and balances of the constitution may remain to all appearance undisturbed, and yet he who can "curse our blessings" may give us over to all the evils of despotism, if we do not "lay to heart" the high duties of that freedom wherewith he has made us free.

I am sensible, young gentlemen, that, to many, these ideas will not be acceptable. And for an obvious reason. "Men like well enough," it is said, "to hear of their power, but have an extreme disrelish to be told of their duties." Yet in a government of equal rights, these are strictly correlative. The rights of each individual are the exact measure of the duties which others owe to him, and of course, of those he owes to others. This is so obviously true, that it needs but be stated, to be recognized at once as a man recognizes his face in the glass. But <u>he</u> "goeth his way, and straightway forgetteth what manner of man he was." Let not us do likewise.

But there is another reason why many will hear with impatience of the difficulties attendant on the proper discharge of duties, which are too often made the low sport of a holiday revel. None can deny the truth and justice of the remarks already quoted from Mr. Blackstone; but few, I fear, are willing to bring them home, and to acknowledge the necessity of such severe preparation to qualify themselves to exercise the franchises of a citizen. Let me hope, young gentlemen, that you will view the matter in a different light, and go to your task with the more cheerfulness, from the assurance that you will thus be qualified to derive a blessing to yourselves and to your country, from the discreet and conscientious exercise of a privilege, which others, from a want of correct information and just sentiments, so often pervert to the injury of both.

Before I conclude, give me leave to offer a few remarks on a subject in which every member of the faculty has an equal and common interest. If there be any thing by which the University of William and Mary has been advantageously distinguished, it is the liberal and magnanimous character of its discipline. It has been the study of its professors to cultivate at the same time, the intellect, the principles, and the deportment of the student, laboring with equal diligence to infuse the spirit of the gentleman. He comes to us as a gentleman. As such we receive and treat him, and resolutely refuse to know him in any other character. He is not harassed with petty regulations; he is not insulted and annoyed by impertinent <u>surveillance</u>. Spies and informers have no countenance among us. We receive no accusation but from the conscience of the accused. His honor is the only witness to which we appeal; and should he be even capable of prevarication or falsehood, we admit no proof of the fact. But I beg you to observe, that in this cautious and forbearing spirit of our legislation, you have not only proof that we have no disposition to harass you with unreasonable requirements; but a pledge that such regulations as we have found it necessary to make, <u>will</u> be <u>enforced</u>. If we did not mean to execute our laws, it might do little harm to have them minute and much in detail on paper. It is because we <u>do</u> mean to enforce them that we are cautious to require nothing which may not be exacted without tyranny or oppression, without degrading ourelves or dishonoring you.

The effect of this system, in inspiring a high and scrupulous sense of honor, and a scorn of all disingenuous artifice, has been ascertained by long experience, and redounds to the praise of its authors. That it has not secured a regular discharge of all academical duties, or prevented the disorders which characterize the wilderness of youth, is known and lamented. But we believe and know, that he who cannot be held to his duty, but by base and slavish motives, can never do honor to his instructers; while we are equally sure that such a system as keeps up a sense of responsibility to society at large, is most conducive to high excellence. We think it right, therefore, to adapt our discipline to those from whom excellence may be expected, rather than to those from whom mediocrity may barely be hoped. Such a system is valuable too, as forming a sort of middle term between the restraints of pupilage and the perfect freedom and independence of manhood. Experience shows that there is a time of life, when the new born spirit of independence, and the prurience of incipient manhood will not be repressed. They will break out in the airs or in the graces of manhood. Between these we have to choose. The youth of eighteen treated as a boy, exhibits the former. Treated as a man, he lays aside these forever, and displays the latter. This system is thus believed to afford the best security against such offences as stain the name of the perpetrator. Of such our records bear no trace; nor is there, perhaps, a single individual of all who have matriculated here, that would blush to meet any of his old associates in this school of honor.

May we not hope then, young gentlemen, when so much is trusted to your magnanimity, that the dependence will not fail us? May we not hope, when we are seen anxious to make our relation, not only a source of profit, but of satisfaction to you, that you will not wantonly make it a source of uneasiness and vexation to us? I persuade myself that you, at least commence your studies with such dispositions as we desire. If this be so, there is one short rule by which you may surely carry them into effect. "Give diligent attention to your studies." This is the best security against all unpleasant collision with your teachers, and against that weariness of spirit which seeks relief in excess or mischief. It carries with it the present happiness, which arises from a consciousness of well doing; it supplies that knowledge which encourages to farther researches, and renders study a pleasure; it establishes habits of application, the value of which will be felt in all the future business of life; and lays the foundation of that intellectual superiority by which you hope to prosper in the world, and to be distinguished from the ignoble multitude who live but to die and be forgotten.

Williamsburg, October 27, 1834.

– 9 –

Simon Greenleaf

A Discourse Pronounced
at the Inauguration of the Author
as Royall Professor of Law
in Harvard University (1834)

Mr. President, and Gentlemen of the University,

In accepting the office to which I had the honor of your invitation, I have not been insensible of the difficulty and peril of the undertaking. To follow out the designs and continue the courses of exact and thorough instruction, projected by men of vigorous and exalted intellect and various learning who have here preceded me, and to act daily and constantly, by precept and example, with all the influences of an elder brother, on the minds of so many young men already the hope of our country, is a work of magnitude sufficient to oppress a stouter heart than mine. And perilous indeed is the position, exposed to the brilliant lights of jurisprudence and of science by which I am surrounded. Yet, believing that an honor like this, unsought, was not to be declined, I have not felt at liberty to withhold this testimony of devotedness to a science of such surpassing value as the law; affecting, as it does, all we hold dear in civil or social life, and imparting, as it may be well or ill understood and administered, either health and vigor, or disease and death to our institutions.

It would not become me to claim for the profession, to which I belong, a rank and importance which are not accorded to it by the suffrages of all enlightened men. Yet, if the moral dignity of any science may be argued from the greatness and variety of its objects, from its intimate connexion with human happiness, and its tendency to mould the characters of men for a period of unknown duration, this attribute may be claimed for the law.

In all civilized communities, especially in those which are free, it affords protection to man from his earliest infancy. It provides for his education; taking care that he shall be imbued with the principles of sound morals and the love of virtue, and trained to science, or the useful arts. While it guards the orphan from the spoliations of fraud and avarice on the one hand, and on the other from the cruel exactions of a merciless master,

it still interposes its kind restraints, to save him from
his own worst enemy, himself.   It presides over the
tenderest and most permanent of the contracts into which
he is permitted to enter; and in the character of parent,
master and guardian, it charges him, in turn, with the
offices which others have already performed towards
himself; establishing, defining and enforcing, with
scrupulous care, the reciprocal duties of those relations.

In the affairs of maturer life, man is constantly
dependent on the aid of law.   While it binds him to the
fulfilment of his engagements to others, it enables him to
demand from others the exact performance of their own.   It
secures the enjoyment of his honest acquisitions, whether
of property or of good name, and enables him to transmit
to his children the legacy not only of wealth, but of
reputation and example.   Its protecting power is felt in
the sacredness of his dwelling, and in the unlimited
extent of his personal freedom and independence of action.

In our own country, the law constitutes the very
element of our social existence.   The present is
emphatically the age of combined operations.   The
enterprises of men are no longer conducted, as in early
times, by solitary and individual effort, and private
capital; nor, as in the middle ages of commerce, by the
regular and proper copartnerships of the mercantile world.
Even these copartnerships, however numerous and extensive,
are now made to assume the place of units in the vast
schemes of the day; and from the puerile society, with its
cent a month, to the magnificent conceptions of manhood,
with his gigantic operations and his millions of capital,
all is effected by condensed and incorporated energies.
The unwritten laws of the social circle, and the statutes
of the commonwealth, alike confer on numbers the character
of individuality; and thus new forces are created, whose
effects are limited only by the utmost extent of human
power.   Every man is a corporator; and the number and
variety of these relations, which every member of the
community will, on reflection, be found to sustain, are no
less important than surprising.   And what is the mighty
power which so smoothly, yet vigorously, moves this vast
complication of machinery, but the all-pervading influence
of law?

Nor is this power discerned only in the encouragement
of industry and the protection of innocence and youth.
With an eye that never winks, it watches the earliest
developments of vice, and explores the deepest recesses of
fraud and criminal intention; preserving the purity and
peace of society, by its preventive process, and the
certainty of its wholesome inflictions.   In this respect
we can never measure the extent of our obligations to the
law, until we can estimate the amount of crime which is
prevented by the restraints it interposes before intent
his ripened into action, or by the well-founded belief
that the hand of justice will, sooner or later, yet
certainly, be laid on the offender, if he shall consummate
the wrong.   And, even now, when the scenes of anarchy and
violence which have scourged the old world are beginning
to be re-enacted among us, next to the immediate vigor of

our own arms, the energetic administration of justice is
our only protection.

But of yet wider extent and higher character is its
sway in the political relations of man. The strength of
every government is in its laws, whether they originate in
the will of one man, or are formed by the deliberations of
many. The efficacy of physical force, as an instrument of
governing, will depend on the depth of ignorance and
corruption to which men are degraded. The nearer a people
are sunk to the condition of brutes, the more appropriate
and successful will brute force be found, to subdue and
control them.   But in free governments, and among
civilized men, its place is supplied in a greater or less
degree by the power of public opinion, regularly expressed
through the medium of law. It is this which measures the
amount of personal freedom and rights which the individual
surrenders to the whole community, in return for its
protection; and determines and secures those which are
reserved for ultimate resort, under circumstances of
extreme peril.   It defines the relations of magistrates
and people, prescribing the limits which neither are
permitted to transcend. The sovereign and the subject,
the public leader and the private citizen, all, in every
situation and circumstance, alike yield obedience to the
supremacy of law.

This, too, is the only successful arbiter of the
destinies of nations. War may still be resorted to, as
unhappily it has been, to avenge real or imaginary
national wrongs; but it will still prove, as it ever has
proved, a most unsatisfactory and ineffectual appeal. The
spirit of man never bows submissively to its decisions;
his bosom still heaves with strong though hidden purpose
of future vengeance. Peace has no stable foundations but
those of compact and voluntary stipulation, entered into
with good faith for reciprocal benefit; and peace and
commerce are regulated and preserved only by the paramount
authority of the code denominated the Law of Nations.
Whence this code derives its high sanctions and exerts its
mighty sway over the while family of mankind, public
jurists may continue to inquire, and philosophers to
dispute; but the true solution is found only in the power
of Him who has ennobled this science by giving it the
impress of his own mind, and in imparting its rules to the
lawgiver of his chosen people.

The effect of law upon the happiness of a community
may be farther illustrated, by considering the personal
influence exerted by its votaries upon that in which they
live. I speak not now of the amount of good they actually
achieve; nor of any respectful consideration with which
individuals may happen to be regarded; but of the extent
of the influence, be it good or evil, which they all, in
various degrees, possess. For though, as was justly
observed by a distinguished jurist, "those who practise
the law, without a knowledge of its principles, are the
most mischievous, as well as the most degraded class of
the community;" yet, wherever the law affords protection,
it is to be expected that those who profess it should be
resorted to and employed, not merely to obtain reparation

of wrongs, but to devise the means to prevent them. And
who so able to advise such means, as they whose
employments lead to familiar acquaintance with the
operation of existing laws, and with the almost endlessly
varied shapes, which crime and cunning assume, in order to
elude them? All alike feel the operation of law; but
those more intimately concerned in its administration may
be presumed best to know the process by which effects,
whether beneficial or not, are produced, and are most able
to suggest the proper mode either of suppressing the
mischief or advancing the remedy. It is therefore equally
honorable both to the people and to the profession in our
country, that its members have been selected to discharge
so large a portion of this important trust. It was
eminently so in the period of our revolution, when the
edifice of civil liberty was reared, whose harmonious
proportions were adjusted by the sages of the law in the
senate-house, while its materials were secured by blood in
the field. In the dark and lowering night, which
succeeded that brilliant day, when the bonds of social
order were loosened, and society was rapidly returning to
its original elements; when the only remedy was the
infusion of new vigor into the social compact by the
adoption of a more efficient constitution of government;
the most distinguished disciples of the law were again
among the framers of that instrument; and to the united
efforts of three of its brightest luminaries, in
expounding the doctrines of the new constitution, and
unfolding its spirit and tendency, in the numbers of the
Federalist, we are chiefly indebted for its final
adoption. And in later days, when the integrity of that
charter has been invaded, its spirit violated, and its
language perverted, whether to gratify the mad ambition of
one partisan, or the cupidity of many; to whom have all
eyes been imploringly directed for its preservation, but
to the living and honored champions and expounders of
constitutional law?
      In the humbler scenes of private life the influence
of the profession is hardly to be measured or imagined.
Consider the variety of the municipal and social
relations, and the legal questions to which they give
birth; the numerous instances of unavoidable and
involuntary trespass upon the rights of others; the errors
into which even the most cautious are sometimes betrayed;
the perpetually recurring misunderstandings and
misconstructions, and the feuds, which arise in every busy
community; capable of being inflamed into wide-spreading
devastation, or of being composed, by timely and honest
interposition, into firm friendship and peace; -- consider
farther the easy and familiar intercourse which naturally
subsists between the members of our profession and their
fellow citizens, and the effect, either salutary or
mischievous, of legal opinions, formally pronounced or
casually thrown out, upon such materials as these; -- and
all which we have asserted will not seem too much to be
said of the law. To whom, in the first instance, do the
injured resort, for redress of their wrongs; the doubting
and perplexed, for the solution of their difficulties; the

oppressed, for relief; the dying, for the final
arrangements of their worldly wealth; the widow and the
orphan, for their violated rights; and all for the
preservation and security of whatever is valuable in life,
or its modes of enjoyment; but to the ministering officers
in the temple of justice?

Thus, as has been quaintly but beautifully written,
"of law there can no less be acknowledged than that her
seat is the bosom of God; her voice, the harmony of the
world; all things in heaven and earth do her homage; the
very least as feeling her care, and the greatest as not
exempted from her power.

It was a similar view of the worth of this science,
and of its importance to the preservation of our
liberties, which led to the provision made for its
cultivation in this place, by the noble liberality of Mr.
Dane, and the enlightened forecast of Royall and of Gore;
whose ample benefactions will continue to bless successive
generations, while the institutions endure which they
sought to perpetuate. They well knew that solitary study
was unfavorable to the acquisition of enlarged and
philosophical views of any science, much more of this;
that individual man is every way circumscribed, and the
limitations of his narrow and brief existence pursue him
in whatever he attempts; that numbers and succession can
alone enable him to attain that, which is great and
perpetual; -- and that in the associations of the
seminary, the union and impulse of kindred minds,
communicating to each other their separate acquisitions,
can accomplish what the maturity of isolated genius may
never be able to effect. It is here that professional
character is best formed, and its elements tempered and
wrought up for future action. And in a government of
laws, the formation of this character, by such a
discipline, is a subject of public interest. It can never
be a matter of indifference to an American State, what
manner of men are employed in its halls of justice, or
mingle with the people as expositors of the laws, or are
concerned in their enactment in legislative assemblies.
It may therefore not be deemed inappropriate to the
present occasion, if the remaining moments allotted me
should be employed in briefly sketching the character,
which it will be my humble endeavor to impress on those,
whose studies I am to direct.

The value, and even the necessity of deep and exact
learning, to successful practice in either of the
professions, is a point now so generally conceded as to
require no argument or proof. The decrier of human
learning at the present day finds neither audience nor
disciples. Even among those whose religious systems were
once founded on the utter worthlessness of learning,
popularly so called, which, of course, was regarded with
contempt, the High School and the Seminary of modern
times, with their splendid halls, their ample endowments,
and their learned professors, however disguised under the
humble title of schoolmasters, and tutors, all concur in
the most consenting and conclusive testimony to the
importance of liberal and thorough education. In the

department of Theology, the necessity of a learned
ministry for the defence of our common faith against the
common enemy has been urged with strength of argument and
fervor of eloquence, and attested by the splendid
offerings of living piety and dying zeal.   In Medicine
too, the same necessity is felt and admitted, in the
princely munificence with which Institutions for the
blind, the deaf, the insane and the diseased are endowed
in all directions around us; and in the care with which
its regular practice is guarded, and regular education
encouraged by positive statutes; expressing, with
remarkable distinctness, the strength and the direction of
public sentiment.   And should less be done for the Law, in
which our liberties have their being, -- for a profession
from which we select our judges, and so many of our
legislators and statesmen, -- and whose influence on the
whole body of civil magistracy is hardly to be conceived?
The age of mere fanaticism and cant, of bold empiricism
and noisy declamation, of passionate appeals to prejudice,
and forensic buffoonery, it is to be hoped, is passed
away.   Men are now to be addressed through their
understandings.   They are to be treated as rational
beings, and convinced by argument and reason.
     I would not confine the education of a lawyer to the
technical learning of his profession, nor to the code of
his particular state.   He can with no propriety be
considered as sufficiently instructed, whose learning is
limited to the remembrance of a few dry maxims, common
places and positive rules; and whose skill consists in the
adroit practice of the mere technicalities of the law.
Rules are of little value, without a knowledge of the
principles on which they are constructed; and the
principles of law are to be sought only at the fountains
of jurisprudence.   In this science, as in the comparative
anatomy of a sister profession, we best understand our own
system of laws by comparing it with those of other
nations.   Man is to be studied in every period of his
social existence, from the savage to the civilized state,
in order to perceive the great truth, that in every
condition of freedom, of intelligence, of commerce, and of
wealth, his habits, his virtues, his vices, the objects of
his desires, and hence the laws necessary for his
government, are essentially the same.   But to us, as
members of a family of sovereignties, it is peculiarly
necessary, that we should understand something of the laws
of the other states in the Union, under which we hold many
of our own rights, and with whose citizens our intercourse
is becoming daily more and more intimate and familiar.
From the primitive ordinances and laws of New England, the
refined and elaborated code of commercial and affluent New
York, the equitable-common-law of Pennsylvania, and the
staid and polished systems of the Carolinas and the
Ancient Dominion, the accomplished jurist of every state
will derive rich illustrations of the jurisprudence of his
own.   In that of Louisiana, he will recognise the living
Institutes of Justinian, transmitted through the codes of
France and Spain, and baptized, reverently so to speak,
with the spirit of American liberty.   In the statutes of

the far West he will discern, as in a daily journal, the latest form and impress of modern law; while the national jurisprudence exhibits in bolder relief the great features common to them all.

It will be apparent, from a slight survey of our institutions, that no lawyer will have mastered his profession by an acquaintance with the common law alone, since this is not the only source from which they have been derived. Its earlier sages themselves drew largely from the vast reservoir of the civil law; and in modern times the most enlightened and ablest judges are found to have been accomplished civilians. We ought, therefore, to be no strangers to this branch of professional learning.

But our studies should not be confined to codes. In the renowned examples of both living and departed jurists we see with what success the cultivation of liberal learning may be combined with the study of law, as a constituent part of professional education. The law should be commended to good taste by classic purity of style, as well as to enlightened reason by the wisdom of its decisions; it is always more respected when administered with courtesy, than when it is morosely inflicted.

In the walks of private life, the character of an upright lawyer shines with mild but genial lustre. He concerns himself with the beginnings of controversies, not to inflame but to extinguish them. He is not content with the doubtful morality of suffering clients, whose passions are aroused, to rush blindly into legal conflict. His conscience can find no balm in the reflection, that he has but obeyed the orders of an angry man. He feels that his first duties are to the community in which he lives, and whose peace he is bound to preserve. He is no stranger to the mischiefs, which follow in the train of litigation; the deadly feuds and animosities descending from the original combatants to successive generations; the perjuries and frauds so often committed to secure success; and the impoverishment so commonly resulting even to the winning party; and in view of these consequences, he advises to amicable negotiation and adjustment. He is a peacemaker; -- a composer of dissensions; -- a blessing to his neighborhood; -- his path is luminous as the path of the just. I look with pity on the man, who regards himself a mere machine of the law; -- whose conceptions of moral and social duty are all absorbed in the sense of supposed obligation to his client, and this of so low a nature as to render him a very tool and slave, to serve the worst passions of men; -- who yields himself a passive instrument of legal inflictions, to be moved at the pleasure of every hirer; -- and who, beholding the ruin and havoc made by a lawsuit, which "two scruples of honesty" in his counsel might have prevented, can calmly pocket his fee with the reflection, that he has done his duty to his client, alike regardless of duty to his neighbor and his God. That such men do exist, to disgrace our profession, is lamentably true; men --

"that can speak to every cause, and things mere
contraries, till they are hoarse again, yet all be
law."

-- We would redeem its character by marking a higher
standard of morals. While our aid should never be
withheld from the injured or the accused, let it be
remembered, that all our duties are not concentrated in
conducting an appeal to the law; -- that we are not only
lawyers, but citizens and men; -- that our clients are not
always the best judges of their own interests, -- and that
having confided these interests to our hands, it is for us
to advise to that course, which will best conduce to their
permanent benefit, not merely as solitary individuals, but
as men connected with society by enduring ties.

In the management of causes in Court, the whole duty
of a lawyer, not only to his client but to all others, is
expressed in the simple yet dignified and comprehensive
formula of his oath of office, as administered in the
national tribunals, -- to demean himself "uprightly, and
according to law." He is to deal faithfully with the
merits and facts of the cause confided to his care; yet
not pressing them beyond their intrinsic value, or the
boundaries of justice. He has not sold himself to obtain,
by right or wrong, a victory for his employer; but is
engaged to see, that the cause is clearly and truly
developed, and that the judgment pronounced upon it is
agreeable to the law of the land. He is to perpetrate no
falsehood; -- he is to practise no chicanery; -- he is to
take no advantage of the mistakes of his brethren; -- he
is to resort to no low cunning; to spread no net for the
unwary. He is to draw a broad line of distinction between
the facts of the case, which are the property of his
client, and the mode of bringing them into judgment, which
is exclusively his own. In the ardor of forensic conflict
he is still to be governed by the standard of morals in
private life, and to personate no man but himself. He is
to lend "his exertions to others, himself to none." He
has no personal abuse to bestow for the gratification of
another's spleen; no gibes upon virtue and religion;
neither is he to neglect the courtesies, which are due to
an opposing brother. If, in the collisions of the bar,
his anger is sometimes roused, it should be, like the
anger of Hooker, but "the momentary bead upon a phial of
pure water, instantly subsiding without sediment or soil."
He is not to forget, that while maintaining individual
rights, he is also addressing the public, and acting upon
minds with which he may never again come in contract; that
he is testifying for or against his profession; whose
character, for the time being, he sustains, and is giving
his suffrage, as a member of the community, either for
virtue or for vice.

But his responsibilities, as the citizens of a
republic, are of peculiar solemnity. Our institutions
were created, not for the pageantry of an elevated
executive, nor the brilliant display of the robes of
office; but for the security of personal liberty and
right, -- for the solid advantages afforded by law, the

means of resistance against lawless aggression and the redress of wrongs; -- for that which enables us to be individual and unitedly happy, in personal quiet, secure in the enjoyment of all which we may call our own. To us, therefore, seeking safety and happiness in a free government, there is nothing of such peerless value as the Judiciary; regulating as it does the movements of the whole machine. It is the only barrier against the desolating flood of wild misrule, and the encroachments of stern and relentless despotism. While the tribunals continue to be filled by men of extensive learning, of minds capacious and highly gifted, of unblenching courage and uncompromising integrity; however the storms of party may beat without the walls of the temple of justice all will be peace, security and confidence within. The equal and upright administration of justice in the courts of law will continue to impart stability to our institutions, operating as the safety-valve, through which occasional effervescences of popular excitement may quietly escape. It will disarm the cloud of faction of its terrors, and conduct them, harmless, to the ground. While men have within their own reach the means of removing the evils, private or political, which they suffer, whether it be through the judicial tribunals or the ballot-boxes, they will patiently endure them till the remedy is perfected by the slow but certain revolutions of time. While courts are open, and legal remedies exist, and public confidence in the integrity and ability of Judges is high and unimpaired, it is here, and here only, that the battle will be fought, in the undoubting confidence of success on the side of liberty and justice. The discharge of this responsible office is of difficulty and magnitude enough to demand the noblest faculties allotted to man. There is no royal road to judicial eminence; no process by which the labors of a judge can be performed without intellectual exertion. He holds the balance of rights as dear, perhaps, as life, to the parties; and the happiness or misery of unknown numbers hangs upon his decision. He cannot but deeply feel his accountabilities. The cases brought to his judgment are of endless variety in their circumstances; often nicely balanced in their merits; and not unfrequently invoking the aid of novel and sometimes of different principles. Justice and law may be on the side of his personal friends; yet not so clearly and obviously as to deliver him from the reproach of partiality, even when obeying the dictates of an honest conscience. Party may assail him; and tyranny may combine with faction to put him down. His life is a round of unceasing toil; delightful, it may be, to a mind enkindled with the love of science and virtue, and dilated with strong and just conception of the value of these labors to his country and his race; yet tasking to the utmost the vigor of his constitution, and rapidly consuming the energies, which bless and improve the circle, in which he moves. The whole man, -- his power of perception, his memory, his understanding, his judgment, -- even his patience and his self-control, are put in requisition by the duties of his station. While the ermine of justice is worn by men capable of these duties and worthy of the trust, public acquiescence in their decisions may justly be demanded.   Yet the wisest judgments will sometimes be questioned by the unthinking; and the losing party will still exert the precious privilege of complaining of the jury or the judge.   But whenever these seats of learning and of law shall be occupied by men unable, through their ignorance, to acquire the respect of an intelligent people, or unworthy, through corruption, to retain it; when the course of justice can be delayed by blind devotedness to party, or led astray by timidity, or obstructed by bribes, the redress of private wrongs will be sought through private vengeance; and public grievances will find their relief in open and bloody insurrection. American liberty can never be destroyed but by first destroying the independence of the judiciary, and bringing its authority into contempt.   While therefore all good citizens should give their united and generous support to this important branch of the government, and preserve the public confidence in its wisdom and uprightness, on no class of men does it devolve with greater emphasis than on members of the bar.   If we are supposed best to understand the difficulties, which the judge is obliged to encounter, and the process by which he arrives at the ultimate conclusion; to be more familiar than others with the habits of his mind, and the strength or weakness of his moral principles; the greater deference will be yielded to our opinions of his judgments; and the greater should be the caution with which we form and express them.   Every rash and undeserved censure of this sort does but impair the protecting power of that, which sooner or later we may find to be the only Palladium of liberty, the only remaining security of our dearest rights.

But it matters little to the peace of society, how wise or upright the judge or the jury may be if their means of ascertaining the truth are feeble and inefficient; since judgments and decisions will be respected only in proportion to their supposed agreement with the actual merits of the case, in fact, as well as in law.   The great instrument of eliciting truth is the hold obtained upon the conscience through the medium of an oath.   The force of this hold will depend on the sense of moral obligation and accountability in the person taking it; and to strengthen, rather than to impair this, seems peculiarly to be demanded of us, who have such frequent occasion to resort to its agency.   The utility of judicial tribunals is thus referred at last to the sanctions afforded by religion.   In this country, religion in all its forms is freely tolerated; but its existence in any form, is left to depend on the support of public opinion. And the founder of our nation has remarked, that "in proportion as the structure of a government gives force to public opinion, it should be enlightened."   Christianity founds its claim to our belief upon the weight of the evidence by which it is supported.   This evidence is not peculiar to the department of theology; its rules are precisely those by which the law scans the conduct and language of men on all other subjects, even in their daily

transactions.   This branch of the law is our particular
study.   It is our constant employment to explore the mazes
of falsehood, to detect its doublings, to pierce its
thickest veils; to follow and expose its sophistries; to
compare, with scrupulous exactness, the testimony of
different witnesses, to examine their motives and their
interests; to discover truth and separate it from error.
Our fellow men know this to be our province; and perhaps
this knowledge may have its influence to a greater extent
than we or even they imagine.   We are therefore required
by the strongest motives, -- by personal interest, by the
ties of kindred and friendship, by the claims of
patriotism and philanthropy, to examine, and that not
lightly, the evidences on which Christianity challenges
our belief, and the degree of credit to which they are
entitled.   The Christian religion is part of our common
law, with the very texture of which it is interwoven.   Its
authority is frequently admitted in our statute-books; and
its holy things are there expressly guarded from blasphemy
and desecration.   If it be found, as indeed it is, a
message of peace on earth and good will to men; exhibiting
the most perfect code of morals for our government, the
purest patterns of exalted virtue for our imitation, and
the brightest hopes, which can cheer the heart of man; let
it receive the just tribute of our admiring approval, our
reverential obedience, and ur cordial support.   I would
implore the American lawyer unhesitatingly to follow in
this, as in the other elements of the law, the great
masters and sages of his profession; and while with
swelling bosom he surveys the countless benefits rendered
to his country by this his favorite science, let him not
withhold from the Fountain and Source of all Law the free
service of undissembled homage.

– 10 –

Daniel Mayes

An Address to the Students of Law
in Transylvania University (1834)

In a discourse, delivered from this chair, at the opening of our exercises in the fall of the past year, I endeavored to prove that law, was not a science only, but that it was a _moral_ science; and to answer the reasoning urged by authors who contend for the contrary. I then selected certain subjects generally supposed to defy analysis and classification, and to be involved in much obscurity; if not in incomprehensibility, and made an effort, so to simplify them, by a complete analysis and classification of their several parts, as to establish the fact, and impress it on the mind of the student, that this science embraced nothing of which it is difficult to obtain a knowledge, by any man of tolerably good capacity, who engages in its study with zeal, and continues that study with untiring ardour, if in addition he avails himself of the indispensable aid of a methodical arrangement of his studies, under the guidance and constant supervision and examination, of a preceptor, competent to discharge the duties of a teacher of law, and who unites in himself inexhaustible patience, and untiring perseverance in the business of instruction. Without which patient application of his time to, and persevering industry in the discharge of his duties, be his acquirments never so eminent, no teacher in this or any other department of learning will confer upon those who become his pupils much benefit.

This I did for these reasons. There are to be found in our profession, as in every other, many, who either have not learned, or who having learned cease to remember, that there is a _science_ of jurisprudence as well as an _art_ of jurisprudence. Who standing in the same relation to law, that the cook does to chemistry, are actively engaged in practice during long lives, ignorant of the principles of the science upon which their art is founded -- giving themselves no more trouble to ascertain the relations, connexions and dependencies, that exist between the numerous rules of law memorised by them, or to inquire into the reasons why those rules are adopted, by which they govern themselves in the practice of their legal art,

than the cook does to investigate the laws, governing the
phenomena, hourly occurring under his observation, whilst
practising his culinary art.   Indeed no more suspecting
the existence of such relations, connexions and
dependencies, and that the rationale of each may be
clearly explained, and readily comprehended, than the cook
suspects the existence of certain chemical laws, uniform
in their action, and universal in their application, which
are upon investigation not only discoverable, but easy of
comprehension, and which give rise to all the wonderful
changes in the form and mode of existence of the
substances which pass through his hands.   The cook has
always seen certain articles compounded according to a
certain receipt placed in a bag, and that bag placed in a
pot, and that pot filled with water, and suspended over a
fire, and has observed, that after it has remained
suspended over the fire a certain length of time, the pot
boiled; and having continued to boil a certain other
length of time, the bag being taken out and opened,
contained a fine pudding.   And having from repeated
experiments, or from information derived from others
become fully satisfied, that the same result is uniformly
produced, proceeds with his manipulations through his
whole life.   Proving a very successful practioner in the
business of pudding making, if he were only informed that
he was engaged in the practice of chemistry, would without
hesitation, take under his direction students, and would
heartily laugh, at any man who should tell him that from
his manipulations Professor Yandell could demonstrate many
important truths in chemical philosophy, or from them
teach his class any thing beyond the mere art of making a
pudding.   He would undertake to prove, that an experienced
cook was the best possible teacher of chemistry, and that
there is no laboratory equal to a well furnished kitchen.
"What care I' he would say, "for professor Yandell's
solids, and liquids, and gases -- his acids and alkalies
-- his attractions of cohesion, and aggregation and
gravitation, with all his long list of affinities and ten
thousand other fooleries which it is almost impossible to
comprehend.   Bring the professor and myself to this simple
and fair test; give each of us the ingredients, I'll go to
the kitchen and let him go to his laboratory, and if I do
not bring to the table a better or at least as good a
pudding as he does, send your sons to Transylvania to
study Chemistry."
      Just so it sometimes is in our profession.   The
lawyer has always seen a particular species of action
brought to obtain remedy for a specific wrong.   The
declaration and subsequent pleadings, drafted according to
an established formula, and the whole proceeding
terminating in a judgment for the plaintiff or defendant,
and remembering the practice, (I will not say having a
knowledge of it,) practices with success in that precise
state of case, nor imagines that the formula he follows,
is framed upon principles of general application, and
susceptible of practical use, in all the modifications of
facts and circumstances, which can arise in the
diversified transactions of men.   He dreams not that there

is any thing of science to be taught from what he has
done, and laughs at the idea, that a sensible reason ought
to be sought for in every thing connected with the
profession.   Understanding little or nothing of the
rationale of his professional operations, and indeed
supposing that this or that is so, for no other reason but
that Coke or Mansfield said it was so, his investigations
and researches terminate in "ita lex scripta est." -- and
if in even that, he is not mistaken he thinks himself
wondrous learned.   His students are engaged in reading,
without comprehending, and impressing on the memory,
without being instructed by adjudged cases, and forms of
proceeding.   Wholly unable to assign a reason for any
thing they do, but acting as the preceptor acted before
them because he so acted, they acquire the art, whilst
wholly ignorant of the science of jurisprudence.   IN the
language of one who has contributed more to the
advancement of legal science, in Great Britain and North
America, than any other man who has lived, we may truly
say, "Making due allowance for a few shining exceptions,
experience may teach us to foretell, that a lawyer thus
educated to the bar in subserviency to attorneys and
solicitors, will find he has begun at the wrong end.   If
practice be the whole he is taught, practice must also be
the whole he will ever know; if he be uninstructed in the
elements and first principles upon which the rule of
practice is founded, the least variation from established
precedents, will totally distract and bewilder him, he
must never aspire to form, and seldom expect to comprehend
any arguments drawn a priori from the spirit of the law,
and the natural foundations of justice."   It is because of
the defectiveness of the legal education of gentlemen of
the bar, who study and pursue the profession as a mere
art, that one of the most eminent writers of the last
century says, "a lawyer now is nothing more, (I speak of
ninety-nine in a hundred at least,) to use some of Tully's
words, "nisi leguleius quidem cautus, et acutus praeco
actionum cantor formularum, auceps syllabarum."   If those
of the present century would escape the reproach, let them
avoid the error which gave rise to it; and which since,
and in a great degree in consequence of the establishment
of the Vinerian professorship of law, has ceased to be
just when applied to the English bar.
     Having long anxiously watched, the development, and
growth, of legal learning in the student's mind, and
ascertained, by observation and experience, that the
greatest obstacle in the way of his successful and easy
progress, is the too prevalent, though false belief, that
he is engaged in the pursuit of a mere practical art, by
which to make a subsistence, I endeavored to maintain the
contrary, by selecting certain subjects, and so treating
them in a brief and purely elementary manner, as to show
all their supposed absurdity, mystery, intricacy,
obscurity or incomprehensibility (for each of these terms
has been freely applied) existed only in the imagination
of those, who have looked upon the learning of the law,
with the same uninquisitive eye, that the cook does, upon
the boiling of his pot.   That in truth it had elementary

principles, founded in reason and the fixed nature of
things, and that these principles were of easy
comprehension, by any ordinarily good mind, if explained
with clearness, and simplicity. That what was true of
these was equally true of the other branches of the
professional learning of the lawyer, and that, that
student laboured under a dangerous mistake, who had
entered or was about to enter, on the study of his
profession, impressed with the opinion, that its learning
is composed of arbitrary rules, not to be examined,
investigated and understood; but only to be memorised,
believed as found in books or pronounced by courts; and
followed, not because sanctioned by reason, but because
they have been followed from time immemorial. I know from
having uniformly found the fact so to be that a student
laboring under such false opinion, has no relish for,
derives no pleasure from, and of consequence engages with
no ardour in, the study of his profession, and nine times
out of ten, he lazily drags himself through it, with pain
and labour, or retires from it in disgust or despair. On
the contrary, the student of no better talents, whose mind
is awakened to and fully sensible of the true nature of
his profession, advances with rapidity, because his
reasoning powers, as well as his memory, are aroused to
action. He derives pleasure from his studies, for he
perceives the reasons upon which he proceeds. Deriving
pleasure from, he prosecutes his labours with zeal and
perseverance; and without zeal and perseverance, it is
worse than useless to persist in the study, as it is
impossible without them to rise to respectability in the
profession. To convince the student, indeed to
demonstrate clearly, that law might be so studied, and so
comprehended, and thus to remove despondence, excite hope,
and awaken zeal, was the object, and the only object,
which I had in view, in the introductory address before
spoken of, and I am led to hope, that the effort was not
wholly unsuccessful.

Permit me now for a short time, to call your
attention to the nature of the science, the subjects to
which it relates, the manner in which I attempt to teach
it, my reasons for adopting the course I pursue, and to
point out why it is (according to my apprehension) that
the student who prosecutes his studies in a well conducted
law school, has decidedly an advantage over him, who
prosecutes the study in the ordinary manner, in the
office, and under the direction, of a practising attorney
and counsellor, who does not make the business of
instruction a part of his regular employment, and the most
successful mode of imparting knowledge the subject of his
daily meditation.

From the limits, within which this discourse, must
necessarily be confined, nothing more will be attempted
than a very general glance at these topics.

The subject, of all law, is man, its object, the
promotion of his happiness. Man being its subject, and
his happiness its object, its rules must necessarily be
framed, in direct reference to his nature; and to this
end, he is to be contemplated in every aspect in which he

is found to exist, and in all the diversified relations which he bears to the persons and things, by which he is surrounded. The law therefore contemplates and treats of him, first as a single individual, unconnected with the rest of his species. But man being according to the constitution of his nature, a social being, is found to exist not in a solitary state but in a state of society, entering into many relations with his species, which relations are essential to his well-being. Upon examination these relations are found to arrange themselves into two classes; Private social relations; such as master and servant, husband and wife, parent and child &c. and political, social relations, such as magistrates and people, or officers of government and private citizens. Again; As the inhabitants of the globe are not formed into one community, but exist, and from the nature of human government must ever exist in many distinct and independent nations, states or communities; the laws contemplate those individual and independent nations or states, and considers and treats of their rights and duties as such. But these independent states do not always occupy the same relations to each other; sometimes they are in a state of peace, at others, war. The law then must contemplate them under each of these conditions, and define the rights of war and those that exist in time of peace. And again. In time of war, neighboring states may be at peace with the billigerent nations. Hence it is necessary to define and fix clear limits to the rights and duties of neutral nations. Further. Either in time of war or of peace, a citizen of one state, or nation, may be found within the territorial limits of another to which he owes no permanent allegiance, and here arises the necessity of ascertaining the rights and duties of alien friends and alien enemies. I might extend this list, of the different circumstances in which man exists, and in which the laws contemplate him, to a length almost indefinite; time however forbids, nor would it be profitable, on this occasion to carry it further.

As the law contemplates, and is predicated of man, in each of these and many other situations, he who would enter into the true spirit of his profession, and understand the reasons upon which its rules of action proceed, must lay the foundation upon which he intends to erect his superstructure, (where and where only a sure foundation can be laid) in an intimate knowledge of man, in these and in all other states and conditions in which he may be found. To use the language of Lord Bolingbroke; "he must pry into the secret recesses of the human heart, and become well acquainted with the whole moral world, that he may discover the abstract reason of all laws; and he must trace the laws of particular states, especially of his own, from the first rough sketches, to the more perfect draughts; from the first causes or occasions that produced them, through all the effects, good and bad that they produced." He must in the first place view man as a single individual, unconnected with persons or things, as a child and as the mature man, and study his physical,

moral and intellectual constitution. Thus contemplated he
will be found subject to many wants and susceptible of
much suffering, when the laws to which he is subjected by
his creator are violated, either as it respects his
physical, moral or intellectual nature; and capable of
much physical, moral and intellectual enjoyment, when his
condition and conduct is in harmony with those laws. It
will be found that he is not only capable of suffering, or
enjoyment as he conforms or fails to conform to those
laws, but that in no instance does he transgress them,
without encountering evil; in none does he conform to them
without experiencing good. To develope, strengthen and
rightly discipline, so as to produce the greatest
attainable perfection of these physical, intellectual and
moral powers of man; to secure to him the greatest
practical amount of happiness and guard and protect him as
far as can be, against physical, moral and intellectual
ill or suffering, is the great leading object of all laws
in a wisely regulated state. Therefore the nature of man
being understood, and the student bearing in mind that the
"design and object of laws" to use the language of
Demosthenes "is to ascertain what is just, honourable and
expedient" and so by requiring men to do such things as
justice, honor and expediency dictate, and to refrain from
such acts as they forbid, human happiness; he will readily
comprehend the reason of all those rules and precepts,
which have reference to man, as a single and unconnected
being. By a single and unconnected being I here mean, a
being not contemplated in the domestic relations, or in
the relation of magistrates and people. But man enters
into private social relations. Occupying then a different
and additional station, we must consider of the essential
character, the true and lagitimate end and object of the
relation contracted. In doing so, we must not forget,
that he is the same compound being that he was when he
stood alone and unconnected; that he carries with him,
into his newly contracted state, all the sources of
happiness and of misery, to which he was subject before,
and that the new sources of happiness, or the reverse,
which are now opened to him, by the alliance he has
formed, do not supersede, but are additional to them.
Wherefore in this newly formed relation, he is still
required to conform to the laws of his nature, or
constitution. He remains the rightful possessor of all
the rights, and subject to all the duties of his former
condition, except in so far as they are necessarily
modified, changed or superseded by reason of some
incompatability with those rights and duties which spring
from the new relation assumed. And as by the creation of
any social bond, the consequences of the acts of him who
enters into it, are not spent upon himself alone, but
extend to those with whom he stands connected, the law
therefore takes cognizance of his conduct, in this his
connected state, and regulates it with a view to the
happiness of each party. He then who understand the
nature, of the private social relations, sufficiently to
perceive what acts of the parties, whether master and
servant, husband and wife, parent and child &c. tend to

the injury, and what to the welfare of those who stand in them, is in possession of the true key, which unlocks all the reason of laws regulating the conduct of persons in such relations.

Men also exist in a state of political society, their natures unchanged, their private social relations unaltered by this additional bond of union. They carry with them into the political community, of which they become members, all the duties that before rested on them as individuals, or as parties to a private social contract, and retain all the rights which belonged to them, when considered in either of the aspects before spoken of, except such as it is necessary to renounce, for the good of the community of which they form a part. The rights they acquire, and the obligations they contract, by this new modification of the circumstances under which they exist, are not in exclusion of their former rights and duties, but are only or mostly cumulative. In this relation additional means are acquired by the parties, of promoting the happiness, or producing the misery of each other. Consequently the lawyer must contemplate men, in the relation of magistrates and people, or officers of government and private citizens; consider of the motives that induce the contracting such relations; ascertain the limits of the rights and duties on the one side and the other; still remembering that the only legitimate object of the parties to the political social compact, like that of the parties to the preceding is the welfare of the individual members of the state or community. That it is the duty of those who govern, so to rule in all things, as to secure as far as practicable, the true well-being of the governed; and the duty of the governed, to submit and yield obedience, to all legitimate regulations of the governing power; upon which simple foundation rests all laws respecting magistrates and people. I might proceed to speak in the same way of laws established in reference to man in the relation he hears to things in contra-distinction to persons; and likewise of those that regard independent states or nations, but might fatigue and exhaust your patience, by dwelling longer on a subject, which admits of little variety in the view of it which I have been taking.

From what has been said, it will be perceived, that whether we consider those laws, that relate to man, in his single unconnected state, or that have reference to him in his private social relations, or that regulate his conduct as a member of a political community, we must contemplate the whole of them, as framed with strict regard to, and an understanding of the nature of his constitution, and with an eye to his happiness or welfare.

What those laws are, which thus have reference to the physical, moral, and intellectual constitution of man, it is not now my province to enquire.

The relations of man to persons and things, and the modification of circumstances by which he may be surrounded, admit of endless combinations, giving rise to the application, in a modified form, of elementary principles; and these elementary principles when treated

of separately and in the various combinations of which
they are susceptible, require volumes to embody, and years
of assiduous study to acquire a knowledge of them.   For
although I have ever contended for the truth, as certainly
the truth is, that law is a science simple in its
elements, and that these when fully understood are easy of
combination, and application to any given state of facts,
yet the stores of its learning, are so inexhaustible, that
although we may readily possess ourselves, of any one of
its parts, if we proceed methodically, much time and
laborious study is indispensible to him, who would possess
himself of all its treasures.   The acquisition of
extensive legal knowledge, may in one respect be compared
to the acquisition of wealth, in which, any man may with
moderate assiduity possess himself of a few hundred
dollars; but he who would gain a princely fortune, must
labour diligently, and labour long.   Not that any one
dollar is more difficult to acquire than any other one;
but because it requires many dollars to make up the sum
total, and they must be acquired one at a time.   And as
each dollar gained, may if judiciously applied, be
converted into an instrument with which to acquire yet
other and larger sums, so each legal principle thoroughly
understood, may be used, to much advantage, in the
acquisition of knowledge of yet other principles; and as
the capital of the student increases (if he perseveres in
study) he may still use the accumulated capital to
increase his revenue of professional knowledge, thus by
application, each day drawing in a compound interest, on
the stock of science which before he had amassed.   What
Doctor Beattie says of knowledge in general, may be said
of that of law in particular; "that to the possible extent
of human knowledge we can set no bounds, and what is very
remarkable, the more real knowledge we acquire, the
greater is our desire of knowledge, and the greater our
capacity of acquiring it."
    The parallel just drawn between the acquisition of
knowledge, and the accumulation of wealth, cannot be
carried through; for money possessed if not profitably
used, may nevertheless be locked up in a strong box and
preserved from loss.   Not so of the lawyer's learning.   In
this respect the study of law, may aptly enough be likened
to rowing a boat against the current of a rapid stream.
When we first tug at the oars, scarcely can we perceive
the vessel moving; continuing to row with vigor, it begins
slowly but perceptibly to glide along, and persevering in
our efforts, the momentum given by preceeding exertions
added to the impulse given by each succeeding stroke,
quickens its progress, and more swiftly and yet more
swiftly rides the bark upon its course, not seeming to
feel the resistance, made by the opposing current.   No
sooner however do we rest on our oars, than the headway is
checked, soon is the ascending momentum of the vessel
overpowered by the descending stream, and speedily are we
swept down the channel, up which we rose with so much toil
and persevering labour, now by the inaction of a short
time rendered fruitless and unprofitable.   The student of

law, like the boatman, must to rise pull with vigour, and
without ceasing.
    It will be perceived by the young student, that there
is a wide field of investigation before him, and of course
he will desire to be informed how it is that I expect to
aid him in exploring it. This I will explain in a few
words. On the various branches of the science including
common law, statute law, constitutional law, and equity,
the best elementary treatises are selected as text books,
and placed in the hands of the students, they being
divided into classes, arranged with reference to the
proficiency made by them in the study of law. Each day a
lesson is assigned to be recited to the professor on the
next day. At the hour of recitation the class assembles.
-- The professor with the book in his hand, examines
sentence by sentence, upon the preceding day's reading,
endeavoring so to frame the questions, as to cause the
student to answer from a correct understanding of the
treatise, and not from memory of the author's words. In
other words, the effort is to bring into action the
reasoning and reflecting powers of the mind, as well as
the faculty of memory; and indeed to give them the lead as
far as practicable in all our exercises. During the
recitations the students are required to be exact and
accurate in all their definitions, neither including in
them, ideas not applicable to the thing treated of, nor
excluding any thing necessary to be understood, or which
may be predicated of it; that is, the definition is
required, exactly to comprehend the thing defined, and to
comprehend nothing else. Accurate analysis is constantly
attended to and as far as practicable the student is led
into a strictly analytical method of investigation; which
in the study of law is indispensable to success. As the
recitations of the class proceed, the professor
incorporates on the text, by a king of colloquial
lecturing, in the most familiar and simple, mode of
expression, of which he is capable, all such ideas as are
necessary to be connected with, in order to a distinct
understanding, of the subject under examination, and
informs the students of all such changes in the laws as
have resulted from the provisions of treaties, acts of
congress, the constitutions of the United States and of
the several states, modern statutes, and adjudged cases;
explaining as he may be able, the circumstances which gave
rise to and the reasons which induced each change if a
reason is known. -- Where a principle is laid down too
broadly, he endeavours to reduce it to its proper
dimensions, where it is too contracted, it is extended to
what is conceived to be its due limits. If the meaning of
the author is obscure, an attempt is made to supply his
deficiency in perspicuity and remove the obscurity; if
incorrect to point out the inaccuracy &c. such
difficulties as present themselves to the mind of the
student, he is encouraged, as far as possible to lay
before the professor, that he may be placed in a situation
to overcome them by his own reflection and reasoning if he
can do so, or may receive such instruction, as the nature
of the obstacle in his way requires; and thus we proceed

by way of question and answer with all necessary remarks
thrown in, when deemed most appropriate, until the subject
is as fully explored, as the nature of things and the
situation of the parties, will admit of.   It only being
required of the students, that whilst they are solicited,
freely to present all their difficulties, and freely state
all their doubts upon the text, or the professor's
commentary, explanation, &c. that they confine themselves
to such questions as are pertinent to the subject under
consideration, and abstain from wandering into foreign
subjects, until they shall in their due order be reached.
In addition to those exercises which are attended to
daily, a moot court is opened on each Saturday.   Here the
students sufficiently advanced to engage in its exercises,
apply their theory to practice.   They are exercised in all
the forms of professional duty, such as drafting pleas,
declarations, bills, answers, &c.; and in debating such
legal questions, as arise in the course of their
exercises; and they are instructed in the practice in
courts of law and equity as fully as the nature of a moot
court will admit of.   This court is not modelled, nor are
proceedings conducted in it, upon the practice in Kentucky
or any other state in the Union.   It is modelled as far as
practicable upon the practice in Westminster Hall.   -- The
reasons for this are these.   The objects of the law
department of Transylvania University are not local --
confined to the state -- they are far more broad and
extended.   It is not proposed to prepare young men
peculiarly for the practice in Kentucky, Tennessee or
Ohio; but to supply them with a fund of elementary
knowledge equally applicable to the practice in every
state in which the common law has been adopted.   As the
practice at Westminster, is the basis upon which rests
that of every state in the Union, with the exception of
Louisiana; it follows that the practice in all those
states are kindred branches, springing from the same root.
This root must be studied; if not the practice which
springs from it will never be understood.   He who
commences his practice upon a mere acquaintance with the
local usages and routine of business in the courts of one
of the states, without tracing it back to, and discovering
its foundation in the practice at Westminster, has
commenced his course as an artist, not as a man of
science, and he must retrace his steps, commence his
studies anew, go back to the practice at Westminster, and
trace it in its origin, rise and progress, explore the
reasons and circumstances which called it into use, the
changes through which it has passed, enquire into and
ascertain the reason of such changes; or if I may be
allowed the expression, he must study its history and
chronology, before he can understand its rules, or
comprehend what he himself does -- before he can at all
understand his own practice.   The student however who has
a sensible understanding of the practice at Westminster,
no odds in what state his lot may be cast, will readily
acquire a thorough knowledge of the practice of the
courts, into which he may enter, because he is already
master of that practice out of which it sprung, and of

which it is merely a modification, and even that in
unimportant particulars. Let me illustrate my meaning by
supposing the language spoken in each state was in some
degree different, but that each word in each dialect
sprang from the same tongue, and a young man ignorant of
them all, wished to study one or more of those dialects;
how would the judicious instructor proceed? Would he
carry his pupil into a community in which one of the
dialects was spoken, and devote him to the study of that?
or, would he not rather say to him, "commence with the
study of the parent language, acquire an accurate
knowledge of that, and having done so you will be enabled
to acquire with ease the dialect of every state in the
Union." How much more valuable would be the attainments
in language of him who had thus mastered the radical
tongue, than of him who by mere practice could speak with
fluency one of the dialects, but who had not studied that
language of which his dialect was but a corruption. These
are my reasons for conforming in my moot court to the
Westminster practice. My course may be erroneous; it is
however sanctioned by my judgment and will be continued
until reasons not yet present to my mind shall induce a
change. It is not pretended that the students here do
become sufficiently well acquainted with the Westminster
practice. They do not continue long enough in the
institution to enable them to do so. The advantage is not
in the quantity, but in the kind of knowledge acquired.
As far as they do go, they proceed on the right rout, and
will have no occasion to turn back. They do not continue
to complete the edifice but lay a good foundation.
     Having assigned the reasons which influence me in the
conduct of the moot court, I will now present briefly,
those by which I am induced in the other exercises of the
school, to pursue the course before spoken of. And here
permit me to remark, that nothing is more common in any
department of instruction, than to pursue the course
pursued by our forefathers, long after the reasons which
induced them to adopt it, and which rendered its adoption
under the then existing circumstances proper, have ceased.
When the practice of instructing by written lectures
originated it was the most judicious course that could
have been adopted. Indeed it was the only course that
could have been resorted to with any well founded hope of
success. Then the lawyer's library scarcely contained a
treatise which deserved to be considered as elementary.
All the learning of the law was in confusion, scattered
without method through the books of reports and the
writings of some few learned lawyers, who had little or no
arrangement in their respective works, or it was buried in
the records of the courts. Even the famous work of Lord
Coke, commonly known as "Coke upon Littleton," which is
one of the best of those works now within our reach,
presents it is true a great mass of learning, but so
totally destitute of method that no student can understand
it, although it is yet frequently placed in the hands of
the mere tyro, in law. Mr. Butler, one of the most
learned lawyers of the age, and one of the ablest editors
of the work, advises in his Reminiscences, that no student

should read Coke, who cannot devote to that single work, three years of laborious study. The elements of law being in a state of chaos, it was to be methodised, arranged and classified. To place a raw and inexperienced youth, who had just finished his collegiate, in the midst of this confused mass, and direct him to read and study, was to embark him on a boundless ocean, without compass or chart, in which to escape shipwreck was next to impossible. The professor, who by years of intense labour, had acquired extensive knowledge of his profession, was under the necessity of bringing order out of confusion, and to do so, wrote and read to his class lectures. He had no alternative, for elementary treatises suited to his object were not in being.

Now, there is no branch of the science, upon which we have not elementary treatises, prepared with all possible care, by lawyers of the first order of talents and learning; treatises at least equal to any which we can reasonably expect to find prepared by a professor in a law school, and which have this decided advantage over lectures read or spoken from notes; the student may take the treatise to his room, read, pause, reflect upon, study it, criticize the reasoning of the author, and repeat this from time to time, until he fully understands the work. It seems to me as absurd at this day to instruct in law by oral lecturing alone, as it would be so to instruct in arithmetic, or mathematics. To make a judicious selection of text books, direct the order in which they shall be studied, point the attention of the student to those parts which should be thoroughly studied and perfectly understood, and to those that may be more slightly read or wholy passed over, carefully to examine him day after day, and supply deficiencies by written or extemporaneous lecturing, is for these brief reasons the course here pursued. The experiment has been fairly made, and has by actual results been proved to be far more advantageous than to read lectures or make speeches to the student from notes, referring him to authorities which if he chooses to do so, and can get hold of them, he may read or omit to read at pleasure, and which if read may be understood or not understood by him. To the professor however it is at the same time much more laborious, and of lower pretentions. More laborious, because he must subdivide his class and attend separately to each subdivision, having as many of these as the varying state of the learning of the students may render necessary, here, generally amounting to four or five, of lower pretentions, because he who reads his own lectures impliedly says, "the library of the lawyer contains nothing equal to this my production," whilst he who places in their hands text books to study, tacitly acknowledges his inability to surpass at least in any considerable degree those who have gone before him. Although there are some very creditable and highly valuable exceptions, I must declare that most of the lectures lately published, are not worth the paper consumed in the writing. They are mostly new hashes, made up of scraps of old dishes, and by using them instead of the materials from which they are prepared, we accept one bad article, to make which, many good ones have been spoiled. It is by no means unusual, to find introduced in the same connexion, things that have no more affinity, than oils and acids. It is a foolish and pernicious pride of authorship, that produces this. No teacher of any branch of knowledge should for a moment forget, that it is no part of his business to display and hold himself up to the admiration of his pupils, that he is not called into employment for any such purpose, but that his exclusive charge is, to develope and educate the minds, or the minds and bodies of those committed to his charge. Of the treasures of literature and science, he should be studious to select and lay before them (certainly in the most alluring manner) such and such only as are suited to their situation, and not endeavor either to dazzle them by his brilliancy or confound and bewilder them by his profundity. The mind of the young student, like the stomach of the infant, should be supplied with aliment, suited to its immature powers of digestion. As the one and the other increases in power, more substantial fare should be presented, and if in this respect the teacher errs, and presents to his student's mind subjects by him either indigestible or too highly seasoned, instead of a healthy, vigorous growth of knowledge, he may well apprehend that an intellectual dispepsia, will be produced by his indiscretion. Injudicious as this course obviously is, it is by no means unusual, to witness instances in which the student, whilst uninitiated in the simplest elements of law, is suddenly plunged into its most dark and hidden labyrinths, and the most profit he finds in the discourse to which he listens is, that he rises from his seat, greatly delighted with the conviction, that it is his good fortune to have a preceptor so very learned that he cannot understand him.

The advantages of studying law, in schools dedicated to that science are almost too obvious to require notice. Yet obvious as they are, such is the force of custom that nine tenths of the youth destined for the bar, never enter a law school. They get admission into the office of some attorney, generally choosing one of eminence, and call themselves his students, not that he acts as their instructor, but because the book they read, is taken off a shelf in his library, and the room in which that book is read is called the office of Mr. A. or Mr. B. Sometimes he tells them what book to read, and when he is told that this is done, the direction is given to read it again or take up another. The difference between having read, and understanding a work, is not much, sometimes not at all attended to. Whether the student has or has not acquired knowledge by his reading, the supposed preceptor is not apt to enquire. If a question is asked it is generally addressed merely to the memory, not to the understanding; and most usually there is not even an attempt at examination, or if attempted, it is hurried over in the most superficial manner. The selection of books is often injudicious, and each book placed in the student's hands is to be read in all its parts, in the same manner. Whether its value be great or small, or whether all its

parts are, or are not connected with our system of laws, the student is uninformed, and consequently reads without the necessary discrimination, between books, or the different parts of the same book. There are but few books of which we may not with truth say, that certain parts of them are not necessary, or useful to read at all, and other parts that deserve only comparatively a slight examination when contrasted with the perfect and thorough understanding that should be acquired of other portions. In the language of Lord Bacon, the prince of philosophers and light of the bar "some books are to be read only in parts, others to be read but not curiously; and some few to be read wholy, with dilligence and attention." How few of the many who receive students into their offices, heed this advice of the distinguished individual just mentioned.   Another objection to studying law in the office of an attorney is this.   Instruction being no part of his regular employment, the best method of imparting knowledge to a student is no part of his study. Experience as a teacher he has none, for he has never attempted to teach.   He has only permitted students to read his books, and occasionally given a hasty answer to a casual question of his pupil, all the while considering him as an incumbrance in his office, rather than in any other light. The student under these circumstances, reads or plays as to him is most agreeable; no one knows his progress; it is unknown even to himself.   Every step he takes is taken in the dark.   No light is held up to illumine his path-way, no hand stretched fourth to support, no voice raised to animate and cheer him.   All the advantages he has, is the use of his preceptor's books, and the empty name of being the student of Mr. A. or Mr. B.   As if Blackstone's commentaries, owned by, and read in the office of Mr. A. or Mr. B. who stand at the head of the bar, would impart more knowledge than Blackstone's commentaries owned by, and read in the office of Mr. Y. or Mr. Z. who stand at the foot.
Not one lawyer out of ten who receive students into their offices, pays any attention to the course of proficiency of their studies.   If they be lawyers of high attainments, the unceasing pressure, of professional duties, demands their continued attention, and they have not the time; if their professional learning is limited, they have not the ability.   Besides which, practice is necessary to proficiency in any employment.*   The same experience and qualifications that cause a man to shine at the bar, do not qualify him for the bench, nor are the qualifications for the bench sufficient in quantity, or the same in kind, to fit him for a professorship of law. Each is to some extent a distinct employment, requiring, in some degree a distinct course of study and mental discipline, and distinct natural aptitudes.   I will not say that there is no man so happily endowed as to be well qualified for either station, but such union of qualities and acquirements, is so very rare, that it is unreasonable to expect to find them united in any particular individual.   It is unreasonable to conclude, that because an individual acquits himself well in the one, he will be

equally fortunate in the other. The superior lawyer may
often be the inferior preceptor. I doubt very much
whether if Doctor Johnson were now living, in full
possession of his whole intellectual vigor, and mighty
attainments, it would not be a very bad appointment were
our trustees to elect him principle of the preparatory
school of this University. It is by no means true that he
who is most learned is generally best qualified for the
business of instruction. All other things being equal he
would be so. He is best suited to the business of
instruction in a given subject, who has a thorough
understanding of the subject so far as it is proposed to
teach it, whose ambition it is to teach successfully, and
who has no views or ambition beyond this; who is gifted
with that peculiar tact which enables the instructor at
once to ascertain the character of mind, and the state of
improvement, of him who is to be instructed; who can
speedily know exactly the wants of the students and most
simply and immediately supply those demands upon him which
grew out of such wants: who can and will let himself down
to the exact level of the beginner's ignorance, and
patiently and perseveringly enlighten that ignorance, and
raise up the pupil step by step, in regular method, to the
desired point of knowledge. -- Sir Isaac Newton would have
found it difficult, possibly impracticable, to let himself
down to the proper level for a teacher of common
arithmetic. Whilst the scholar was perplexing himself
with simple division, and requiring his assistance, his
towering mind would sicken at the humble employment, and
soaring aloft into the immensity of space, fly from
divisors, dividends and quotients, to the stray heavens,
there to find scope for the exercise of its mighty and
cultivated powers.

My professional brethren therefore, will not believe
it proceeds from the absence of a due sense and
appreciation of their superior learning and talents, that
I come to the conclusion, that as a general rule, they are
not the best instructors. Whilst candour requires that I
declare my opinion, that there are many who undertake the
charge of the legal education of youth, who are worse that
"blind leaders of the blind," justice demands that I
admit, that there are those in respectable numbers, who
would be well qualified to instruct him, who would be
better qualified to teach the beginner, than they
themselves would be. Just as Newton would have been well
qualified to teach those, who would be far his superiors
as teachers of common arithmetic. To repeat what I have
before in substance said, he is best qualified to instruct
youth, who can with ease let himself down to the level of
their knowledge, ascertain precisely their wants, and in a
manner the most easy and familiar impress upon their minds
the knowledge desired -- and he is generally best able to
----
*No man however pre-eminent, his acquirements in any
department of learning, will be a successful teacher,
until he has trained himself to the business of teaching
as a distinct employment.

do this, whose daily habit it is patiently and earnestly to make the effort, observing carefully the success or failure of his exertions and profitting by his experience.

We are informed that in continental Europe, no gentleman considers his education complete, until he has attended several courses of instruction, in the laws and constitutions of his country, under the professors of law in their institutions of learning. With us the constitutions and laws of our country form no part of the regular system of education, and indeed save in one practical profession, a knowledge of them is not at all cultivated. Hundreds of our pretended statesmen, enter the halls of legislation without having in their whole lives devoted one single hour to the study of the form, structure, constitution, and laws that govern that body politic for whose diseases they are about to prescribe. They are, as it is taken, statesmen and legislators by inspiration, a kind of political _faith_ or _steam_ doctors to the body politic. The thinking, and informed, can but perceive the mischief that must in time grow out of this defect in the education of those who are to be our lawmakers, if the evil is not remedied.

Who can look upon the present state of the healing art, and believe for one moment that it could have arisen to the rank it now deservedly occupies, was medicine, like law, taught exclusively (almost), in the offices of private practitioners, and the halls of science abandoned by the sons of Aesculapius. To the honour of that learned body, and to the benefit of the human race, no young man who aspires to eminence in that profession, fails to avail himself of Academic instruction. With one unanimous rush they spring forward to drink in the streams of professional learning, poured forth by our learned Faculty. When will the legal corps arouse itself from its lethargy and emulate so laudable an example? When shall we see our halls crowded with youth, pressing forward with ardour in the cause of legal learning, and the whole body of our lawyers like the whole body of physicians, exerting themselves to increase the facilities of legal instruction? Look upon the Medical Hall, its libraries -- its lecture rooms -- its perfect apparatus, and all the means of instruction collected there. Thousands and thousands of dollars are easily raised by physicians to advance the learning, and rank, and usefulness of their body. Then look upon our law room, no single monument does it exhibit of the liberality or love of professional learning. Of a single lawyer who has lived. Even a solitary volume is not to be found in its library, as the gift of private endowment or public liberality, five volumes, and five alone excepted. When shall we awake to a sense of what is due to our profession?

There is one remarkable fact to which I would call your attention, and which deserves your serious consideration. Within the last half century every branch of useful knowledge, one and only one excepted, has advanced with rapid strides. That one is the science of jurisprudence -- whilst all others have made rapid strides towards perfection; jurisprudence and jurisprudence only has remained, as if by enchantment, spell bound. To what causes can this be attributed, ponder it well; as a portion of the future hope of the profession, it is your duty to do so. Will we not find the cause in the absence of the l'esprit du corps and its almost entire banishment from academic halls.

I rejoice to perceive that the public mind, or that at least of the most eminent lawyers of our country, is taking a proper direction. -- That our classes are constantly increasing in members. The best evidence of the increasing conviction in the minds of eminent lawyers that law schools are of great utility, and decidedly preferable to private instruction, is the fact, that there is no lawyer in Kentucky (at least within my knowledge,) whose rank in the profession is high, and who has done us the justice to inform himself correctly of the course pursued here, who has not, if he had, sons, brothers, or other near relations engaged in the study of law, sent them to join our classes. I know there are gentlemen of high professional attainments, who oppose law schools, but I would appeal to their candour and ask of them, have they fully informed themselves, or indeed informed themselves at all on the subject? Have they enquired into and do they distinctly understand, the course of instruction here pursued. Does not their opposition grow out of a knowledge of the old course, which I heartily concur with them in supposing to be at least unprofitable. Is it not due to the profession that they should not condemn, before they have examined? It is asking too much of them as lovers of legal learning, to request them to embrace some opportunity of being present at our exercises each day during one week?

I doubt not but the day will come, when no man will place his son in the office of a practitioner, but will be as certain to provide for him a preceptor devoted to the business of instruction in this department of learning, as he would to provide him a competent classical teacher, if engaged in the study of the languages. This event would sooner take place in this section of country, were it not for one mistake into which a portion of our distinguished professional brethren have fallen, with respect to our law department since its reorganization. The mistake is this. Whilst the old course of instruction by written or spoken lectures was pursued, a student to derive advantage to any considerable extent; indeed to be able to understand the language in which the lectures were delivered, must have prepared himself by a previous course of legal study. This previous study is still considered necessary to prepare the student for our classes, whereas the course now pursued is intended to embrace the whole course of study from the commencement or A. B. C. of the profession, up to the preparation of the student to receive the degree of Bachelor of laws. In consequence of young gentlemen's reading a part of their course in different offices, under different preceptors, they reach this place with widely differing ideas of those branches of the law, not studied, but superficially glanced over by them, before their arrival. The classes are made up of materials not at all

prepared in the same manner to receive instruction. Bad
habits of reading, or study have been formed.   One by
having been injudiciously set to reading works which he
was not prepared for, proceeds as if it were rooted into
the very constitution of his mind, that law was not to be
understood, but that the words only of authors were to be
remembered.   Another has acquired the habit of skimming
through a law book, as a young Miss would hurry over a
novel. -- Another by having been employed in reading
reporters, has no idea of the value of method, and no
suspicion that there is any such thing as first
principles, and almost without an exception, the habit is
acquired of speaking on legal subjects, in language as
loose and indefinite as that which is used in common
conversation.   So that our language is devoid of
precision, which is a great hindrance to accurate thinking
and reasoning.   Nothing is more difficult than to learn
precisely and certainly what are the students' opinions on
any subject.   Whilst we should all speak one language, our
tongues are as various as those of Babel.   Growing out of
these and many other causes, the wants of the students are
almost as diversified as their numbers, and the first
session of four months is often necessarily expended, in
divesting their minds of the seeds of error, and preparing
them to receive those of truth.   The session being ended,
and the student prepared to prosecute his studies with
success, returns to his former preceptor, falls back into
his old habits, and returns the next fall not quite so
good a lawyer as when he departed.   That is, if he has
read any thing he has been engaged in laying in another
stock of errors to be removed, and mistakes to be
corrected, and his second session is spent before he gets
back to the point at which he was in the preceding spring;
that is, prepared to prosecute his studies with a prospect
of success.   Hence I am generally engaged in preparing
materials, on which I have not an opportunity of
labouring, until they shall have passed through the hands
of others, who enter into none of my views, and second
none of my efforts.   Indeed it is to me somewhat
surprising, that under circumstances so inauspicious, the
institution has continued constantly to grow upon the
public favour.   Its having done so under such untoward
circumstances; is no mean evidence of the value of law
schools.   The full benefits to result from them never can
be ascertained, until the student shall commence and
complete his studies preparatory to practice in them.
    But if the student will not spend the whole time
devoted to preparatory study here or in other regular law
schools, at what period should he attend.   As to other
institutions I cannot answer.   I am not sufficiently
informed to decide?   As to this, I say most
unhesitatingly, when he commences the study.   If there is
any one time when he needs the assistance of a preceptor
more than at any other, it must be, when he is most
ignornnt of the subject upon which he enters.   The child
never needs the schoolmaster more than when learning the
Alphabet.   I would not make the remark myself had it not
been made by others who have had good opportunities of

judging, that generally, all other things being equal, the student who has not opened his Blackstone, until he has arrived at this place, is at the end of the session, in advance of him, who entered the class at the same time, but with six months previous reading. The reason of this is obvious. In the first case, there is nothing to do but instruct the ignorant; in the last, the ignorant is to be instructed, and his errors and prejudices combatted and overcome, before he is prepared to receive instruction. Such is a slight sketch of the reasons which have led me to the opinion, that law should be studied in schools; an opinion which I have not for the first time adopted since my connexion with this institution, but which I have long entertained, avowed, and advocated.

Having assigned young gentlemen in a brief and imperfect manner, some of the reasons which establish in my own mind the belief that in a law school you have a decided advantage; permit me to add, that no odds what nature or education may have done for you, no odds with what assiduity I may labour for your advancement, without your hearty, devoted, and untiring exertions, it will all profit nothing. All that your friends can do is to place you in the school, all that your preceptor can do is to scatter the seeds of legal learning amongst you -- let this be done with a hand never so liberal, on you and you alone depends the abundance or poverty of the harvest. It is yours diligently to warm and water and cultivate.

Upon the use which each of you shall make of a few fleeting months, depends, certainly in some degree, possibly entirely, the future destiny of your lives. It is a serious matter, let us not forget it. A few words by way of advice and I have done. I shall use the language of one whose great experience, extensive learning and distinguished talents, justly give to his advice a weight, to which my own could have no just pretentions. "To improve, you must cultivate habits of strict attention, not only when you read books, and hear discourses, but also in conversation, and in every part of your daily business. It will also be prudent to study according to a plan; to dispose your affairs methodically; and to study nothing but what may be useful. To read a great variety of books is not necessary, but those you read should all be good ones, and you will do well to read them slowly and considerately, often recollecting what you have read, and meditating upon it, and you should never leave a good author, until you be masters of both his language and his doctrine. In general when you would preserve the doctrines, sentiments, or facts that occur in reading; it will be prudent to lay the book aside and put them in writing in your own words. This practice will give accuracy to your knowledge, accustom you to recollection, improve you in the use of language, and enable you so thoroughly to comprehend the thoughts of other men, as to make them in some measure your own."

Much young gentlemen, depends on you who enter our classes. -- You are to go forth into the world as practical illustrations of the advantages or disadvantages of the study of law in schools. The question is not yet

fully decided.   The cause of Academic instruction in law
is rising in the estimation of the public.   In this part
of the Union it is much indebted for its growth in the
public favour to the youths who have preceded you; upon
you in some degree the decision of the question depends.
May you, and may I, through the session on which we now
enter, never lose sight of the influence the labours of
the winter will surely have on our destiny as individuals,
and may have upon the cultivation of that branch of
knowledge which I have engaged to teach, and you to learn.

– 11 –

Benjamin F. Butler

A Plan for the Organization of a
Law School in the University of the
City of New York (1835)

NEW-YORK, July 6th, 1835.

TO REV. J.M. MATHEWS, D.D., Chancellor of the University
of the City OF NEW-YORK.

SIR,

In compliance with your request, I proceed to commit to
paper, the details of the Plan for organizing a FACULTY OF
LAW, and for establishing a System of Instruction in Legal
Science, in the university of the City of New-York,
heretofore submitted to the consideration of yourself and
your associates in the government of that Institution.
    In order to a correct understanding of the object and
merits of this plan, it will be necessary to state at the
outset, the leading principles by which I have been guided
in arranging its provisions.
    1. I remark then, in the first place, that a Law
School in the City of New York -- and especially one which
is to form part of an University -- to correspond with the
advantages of its geographical position, and to meet, in
any adequate degree, the necessities which call for it,
should be organized upon an extensive scale; and that its
courses of study and instruction should accord with the
magnitude and dignity of the science intended to be
taught, and with the enlarged and practical philosophy of
modern times.
    It is true that an institution which should furnish
even a moderate amount of sound instruction, to only a few
of our Law Students, would under existing circumstances,
deserve to be regarded as a public blessing. But though
the means of professional education in this city, are at
present so defective, as to render any relief, however
partial, a matter of great importance; the wants, in this
respect, of our great and growing metropolis, are not to
be satisfied by any half-way provisions. They demand a
Scientific Institution for Legal Education, founded on a
plan at once stable, appropriate, and expansive: an
Institution which shall be capable of supplying to all who

may desire to resort to it, -- and this not for a few years only, but so long as the Law shall be cultivated as a science -- the means of acquiring an accurate knowledge of its Principles and Practice: an Institution which shall be fitted to elevate the standard of professional attainments, and to exert an extensive and healthful influence on the character and conduct of the Bar, and through them, on the great interests of legislation and justice, and on the other departments of social life with which Lawyers are, in our country, so intimately connected.

Without enlarging on this fruitful topic, I will briefly advert to one or two points of prominent importance.

The great principle of division of labor, adopted with so much success in other departments of industry and science, is equally applicable to a Law School. The science to be taught embraces a great number of branches, many of which have but little connection with each other, and some of which are so difficult and extensive, as to furnish to him who attempts their complete investigation, ample materials for years of laborious research. It admits, and to be taught with the utmost perfection, requires, as minute a subdivision of labor as Theology or Medicine. In the Law Faculties of those Universities on the continent of Europe, in which the Law is taught in a scientific and thorough manner, we accordingly find a professor for each of the important divisions. In some cases there are nine or ten professors of Law, ordinary and extraordinary, at a single university.

Whilst it would be far in advance of our condition and necessities, to copy the extended organization of the institutions just referred to, it yet appears to me, that it will be useful, so far as circumstances may allow, to adopt, in this respect, the principles by which they have been governed. A Law School conducted by a single individual of competent abilities, would, no doubt, be highly useful to its pupils, and probably more lucrative to its principal, than one organized upon a different plan. But no one man, even supposing him to possess such a knowledge of the various branches of the Law, as to qualify him to instruct in all of them, can find the time, or endure the labor, which such a task would require. After bestowing, on this part of the subject, the most deliberate reflection, I do not hesitate to express the belief, that you will not only find it safe in a financial view, but really indispensable to the success of your endeavors, to employ at least three regular Professors.

A suitable classification of the students, with a view to the adaptation of their studies to their respective years and attainments, is perhaps next in importance to a division of labor on the part of the Professors. The necessity and advantages of such a classification, in cases which admit of it, are too obvious to need comment; but it is only in schools attended by a considerable number of students, and possessing an extensive Faculty, that this arrangement can be adopted with convenience or success.

2. The organization of the school, and its whole
system of instruction, should be specially adapted to
students who design to pursue their professions within
this State.
Independently of the duty of providing in the first
instance for our own wants, it may also be mentioned, that
there are already in various parts of the Union, and
particularly in the neighboring States of Connecticut and
Massachusetts, several Law Schools of established
reputation, which are fully adequate to the necessities of
the States in which they are respectively situated. The
opinion is, moreover, becoming generally prevalent, that
an attendance on institutions of this sort, is a very
necessary part of the education of a Lawyer; and under its
influence, we may reasonably expect them to become still
more numerous. At Hamilton College, in the western part
of our own State, such an institution is soon to be
organized, under circumstances highly favorable of its
stability and usefulness, and which are likely to draw to
it, a great proportion of the Law students in that region.
Your School is therefore to be attended, for the most
part, by students from this city and its vicinity; and
though some of them may ultimately settle elsewhere, by
far the greater part may be expected to remain with us.
to this state of things, all your arrangements should be
carefully conformed.
In the higher Courts of this State, we have two
professional degrees. The first degree in the Supreme
Court is that of attorney, in the Court of Chancery that
of Solicitor; the second and highest degree in both Courts
is that of Counsel. The several offices of Attorney,
Solicitor, and Counsel, in time, may be, and usually are,
united in the same person. Attorneys and Solicitors are
not entitled, until three years after having been licensed
as such, to apply for admission to the further degree of
Counsel. The full term of preparatory studies, classical
and legal, for the Attorney and Solicitor, is seven years
after the age of fourteen. In no case can more than four
years be allowed for classical studies; and where the
party has not pursued such studies for that period, after
the age of fourteen, his legal clerkship will be from
three to six years, or more, according to circumstances.
The graduates of our Colleges being generally entitled to
a deduction of the longest time allowed for classical
studies, their term of professional education is usually
three years; and as the means of Academical instruction
are daily becoming more abundant in our country, it may be
hoped that few persons will hereafter apply themselves to
the study of the Law, in this city at least, without
having first pursued classical studies for the whole
period allowed.
We may therefore assume, that the ordinary term of
Law studies in this city, will hereafter be three years;
and I would also make that period the term of instruction
in the Law School, so that the student may avail himself
of its advantages, during his whole clerkship. This will
be a longer course than is usually required in our
American Law Schools; but it is very certain, that even

this term will be quite too short for a complete course of instruction, theoretic and practical, in all the branches of a science, so extensive and complicated as the Law of this State. And yet it is equally certain that our young men will always present themselves at the earliest allowable day, for admission to the Bar. The regular period of clerkship, although short and insufficient, is therefore all that will be appropriated to the initiatory studies. What then is to be done? Are we to abandon the idea of teaching the Law as a Science? Not at all. The very fact that sufficient time is not allowed for thorough information in all its branches, makes it the more important to the student, that the limited instruction he may receive should be as scientific in its nature, and as perfect in degree, as it is possible to make it. Instruction of this sort can scarcely be obtained, except in a regular Law School; and even there it must be confined to the most important Titles, and in many cases to a mere outline of the Law on such Titles. The subjects selected may, however, so far as they are pursued, be treated scientifically, and as parts of a great system; and the mind of the student may thus be imbued with principles which will not only guide him in his subsequent investigations, but qualify him, to a considerable extent, for immediately engaging in professional employments on the expiration of his legal clerkship.

The selection of Titles for study and instruction, should be accommodated to the period of clerkship, and to other attending circumstances; and as a general rule, scientific method must also bend to the necessities of the case. The great object of the School should be, to impart, within the given time, the largest amount of that kind of knowledge, which is best calculated to qualify the student for the practical duties of his profession; leaving it to him, in after years, and by diligent self-instruction, to fill up deficiencies. The term which intervenes between the two professional degrees, furnishes a good opportunity for this purpose; and under the imperfect system of legal education which has hitherto prevailed in this state, our junior Attorneys and Solicitors have found it indispensable, to devote a great portion of this period to a regular course of private study, preparatory to their admission as Counsellors. The Law School may be made extremely useful to such persons; and its instructions should be so regulated, also to induce them to attend it for one or more years. Of the junior Attorneys and Solicitors now established in this city, many, I should think, would be glad to avail themselves of such advantages. And as there will always be in this place, many members of the Bar who will not have enjoyed, during their clerkship, the benefits of a Law School, you may reasonably count, at all times, on some students of this class.

Lawyers in this State, as well as in other parts of our country, are generally obliged to apply themselves to the business of the Attorney and Solicitor, in connection with that of the Counsellor and Advocate; and to a greater or less extent, the multifarious duties of the different departments of the legal profession, are usually performed by the same individual. This renders it indispensable that the American Barrister should possess a thorough knowledge of Conveyancing, and of the practice in the Common Law and Equity Courts; and such knowledge is only to be acquired, by spending the whole, or nearly the whole, term of study, in the office of an extensive and accurate practitioner. Every man knows that the mere reading of books on naval architecture, or nautical science, will never qualify one to build, or to navigate, a ship. In like manner, the most laborious course of Law reading, superadded to the ablest lectures on the theory of the science, will be equally insufficient, without some practical training, to prepare the student for the arduous and responsible labors of the legal profession. Hence it is that our Courts require, as a general rule, that the whole term of clerkship shall be spent in the office of a practising Attorney and Solicitor, and under his direction, except when some portion of the term has been spent in the regular studies of a respectable Law School; and that only one year is usually allowed for such studies. This latter regulation has been the more necessary, because our American Law Schools, have, for the most part, been situated in small towns containing but few practising lawyers, and have therefore furnished little or no opportunity for instruction in the Modes of Proceeding. For the like reason their pupils have usually been required to devote their exclusive attention, to the lectures and other exercises of the school. In the few instances in which such institutions have been established in our great cities, similar regulations, have, I believe, been generally adopted, although not enforced by the same necessity. The location of your school, the peculiar wants of Law students in this place, and the comprehensive and permanent provisions you desire to make, all require that you should arrange them on a different plan.

The great number of Law offices in this city, in which a varied and instructive business is carried on, will afford facilities for the acquisition of practical knowledge which may be turned to great account. Instead of withdrawing the Law Clerks from the labors of the office, the University should endeavor so to regulate its Law Department, as to give new value to those labors, and to render them auxiliary to a systematic course of instruction in the principles of Legal Science. This, I think, may easily be done; and unless it be accomplished by your arrangements, you will confer but little benefit on those who are to form, in future times, the bar of the city and state. For if a choice is to be made between the School and the Office, on the supposition that the advantages of the former can only be enjoyed, at the expense of an entire abandonment of the latter, you may rely on it, that the system which has heretofore obtained, will be kept up. The necessity of acquiring an early and thorough knowledge of the practice, will, in the estimation of a great majority of the students, far outweigh the benefits of theoretic tuition. Most of them will prefer the Law Office for the whole term; and those

who resort to the Law School, will not remain in it more
than a single year.

But whilst I would so connect the instructions of the
School, with the business of the office, as to give to the
student, the benefits of both, I would not make it
indispensable, that he should, in all cases, actually
attend as a Clerk in a Law Office. It has already been
suggested, that the courses of study should be so
regulated, as to be appropriate to junior Attorneys and
Solicitors.   They may also be so arranged, in perfect
consistency with the other features of the plan, as to be
well adapted to those persons who may choose to apply
themselves exclusively to the lectures and other exercises
of the school, without devoting any portion of their time
to practical labors.

In the further application of these principles, the
following has occurred to me, as a suitable plan for the
organization of the school, and for the courses and method
of instruction to be adopted in it.

I.   ORGANIZATION OF THE SCHOOL.

This branch of the University may, with propriety, be
divided into three separate Departments: -- the SENIOR,
to include those students who are in the last year of
their clerkship; the JUNIOR, those who are in the
intermediate year or years; and the PRIMARY, those who are
in their first year.   To each Department, a Professor
should be assigned -- the Principal Professor, who will
also be the Head of the Faculty, being assigned to the
Senior Department.   Each Professor should instruct his
Department in an appropriate course of study, to be
completed in one year.

These three courses should embrace those Titles of
our Law, which are of the most general and constant
application, and in which early and thorough instruction
is most needed by the student.   The study and exposition
of the branches thus assigned to the several Departments,
will accordingly constitute the great business of the
school, and to these branches the attention and labors,
both of the Professors and the students, will be chiefly
devoted.

In order to bring the students into contact with each
other, and to make the institution a single school instead
of three separate schools, as well as to supply
deficiencies in the regular courses, there should also be
a GENERAL or PARALLEL COURSE, to be given by the Principal
Professor to the three Departments combined, upon subjects
not embraced in the regular course of either Department.
This General Course should embrace three years; so that no
part of it may be repeated to students who go through all
the Departments.   In the selection of Titles of this
course,some regard should be had to general method, and
also the regular studies of the several Departments.   The
subjects chosen for it should be less didactic and
abstruse, than those allotted to the regular courses, so
as not to require the same degree of labor on the part

either of the Professor or the student; and so also as to
furnish to both an agreeable change of study. Instruction
in this course will accordingly be confined to elementary
principles, and they will be discussed for the most part,
in a very general manner.

II. COURSES OF INSTRUCTION. PRIMARY DEPARTMENT

1. Beginning with the primary department, I would
propose an important departure from the ordinary
scientific course pursued by the institutional writers.
They more usually commence with the law of nature, as the
foundation of all legal science, and go through a course
of instruction in the law of nations, and in the Political
or Constitutional Law of the country for which they write,
before entering upon the peculiar system of Municipal Law
which composes the great body of its civil and criminal
jurisprudence. In treating of the Municipal Law, they
commonly begin with the rights of persons and the
relations of domestic life, which branches, as well as the
whole Law of property, real and personal, are all
expounded, before the modes of applying the rules of Law
and of administering justice in pursuance of them, are
taken up. The courses of instruction in Law Schools are
generally arranged upon the same plan; though as before
suggested, they do not often pay much attention to mere
Practice.
The course adopted by the elementary writers, as just
stated, is undoubtedly the philosophical order in which
the Law, as a general science, ought to be unfolded. And
when the term of study is long enough to allow it, the
same method may, with advantage, be pursued in a Law
School; but then the student, until he reaches the
practical branches of the Municipal Law, should not enter
the office of the Attorney or Solicitor.
Proceeding on the supposition, that the members of
the Primary Department will all have taken their places in
Law offices, I would here, in accordance with the
principles above suggested, carefully adapt the course of
instruction to their circumstances and wants.
To enable the student to derive any considerable
advantage from the labors of the Law office, they should
be elucidated by a corresponding course of study and
instruction. This is rendered the more necessary at the
commencement of his clerkship, by the peculiar character
of legal proceedings, which, it must be confessed, are not
very intelligible to a tyro.
On entering a Law office, the student is immediately
brought in contact with the forms of conveyancing, and the
proceedings in suits, many of which forms and proceedings
he is required to read, copy and prepare. Nothing can be
more inappropriate, and if custom had not made it common,
nothing would strike us as more absurd, than to place in
his hands, at the very commencement of these labors, and
as his chief subjects of study, books treating of the Law
of Nature and Nations. The first and second volumes of
Blackstone, and the whole of Kent's Commentaries, are at

this time almost equally inappropriate, because they have little or no connection with the practical business of the office, which will therefore be utterly unintelligible, unless his principal can make time to give him oral explanations -- an advantage rarely enjoyed in our Law offices, and least of all, in those which afford the greatest amount of diversified and instructive practice.

Strict philosophical method must therefore give way to the necessities of the case; and what might otherwise be left to a later period, should, under the circumstances and for the reasons just stated, be taken up at the beginning. I would accordingly so far invert the present order of study as to direct the attention of the student, during his first year, chiefly to the science of Practice and Pleading, and though I would not entirely overlook the Law of Nature and Nations, and the other fundamental branches usually taught at this period, I would give them a secondary place, by transferring them to the General Course. To the Primary Department I would assign a full course of instruction upon <u>the Organization and Jurisdiction of Courts; their modes of proceeding in suits at Common Law, and in Equity, Admiralty, and Criminal cases; and the System of Pleading, generally, and in each of the Superior Courts.</u> As these subjects comprise a large portion of Blackstone's Commentaries, and of our own Statute Laws, as well as several extensive treatises on Practice and Pleading in the different Courts, a full year will be barely sufficient for proper instruction in them. They will therefore furnish abundant employment for one of the Professors. Nor will the task of instructing in these branches be unworthy the efforts of an able and learned jurist. Our forms of proceeding, though generally prolix, and often encumbered by needless technicalities, are yet intimately connected with the principles of the Law. And as a general rule, he who best understands the nature and design of the instruments which the Law employs, will not only be most expert in the business of his profession, but be best qualified to look above the mere form, and to lay hold of, and appropriate to their true uses, the higher parts of his profession.

The advantages of this plan of study will, as I conceive, amply compensate for its departure from a strict scientific arrangement. The ordinary labors of the Law Office, properly explained to the intelligent student, will immediately become to him subjects of interest, and sources of improvement. What might otherwise be regarded as intolerable drudgery, will now be valued as instructive occupation; and he will therefore apply himself to his duties as a clerk with alacrity and diligence. His services will soon become sufficiently useful to his principal to remunerate him for the use of his library, and for the occasional instruction he may be able to give. One of my purposes, indeed, in this part of my plan, is to render the connection between the practising lawyer and his clerks a source of mutual benefit.

Another advantage will result from this course of study. In this city, some Court is almost constantly in session, which the student, after he has acquired such a knowledge of the modes of proceeding as to enable him to understand the reasons on which they are founded, and the purpose to be accomplished by them, will find it very useful occasionally to attend. Under the present system, he can derive but little advantage from attendance in the Courts, in the earlier parts of his clerkship; but upon the plan above proposed, he will be qualified to understand proceedings and discussions in Courts of Justice at an early day.

The course of instruction thus proposed to be allotted to the First Department, though specially designed for those who intend to pursue their professions in this State, will not be without its use to those who may establish themselves in other parts of the Union. The general rules of Pleading are every where the same; and our system of Practice, though more complex and laborious than that of any one of our sister States, will yet confer on the Lawyer who has once mastered it, two decided advantages. From the similarity of our Practice to that of the English Courts, he will more readily understand their decisions, so frequently the subjects of reference in our legal discussions, than if he had been educated in a State where the Practice is more simple, and less analagous to that of England. And if occasion demands it, he will also be enabled to acquire, very easily, a correct knowledge of the practice of any other State; for it may be said with truth, that almost every form of action in use in the United States, is substantially embraced in some one or other of our multifarious modes of procedure. This remark may even be extended to the Civil Law Practice of Louisiana -- our Equity proceeding being a good introduction to that system.

The separation of the Department of Practice and Pleading from the other classes, will, however, enable those students who may prefer to apply themselves to other branches, to do so without difficulty; and to consult, in the term and subjects of their studies, their respective wants and inclinations. This remark is equally applicable to junior attorneys and solicitors; who, as before suggested, will be enabled to select from the Regular and General courses, such Titles as they may prefer.

2.   For the JUNIOR DEPARTMENT, I propose as a regular course of study, the Law of the Domestic Relations and the various Titles forming the Law of Personal Property, including Commercial and Maritime Law. By far the greater part of our suits, and especially in this city, belong to these branches. An early introduction to them so that the student may be enabled, as speedily as possible, to understand the principles involved in the business of the office, will greatly facilitate his progress. It is almost needless to say that the numerous and important subjects embraced in this course, will open to the professor to whom it may be assigned, an important and laborious field of duty. They compose the Second and Third Volumes of Kent's Commentaries; several of their particular Titles have been made the subject of extended treatises, and in some of them the explanations of a competent teacher, are peculiarly requisite.

3.   The Law of Real Property, on account of its
abstruseness and difficulty, should, in my judgment, be
reserved until the last year.   For this arrangement, I
have also the authority of the distinguished Commentator
on American Law, who has treated this subject in his last
volume, and after having given a full exposition of the
Law of Personality, departing in this respect from the
analysis of Hale, and the works of Blackstone, and other
Institutional writers.   I would also assign to the SENIOR
DEPARTMENT, the Law of Corporations, and the Law of Equity
-- the former having become in this country, a most
important title, the latter constituting a system by
itself, and both being more or less connected with the Law
of Real Property.

4.   For the GENERAL or PARALLEL COURSE to be given to
the whole School, and to occupy three years, it will be
easy to select a sufficient number of appropriate and
interesting subjects.   The following have occurred to me
as combining the various requisites proper to this course.

FIRST YEAR.   Law of Nature and Nations; History of
American Jurisprudence; Constitutional Law; Principles of
Legislation; and Interpretation of Statutes.   As these
subjects lie at the beginning of a systematic analysis of
Legal Science, the propriety of placing them in the first
year is too obvious to need comment.   And though the time
and labors of the student will be principally devoted to
other and very different branches, there will yet be
opportunity to give him such information on the Titles
just mentioned as may impress upon his mind their leading
principles and relations.

SECOND YEAR.   Criminal Law; and Law of Evidence.   In
going through the regular courses of the several
departments, the rules of Penal Law, and of Evidence will
frequently be referred to, and some of them will be more
or less discussed; but as each of these branches forms an
entire system, which not only admits of scientific
analysis, but of many interesting illustrations, they may,
with great propriety and advantage, be made the subject of
particular instruction.   This course will also very
usefully connect itself with the regular studies of the
Junior Department.

THIRD YEAR.   Selections from the Roman Law and for
the last term of the year, which will immediately precede
the examination of the students for admission to the Bar,
Forensic Duties and Professional Ethics.

The immense extent of the Civil Law, the time and
labor which are necessary to the acquisition of even a
moderate knowledge of its details, and the fact that the
greater part of it has little or no connection with our
system of Jurisprudence, all conspire to demonstrate the
impropriety of devoting to this subject, any very large
portion of the usual period of clerkship.   On the other
hand, the laws of so many nations have been founded on the
Roman code, and so much of what Gibbon calls its "public
reason" has been transfused into particular branches of
our own Law, that to overlook it entirely, would be
equally objectionable.   A general view of its history and
spirit, and a reference to some of its most useful Titles,

rather to guide the student in his subsequent
investigations, than for immediate instruction, are all
that can be attempted with advantage. It will, however,
be easy for the Professor, in his treatment of this
subject, to make it illustrative of the regular studies of
the Senior Department. By contrasting the rules of the
Civil Law in regard to Real Property, with the Feudal
principles on which that portion of the Common Law is
founded, the peculiarities of the latter system may be
developed in a more striking and impressive manner, than
if it were considered by itself. Other parts of the Roman
code will discover the sources, and explain many of the
rules, of the Law of Equity and of Corporations.

     The other topics proposed to be assigned to the
Parallel course during the third year, are not, strictly
speaking, branches of Legal Science. And yet it is
obvious that they constitute very important parts of a
thorough professional education. Under the head of
Forensic Duties, may be included such suggestions and
advice concerning the preparation of cases for trial and
argument, the composition of briefs, the examination of
witnesses, and the style and manner of legal discussions
and forensic eloquence, as the learning and experience of
the Professor may enable him to offer. Professional
Ethics will include every thing that relates to the duties
and deportment of members of the Bar, in respect to each
other, to their clients, to the courts in which they
practice, and to the public generally. Under this head,
the advantages of diligence and integrity may also be
enforced; and the true methods of acquiring public esteem,
and of rising to eminence in the profession, may be
pointed out and recommended. On this subject, early and
sound instruction is of the first importance. It is true
that our courts, by their rules and decisions carefully
inculcate on Gentlemen of the Bar the high obligations of
fidelity and justice, and when occasion requires, they
enforce these precepts by appropriate penal sanctions.
But there are cases of chicanery and illiberality in
practice, and sometimes of professional delinquency of a
more serious character, which cannot be brought to the
notice of the courts, and which must therefore pass
without judicial censure. And even were it certain that
every such instance would be detected and punished, how
much more conducive to the interests of the community, and
to the honor and usefulness of the profession, to secure,
if we can, on the part of all its members, such a line of
conduct as shall furnish no occasion for judicial rebuke
or popular reproach?

     One of the most effectual methods of promoting so
desirable an end, is to combine moral training with
professional education, and to imbue the mind of the
student with correct notions of the nature and purposes of
his calling, and of the responsibilities which belong to
it. He should be taught, that though many of its duties
grow out of the misfortunes, the errors, and the vices of
mankind, the great object of his profession is not, as
supposed by many without, and by some within, its pale, to
derive wealth or livelihood from those evils, but to

mitigate and correct them. He should also be informed,
that the display of rare ingenuity or of great
intellectual power, in forensic discussions, is by no
means the most useful of Professional labors.   On the
contrary, he should be instructed, that it is an important
and very honorable part of the business of a lawyer, by
his learning, skill, and sound advice, to aid his fellow
citizens in the correct transaction of their affairs, in
the solution of difficult questions without resort to
litigation, and in the amicable settlement of angry
controversies. Above all, he should be impressed with the
conviction, that in conducting such legal proceedings,
either in or out of court, as may be necessary to the
interests of his clients, he is called to the high dignity
of ministering in the sanctuary of Justice, and that it
behooves him to come to the altar "with clean hands" and
"a pure heart" -- that frankness and integrity towards his
antagonists, are perfectly compatible with the manly
support of the rights of his employers -- that chicanery
and artifice are not only, in the long run, injurious to
professional success, but utterly inconsistent with the
first principles of a science, whose grand business is "to
command what is right and to prohibit what is wrong" --
and that to form the character of a great jurist, it is
necessary, first of all, to be a good man.
    In the development of these principles, and in their
application to the circumstances and relations of members
of the Bar, there will be room for considerable detail.
And I apprehend that no one who duly reflects upon the
subject will doubt the importance of assigning to it a
prominent place in the exercises of the School.

III.   MODE OF INSTRUCTION.

    Instruction in Law Schools is usually communicated
through the medium of lectures; and when properly managed,
this mode of teaching may undoubtedly be made extremely
useful to the student.   In most of the English, and in
some of our American Law Schools, is has been used as an
original means of exhibiting the elements of Legal Science
-- that is to say, the students have come to it with
little or no previous knowledge, and with the expectation
of deriving from it, their first impressions of the rules
and principles of Law upon the subject intended to be
discussed.   The lectures in these cases have usually been
in writing, and not unfrequently prepared with such
accuracy and precision, as to fit them for the press on
the completion of the series.   This is an admirable method
of composing institutional books; and we are indebted to
it for the Commentaries of Blackstone and Kent, Woodeson
and Story; but it appears to me not well adapted to the
business of instruction in Law School.
    When the elements of a science are few and simple, or
of such a nature as to address themselves to the
affections as well as the understanding; and above all,
when they admit of demonstration to the eye, the lecture
alone, may often be found a fit method of teaching them;

though even in such cases its usefulness will be increased by some prior knowledge or preparatory study of the subject. The Law, as a science, is addressed almost exclusively to the mind; and of all mental sciences it is at once the most extensive, multifarious and complex. Each leading Title embraces so many minor divisions, and is so intimately connected with other kindred topics as to require, in order to its complete exposition, a fullness and accuracy of treatment which cannot well be given in the lectures of a Law School, without overlooking other branches of equal, or perhaps of greater, importance.

The most useful kind of Law lectures, (I had almost said the only kind from which much benefit can be derived) is that which is designed to elucidate a preparatory course of Text reading previously assigned to the student, and to impress on his mind and memory, its leading principles. And for this purpose the oral lecture is by all means to be preferred; for whoever undertakes to discuss, in writing, any particular Legal subject, will necessarily find himself compelled to write a treatise or dissertation. But if treatises or dissertations are to be read, the pupil had better do it for himself, and under such circumstances as to enable him to peruse and digest them at his leisure. Besides, the rules of Law on almost any given subject, are too numerous and sometimes too abstruse, to be treasured in the memory without the aid of notes and memoranda which cannot be made whilst listening to a fluent reader. Many legal principles are also so artificial and refined, and others qualified by distinctions so subtle, as not to be understood without the closest attention, even when presented to the mind in a written page -- much less when pronounced with the rapidity of ordinary reading.

The oral lecture is not only far more attractive and inciting, but it furnishes the opportunity of supplying the defects of the Text books, and of giving much useful information which would never be incorporated in a written lecture. The speaker not being confined to the precision of written language, nor to a strictly scientific examination of his subject, and his great object being to expound and illustrate the Text reading, he may select such topics as are most important, and when necessary may amplify and repeat, in a manner which may be very useful to his hearers, but which would not be allowed in written composition. Lectures, more or less of this nature, are now taking the place of the written dissertations formerly read in our Law Schools; and as their superiority to the old method is too obvious to need further remark, I proceed to point out the mode in which I think they should be given.

Each course of instruction should be divided into a convenient number of lectures, a Syllabus of which should, from time to time be printed for the use of the School. After stating with suitable minuteness, the subject and divisions of each lecture, and the time when it is to be delivered, the Syllabus should carefully specify the preparatory studies. They should consist of appropriate selections from the most approved elementary books, with

references to the Statute Law, if there be any applicable
to the subject, and to one or more leading authorities
from the Reports. This preparatory reading should not be
so voluminous, but that an intelligent and industrious
student may go through it with care, during the interval
between the lectures, and at the same time attend with
fidelity to his office duties. On the other hand, it
should be sufficiently extensive, to impart to such a
student, a general knowledge of the state of the Law on
the given subject. The Professor to be qualified for his
lecture, must not only be thoroughly acquainted with the
preparatory Text reading, but he must also extend his
researches to other kindred sources; and without
attempting to write a formal dissertation, he should yet
draw up such a brief, as may enable him to speak on the
topics he may select, in a fluent, perspicuous and
accurate manner. With this special preparation, added to
his general learning and experience, he will be enabled to
elucidate the Text-reading, and to communicate a large
amount of valuable instruction. In his remarks he should
endeavor to bring before the mind, in a distinct and
forcible manner, the general principles which belong to
his subject; to state the leading rules, with their
exceptions; and to develope the history and reason of all;
with such illustrations as may be likely to impress on the
memory the substance both of the Text books and of the
Lecture.

To derive from such a lecture all the instruction it
is capable of imparting, the preparatory course must have
been faithfully studied and clearly understood; and to
ascertain whether such be the fact, recourse must be had
to personal examinations. These may, I think, be
connected with the lecture, by interspersing it with
appropriate questions, at the pleasure of the Professor,
in such manner as to put at least one question, during the
lecture, to each member of the class. If it be too large
to admit an interrogatory to each pupil, the object may be
sufficiently attained, by dividing the questions among the
students at the pleasure of the Professor. These
interrogatories should be connected with the points
intended to be explained in the lecture; and should in no
case be known to the student, except so far as his
preparatory reading may have enabled him to anticipate and
prepare for them. The answers to such interrogatories, if
correct, will furnish instruction to the whole class; and
in proportion to their fullness and accuracy, and to the
promptitude and clearness with which they are given, will
confer honor on the students from whom they come. If
wrong in whole or in part, they will indicate the topics
on which full and accurate illustration is particularly
needed, and thus draw out such remarks from the Professor,
as will be likely to make a lasting impression upon the
understandings and memories of all.

Where the lecture is confined to the mere business of
reading or speaking on the one side, and of listening on
the other, it must soon become monotonous and tiresome,
unless the teacher be endowed with considerable powers of
language and elocution. And even when those advantages

are possessed, though they may secure for the moment the attention of the audience, it is by no means certain that any lasting impression will be made on their memories. This sort of teaching is also defective in not sufficiently awakening and exercising the mental faculties of the students. The use of occasional interrogatories will not only give animation and excitement to the lecture; but accomplish other and more important purposes. It will compel the students to go through the preparatory course, in a careful manner; and to listen with interest to the lecture during its delivery. They will frequently be obliged to reflect, to reason, and to judge; their minds will be brought into contact with each other and with the mind of their teacher; and as the answers made to the questions which may be put to them, will furnish a decisive test of the industry and intelligence of those who give them, a generous and useful spirit of emulation will be excited in the class. Special recitations on the lectures as delivered, should also be attended to at stated intervals.

As a further means of promoting emulation, and with the higher view of preparing the students for speaking and writing on legal subjects, it will be useful to exercise their minds by forensic debates in moot courts, and by requiring from them written opinions on questions of law, and readings and dissertations on statutes and other themes, as circumstances may admit.

To avoid any interference with the attendance and duties of Law clerks in the offices of their principals, the exercises of the School may all be had in the afternoon and evening. Such an arrangement will also answer another valuable purpose: it will bring such students under the care of the Law Faculty, at hours when they least enjoy the supervision of their principals, and are most exposed to the temptations of a great city. The mornings of each day before office hours and the numerous intervals of leisure when in the offices, will be abundantly sufficient for reading and study.

To keep up with the lectures, to sustain with credit the examinations and other tests to which he will be subjected, and to derive any considerable advantage from the course of instruction here delineated, it will doubtless be necessary that the student apply himself with method and industry, to the studies and exercises of the School. For however able or unwearied may be the exertions of his teachers, his improvement will mainly depend on his own capacity and diligence. But this is an unavoidable condition of every scheme which may be projected for instruction in the science of the Law. Every man who is at all acquainted with the nature and history of the Legal Profession, will admit, that without a considerable degree of intellect, and a large amount of industry and perseverance, it is impossible to acquire even a moderate knowledge of its Principles and Practice. In a Law School well conducted on the plan above sketched, the intellectual and other qualifications of the students will very soon be developed; and those who are more than commonly deficient in natural endowments, in industry, or

in any other requisite, will probably be induced to
abandon the study of the Law, and to select some other
calling more appropriate to their character and habits.

_____

The foregoing plan has never, as a whole, been
subjected to the test of actual experiment; but as many of
its details have been successfully employed in our own
country and elsewhere, it cannot be considered as entirely
untried.   In digesting it, I have endeavored to select
from other institutions, whatever I thought valuable and
appropriate; and to combine therewith such additions and
improvements as were suggested by my own experience, or
demanded by your location and by other attending
circumstances.   I am also indebted to several of my
professional brethren, for valuable suggestions on the
subject; and in this connection it may not be improper to
add, that those of them to whom the scheme has been
explained (and the number is not small) have stated, in
very decided terms, their approbation of its general
arrangements.
Under these circumstances, it will not be thought
chimerical or presumptuous to express the belief, that an
Institution conducted with ability on the above plan, with
such modifications as experience may require, will prove
extensively useful to the Bar, the City and the State.
With reasonable diligence on the part of Professors and
students, the progress of the latter in acquiring a
knowledge of their profession, will be far more rapid than
under the present system.   Indeed, I have no doubt, that
intelligent students who shall attend with fidelity on the
whole course, will possess, at the end of the three years,
a larger amount of elementary science, and more practical
skill, than is now usually possessed by Attorneys and
Solicitors, of two or three years standing.   It may
therefore be expected, that the Courts will think it
expedient to hold out some inducement to a general
attendance on the school, by admitting those who shall
have attended all the regular courses, to examination for
the degree of Counsel at the end of a single year after
their admission as Attorneys and Solicitors, or in some
other fit way.   In the law concerning the practice of
Medicine, there is a precedent for such a provision; --
those who attend all the lectures delivered in a Medical
College, being entitled to a deduction from the term of
study which would otherwise be required.   An attendance on
these lectures, is also a necessary prerequisite to the
degree of Doctor of Medicine from the Regents of the
University.   These regulations were designed to elevate
the standard of Medical Science; and so extensive has been
their influence, that a compliance with them is now
generally considered a necessary introduction to the
practice of Physic.   As the like reason will apply to Law
students whenever suitable Law Schools shall have come
into existence in our State, it may be presumed that
similar encouragements to frequent them, will be proffered
by the Courts.
It is unnecessary in this place to enter into details
in respect to financial arrangements, but it may be useful

to offer two or three suggestions on the subject. Those
students who are engaged as clerks in the Law offices,
will probably find in them the requisite books; and of the
Professors, each, doubtless, will have his own library.
For the occasional use both of professors and students,
and especially with a view to the collection of rare and
expensive works, the University should take measures to
provide a Law Library. You will of course furnish the
appropriate lecture rooms, and perhaps defray the
contingent expenses, but the Professors should rely, for
their compensation, on the tuition fees. If the
institution be such as to deserve support, they will
amount to a considerable sum, which may be more or less
increased by the private practice of the professor. On
this latter point, however, it will be necessary that
definite limits should be prescribed and religiously
adhered to. To do honor to themselves, and to make the
school what it ought to be in usefulness and reputation,
the Professors must give to it their best efforts: -- it
must be their principal employment. Nothing short of this
will ensure success; without it, however able the
Professors, whose names may figure in your catalogue, the
whole scheme will prove abortive; and the mortification
and disgrace of the failure, will be proportioned to the
theoretical perfection of the plan, and to the promises of
good it may have held out to the community. The duties of
the Professorship must therefore be paramount to all
others; and the members of the Faculty should engage in
professional business, so far only, as may be necessary to
keep up their connection with the courts and the bar; to
retain and extend their practical knowledge; and to supply
any deficiencies in their support. To accomplish these
objects, without prejudice to the school, each professor
will be obliged to confine himself to the business of
Chamber counsel, and of some particular Court or Courts.
But I forbear to enlarge on these topics, as they can more
fitly be discussed and settled hereafter.
      Before closing this exposition it should be remarked,
that the organization and system of instruction above
proposed, may be readily enlarged or varied, as the
increased number of students, or other circumstances may
require. The three departments, the general
classification, and the regular courses of study may be
substantially preserved; but the Faculty may from time to
time be enlarged, as success shall justify, or necessity
demand such a step. Each of the branches proposed to
assigned to the Parallel course, may very usefully be made
the subject of fuller instruction than such as can be
given on the above plan; and the labors of the regular
courses may also be divided. In this way the institution
you propose to establish, may gradually extend its means
of usefulness, until at length it may be enabled to afford
thorough and complete tuition in all the branches of Legal
Science.
      I have now, I believe, stated the more material
particulars of the plan heretofore submitted to the
Council. It has given me great pleasure to learn that its
principles have been approved and adopted by that body;

and I have also received, with becoming sensibility, the
notice you have given me of my appointment as Principal
Professor.   In regard to that appointment, I can only
repeat what I have before said to you in conversation.
Such is my conviction of its importance and real dignity,
that were I now at liberty to enter on its duties, I would
do so with no other hesitation than that occasioned by a
sense of my utter inability to realize, in any efforts I
may make, my own conceptions of the manner in which those
duties should be performed. You are fully acquainted with
the circumstances which forbid, at present, any such
attempt, and which may perhaps continue to forbid it until
March, 1837.   If life and health shall be spared to me
until that date, and the University think it proper to
wait for my services, they will then be at your command.
     In the meantime, however, the other Professors may be
appointed, the Primary and Junior departments organized,
and the courses of instruction assigned to them,
commenced; and all this, I trust, will be done at an early
day.   In these incipient measures you may rely on my
hearty co-operation, so far as my official duties, and my
other avocations may allow.   And should any unforeseen
contingency prevent, on my part, any further participation
in the enterprise I shall yet feel, that in thus
contributing to the establishment of a Law School in this
place, on a foundation commensurate with the dignity of
the science, the character of the age, and the wants of
our community, I shall have done something towards
discharging the debt, (in my case a very large one) which
every Lawyer owes to his Profession.
     I have the honor to be,
          With great respect and esteem,
            Your obedient servant,
               B.F. BUTLER.

Samuel Warren

A Popular and Practical Introduction to Law Studies (How the Common Law Pupil should Commence His Studies) (1836)

How he who has determined on devoting himself with energy to the Common Law branch of the profession should commence his studies, is a question which has received very different answers; and if Bonaparte's celebrated axiom, before quoted, c'est le premier pas qui coute, be really applicable to the legal campaign, such a contrariety of opinion on this subject as the inquirer is fated to encounter, must certainly not a little embarrass and disconcert him. Solitary reading -- but of what books no two can agree -- is the advice of some; others urge the propriety of a six or twelve months' attendance in an attorney's office; a few suggest a course of law lectures; others insist on a six months' study of conveyancing; while many strenuously recommend the student's entering, in the first instance, the chambers of a special pleader. Very numerous inquiries and anxious reflection have emboldened the author to express a confident opinion in favor of the last of these methods; and he will proceed at once to state the reasons on which this opinion is founded.

By the solitary study of appropriate elementary works, if vigorously and systematically pursued -- and how rarely is this the case! -- some glimmering may certainly be obtained of the theory of the law, -- of its general scope and principles; and by an assidious attendance for a few months in an attorney's office, a smattering of practice may be obtained; but, in the name of common sense, why not blend theory and practice together? and that, too, in the most efficient manner possible, by a diligent attendance on a competent teacher? If the third volume of Blackstone's Commentaries is to be read, why not read it under the eye of an able and experienced practitioner of the branch of law there so beautifully delineated? -- of one who may infuse life and interest into the dull "dead letter" of the law, correct erroneous impressions as they are formed -- more frequently, however, preventing their formation -- and point out the various changes which the law has since then undergone,

all the while illustrating doctrine by actual practice,
and accommodating his instruction to the capacity and
progress of his pupil?   "There is a monotony," truly
enough observes Mr. Ritso, "attending retired study, by
which the attention is apt to be fatigued, and the spirits
exhausted; while, on the contrary, the effect of oral
communication is to keep the mind on the alert, and to
render the understanding more active.   Besides, if any
doubt presents itself, it may be instantly cleared up,
every mistake corrected, and every difficulty removed."
The most attentive perusal of the very best elementary
works, will leave only an indistinct and imperfect
impression upon the mind, even after a year or two's
devotion to such a task; and then, -- this space of time
thus unsatisfactorily spent, it is thought time enough
forsooth, to apply to a teacher, who may lead the learner
again over the ground already traversed, -- retrace the
faded, correct the erroneous impressions, and point out
his future progress!   Take it at the best: let it be
granted that the student comes into a pleader's chambers
never so well possessed of general views on legal
subjects, that something is known of the various species
of rights, wrongs, and remedies, and of the machinery of
courts of justice in dealing with them.   And what then?
He find himself -- especially if he fall into the
prevalent error of going in the first instance to an
eminent pleader -- turned into a pupil's room, where he is
set down to draw pleadings, and advise on cases for which
he faces himself by no means unqualified, -- matters
involving the accurate and incessant application, not only
of his previously-acquired and often ill-assorted
knowledge, but of a vast variety of new knowledge; so
that, if the former be not utterly driven away, it is
wofully deranged, the whole framework dislocated, and
himself hurried, fretted, and disheartened, by the
consciousness of having so long postponed, if not impeded,
the real practical commencement of his professional
studies.
     By watching the current of business that runs through
a pleader's chambers, carefully noting the manner in which
it is despatched, an attentive student will soon perceive
what portions of law demand his earliest and best
attentions; which of them ought to be known thoroughly and
minutely, and which it may, for the present, suffice to
know generally, and by way of reference only: in other
words, he will see how to direct and apportion his
application -- will see law, not as it was, or may be, but
as it is, -- as he must learn, and presently practise it.
No doubt, a man of powerful and disciplined intellect may
reap considerable advantage from such a course of
preliminary reading as he might adopt, and would
subsequently come better prepared to the practical study
of law in chambers; but, even in his case, no valid reason
can be assigned why, circumstances permitting, he should
not avail himself, in the first instance, of a pleader's
instruction and business.   But how many are unequal to
such a course of consecutive reading in private, without
falling, at length -- through incessant difficulties only

half mastered, or passed over altogether -- into a
slovenly superficial habit, which may not be so easily
cast aside! "The ordering of exercises," says Lord Bacon,
"is matter of great consequence to hurt or help: for as
is well observed by Cicero, men, in exercising their
faculties, if they be not well advised, do exercise their
(FAULTS,) and get ill habits as well as good: so there is
a great judgment to be had in the continuance and
intermission of exercises." Let it be borne in mind,
also, that the age at which the legal profession is
generally adopted, is one that, in the majority of
instances, renders it important that no time be Lost in
preparing for actual practice. For this purpose, at least
three years' sedulous attendance on chambers is necessary:
and -- without supposing that any one will think of
substituting, for one of the three, a year of solitary
reading -- why add to them such an one? "But," says the
student, "I cannot be called to the Bar for five years."
Then, by all means, spend the first three years as we are
recommending, and devote the two remaining, if you will,
to reading -- the most laborious and successful. Or, why
not pursue a middle course -- one which may, in particular
instances, be on many accounts the most desirable: spend
the first year in a pleader's chambers, devoting the
second to a course of careful private reading, grounded on
the knowledge obtained in chambers, and then return to
them, with redoubled energy and ability? Or, spend one
year with a pleader, another with a barrister, and devote
the next to careful and systematic solitary study? The
truth is, that law is so much a matter of detail, --
"consisting," as Lord Coke says, "upon so many, and almost
infinite particulars," general principles, -- fettered as
they are by innumerable exceptions and restrictions, are
so unsafe, either in their use or acquisition, that the
utmost industry and energy of the pupil, unassisted by a
judicious and experienced tutor, will but conduct him into
error and confusion. "Begin with general principles; get
a store of these," says one class of advisers. Nothing,
however, can be at once more plausible, erroneous, and
unphilosophical.
        "In order to proceed with safety in the use of
general principles," says Dugald Stewart, "much caution
and address are necessary, both in establishing their
truth, and in applying them to practice. Without a proper
attention to the circumstances by which their application
to particular cases must be modified, they will be a
perpetual source of mistake and of disappointment, in the
conduct of affairs, however rigidly just they may be in
themselves, and however accurately we may reason from
them. If our general principles happen to be false, they
will involve us in errors, not only of conduct but of
speculation; and our errors will be the more numerous, the
more comprehensive the principles are on which we proceed.
It is evidently impossible to establish solid general
principles, without the previous study of particulars: in
other words, it is necessary to begin with the examination
of individual objects and individual events. It is in
this way only that we can expect to arrive at general

principles, which may he safely relied on, as guides to
the knowledge of particular truths; and unless our
principles admit of such a practical application, however
beautiful they may appear to be in theory, they are of far
less value than the limited acquisitions of the vulgar."
These observations it is of importance that the legal
student should bear in mind, especially at the outset of
his career; and they will greatly assist him in the
formation of just views of his profession -- of the mode
of practically initiating himself into its studies. His
constant aim should be to acquire, as soon as possible, a
legal habit of viewing facts, their connexions, and
consequences: and there is no other mode of doing this,
than under the strict surveillance of an intelligent and
conscientious teacher. Principles should be the results,
not the precursors of practice.

This brings us to a subject which has been already
alluded to, towards the close of the "Introduction," to
what may be called, with sufficient accuracy for our
present purpose, the author's preference of the analytic
over the synthetic method of learning law; in other words,
of pupilage over private and solitary reading. An
attentive consideration of the passage there quoted from
Dr. Whately's Logic, will, in the author's opinion, set
the matter at rest. An appeal may, however, be here made,
briefly and confidently, to experience. Look, for a
moment, to the various other professions -- even the
trades, to which youths are apprenticed. How does the
tyro, as soon as ever his articles are executed, commence
his study, -- for instance, of the medical profession? Is
he forthwith ordered off to a private chamber, with a
treatise to chemistry, to master its elementry principles
before he is allowed to enter the surgery and compound
medicines? ·Is he sent down to the hospital to attend
lectures on that science? -- on the principles of
physiology -- on medicine, surgery, and anatomy? Surely
never; but is plunged at once in medias res; under the eye
of his master, or a senior pupil, he is set immediately
upon the ordinary business that is going forward; he
pounds pills, spreads plasters, mixes ointments, draughts,
&c. &c. -- he even administers this medicine on ordinary
occasions, and performs the little practical operations of
surgery, his tutor occasionally explaining the mode of
doing them, their uses and objects. Having acquired this
manual, this technical dexterity, be begins to feel
interested in the reasons and principles of the sciences
he is practising; and the latter years of his
apprenticeship are devoted to vigorous study, -- to
walking the hospital, as it is called, where he devotes
all his energies to the acquisition of a theoretical and
systematised knowledge of those general principles which
regulate the practice with which he has been so long
familiar. Thus also is it with the young attorney --
with, in short, the learner of any "art of mystery"
whatever: and why should it be otherwise with the embryo
pleader or barrister? Why should the maxim, that
"practice makes perfect" be inapplicable only in the case
of the higher walks of the law?

The system of legal education suggested by the author may be considered, perhaps, as blending the analytic and synthetic methods of study; the latter being carried into effect by daily reading with the preceptor for an hour every morning, the pupil being carefully interrogated each day on the preceding day's prelections; and the former, by copious explanations of the current business of chambers. The one will convey an accurate and comprehensive view of the legal system, carefully combined, as the pupil advances, with practice; which latter will fix and strengthen his knowledge of principles, begetting a constant habit of reflection, and reference to authorities -- augmenting thus, with sensible rapidity, both his knowledge and his power of using it.

Let us now suppose a student in his solitary and diligent perusal of the second volume of Blackstone's Commentaries, to have arrived at that part of the thirtieth chapter which relates to the very important and extensive subject of "Title to things personal -- by Contract." He will find the law thus laid down, concerning the sale of goods: --

"If a man agrees with another for goods at a certain price, he may not carry them away before he hath paid for them; for it is no sale without payment, unless the contrary be expressly agreed: and, therefore, if the vendor says -- the price of a beast is four pounds, and the vendee says he will give four pounds, the bargain is struck; and they neither of them are at liberty to be off, provided immediate possession be tendered by the other side.   But if neither the money be paid, nor the goods delivered, nor tender made, nor any subsequent agreement be entered into, it is no contract, and the owner may dispose of the goods as he pleases.   But if any part of the price is paid down, if it be but a penny, or any portion of the goods delivered by way of earnest (which the civil law calls arrha, and interprets to be 'emptionis venditionis contractze argumentum,') the property of the goods is absolutely bound by it; and the vendee may recover the goods by action, as well as the vendor may the price of them.   And such regard does the law pay to earnest, as an evidence of a contract, that, by the statute 29 Car.II., c. 3, sec. 17, no contract for the sale of goods to the value of 10l., or more, shall be valid, unless the buyer actually receives part of the goods sold, by way of earnest on his part, or unless he gives part of the price to the vendor by way of earnest to bind the bargain, or in part of payment; or unless some note in writing be made and signed by the party or his agent, who is to be charged with the contract.   And with regard to goods under the value of 10l., no contract or agreement for the sale of them shall be valid, unless the goods are to be delivered within one year: or unless the contract be made in writing, and signed by the party or his agent, who is to be charged therewith.   As soon as the bargain is struck, the property of the goods is transferred to the vendee, and that of the price to the vendor;   but the vendee cannot take the goods until he tenders the price agreed on.   But if he tenders the money to the vendor, and he refuses it, the vendee may seize the goods, or have an action against the vendor for detaining them.   And by a regular sale without delivery, the property is so absolutely vested in the vendee, that if A sells a horse to B, for 10l., and B pays him earnest, or signs a note in writing of the bargain; and afterwards, before the delivery of the horse, or money paid, the horse dies in the vendor's custody, still he is entitled to the money; because by the contract, the property was in the vendee.   Thus may property in goods be transferred by sale, where the vendee hath such property in himself."

Now almost every sentence in the above paragraph contains the enunciatio of a <u>principle</u> so important and difficult in its application, as to have called forth several dozens of reported decisions; and if only one of each of them were proposed to the ablest and most laborious reader, fresh from his perusal of Blackstone, -- before his recollection of it had been at all impaired or confused, -- he would find, that the foregoing sentences would be about as serviceable in conducting him to a correct conclusion, as a chorus out of Sophocles.   Reading them is really -- so to speak -- <u>feeding upon essences</u>. If they were even to be learnt off by heart -- frequently repeated -- and imaginary cases framed upon them, the student, when asked the simplest practical questions by commercial men, would find himself as much puzzled as if he had never seen or heard of the paragraph in question; and yet, perhaps, imagine himself fully possessed of the materials for forming a judgment upon them.   But he passes on to the next subject, and the one after, to the end of the volume: and what sort of a serviceable recollection can he be supposed to retain of the multitude of principles which have thus fallen consecutively under his notice?   "There is another observation to be made on the subject of the Commentaries," says Mr. Starkie, "which is this -- that where the student extracts general rules and principles from decided cases, by the aid of his own talents and industry, he is not only possessed of the general rule or principles, but he has also learnt its <u>practical operation</u>, and therefore the confines and limits to which it extends, the boundaries, the <u>fines</u>, <u>Quos</u> <u>utra</u> <u>citraque</u> <u>nequit</u> <u>consistere</u> <u>rectum</u>.   But, in the Commentaries, where the principle is <u>already</u> <u>extracted</u> <u>for</u> <u>him</u>, he learns the principle, with less trouble, it is true, -- but then, this is a dispensation with labour which is one of the most useful exercises to the mind of a lawyer; and which leaves the mere idea of an abstract rule, without any knowledge of its practical application, or of the legal limits which the principle serves to define."   "With respect to the application of the general principles of justice, they are usually obvious; opinions do not generally differ about them; it is in the searching out the proper principles in confused and complicated cases of fact, to which the almost infinitely-varied combinations and transactions of life constantly give rise, and in the skilful use of the discovered or acknowledged principle, for the defining the boundary line between right and wrong, that its practical excellency

consists." When the student at length thinks fit to
betake himself to a pleader's chambers, he will be in a
twinkling convinced of the truth of these observation --
hurried as he will find himself, probably, from case to
case, from pleading to pleading, in such a manner as to
confuse all his recollections of past reading.

Let us, suppose, on the contrary, a man taking the
course which is here recommended -- of entering at once on
the scene of actual business under the eye of one who make
a point of such daily prelections with his pupils as will
be hereafter described; his mind being a complete 'rasa
tabula' -- as far as law learning is concerned. Some two
or three hours after his morning's 'reading.' the
following statement of facts is laid before him by his
pleader, who requests him to read it over alone, and then
come and confer with him upon it: --

"Mr. _____ is requested to advise whether,
under the following facts, this action can be maintained;
and if so, to draw the declaration.

"A, a gentleman farmer, having cow which was near
calving, was asked by B, one of his neighbours, what sum
he would take for her. The cow was then in a field
belonging to A; who -- one of his servants being present
-- mentioned 131. as the lowest price. After a good deal
of bargaining, B agreed to give that sum, (but nothing
passed as to the time of payment,) and paid A half-a-crown
to bind the bargain. A said, "When will you take her
away? -- you may, if you choose, at this moment." "You
had better let her remain in your field till this day
week,"replied B. "Very well -- but I remember the cow is
yours -- and if anything happens to her, I will not be
answerable." "I understand," said B, and they parted.
Three days afterwards A send his servant to tell B that
the cow seemed ailing, and he had better take her
immediately away: -- but B said, "I don't care -- I'll
have nothing to do with her; I don't want her, now. I'm
content to lose the half-crown." The cow got worse, and A
sent twice to inform B of the fact, who returned similar
answers.   After the expiration of the week above
mentioned, the cow died in calving. A sent immediately to
tell B of the fact, but he had gone to a distant part of
the country; on hearing which, A sold the carcass for four
pounds, and kept the proceeds. Can he, under these
circumstances, recover the balances of 81. 17s. 6d. due to
him on the bargain? If so, Mr. _____ will please,"
&c. &c.

Can there be a simpler state of facts than this?
inquires the pupil. 'The cow was clearly sold,' replies
the tutor, 'but was she delivered to B? for that is a
circumstance most materially influencing the form of
action which must be adopted to recover the sum demanded
by A, i.e. whether it should be a special count for not
accepting the cow -- a common count for goods bargained
and sold, or one for goods sold and delivered. If the
first if these, assumpsit will be the proper form of
action; if either of the two latter, it may be
indifferently either assumpsit or debt. Under the old
system we should have had no difficulty; we should have

stated our case in all three ways, and so _must_ have
recovered under one or other of the counts. Recollect,
however, that we are now restricted to the use of _one_!"
The student is possibly apprised of the distinctions
between these three modes of 'declaring,' and is requested
by his tutor to state the facts of the case _memoriter_, to
show that he is in full possession of them. This he can
do, but owns he is quite at sea about the _law_ of the of
the case. "And well you may be,"replies his tutor, "for
this, which is so common, and seems so easy a case, really
involves a knowledge of one of the most extensive and
difficult branches of law. There are here nearly a dozen
important questions to be considered. Observe that this
was only a _verbal_ contract; that no time was mentioned for
paying the money; that earnest was given; that immediate
possession of the cow was tendered, but dispensed with,
and the vendor requested, for the vendee's convenience,,
to keep it for a week: that the vendor assented to this
-- expressly telling the vendee that the cow remained at
his (the latter's) risk. He is subsequently informed of
the dangerous state of the cow; and then, unexpectedly,
repudiates the whole transaction. The cow dies; and what
is the effect of the vendor's selling the carcass? Had he
a right to do so? If not, what course ought he to have
pursued? Was the carcass to lie rotting on the field?
Who, at the time of the cow's death, was its _owner_? If
the vendee, did the vendor's sale of the carcass operate
as, on his part, a recision of the contract? What should
he do with the half-crown received as earnest-money? Can
he treat the contract as still subsisting, and therefore
sue the vendee for the price? If he can do this, then,
was the cow constructively _delivered_ by the payment of
earnest, and _offer_ of immediate possession? No time for
paying the remainder of the price having been named, was
it incumbent on the vendee to tender it, before he could
have taken the cow? In other words, did the vendor,
notwithstanding all that had passed, retain a _lien_ on the
cow for its price? If so, could the cow be considered, in
any sense of the word as _delivered_? You see, now,"
continues the tutor, "the multitude of questions that may
arise on so simple a transaction as the present, and the
vast importance of having the mutual rights and
liabilities of the parties well settled and defined, which
cannot possibly be done, in case of a dispute, without
resorting to the subtlest distinctions. When it comes to
so nice a point as this, cannot you see the obvious danger
of the eager parties perjuring themselves, if, in the
absence of any _written_ terms of contract, there should be
occasion to supply defective evidence? Now, look at the
present case. What reason has been _assigned_ by the
vendee, for breaking his engagement, does not appear.
What will he assign _at the trial_? Are we now, were we
ever, in a state to sue him? Have we acted according to
law? Have we neglected to observe any statutory
regulations? -- those, for instance, of the Statute of
Frauds? Can you imagine any defence that he may be
relying upon? Perhaps you will take this book into the
pupil's room -- (probably Chitty on Contracts, or Smith's

Mercantile Law,) and having carefully perused the sections on the 'Sale of Goods,' try to apply them to our present case." He goes and reads what is entirely new to him -- but nevertheless, if <u>carefully</u> read, by no means unintelligible. Having gained a general notion of the law bearing on this subject, he finds that his case falls within the sec. 17th of the Statute of Frauds, unless the payment of earnest and the tender of the cow, coupled with the subsequent conversation, exempt it. He reads the <u>cases</u> which have been decided on that subject, as well as on others connected with it -- and having come to the conclusion that the <u>property</u> in this cow was clearly vested in B, he finds himself somewhat puzzled to adjust the legal consequences of A's subsequent acts, particularly his sale of the carcass: and returns to his tutor, who briefly discusses the subject with him. "The cow, on payment of the earnest money, became the property of B, whether A did or did not retain a lien upon it for the payment of the remainder of the purchase-money. If A <u>had</u> a right to detain the cow on the ground of lien, it cannot have parted from his possession, and been <u>delivered</u> to B; since neither an actual nor constructive <u>delivery</u> could have taken place, till A had divested himself of all claim, on any pretence, to the further <u>possession</u> of the cow. The contract of <u>bargain</u> and sale remains, therefore, in full force; and B is liable to an action for 'goods bargained and sold' at the suit of A, whose re-sale of the article, or rather disposal of the carcass, would not, under the circumstances, interfere with his remedy, as it clearly could not have the effect of annulling the contract."

Having a length come to a determination on the case, our pupil betakes himself again to his room, draws the appropriate 'declaration,' and writes down the result of his inquiries in the shape of an <u>opinion</u>; which, when it has been, perhaps, remodelled, and adopted by his tutor, he copies into a book, and devotes the remainder of the day to the subject of discussion -- the sale and deliver of goods -- the mutual rights and liabilities of vendor and vendee.

It is obvious that he has by this means gained a practical insight into a very important and difficult head of law, sufficient to guide his researches when he shall have leisure to pursue them into the ultimate grounds and reasons of the rules he has become acquainted with, and thus pleasantly applied to practice. He knows where to look, on any future occasion, for all the law of <u>earnest</u> -- what constitutes acceptance, and delivery, -- with reference to the Statute of Frauds; and his copy of the "opinion," in the case above mentioned, serves to connect and arrange his materials for a future occasion. Probably within a day or two, his attention is again called to this subject, by a case involving another application of the law he has collected on the subject of the <u>delivery</u> of goods -- one tending equally with the former to fix in his mind the principles which regulate such transactions. With what interest and intelligence will the student enter upon the examination of such a case, for instance, as the following: --

A gentleman went in to a tobacconist's shop and ordered 25l. worth of cigars, on terms of ready money, desiring them to be packed and sent to "The Tun," in Jermyn Street.   Having sent his own boxes to the tobacconist's shop, for this purpose, he followed them, superintended the packing of the cigars, and taking some of them up, countermanded his first direction (i.e., that the goods should be sent to "The Tun,") and requested the tobacconist to keep them for a day or two, when he would call, pay for, and take them away in his gig.   This, however, he failed to do; and the seller brought an action against him for the price of the cigars.   Now, had there been a delivery of them?   The tobacconist thought that there had; and accordingly brought his action for "goods sold and delivered."   His counsel contended that the delivery to the defendant was completed by the seller's filling the boxes furnished to him by the buyer, "which they became the buyer's warehouse for that purpose, so as to entitle the seller to payment of the ready-money price agreed upon, and to preclude him from any right to unpack them."   This may be considered a striking way of putting the case -- but hear the ready and decisive answer of the judge (Bayley).

"I do not assent to the proposition that the buyer's boxes are to be considered as his warehouse -- and think that the seller might consider his goods as being still in his own possession.   Goodall v. Skelton is directly in point against the seller's right to recover in this action.   There, the plaintiff agreed to sell wool to the defendant, who paid earnest.   The goods were packed in clothes furnished by the defendant, and were deposited in a building belonging to the plaintiff, till the defendant should send for them -- the plaintiff declaring that the wool should not go off his premises till he had the money for it; and the court held that no action for goods sold and delivered would lie, for want of delivery."

Such are specimens, selected at random, of the current business passing under the pupil's eye, in his pleader's chambers: and, supposing him to feel an interest in his profession, and exhibit but moderate industry, can anything be conceived more calculated to excite his attention -- to lead him easily and at once into the "art and mysters" of law -- to work his own way both into and out of its greatest difficulties, to deduce accurately the principles by which its details are regulated, and fix them deeply in his mind?   "Who so valueth, or eateth with so keen a relish," says an ancient worthy, "the fruit he buyeth of the stall-woman in a market, as that which his own hand hath gathered, after great pains, and, it may be, peril, encountered in the search?   Our cow-case literally bristles with points of law -- law that is involved in three-fourths of the most ordinary business of life, in every shade of variety and degree of complication.   Facts, such as those in the two cases above narrated, are comprehended and retained without difficulty, and serve to suggest the principles by

which their legal consequences are ascertained and
adjusted: and if a little perseverance in frequently
referring to them, be but exhibited, and a spirit of
further investigation cherished, the student will, it may
be safely asserted, reap more solid instruction from a
month of such labour, than from years of solitary reading,
or attendance on the most learned lectures that can be
delivered. The daily recurrence of such instances cannot
fail to put him into working trim, to stimulate his
energies and accelerate the rapidity of his progress.
Scenes such as these are calculated to enlist, in a
certain degree, his feelings -- his self-love -- as a
motive and stimulus to exertion. He is anxious to acquit
himself well in the sight of his tutor and fellow pupils.
Emulation sets an edge upon his attention, and, as it
were, glues him to his task. He feels conscious, besides,
that he has entered at once upon the species of employment
that will occupy him throughout life, that he is every
hour qualifying himself for the fit discharge of it. He
learns law by using it, -- vires acquirit eundo. Theory
thus illuminates practice, and practice, in return,
developes, illustrates, and supports theory: they act and
react upon each other. This judicious intermixture of
speculative and practical pursuits will infallibly be
found the quickest and surest method of access to a
thorough and masterly knowledge of legal science.

     "I may venture to assert," says Mr. Starkie, "that
there is nothing which more effectually facilitates the
study of the law, than the constant habit, on the part of
the student, of attempting to trace and reduce what he
learns by reading or by practice, to its appropriate
principle. Cases apparently remote, by this means are
made to illustrate and explain each other. Every
additional acquisition adds strength to the principle
which it supports and illustrates; and thus the student
becomes armed with principles and conclusions of important
and constant use in forensic warfare, and possesses a
power, from the united support of a principle, fortified
by a number of dependent cases and illustrations; whilst
the desultory, non-digesting reader -- the man of indexes
and abridgments, is unable to bear in his mind a
multiplicity of, to him, unconnected cases; and could he
recollect them, would be unable to make use of them, if he
failed to find one exactly suited to his purpose. The
good fortune to meet with a case fully in point, is not
very frequent -- not without the voluminous digests of the
still more voluminous reports, which, having increased to
an enormous extent, are still further increasing in a
fearful ration. A case seemingly in point, is not to be
relied on without danger, when it is considered, how
frequently nice distinctions are resorted to, as an
expedient for attaining justice; and that, sometimes, by a
bolder course, the precedent is condemned, and overruled
as untenable."

     No one can have devoted himself to the perusal of our
early legal writers -- our Cokes and Plowdens -- without
discovering an amazing accuracy, extent, and profundity of
knowledge which may be in vain looked for in modern days.

How was it obtained?   Where were then the elementary
treatises upon -- the synthetical compendia of law, with
which our times are so prolific, and on which now so much
reliance is placed?   Where then a Blackstone, a Woodeson,
a Sullivan, a Fearne, a Watkins, a Sugden, a Preston, a
Selwyn, a Starkie, a Phillips, a Burton, a Wynne, a
Chitty?   Littleton may be said to have been "alone in his
glory!?   It was the incessant and systematic study of
individual cases alone, both oral and written -- constant
attendance on the courts, and perusal of the reports --
that then conduced to the formation of legal greatness.
Our "fathers in the law" acted entirely in the spirit of
the philosopher whose sentiments have been already quoted
in this chapter -- they felt that it was "impossible to
establish solid general principles, without the previous
study of particulars," that it was "necessary to BEGIN
with the examination of individual objects and individual
events:"   which is precisely the point for which we are
now so anxiously contending.   But do we wish
presumptuously to undervalue the numerous admirable
elementary works -- the treatises, abridgements, and
digests produced by modern learning -- by those who are
now so successfully "labouring to systematise what the
experience of our ancestors has collected, and to unite it
with more simplicity and clearness?"   By no means; we wish
rather to enhance the value of such works a thousand fold
-- to secure their thorough appreciation -- to enable
their readers to do them far ampler justice than they now
receive.   Prepared as they will be by such a mode of
procedure as is here recommended, Blackstone's
Commentaries, -- Coke upon Littleton, will seem "a NEW
book;" every page, every line even, will be luminous with
a meaning which before was hidden from their eyes.   The
fact cannot be too frequently adverted to, it cannot be
too anxiously borne in mind by the student, that but a
short interval elapses between his acquisition and USE of
legal knowledge; that if he chooses to devote -- say a
year or two, to the formal and systematic study of
abstract principles, -- however well he may succeed in his
labours, he must necessarily retard his acquisition of
those habits of mental exercise, of that species of
practical knowledge, which alone can warrant him in
undertaking, on his own account, and unaided
responsibility, the active duties of the profession.   Let
him also bear in mind that it is pre-supposed he will
engage with a tutor, who pursues a daily course of
consecutive reading, commenting as he goes on, and by all
means in his power connecting its topics with the actual
business of his chamber: a system, this, which is rapidly
gaining ground.   The author does not hesitate to avow his
opinion, that that student is blind indeed to his own
interests, who would enter, in the first instance, at any
pleader's chambers, where such prelections are dispensed
with.
        Surely, however, no more need be said to convince the
reader of the great advantages attending the adoption of
the mode here pointed out for commencing his legal career.
Does he wish to read connectedly, and with effect?   His

experienced tutor is reading <u>with</u> him. Does he wish to
pursue his researches into obscure objects? A library is
at hand -- in the very room in which he is sitting -- by
the aid of which, and the occasional assistance of his
tutor, all doubts may be satisfactorily cleared up. His
learning is continually stirred and freshened by
conversation with his preceptor, and discussions with his
fellow-pupils. "The very practice," says Mr. Ritso, "of
discussing verbally has its peculiar advantages; the
information which is to be had from any written
commentary, however explicit or circumstantial, is by no
means to be so speedily acquired, nor is it so likely to
be retained in the memory, as that which is communicated
by word of mouth, and made the subject of discussion
between man and man."

Hear, also, the words of a consummate teacher - Lord
Coke: "In truth, hearing, reading, conference,
meditation, and recordation are necessary, I confess, to
the knowledge of the common law; because it consisteth
upon so many and almost infinite particulars: but an
orderly observation in writing is most requisite of them
all; for reading without hearing is dark and irksome; and
hearing without reading is slippery and uncertain; neither
of them, truly, yields seasonable fruit, without
conference, nor both of them, with conference, without
meditation and recordation: nor any of them together
without due and orderly observation. <u>Scribe</u> <u>sapientiam</u>
<u>tempore</u> <u>vacuitalis</u> <u>tuae</u>, saith Solomon."

"But," may whisper some, "is not this a very
unphilosophical mode of applying to the study of the law
-- thus to perplex, embarrass, and discourage the tyro
with the <u>use</u> of forms and the hasty application of
principles of which he is entirely ignorant -- is it not a
most precarious and unsatisfactory method of picking up
points of law?" No such thing -- as every practical
lawyer, however eminent, will testify. The author hopes
he is as fully aware as any one can be, of the necessity
of a thorough and comprehensive knowledge of the elements
of a science. He has well considered the sentiments of
Lord Chancellor Fortescue.

"Whoever desires to get a competent understanding in
any faculty or science, must, by all means, be will
instructed in the principles; for by reasoning from the
principles which are universally acknowledged and
uncontested, we arrive, at length, at the final causes of
things: so that whoever is ignorant of these three -- the
principles, causes, and elements of any science -- must
needs be fatally ignorant of the science itself. On the
other hand, when these are known, the science itself is
known too -- at least, in general, and in the main, though
not distinctly and completely."

And the opinion of the learned Mr. Watkins --
"A general outline the mind can easily embrace, and
the general principles of law it can easily remember.
When acquainted with a whole, we may discern the symmetry
of the parts; but an insulated position will appear
arbitrary, and its connexion will not be seen. As
difficulties arise, or new matter presents itself, a

general principle will afford us a rallying point, and we shall find ourselves possessed of premises from which we may argue."

"There is, I am persuaded," says, again Mr. Starkie, "no doctrine which can be more beneficially, and consequently, which ought to be more frequently and zealously inculcated, than the necessity of a constant reference to principle; whether the object be the acquisition of legal knowledge, the successful application of that knowledge in practice, either to the explanation and illustration of the existing law; or to the improvement of the law, by the removing of anomalies, on repairing the ravages which time, that maximus innovator, never fails to make, even the most perfect of human institutions."   To these sentiments the author most implicitly subscribes; and ventures to assert that the method of procedure above suggested, will be found the most rational, speedy, and effectual, for attaining the desired object -- a thorough, practical, and systematic knowledge of legal science.   By all means, student, get this intimate acquaintance with "principles, causes, and elements" -- this "general outline" -- these "general principles:" but, if you wish to get them early, long to hold them fast, and turn them to good account -- seek them as above directed; "deduce them" in Lord Coke's language, "from an infinite variety of particulars," for, to recur once more to Dugald Stewart, "it is in this way only that we can expect to arrive at general principles which may be safely relied on, as guides to the knowledge of particular truths: and unless our principles admit of such a practical application, however beautiful they may appear in theory, they are of far less value than the limited acquisitions of the vulgar."

With respect to attendance on a course of lectures, the author has but little in this place to add, further than to refer the reader back to pages 8 and 9, where will be found some observations on the subject corroborated by quotations from Dr. Johnson, Dr. Copleston, and Dr. Parr. He cannot ·help expressing his opinion, with all due deference to that of other and abler persons, that it is a mere loss of time to commence legal other studies by attending a course of lectures, however masterly -- however useful as an auxiliary source of instruction; that these are of but little practical utility at any stage of his studies, to a pupil who has the opportunity of attending at a pleader's or barrister's chambers, with such daily prelections as we have been speaking of, and access to a good library.   He has known several who, however sanguine at the first, have regretted the time and labour bestowed upon lectures.   There are so many excellent treatises on every leading head of law -- they are, in general, so accurately digested and arranged, as to supersede altogether the necessarily hasty summaries of the most able lectures.   It is in the introductory lecture alone, generally speaking, that any allusion is made to the manner in which the student should apply himself to the study of the law: and all the remainder of the course is devoted to the epitomising of various heads of law --

subjects so abstruse often and complicated as to render it
utterly impossible for any but an expert short-hand
writer, and one familiar, too, with technical terms, to
follow the lecturer with anything like competent accuracy.
But in the great majority of instances, how liable are the
hearers to catch at wrong notions -- wholly to
misunderstand the drift and tendency of what is uttered!
Only think of the following fearful summary of the topics
discussed in a single lecture of Mr. Amos!   It is
extracted from the authorised published copy.

> "Corporeal, Incorporeal, and Derelict Property;
> Blackstone' Classification; Property why called
> Incorporeal; Corporeal Profits and Incorporeal
> Property; Modes of transferring Property; Livery
> of seisin; Statute of Frauds; Uses; Effect of
> Stat. Hen. VIII.; springing and Shifting Uses;
> Transfer by Deed: Effect of Delivery; statutes
> requiring Signature contrasted with the Common
> Law; Authorities respecting execution of deeds
> collected; Escrows: Antiquities of Deeds;
> Maddox's Formulare; Spelman's Posthuma; Hicke's
> Dissertation; Fortescue De Laudibus; Antiquities
> respecting witnesses to Deeds; Saxon Deeds;
> Things in Livery and in Grant; Easements and
> Interests in Land; Opera Tickets; Fisheries;
> Drains; seizure in demesne; Derelict Property;
> Occupancy; Running Water; Public Property; Right
> to Fish, and Shells in Sea; In Arms of Sea; On
> Shore of Sea; Hale de Jure Maris; Free Fishery;
> Several Fishery; Common of Fishery; Right of
> Towing; Of Gleaning; Of Bathing; Treasure-trove;
> Waif; Anecdote respecting Trasure-trove; foreign
> Codes respecting Public Rights; Royal Rights in
> Unclaimed Property; Wreck; Royal Fish; Game;
> Free Warren; Chace; swans; Pepysian Library;
> Bastards' Effects; Maritime Accretions; Town of
> Hastings; Lincolnshire Coast; Manuscript
> Treatise, temp. Elisab."

Another Lecture is headed thus: --

> "Real and Personal Property; Terms for Years;
> Derivation of the term 'Chattel;' Diversity of
> Situations between Tenant for Years and Tenant
> for Life or in Fee; Causes of this Difference;
> Changes effected by 21 Hen. VIII. c.15; History
> of the Action of Ejectment; Limitations by way
> of Executory Devise; Doctrine of Uses; Duke of
> Norfolk's Case; Mr. Butler's Note on that Case;
> Fearne's essay on Executory Devises; Leasehold
> Qualification to kill Game; to become Jurors;
> Repeal of the declaration of Rights, by Mr.
> Peel's Jury Act; Wife's Right of Survivorship to
> Chattels Read; Writ of Elegit; Effect of this
> writ upon trust Estates; Liability of Real
> Property to satisfy Debts; Lands of Bankrupts;
> Estates by Statute Merchant, Statute Staple and

Elegit; Devises for Payment of debts;
Presentations of Advowson; Ancient Principles
upon which Distinctions between Real and
Personal Estates are founded; feudal System;
Different Senses of the word Freehold."

It is not impossible that the lecture may be a mere
rifacciamento of a section in -- for instance -- Bacon's
Abridgment, which its deliverer, often a man in
considerable practice, may not have had time to
accommodate the varied capabilities and acquirement of
learners, or scientifically interweave into it the
alterations subsequently effected by statutes and
decisions.   Supposing, however, the lecture to   be
unexceptionable, how few are the pupils who give due
attention to it-- who attempt, or are able to follow the
lecturer -- to connect each lecture with the preceding --
to take copious and accurate notes, and work them out in
private reading! How great are the temptations to
idleness and irregularity, arising out of a promiscuous
intercourse with numerous fellow-pupils! What a disparity
between their tastes, talents, acquirements, pursuits, and
objects! Mr. Amos has himself drawn a lively picture of
the difficulties to be encountered by one undertaking this
office.
"The person undertaking to lecture law students,
stands under circumstances which lecturers on other
subjects have rarely to encounter.   Each student is
interested almost exclusively in that circumscribed range
of legal knowledge, which he is likely to have occasion
for, when he practices for himself. And thence it happens
that what will keep the eyes of one student broadest
awake, will set the eyes of another student fast asleep.
Again, there is found every shade of disparity in the
acquirements of pupils, to say nothing of their abilities.
Some have yet to learn the veriest elements of law, others
want only some finishing touches to their education.   In
this difference, they may be compared to vessles in a
fleet, where the swiftest sailers are always on the point
of upbraiding the delay of their commodore; and the slower
are always apprehensive of being left behind. Again, the
law student has, most probably, been engaged during the
day in some kind of legal pursuit or another; he comes
will a full stomach of law, and is, therefore, not a
little dainty about his food. He comes, also, of an
evening, when not very unfrequently, from very natural
causes, his spirits invite him rather more to occupations
of an allegro than of a penseroso kind."
The author begs to add that he has spared no pains to
gather the sentiments on this subject of those whose
learning, rank, and experience, enhance the value of their
opinions -- and has found them almost uniformly in
accordance with those which he has ventured to advance in
the foregoing pages. He has also made a point of
attending several law-lectures -- all of them
intrinsically excellent, -- with a view to the correction
or corroboration of his views on the subject; and

conversed with several students who have assured him that
they were much disappointed with the system.

Nor is the author partial to the practice
occasionally resorted to, of visiting an attorney's office
for six months or a year, <u>before commencing</u> with a
pleader. That information of the most valuable kind --
the practical working of the law in all its departments --
may be obtained in these quarters, is indisputable. The
short period, however, usually allotted to such a visit
necessarily precludes the possibility of materially
benefitting a student, entering in total ignorance of the
business there transacted. Considerable advantage would
undoubtedly result from a six months' attendance in the
office of any attorney in respectable business, <u>after</u> a
year or two's study in a pleader's chambers; as he would
by that time be enabled to comprehend quickly the drift of
all that was passing before him, and direct his attention
to those points which he had found elsewhere most
difficult to be thoroughly understood. He would then <u>see</u>
the practice, of which he had before only read and heard:
and <u>seeing</u> would be, understanding. He would not easily
forget the time and mode of conducting the different
stages of a suit, with all its formal preliminaries,
incidents, and consequences, who had himself been engaged
in conducting them; who had witnessed the serious effects
of negligence and erroneous practice. A day's insight
into the actual management of an action -- of filing or
delivering, declarations, pleas, replication, &c.; of
compelling, or obtaining time for, pleading; of preparing
for trial, signing judgment, and issuing execution; of
arresting judgment, writs of error, &c.; of the various
practice of summonses, orders, rules, &c. -- will convey a
far more distinct and lively notion of these matters, than
could be obtained by mere cursory reference, however
frequent, to the <u>books</u> of practice. An intelligent
common-law clerk will be an excellent instructor in all
these matters; more especially at the present time, when
such incessant alterations are taking place, as render the
acquisition of the knowledge of practice almost
impossible, except to one who is actually engaged in it
from morning to night.

It is, lastly, a question frequently asked, whether
the common-law pupil should <u>commence</u> his legal education
by a six or twelvemonth's sojourn in the chambers of a
conveyancer. The author is of opinion decidedly in the
negative. Such a period is too short for any one,
especially if wholly ignorant of legal subjects, and
unversed in legal thinkings, to make any sensible,
available progress in the study of real property law. The
scanty knowledge to be acquired under such circumstances
in six or seven twelvemonths, is likely to be soon
forgotten in the hurry and anxiety of special pleading --
of the varied and minute technical learning to which he
must then apply himself, which will not bring into play
his conveyancing acquirements, for at least twelve months.
What occasional need he may have of such knowledge in
actions of ejectment, replevin, trespass to realty, and
for rent, &c. can be easily supplied, for the present, by

the perusal, under his tutor's superintendence, of the
second volume of Blackstone's Commentary, Watkins on
Conveyancing, and the various articles on "Landlord and
Tenant," to be found in the ordinary textbooks. He will
soon perceive the necessity, the very great advantages, of
a sound knowledge of the law of real property: and cannot
take a more prudent step than to spend six months in a
conveyancer's chambers after completing his course of
pleading. He will then bring to the task a well
disciplined mind; experience will have taught him which
are to him the subjects of greatest practical importance;
and he will, in short, be better able to avail himself of
a conveyancer's instructions. He will, for instance, pay
particular attention to the construction and elucidation
of those instruments which oftenest become the subjects of
litigation; so that when hereafter they may come under his
notice, he may not be confused or misled by their
multifarious and intricate contents. It is a step,
however, not very frequently taken by the young pleader --
who, if duly attentive to what is passing about him,
generally contrives to pick up sufficient conveyancing for
his purpose, from the exigencies of practice, and a
perusal of the standard works on that branch of law to
which his attention is perpetually called.

There is a very striking and important observation to
be found in Dugald Stewart's "Philosophy," which tends to
illustrate and confirm the general view contained in this
chapter: --

"I have heard it observed, that those who have risen
to the greatest eminence in the profession of law, have
been, in general, such as had at first an aversion to the
study. The reason probably is, that to a mind fond of
general principles, every study must be at first
disgusting, which present to it a chaos of facts
apparently unconnected with each other. But this love of
arrangement, if united with persevering industry, will at
last conquer every difficulty, -- will introduce order
into what seemed, on a superficial view, a mass of
confusion, and reduce the dry and uninteresting detail of
positive statutes into a system comparatively luminous and
beautiful."

The author repeats, in conclusion, his conviction
that when a man has determined upon commencing the study
of the Common Law, especially with a view to practising
under the Bar, the sooner he gets, so to speak, into
harness -- the sooner he enters upon the practical details
of business -- the earlier he begins to habituate himself
to the rigorous exercise of his faculties, the better. If
his industry be steady and well-directed, he will quickly
gain that confidence in his own resources, that
familiarity with the doctrines and practice of the law,
which will ensure his safe and rapid progress. Supposing
him, then, to have arrived at such a decision, it is hoped
that the brief outline of the system of special pleading
contained in the ensuing chapter, will distinctly apprise
him of the nature of the arduous and responsible
department to which he has devoted himself.

– 13 –

Anon.

Study of the Law (1837)

It is a circumstance of frequent occurrence to behold a young man of superior intellectual attainments, ardently commencing the profession of the law, buoyed up by the friendly predictions of his associates, and a just consciousness of his own abilities. The road to high and honorable legal eminence appears to lie free and open before him: emulation excites him to present exertion: wealth and fame invite him from the distance.

Yet in nine cases out of ten, the confidence of the young legal aspirant turns to doubt, distrust, despair -- and the hopes of his friends end in disappointment and sorrow. And wherefore? Not because his mental faculties relapse into mediocrity, but because he was not duly prepared for the arduous journey undertaken. His progress is slow -- almost imperceptible. Every day teaches him the deficiences of his knowledge, and opens to his view larger and larger fields of inquiry. The path is difficult, and he meets with a thousand undreamed-of obstacles to his progress. Human nature in its worst aspect is presented to his view, and sordid interest, vindictive malice, envy, hatred and all uncharitableness, are the passions he has to combat, or is called on to sustain. His temper is thus tried in a hundred ways, and, it may happen that though he has a just cause, and a general knowledge of the law as connected with it, a single mis-step in practice, a want of confidence in addressing court or jury -- an ignorance of the great and broad principles of the branch of law under consideration -- a deficiency of application to the details of his case, physical weakness, or mental or nervous irritation, will accumulate difficulties in his progress -- and utterly debar him from success.

Some, it is true, by an inherent force of mind bear up against the pressure, and in the end attain the high reputation of great lawyers. But how much oftener does the study of the law, once so inviting, become disgusting and tedious, and the brilliant promise of the youth, fade away in the obscurity of the man.

This result is mainly attributable to our erroneous system of preparation. Somewhat, it is true, is owing to the miscalculations of young men themselves, to their misunderstanding the nature of the profession, their deeming it to be an easy as well as an honorable life, their considering the vocation of the law as the highway to political preferment, and, in too many instances, their mistaken belief that genius alone, without assiduity, is equal to the accomplishment of any object. The most general plan of preparation is this: A young man, after having been immaturely graduated at a college, wherein a four years' course of miscellaneous study on a variety of subjects has given him no thorough knowledge of any, and sometimes, though rarely, with the advantage of a one year's course of legal lectures, enters the office of a practising attorney, there to abide until the lapse of the probationary period of three years, at the utmost, entitles him to claim the honors of a licence.

Of the mass of students, some consider their respective offices as prisons, in which they are unwillingly immured for an hour or two each day; while others zealously devote themselves to the acquirement of legal knowledge. But mark the fate of the latter. Short as the allotted term of study is for those who ardently desire a knowledge of the law, their hours of study are liable to all sorts of vexatious interruptions. No matter at what point the student's reflections have arrived, no matter to what critical period his investigations have carried him; at a moment when, perhaps, the reason of all he has read is yet wanting to fix it on his memory, the whole train of thought may be dispersed in an instant, and his struggling knowledge thrown irreclaimably back into ignorance. The practice of the law has set periods and times for its operations, and the machinery of a suit cannot be stayed that the student may profit by the perusal of a case, or the opinion of some legal sage. Causes must be pushed on to judgment or decree, and the attention of the anxious student is so often interrupted and averted that at last he despairingly ceases to bestow it, and worse than all, he falls into habits of idleness, always difficult to be eradicated.

Such is the present state of things: such is the present method of studying law. And as well might one attempt to teach an apprentice the art of engraving, by employing him constantly in working at the press, or bearing the impressions to the print-sellers, as to instruct a student in the science of law by initiating him in the deep mystery of copying papers or counting their folios.

Qui student optatam cursu contingere metam,
Multa tulit fecitque puer, sudavit, et alsit,
Abstinuit venere et vino:

Such of old was deemed the discipline necessary to one ambitious to excel in a mere physical excellence; while now, he who aims at eminence in a science confessedly intricate and hard of mastery -- a science requiring undivided attention and indefatigable application -- has his attention rendered diffuse, and his application divided and minutely severed. This may tend to make what is called a sharp practitioner, one who will undertake any cause however perilous, in hopes by tacking and manoeuvering and running to windward, to take advantage of his adversary -- one of those thin, dried up, vulture-looking attorneys, whose little eyes twinkle with the light of long-kindled cunning, and who amass wealth, and bring disrepute on the law -- men whose feelings are divided between their pleadings and their cost books, like Garrick betwixt Tragedy and Comedy, vibrating between their offices and the courts, erudite in special demurrers, and deeply learned in the fee bill or even beyond it, but with no more correct idea of the true object and high aim of the law, than the garbage-fed Hottentot possesses of the perfectibility of human nature.

It is this that has brought the saying to pass, that the studying of the law tends to the narrowing of the mind. It is this which has almost ripened the heresy into doctrine, and given to a dogma the force of an axiom. The paradox has become current in the schools and the senate, and, in spite of multifarious practical contradictions to its truth, it has grown and flourished almost beyond eradication. Plausible reasons and specious arguments are cited in support of it, and if we consider the study of the law merely as a means of livelihood there may be some reason for the assertion. But to consider the study of the science of the law as one tending to contract the understanding, is irrational and absurd. Instances innumerable could be cited to disprove it. Demosthenes, Pericles, Cicero, the elder Antony and the elder Cato, were all lawyers in the strictest sense of the term; and minds more comprehensive than theirs seldom fall to the lot of man. The profession of Bacon, the man of universal lore, and who marked out the path for the progressive knowledge of succeeding centuries was the law. The names of More, of Mansfield, of Jones and of Brougham, need no comment, nor does that of Hamilton, the skillful warrior, legislator and statesman. These are not one tithe of the names of lawyers, distinguished for their extensive views and liberal minds, that could be adduced. They are given for illustration and not for proof, for there is nothing in the subject itself that should tend to narrow the mind. Law is a science and a lofty one. It is based on the rights of man by nature and society; its object is the elucidation of truth; its end the attainment of justice. Besides the rights of man, international differences and the claims of sovereigns may demand the attention of the lawyer. These certainly require a comprehensiveness of views incompatible with a narrowed intellect. The subjects of suits at law are co-extensive with human knowledge and pursuits, and the advocate may not only have need of an acquaintance with the moral sciences, but with the doctrines and principles of the mechanic arts and the customs of trades. Can there be then aught better calculated to elevate the mind, to cause it to break off the shackles of prejudices, and attain to high moral beauty, than the full, faithful and conscientious studying of the law?

But in what manner is a remedy to be applied to the imperfections which exist in the study, and the evils which result from its practice? This is a serious question, and one in which every citizen is interested, and like many others of the same nature, one about which no citizen is concerned. It is a subject interesting, not only to the profession, but to the community at large. There is no person, be his pursuit what it may, that it does not touch. The law in its theory is truth and justice, and if properly administered it could not be made as it too often is, an engine of incalculable evil.

The opinions I present are crude, but I am induced to hazard them, by a feeling solicitous to awaken attention to the subject.

As indolence in youth will hardly ripen into industry in age, and as the blight in the blossom produces rottenness in the fruit, so an imperfect and erroneous studying of the law will produce an imperfect and erroneous knowledge of it, and a deficiency of moral rectitude in the student will leave room for roguery and knavishness in the practitioner. The latter of these evils cannot be universally guarded against, but much can be done to correct the former.

In the first place, the adoption of the law as a profession should be maturely weighed in the mind by the young student before venturing on it. He should examine his mind thoroughly; he should question his passions, his habits, his capacities. He should look upon the study of the law abstractedly from every thing else. He should ask himself if he will be contented with a life of constant labor and secluded study. He should review his course, and observe if he has exhibited unwavering perseverance in any thing. He should separate the pursuit of the law from its incidental honors, its fame and the acquirements it begets, and reflect whether he can love it for its own sake. He should be assured that he will be able to abandon all allurements for the sake of its study. If he cannot solve all these points satisfactorily, let him abandon all idea of pursuing the study of the law, or resolve to be contented with a mediocrity of attainment.

There are mental and moral requisites to the study and to the practice of the law. I believe sincerely that the standing and acquirements of a man depend upon himself, and that it is only the greater or less discipline and culture that the mind is subjected to, that makes the difference. It may be objected, that differing circumstances affect the result; but superiority to circumstances is exactly what marks and distinguishes the great man. He, therefore, who is about commencing the study of the law, should question himself closely to what he has wrought up his moral faculties: to good or to evil; to industry or to idleness. If to evil or idleness, let him first correct his error, or give up his resolve. If to good and industry, he may with strong hope carry his scrutiny farther. The mental and moral requisites to the study of the law and its practice are, perseverance of purpose, a love of truth, a logical conformation of mind, a close discrimination, a quick and correct perception; or, if a slow perception, then a faculty of shutting out partial conclusions until the whole subject is before the mind; an abhorrence of vice, a freedom from dissipation in any shape, a scrupulous, unswerving, indomitable integrity, an unshaken equanimity of temper, and an undeviating courtesy of manner.

The mental preparatory attainments necessary are, a knowledge of the Latin language, both the classic and the modern; a general acquaintance with miscellaneous classical literature, and with the arts and sciences; practised skill in metaphysical analysis and mathematical demonstration.

This may appear a startling enumeration to the student, but I am convinced that with industry and judgment all these are within the reach of every one. If a student possesses an upright heart, he embraces in that alone one half the list. As to the rest, it is true they will require assiduous application, and without that it is very useless to undertake the study. Any gentleman would be ashamed of himself, if his attainments did not reach to at least one half of what we have set down; and as to the mental habitudes spoken of, they are so concatenated together and dependent on each other, that the student who attains one link may easily draw the whole chain of his possession. The acquiring of one, will constitute a relaxation to the pursuit of the others; and so long as the student recollects his aim and object, his multifarious studies will all conduce to his advancement.

The intellectual discipline of the intended lawyer must be strict and constant. He must lay the foundations broad and deep ere he attempts to rear his structure. As the healthful operations of the corporeal functions is of the deepest importance to every student, let not the sanguine student of the law consider that time wasted, which within proper limits is devoted to exercise. Vigorous exercise regularly pursued imparts activity to the mental faculties, whereas indolence of body gradually spreads a damning influence over the mind. Regularity in mental pursuits is also a requisite of the highest moment. The student should apportion his time to his different necessities and avocations. In the spirit of the lines quoted by Lord Coke, I would say to the student,

> Sex horas somno, totidem des legibus aequis,
> Quatuor orabis, des epulisque duas;
> Quod superest ultra saeris largire camaenis.

Having settled these points, let him next decide upon the best means of fulfilling the term of study required by the rules of court. Since it is necessary to spend a certain time in the office of a practising attorney, the choice in this respect is limited to the advantages of different offices. And here may be suggested to the student the fallacy of the prevailing idea, that the office of an old practitioner is preferable to that of a young one. The actual knowledge gained in either, cannot

extend much beyond an acquaintance with the <u>routine</u> of
business. The knowledge of practice that may be gained in
an office where considerable business is carried on, is
limited, and the attainment of it illy compensates for the
heavy sacrifice it requires. In a "large office" no
regular course of study can be pursued, nor can even a
desultory one be very extensive. It may be said that the
supervision of the student's reading by an experienced
lawyer is of great advantage, and so it probably is, when
exercised; but the lawyers best qualified for such
superintendence, are those who in general are too much
occupied with their business to bestow much time on their
students, or, as the rules more correctly style them,
their clerks. What is generally the fact? When the legal
tyro first enters an office, Blackstone is placed in his
hands, and after that he is left to his own guidance,
until, admonished by his approaching examination, he
instinctively directs his attention to the rules of
practice. Blackstone is an invaluable treatise, and
worthy of all commendation. It is so orderly in its
arrangements, so clear in its positions, so rational in
its spirit, and so full, yet just, in its learning, that
it may well be doubted if any scientific work was ever so
well executed. Coke probably possessed more abstruse
learning, but we may vainly seek for hours for any
particular point in his chaos of legal erudition. His
deep learning and acute intellect give an oracular stamp
to all his writings; but as if uttered in the inspiration
of the moment, they are as much distinguished for their
irregularity as their infallibility. But Blackstone is at
once learned and clear, correct and methodical.
Nevertheless, Blackstone is not the work that should be
first placed in the hands of an American student. Should
it be, he will learn what afterwards he must unlearn; and,
as Bolingbroke remarked, it is an easier road to knowledge
from ignorance, than from error; and much of Blackstone's
Commentaries, applied to American law, would be erroneous.
The law of England, though it is the source of our law,
differs from it in many respects extremely, and in others
in such slight degrees, that to separate them will require
a subtle memory ingeniously exercised. The constitution
of England should be studied, but not before our own. The
legislation of England should interest us, but our own
should be paramount. Again, America has remedied many of
the imperfections, and abolished many of the evils of the
English code. Our doctrine of real estate has also been
remodelled and simplified. Fifty years since, the
barrister from Westminster might have argued the briefs in
our courts with as little special preparation as at home.
Fifty years hence, the language of the one bar will be as
it were different dialect from that of the other, unless
England should, as she now seems inclined, keep pace with
our improvement. Why, then, should the student first
peruse a work which, if trusted to as law, will lead to
error, and if not yielded credence to, will unsettle and
disturb his mind? After he has acquired an outline of
American law, a perusal of Blackstone will be beneficial.
But admitting that the "Commentaries" constitute the

proper work for a beginner, the supervising power ends
with that; and it may well be doubted if most lawyers
would not be perplexed by the question, "What course of
reading do you recommend to your students?" This fancied
advantage of an eminent lawyer's office is none in
reality; while in the office of an attorney of limited
practice, the student would have ten times more leisure
for his studies.

But supposing the student to have made choice of his
office, and that he has opportunity for study, and uses
it; he cannot have those advantages which he should have.
The system itself is wrong, fundamentally wrong. For
those young gentlemen of independent fortune, who take up
the profession of the law, merely because, in this
country, a young man without any pursuit or profession
would be an anomaly; or for those who adopt it because it
is eminently honorable, or because it is considered the
high road to place and power, without any determination of
trusting to it as a profession, the present course of
study is fully sufficient. But for him who desires, if
entrusted with power, to use it rightly, or who intends to
make the law his business and his study -- who is anxious
to become master of the law and its spirit -- who expects
to devote his whole life to its ardent pursuit, -- to such
a one, how utterly inappropriate and inadequate is the
present method of study! It allows barely sufficient time
to obtain a general knowledge of the local laws, but is
altogether incompetent to imbue the mind with a deep and
solid acquaintance with its broad and general principles.
He cannot go up to the source of the stream and drink from
its fountains, but he must receive it polluted and
adulterated, as it has floated down to him. His time is
divided between the business of the office and his
studies; and in the regulation of the latter, he has to
trust to his own judgment, or at best, to the casual
advice of one more competent. Why should such a plan be
pursued in regard to students of the law, when one so
different is deemed necessary for those of other liberal
professions. Students of medicine must spend all their
time in the pursuit of that science; they must follow a
collegiate course exclusively relating to their
profession, undisturbed by other pursuits. Why, then,
should not the student of the law pursue a similar plan,
and his time be exclusively devoted to his studies?

The establishment of a law university, in which the
pursuit of the science should be the primary object, and
in which it should be pursued assiduously, methodically,
and on a broad and philosophical basis, is to our country
a matter of the highest moment. From the profession of
the law rise up a large proportion of our statesmen,
legislators and judges; the originators, the makers, and
the expounders of the law. And when we consider how much,
in our constitutional governments, we are directed and
restrained by the law -- how necessary it is to our safety
and protection -- how it is interwoven with our daily
avocations, and with all our relations to others, it seems
indispensable to our happiness and security, that those
who make, and those who practically direct the application

of our laws, should be men of deep and extensive learning
in the principles of human nature -- of a general and
intelligent acquaintance with the arts, sciences and
pursuits of the community -- of a great and pervading
knowledge of the practical operation of principles in
times past and the present; that they should be men
skillful in matters of finance, commerce, trade,
manufactures, agriculture, and all the modes in which the
talents and propensities of citizens are manifested; that
they should be above bribery and corruption; in short,
that they should be of such honesty, knowledge and
judgment, that the laws of their making should be obeyed
through a sense of their justice, rather than their
weight, and their expositions of laws made, should
maintain the right, and right the wrong.

But, independent of the senate and the bench, how
necessary it is that the practising lawyer should be a man
of extensive acquirements and learning -- that he should
be able clearly to discern the right, and detect the wrong
-- to understand fully the principles of law, and be able
to apply them accurately to the case before him. How much
of useless, expensive litigation would then be avoided --
how much wear and tear of feeling would be saved -- how
many a family be prevented from dividing against itself --
how much knavery and roguery blasted in its incipiency --
how many a man saved from beggary and despair -- how many
a wife from sadness and a broken heart -- how many a child
from vice, from guilt, from the dungeon.

A knavish lawyer is productive of a wider extent of
misery than is generally supposed, because, although the
misery be evident, the cause is unsuspected. Look through
the circles formed by his clients and their opponents --
you behold bankrupts, profligates, knaves, rogues -- the
last in all their infinite variety, from the
dollar-extorting cheat, who but just escapes an indictment
for larceny or highway robbery, by his knowledge of law,
to the splendid rascal, who confiscates estates by legal
ingenuity, and proves himself statute-honest by the
subtlety of his villainy, and the depth of his casuistry
in the ethics of the law. It requires no faith in animal
magnetism to support the belief that, when finesse,
chicanery, and knavishness inhabit the mind of the lawyer,
they soon pass into the mind of the client.

Next, take the case of an unskillful advocate. To
his hands may be confided cases of the greatest
importance. Confiding friends may entrust to his guidance
matters involving their fortunes, their estates, their
credit, or their reputation. Step by step he blunders on,
in his short-sighted ignorance, believing each step
correct, until at last his client is involved in
harassing, expensive, ruinous litigation. It is of the
essence of ignorance to believe itself wise, and the
conceited and superficial smatterer in the law hardens
himself in his unbelief, like Pharaoh, though portents and
miracles contend against him; and hence the danger: for
the experience that a client gains by schooling in
litigation, is among the dearest he can purchase; the
light it gives is not a beacon to conduct his vessel to

its haven, but the burning of the fragments of the wreck
by which he would fain comfort and cheer himself in his
despair.   If a lawyer of this cast is defeated, he rails
against judges and juries; they are all numsculls and
blockheads -- the judge had some personal or political
bias against him, or the jury decided "clear against the
judge's charge" -- the case must be appealed from, or
there must be a new trial, or the like; and thus he will
run a cause through the whole scale of legal tribunals, up
and down the forensic gamut, until the costs outswell the
subject matter of dispute -- until there is no longer a
higher Court of Appeals, except that beyond the grave,
whose grand summoner is Death, and where no advocates
avail, save good deeds done in the body, and the mercy of
the Great Judge himself.

Again, suppose the case of an upright and
conscientious advocate, who, believing that a cause
entrusted to him is just, has devoted to it hours, days,
weeks of preparation; who has omitted no care, no toil, no
research; who has conducted his cause safely to his
argument, through all the snares and pitfalls of practice
and pleading; and then, after expending on it all the
stores of his knowledge, and allowing his feelings to be
engrossed by it, is at last hopelessly defeated.   Suppose
him to have been right, yet overcome.   This may be.
Courts are fallible; rules of law imperfect.   But has he
not been too sanguine -- has he not given his attention to
the details of his case, when the elucidation of the
principles involved required it; has he not overrated his
capability for argument; was there no fault in his logic;
was he prepared to render his case as clear to others as
it seemed to his own mind; he has not, in his conviction
of the equity of his case, forgotten that in society,
equity is fenced in by laws, and that in pursuit of the
former we must obey the directions of the latter?   From
these considerations, and such as these, let the ingenuous
student draw a profitable lesson.

Again, how much litigation arises from the imperfect
or erroneous wording of laws, and how essentially
requisite for the guidance of the citizen, is clearness
and lucidness in the statute.   Municipal law has been well
defined to be a rule of civil action prescribed by the
superior power in the state, and which the citizen is
bound to obey.   Every good citizen acknowledges the
obligation, but in many cases, may be extremely puzzled to
ascertain what the rule is, and be no better off than the
subjects of that tyrant who caused his edicts to be
written in small characters, and posted on high pillars,
so that they were illegible to all.   This difficulty in
ascertaining the meaning of some statutes, does not arise
from the imperfection of language, or any inherent
obstacle to the proper expression of the meaning of the
law-giver, but to carelessness or ignorance in those who
indite the laws.   They leave a loop to hang a doubt on,
use words of disputable meaning, particularize to the
exclusion of a general principle, and in their anxiety to
enumerate every case, omit many points which without the
enumeration would have been covered by the rule.   Men not

properly educated and informed are often raised to the rank of legislators, and of course entrusted with the drafting of laws; and the consequence is, that loose verbose, ambiguous, crude, hastily conceived statutes are enacted and declared to be law. Such laws are but firebrands in the community, and the subtlety, the ingenuity, the acuteness, or the astuteness of lawyers, clients and judges, lead the meaning of the statute a dance of fifty or a hundred years before it becomes settled and adjudged. And then such adjudications! -- such violent wanderings of significations! -- such felicitous conjectures of the meaning of the legislature! -- and in the meanwhile such insecurity in contracts! -- such glorious fields for litigation -- such harvests of fees and costs -- all which would have been unnecessary or uncalled for, if the sapient Solon who started the apple of discord, had been a man fitted for his sphere.

Now let us suppose that in every legislative body there were a few men who had been properly nurtured by the principles and educated in the bearing of laws -- skilled in human nature and its practical workings -- elevated to moral dignity and inspired by love of truth; let us suppose that our lawyers also were such men, and that our judges were the like: could any of the results depicted in the few last paragraphs occur? Would not the influence of such men be felt throughout all the ramifications of our laws; and would not the pursuit of law be the most ennobling of human sciences, if directed merely to the attainment of justice, rather than to the shrouding of guilt and wrong under the dubious expressions of statutes, or counterpoising the iniquity of a client by the ingenuity of his advocate?

To give a legal university the importance and influence it ought to possess, many things are requisite. Students ought not to be admitted into it until their general education is completed. They should be scholars in general knowledge ere they become students of law. They should have attended to the requisites enumerated in the former part of this essay -- and should enter the university with healthy constitutions, correct habits, good morals -- the morals of principle and not merely of circumstances, and a resolution to master the science, and for the term of their studentship to pursue it unwaveringly and uninterruptedly. Then if the means of instruction be commensurate, and the mode proper, the students of the law might become, what too often they are not -- fit and faithful trustees of the rights of the community, composers of strife, eludicators and guardians of right and equity, upright men, influential citizens, polished and intellectual scholars.

The writer's want of leisure prevents his entering at present into a full detail of his idea of what a law university should be, and this is the less important, as this essay is rather suggestive than practical. It is but a survey of the ground on which the edifice is to be erected, the architect will come afterwards. But it may be proper here to indicate the general plan and principles, to sow seed for thought -- and leave the

development and maturing for reflection and experience.
It is now time, that in the more thickly settled portion
of our country the practice of the law should be divided,
and consequently the studies at the university so
conducted that each student might apply himself
particularly to that branch of the profession which he
might intend to pursue.   Conveyancers attorneys and
solicitors, and counsellors and advocates, the divisions
that seem proper. To conveyancers the drawing all papers
relating to the transfer incumbrancing of real estate,
such as wills, deeds, mortgages, leases, settlements,
trusts, uses, powers, fines, recoveries, abstracts of
titles, and the like.   To the attorneys and solicitors,
the practical conducting of all suits, the drafting of
pleadings and proceedings, the collecting of evidence, &c.
To the counsellors, who might be again divided into
chamber counsel, and advocates at the bar would appertain
the giving of advice upon legal rights and liabilities,
upon settling or compromising matters of dispute, the
settling of the form of pleadings and proceedings, and the
attending to the trial of causes, and arguments of cases.
      It may be objected that there would be few willing to
confine themselves to the rank of attorneys and
solicitors, but that all would aspire to be counsellors.
To this we may reply both by fact and argument, that in
England where a similar division has obtained, no such
inconvenience occurs; and further, that whatever
aspirations the mind may entertain for a higher exercise
of its powers are checked and confined within their proper
sphere by the actual limitation of those powers.   And
moreover, it would be found that those persons who had
been well schooled as attorneys and solicitors, would make
the most accomplished and ready, and therefore most
successful counsellors, when they should choose to change
their vocation.
      As to the professorships in our university, there
should be one of logic -- that the student's mind might be
trained to close and severe reasoning, induction,
analysis, comparison, the detection of sophistry the most
subtle, and of fallacy the most plausible.   There should
be one of rhetoric -- that he might deliver a deduction of
reason or a statement of facts in a clear and lucid order,
in language choice yet determinate -- nervous yet
graceful.   A professorship of moral philosophy would be
requisite, for by a contemplation of their duties as
members of God's great family, the students would discover
that the streams of the law descend from the great
fountains of truth and justice, and thus incline to
cherish in their hearts a deeper attachment for their
profession, and a deeper desire to pursue it uprightly and
honorably.   A professorship of history and historical
jurisprudence would be essentially necessary, for the
"thing that hath been is the thing that shall be," and
experience is the great corrective of legislation.   This
presents a wide field; for the law keeps progress with
science, trade, commerce, and all other branches of human
pursuits; it has often changed the destiny of a people --
and to trace out the effect of laws on morals and of

morals on laws would be curious and instructive. International law, so essential to the admiralty pleader, so necessary in the pursuit of rights springing from treaties, or of rights delayed or destroyed by war, would demand a separate professor. So, too, of the civil law, which as regards all matters of contract (a comprehensive title in the law) is "fons et principium," and which though not law here by enactment, involves and elucidates the principles of justice so fully, so clearly, so justly, and has furnished so large a portion of the basis of the law of all civilized nations, that he who is well skilled in its teachings, shall have little else of general principles to learn.   In regard to constitutional and municipal laws, and their various divisions, statute law and common law, and the subdivisions, maritime, commercial, criminal &c. no remarks are necessary.   They are too essential to be overlooked by any.

Although I have now fulfilled all I proposed to embrace in this essay -- fulfilled not according to the importance of the subject, but to the extent of my leisure and present object, I cannot forbear citing one or two passages from Lord Coke's English Prefaces to the second and third parts of his Reports.

"Now for the degrees of the law," says he, "as there be in the universities of Cambridge and Oxford divers degrees, as general sophisters, bachelors, masters, doctors, of whom be chosen men for eminent and judicial places, both in the church and ecclesiastical courts; so in the profession of the law, there are mootemen, (which are those that argue readers cases in houses of chancery, both in terms and grand vacations.)   Of mootemen, after eight years study or thereabouts, are chosen utter barristers; of these are chosen readers in inns of chancery: Of utter barristers, after they have been of that degree twelve years at least, are chosen benchers, or ancients; of which one, that is of the puisne sort, reads yearly in summer vacation, and is called a single reader; and one of the ancients that had formerly read, reads in Lent vacation, and is called a double reader, and commonly it is between his first and second reading, about nine or ten years.   And out of those the king makes choice of his attorney, and solicitor general, &c.   And of these readers, are sergeants elected by the king, and are, by the king's writ, called ad statum & gradum serrieatis ad legem.* * *"

"For the young student, which most commonly cometh from one of the universities, for his entrance or beginning were first instituted, and erected eight houses of chancery, to learn there the elements of the law. * * * Each of the houses of court consists of readers above twenty; of utter barristers above thrice so many; of young gentlemen about the number of eight or nine-score, who there spend their time in study of law, and in commendable exercises fit for gentlemen: the judges of the law and sergeants being commonly above the number of twenty, are equally distinguished into two higher and more eminent houses, called Sergeant's Inn: all these are not far distant one from another, and all together do make the most famous university for profession of law only, or of any one human science that is in the world, and advanceth itself above all others, <u>quantum iter viburna cupressus</u>. In which houses of court and chancery, the readings and other exercises of the Laws therein continually used, are most excellent and behoofful for attaining to a knowledge of the law. And of these things this taste shall suffice, for they would require, if they should be treated of, a treatise by itself."

Thus far runs the eulogy of our quaint old master in regard to the English University; and thus would his humble student close his remarks by an eulogy on the law itself.

The spirit of true law is all equity and justice. In a government based on true principles, the law is the sole sovereign of the nation. It watches over its subjects in their business, in their recreation, and their sleep. It guards their fortunes, their lives, and their honors. In the broad noonday and the dark midnight it ministers to their security. It accompanies them to the altar and the festal board. It watches over the ship of the merchant, though a thousand leagues intervene; over the seed of the husbandman abandoned for a season to the earth; over the studies of the student, the labors of the mechanic, the opinions of every man. None are high enough to offend it with impunity, none so low that it scorns to protect them. It is throned with the king, and sits in the seat of the republican magistrate; but it also hovers over the couch of the lowly, and stands sentinel at the prison scrupulously preserving to the felon whatever rights he has not forfeited. The light of the law illumes the palace and the hovel, and surrounds the cradle and the bier. The strength of the law laughs fortresses to scorn, and spurns the intrenchments of iniquity. The power of the law crushes the power of men, and strips wealth of every unrighteous immunity. It is the thread of Daedalus to guide us through the labyrinths of cunning. It is the spear of Ithuriel to detect falsehood and deceit. It is the faith of the martyr to shield us from the fires of persecution. It is the good man's reliance -- the wicked one's dread -- the bulwark of piety -- the upholder of morality -- the guardian of right -- the distributor of justice. Its power is irresistible -- its dominion indisputable. It is above us and around us, and within us -- we cannot fly from its protection -- we cannot avert its vengeance.

Such is the law in its essence; such it should be in its enactments; such, too, it would be, if none aspired to its administration but those with pure hearts, enlarged views and cultivated minds.

– 14 –

Anon.

The Legal Profession (1839)

It is undoubtedly a matter of congratulation to those of our readers who are aware of the fact, that the newspaper press in many parts of the country has manifested unusual solicitude of late, for the welfare, spiritual and temporal, of the legal profession. We have before us a pile of newspapers of no inconsiderable dimensions, which contain so much entertaining matter on this subject, that we are tempted to make some choice extracts for the benefit of those, who are not so fortunate as ourselves.

One of these periodicals, published, we believe, some two hundred miles eastward from the spot "whereon we stand," and which rejoices in the high sounding title of the Northern Statesman, appeared on the 18th ultimo, with a leader of some three columns, in which is discussed, as appears by the title - The Profession of Law - its tendency and importance - The Practioners of Law, their influence in society and their means of doing good or evil.

After some remarks, showing what lawyers may be, and sometimes are, the editor proceeds, -

"It is, however, too often the case, that young men, either of their own volition, or that of friends, enter the profession, without the principles, talents or industry, suited to its multifarious duties. They enter the office of some lawyer, who is postmaster, or holds some other office, the duties of which require one third of the student's time - another third is devoted to pleasure and politics - leaving the remaining third to study - and after thus wearing away three years of the prime of life in his pretended studies, he is admitted to practice with less actual knowledge of the science and philosophy of law, than a smart, industrious man would acquire in six months, assiduous study - or than many of our best informed merchants really possess. During a few of the first terms of the court after his admission, he will be very attentive to his business, in the preparing and arranging of his causes - in closing them up, and paying over the proceeds to his clients. But in too many instances he soon settles down into a kind of listless indifference, passes most of his time sauntering about town, or dabbling in politics; seldom shaking the dust from his stinted and forsaken library, and by neglecting his business - permitting his clients' demands to remain in his office unattended to - their causes to hang along year after year, either undecided in court, or in uncollected executions in the hands of some long-winded office-seeking sheriff - until the costs and interest have equalled the principal - the defendants have died or moved away - the client's patience becomes worn out, and his spirits broken down, between injustice and oppression on the one hand, and professional imbecility and neglect on the other. The natural and legitimate result of all this, is, the lawyer's loss of confidence, business and resources - and to his clients and the community, a disgust of legal proceedings, and a contempt for the practitioners of law. Such counsellors do great dishonor to themselves and to their profession - and set a bad example to their juniors. They appear to think, in the language of a celebrated modern politician, that "It is glory enough to have served under such a chief," as the name of 'A LAWYER.' The Poet, however, says that,

        Honor and shame from no condition rise,
        Act well your part, there all the honor lies.'"

Our editor then comes to the second branch of his subject, to wit: - "Unprincipled Lawyers;" and here his indignation knows no bounds. He accuses this class of men of all manner of evil things, such as exciting suspicion and ill will between neighbors - forging and altering notes - buying up notes - commencing vexatious suits, and he asserts, that "they will trustee clergymen, deacons, and others, without the least cause or reason whatever." They will also bring fictitious suits in order to "give themselves and opportunity to 'cut a great swath,' in a distant court, and appear more like a disgusting 'bag of wind,' than any thing that is just, liberal and manly."
    By way of "Conclusion," it is objected, among other things, that lawyers are inordinately selfish, because they sometimes refuse to labor unless they are sure of receiving an adequate compensation. In such cases, it is said, "they almost invariably say, that they 'don't do any such business,' and that the applicant 'better go to squire such a one, he does all such business.' Now to our mind these transactions show a cold-hearted selfishness, and a disposition to monopolize all the pleasant and lucrative portions of legal business, and at the same time to shove upon other shoulders all the unprofitable, laborious, and vexatious portions which often subject a magistrate to great inconvenience, and to the lasting ill-will of the complainant or accused, which are highly unjust and disreputable to the profession - and deserve the severe animadversion of the public. In a country like this, every man ought to be willing to take the bitter with the sweet of his calling, and to bear his just proportion of the public burthen."

So much from the <u>Northern Statesman</u>.   Throwing this aside, we next come to some score of newspapers, English and American, in which is copied a paragraph, attributed to Lord Brougham, and which is generally followed by editorial remarks, more or less interesting, but for which, we are sorry to say, we have no room at present. The editor of the Boston Mercantile Journal, in particular, expresses himself sorely puzzled to know how a lawyer can act conscientiously in taking up with any and every case, and his difficulty is increased by his Lordship's <u>dictum</u>, which is as follows.

An advocate, by the sacred duty which he owes his client, knows in the discharge of his duty but one person in the world - that client, and none other.   To save the client by all expedient means, to protect that client at all hazards and costs to all others, and among those others to himself, is the highest and most unquestioned of his duties; and he must not regard the alarm, the suffering, the torment, the destruction, which he may bring upon any other.   Nay, separating even the duties of a patriot from those of an advocate, and casting them, if need be, to the wind, he must go on, reckless of the consequences, if his fate should unhappily be to involve his country in confusion for his client's protection."

The Boston Morning Post, thinks that the following rule for advocates, laid down by Mr. Parker, the Commonwealth's Attorney for Suffolk, in a recent trial, are "rather more plausible than Brougham's."

It is the duty of of a counsel not to be a witness against his client, either by work or act.   Even if his client should tell him that he is guilty, he is bound not to take it to be so; for his client, through ignorance of the law, or the nature of the evidence requisite to warrant a conviction, may suppose himself guilty, under the law, when in fact he is not, although he may have committed some great moral wrong.   Even if the counsel be morally convinced of his client's guilt, he is not to act on that presumption, for he, in his turn, may also be mistaken in the weight of the testimony, and some principle of law involved in the case.   Every man is to be tried by the law and the evidence, and the court and the jury are the only judges, known to the law, upon those two points, and not the counsel.   His duty is simply to strive to lead the jury to a verdict of 'not guilty;' and if he misleads them to such a verdict, the responsibility is theirs, and not his.

If professional gentlemen, after reading the foregoing, are not enlightened as to their characters and duties, it would seem to be their own fault.   It might be deemed presumption in us to offer any remarks upon a subject, which, as popular orators love to say, has been so completely exhausted, and we shall conclude with an extract from Mr. Montagu's eloquent and interesting Essays and Selections, lately published. (1)   Previous to this, however, we will extract the concluding sentence of a most excellent Introductory Lecture, delivered at the present term in the Law School in Cambridge, by the Royall Professor of Law.

"Here, for the present," says Mr. Greenleaf, "I leave the subject; but not without first calling your attention to a plain duty of the advocate, resulting from this view of the common law. I mean the duty of never misleading the judge, but rather of always endeavoring to assist him in coming to a right decision. He should present the case of his client, fairly, fully, and truly, before the court; but should remember, that, in the judgment to be pronounced upon it, the whole community are concerned, as it may form a precedent for future decisions; and that, however interesting a victory may be to his client, the public, as well as himself, have a far deeper interest in the triumphs of the law."

Mr. Montagu's essay, which is after the manner of Fuller, is upon THE DUTIES OF A BARRISTER, and he considers the subject in two points of view. 1. <u>His duty to himself</u>, and 2. <u>His duty to his client</u>. We have room for the first part only, at present, which is as follows:

1. <u>Before he engages as a student he considers his health</u>. - Whether it will enable him to encounter sedentary confinement, continued intensity of thought, the exertion of long and frequent pleadings in hot and crowded courts, and the anxiety ever attendant upon the consciousness of being intrusted with the happiness of others.

2. <u>He considers the fitness of his intellect for the profession of the law</u>. - Whether he has invention to find, judgment to examine, memory to retain, and a prompt and ready delivery. He is mindful that a man may be miserable in the study of the law, who might have been serviceable to his country at the spade or the plough.

3. <u>He duty considers his motive for engaging in the profession</u>. - It is not fame, but honorable fame; it is not wealth, but wealth worthily obtained; it is not power, but power gained fairly and exercised virtuously; it is not the promising and pleasing thoughts of litigious terms, fat contentions, and flowing fees, but the heavenly contemplation of justice and equity. His plans will not be subservient to considerations of rewards, estate, or title; these will not have precedence in his thoughts, to govern his actions, but follow in the train of his duty.

He enters his profession mindful of the admonition of Lord Bacon. "We enter into a desire of knowledge, sometimes from a natural curiosity and inquisitive appetite; sometimes to entertain our minds with variety and delight; sometimes for ornament and reputation; sometimes to enable us to victory of wit and contradiction; and most times for lucre and profession; and seldom sincerely to give a true account of our gift of reason, for the benefit and use of man: - as if there were sought in knowledge a couch whereupon to rest a searching and restless spirit; or a terrace for a wandering and variable mind to walk up and down, with a fair prospect; or a tower of state for a proud mind to raise itself upon;

----

1. Essays and Selections, by BASIL MONTAGU, Esq. London. Pickering, 1837.

or a fort or commanding ground for strife and contention;
or a shop for profit or sale; and not a rich store-house-
for the glory of the Creator, and the relief of man's
estate."

    4. <u>He is careful of his health.</u> - He remembers that
the foundation of happiness in life, and of excellence in
his profession, is health of body. His rule, therefore,
is <u>ne quid nimis.</u> He is warned by an eminent lawyer, who
said, "I will not set up more than three nights together
for any attorney in London." He remembers the admonition
of Lord Bacon "Although the world to a christian
travelling to the land of promise be, as it were, a
wilderness, yet that our shoes and vestments be less worn
away while we soujourn in the wilderness, is to be
esteemed a gift coming from divine goodness."

    5. <u>He is industrious.</u> - "I have two tutors," said
King Edward to Cardan," Dilligence and Moderation." So
our student will be on his guard against indolence,
fickleness, irresolution, immoderate love of amusements,
and against every ensnaring and dissipated habit; the
natural effect of an overgrown, wealthy, and luxurious
capital.

    6. <u>He stores his mind with the general principles of
law.</u> - The tutor to King Edward the Sixth said, "I will
not debase my royal pupil's mind with the nauseated and
low crumbs of a pedant, but will ennoble it with the free
and high maxims of a statesman. The stream must fail which
is not supplied from the fountain."

    Lord Bacon, in his entrance on Philosophy, says:
"And because the partitions of sciences are not like
several lines that meet in one angle; but rather like
branches of trees, that meet in one stem; which stem, for
some dimensions and space, is entire and continued, before
it break and part itself into arms and boughs; therefore
the nature of the subject requires, before we pursue the
parts of the former distribution, to erect and constitute
<u>one universal science</u>, which may be the mother of the
rest; and that in the progress of sciences, a portion, as
it were, of the common highway may be kept, before we come
where the ways part and divide themselves." And in his
entrance on the science of Human Nature, he thus speaks to
the same effect:

    "Now let us come to that knowledge, whereunto the
ancient oracle directeth us, which is the knowledge of
ourselves: which deserves the more accurate handling by
how much it toucheth us more nearly. This knowledge is to
man the end and term of knowledges; but of nature herself,
a portion only. And generally let this be a rule, that
all divisions of knowledges be so accepted and applied, as
that they may rather design forth and distinguish sciences
into parts, then cut and pull them assunder into pieces;
that so the continuance and entireness of knowledges may
ever be preserved. For the contrary practice hath made
particular sciences to become barren, shallow and
erroneous, while they have not been nourished, maintained,
and rectified, from the common fountain and nursery. So
we see Cicero, the orator, complained of Socrates, and his
school, that he was the first that separated philosophy

and rhetoric; whereupon rhetoric became a verbal and empty art."

Our lawyer, therefore, studies the law of laws - "justitia universalis," - the fixed poles which, however the law may turn, stand immovable.

7. <u>He studies human nature</u>. - He remembers the maxim, "Poor diriger les mouvemens de la poupee humaine, il faudroit connoitre les fils qui la meuvent." He remembers the words of Lord Bolingbroke: "I might instance in other professions, the obligations men lie under of applying themselves to certain parts of history, and I can hardly forbear doing it in that of the law; in its nature the noblest and most beneficial to mankind, in its abuse and abasement the most sordid and the most pernicious. A lawyer now is nothing more, I speak of ninetynine in a hundred at least, to use some of Tully's words, '<u>nisi leguleius quidum cautus, et acutus, praeco actionum, cantor formularum, auceps syllabarum</u>:' but there have been lawyers that were orators, philosophers, historians: there have been Bacons and Clarendons. There will be none such any more, till in some better age, true ambition of the love of fame prevails over avarice; and till men find leisure and encouragement to prepare themselves for the exercise of this profession, by climing up the 'vantage ground' of science, instead of grovelling all their lives below, in a mean but gainful application to all the little arts of chicane. Till this happen, the profession of the law will scarce deserve to be ranked among the learned professions: and whenever it happens, one of the 'vantage grounds to which men must climb, is metaphysical, and the other historical knowledge. They must pry into the secret recesses of the human heart, and become well acquainted with the whole moral world, that they may discover the abstract reason of all laws: and they must trace the laws of particular states, especially of their own, from the first rough sketches to the more perfect draughts; from the first causes or occasions that produced them, through all the effects, good and bad, that they produced."

8. <u>He studies the law which he is to practise, with due consideration of the law of other countries</u>, - and, that he may practise with effect, he is not unmindful that eloquence is to knowledge what colors are to a picture.

9. <u>He is careful of his times of recreation</u>. - He never forgets the old adage, "Tell me your amusements, and I will tell you what you are." He knows that the employment of times of recreation, is susceptible of every variety between the lowest sensuality and the highest intellectual pleasures: between the "silence of Archimedes in his study, and the stillness of a sow at her wash;" between the drunken revelries of Jefferies, and the calm occupations of Sir Matthew Hale.

When a magistrate," says the author of the life of the Chancellor de l'Hopital, "returned to his family, he had little temptation to stir again from home. His library was necessarily his sole resource; his book his only company. To this austere and retired life, we owe the Chancellor de l'Hopital, the President de Thou,

Pasquier, Loisel, the Pithous, and many other ornaments of the magistracy."

    10. When his name is up, his industry is not down. – He does not think it virtuous to plead by his credit, but by his study. This is the duty of the good advocate; but commonly physicians, like beer, are best when old; and lawyers, like bread, when they are new and young.

    11. He relies with confidence upon the power of industry and integrity. – He does not doubt the truth of the old maxim, "Good counsellors never lack clients." Long suffering is a lesson in every part of our lives; in no part of life is it more necessary than in the arduous profession of the law: the greatest men it has produced, have, at some period of their professional lives, been ready to faint at their long and apparently fruitless journey; and they would have fainted, had they not been supported by a confidence in the power of character and industry by which they broke out into light and glory at the last, exhibiting the splendid spectacle of great talents long exercised by difficulties, and high principles never tainted by any of the arts by which men sometimes become basely rich or dishonorably great.

    I have heard it observed," (says Dugald Stewart,) "that those men who have risen to the greatest eminence in the profession of the law, have been in general, such as had at first an aversion to the study. The reason probably is, that to a mind fond of general principles, every study must be at first disgusting which presents to it a chaos of facts apparently unconnected with each other. But this love of arrangement, if united with persevering industry, will at last conquer every difficulty; will introduce order into what seemed on a superficial view a mass of confusion, and reduce the dry and uninteresting detail of positive statutes into a system comparatively luminous and beautiful.

    "The observation, I believe, may be made more general, and may be applied to every science in which there is a great multiplicity of facts to be remembered. A man destitute of genuis may, with little effort, treasure up in his memory a number of particulars in chemistry or natural history, which he refers to no principle, and from which he deduces no conclusion; and from which his facility in acquiring this stock of information, may flatter himself with the belief that he possesses a natural taste for these branches of knowledge. But they who are really destined to extend the boundaries of science, when they first enter on new pursuits, feel their attention distracted, and their memory overloaded with facts among which they can trace no relation, and are sometimes apt to despair entirely of their future progress. In due time, however, their superiority appears, and arises in part from that very dissatisfaction which they at first experienced, and which does not cease to stimulate their inquiries, till they are enabled to trace, amidst a chaos of apparently unconnected materials, that simplicity and beauty which always characterise the operations of nature."

12. <u>He considers how his profession may tend to warp his mind</u>. - He remembers the words of Lord Bacon: "We every one of us have our particular den or cavern, which refracts and corrupts the light of nature; either because every one has his respective temper, education, acquaintance, course of reading and authorities, or from the difference of impressions, as they happen in a mind prejudiced or prepossessed, or in one that is calm and equal." As the divine, from constantly teaching, is in danger of being wise in his own conceit; the physician, from constantly seeing man in an abject state, of losing his reverence for human nature; the soldier, of being ignorant, debauched, and extravagant; so against the idols of lawyers, moral and mental, our lawyer will be upon his guard.

13. <u>He is cautious that the indiscriminate defense of right and wrong does not lower his high sentiments, or weaken his love of truth</u>. - In the constitution of our courts, and of the courts in most, if not in all civilized countries, it has been deemed expedient, for the purpose of eliciting the truth, both of law and of fact, that the judge should hear the opposite statements of experienced men, who in a public assembly, may be more able than the suitors, to do justice to the causes upon which their interests depend. A more efficacious mode to disentangle difficulty, to expose falsehood, and discover truth, was, perhaps, never devised. It prevents the influence of passions, by which truth may be disturbed, and calls in aid every intellectual power by which justice may be advanced.

But however useful this practice may be for the protection of public justice, it is not without danger to the individual by whom it is practised. It has a tendency, unless counteracted by strength of mind and vigilance, to generate in him indifference to truth on other occasions; and, when the distant prospect appears desirable, to induce him not to be very scrupulous as to the foulness of the road over which he has to pass to attain it.

14. <u>He does not suffer himself to be inflated by imaginary importance</u>. --Instrusted with the management of other men's concerns; consulted and paid for advice; living in private, or within the circle of men engaged in similar pursuits, have a tendency to inflate us into self-importance. Our lawyer, therefore, does not forget the hint given by Chaucer, in his description of the sergeant-at-law -

No where so busy a man as he then was,
And yet he seemed busier than he was."

Nor does he forget the lawyer in the novel, who was "hurried, and driven, and torn out of his life; and repeated many times, that if he could cut himself into four quarters, he knew how to dispose of every one."

When Cromwell was displeased with Sir Matthew Hale, for having dismissed a packed jury, and, on his return from the circuit, said to him in anger. "You are not fit to be a judge;" all the answer Sir Matthew made was, "It was very true."

15.   His general caution is increased, if he has risen from an obscure situation. - It is said that mud walls are apt to swell when the sun shines upon them.   A quack struts with more solemnity than a regular physician.

16.   He is cautious not to form an improper estimate of the nature of power: not to mistake what is of the earth, earthly, for what is of the Lord from heaven. - Power to do good is the true and lawful end of aspiring; for good thoughts, though God accepts them, yet towards men, are little better than good dreams, except they be put in act; and that cannot be, without power and place as the 'vantage and commanding ground.   Merit and good works, are the end of man's motion; and conscience of the same is the accomplishment of man's rest; for if a man be partaker of God's theatre, he shall likewise be partaker of God's rest.   Et conversus Deus, ut aspiceret opera, quae fecerunt manus suae, vidit quod omnia essent bona nimis, and then the Sabbath.

17.   He is vigilant that his profession may not contract his mind. - True vision depends upon the power of contracting and dilating the sight.   The elephant can rend a tree and pick up a pin.   Our lawyer, therefore, remembers that, if law has a tendency to quicken and invigorate the understanding, it may not have the same tendency to open and liberalize the mind.

18.   He does not imagine that knowledge is centered in the law. - It is said, of a lawyer of the present times, that he used to boast of his never have opened any book but a law-book.   The poor man is dead, and will be forgotten with his own pleadings.

Another celebrated lawyer, after a high encomium upon the powers displayed by Bacon in his reading on the statute of uses, says, - "What might we not have expected from the hands of such a master, if his vast mind had not so embraced within its compass the whole field of science, as very much to detract from professional studies."

In the presentation-copy, by Bacon, to Sir Edward coke, of the "Novum Organum," there is written by the hand of Sir Edward, under the handwriting of Bacon -

Auctori consilium,
Instaurare paras, veterum documenta sophisma
Instaura leges, justitiam que prius.

And, over the device of the ship passing between Hercules' pillars -

It deserveth not to be read in schools,
But to be freighted in the ship of fools

19.   He is cautious that his habitual attention to forms does not make him lose sight of the substance. - In the year 1765, the important question with respect to the propriety of taxing America, as she was not represented in parliament, was discussed in the house of commons; the debate occupied the attention of the house for three

successive days, and called forth all the ability of the
country. At the conclusion of the third debate, at three
o'clock in the morning, Sir James Marriott, judge of the
court of admiralty, rose. He said, "That upon this
important subject he could not conscientiously give a
silent vote, particularly as the question appeared to him,
during the whole argument, to have been entirely mistaken;
the question discussed had been with reference to the
propriety of taxing America, as she was not represented;
whereas in truth and in fact, America was represented: for
upon our first landing in America, we took possession of
that continent as part and parcel of the manor of East
Greenwich, in the county of Kent."

Upon hearing the witches in Macbeth say, "We are
doing a deed without a name," a lawyer in the pit
exclaimed, "Then it's not worth a farthing."

The lawyer in Hogarth insists that an elector who had
lost his arm cannot be sworn, as he cannot take the book
in his hand.

20. He does not suppose all his fellow-creatures
under the influence of bad passions, from the effects of
vice which he daily witnesses. - Against this tendency
Lord Bacon warns all students; saying, "As the fable goes
of the basilisk, that if he see a man first, the man dies;
but if a man see him first, the basilisk dies; so it is
with frauds, impostures, and evil arts; if a man discover
them first, they lose their power of doing hurt: but if
they prevent, then, and not otherwise, they endanger."

The young physician, when he attends the hospitals,
sees the ruins of human nature; bodies laid up in heaps
like the bones of a destroyed town, hominus precarii
spiritus et male haerentis, men whose souls seem borrowed,
and kept there by art and the force of medicine; whose
miseries are so great, that few people have charity or
humanity enough to visit them; or visiting them, do more
than pity, in civility, or with a transient prayer; but
the young man does not, from these sad scenes, infer that
all man are thus afflicted. So, our lawyer does not, in
his haste, say that all men are liars. When he assists in
punishing the robbers, he does not forget the good
Samaritan, who bound up the wounds of the way-faring man;
and, when called upon to censure the sins of the woman at
the feast, he is not unmindful that she may have her store
of precious ointment to pour on the feet of her master.

Christian Roselius
Introductory Lecture (1854)

GENTLEMEN,

The science of jurisprudence, on the study of which it is our purpose to enter, is so vast and comprehensive in its range, and often, apparently, so contradictory and complicated in its details, that, in order to avoid perplexity and confusion, we must, at the outset, take a survey of its general elements and prominent outlines. It is proper, therefore, in this introductory lecture, that I should spread before you, as it were, a map of the extensive field we are about to explore. By pursuing this course we shall discover at the very threshold of our inquiries that law is not composed of a collection of heterogeneous and incongruous rules, dictated by the mere whim and caprice of the law-maker; but that it is a beautiful and harmonious system, devised by the profoundest wisdom and foresight, to regulate the multifarious rights and obligations arising from the complex relations of social life, and founded, substantially, on the great and immutable principles of right and wrong, inscribed on the mind of man by the hand of his Creator.

Law, in the most enlarged sense of the word, is that power which exercises its dominion over every thing, both in the physical and moral world. Hence law is divided into physical and moral law. The former is despotic and resistless in its sway;--it governs and controls every thing in the material world, from the smallest particle of dust we tread upon, to the countless heavenly bodies that roll in illimitable space. The latter consists of rules of action for the guidance of man alone, as a moral, intellectual and accountable being. Although the precepts of the moral law are obligatory and binding, yet man as a free agent, has the power of violating them, at his risk and peril. All nature is bound down to implicit obedience to irresistible laws, except man, who is left free to violate the special law given to him for the government of his moral conduct, because he acts under a fearful responsibility both here and hereafter. This moral or natural law is coeval with the human race, for history does not inform us of the existence of any people without it.

In the progress of society these original principles, or that primeval perception of right and wrong, were developed to meet the exigencies and wants of the people, and hence was gradually formed that regular system of laws, consisting of those rules of civil conduct, an observance of which can be enforced by the power of the State, and which is known by the appellation of the municipal or civil law.

But, although the municipal law is, in the main, founded on, and a mere development of the natural law, it must not be supposed that the one is invariably conformable to the other. Motives of public policy, based on an infinite variety of considerations, frequently induce a people to adopt anomalous laws conflicting with those of nature.

A preposterous pretension has been advanced by certain deluded individuals, in connection with the Act of Congress, generally known as the Fugitive Slave Bill. They attempt to justify their resistance to that law on the ground that its enactments are contrary to what they are pleased to style an anterior or a higher law of paramount obligation, by which they mean, I presume, the natural law. The absurdity of such a position must strike the mind of every reflecting person at once. Let me ask what would become of government, nay, of society itself, if every individual could interpose his own crude notions of natural right between the law of the land and its execution? Take, for instance, the opinion expressed by one of the leaders of the French Socialists, Prudhon, that all property is theft! Here we have a person of education and intelligence seriously asserting, in the councils of one of the most enlightened nations of the earth, that the whole frame-work of the social system is founded on iniquity and crime; that all laws enacted for the protection of property are contrary to natural right, and should, therefore, be disregarded; that the thief, the burglar, the robber, the forger, and the swindler, instead of being punished, should be held up to an admiring world as models of virtue and philanthropy! Yet what is the difference in principle between the tissue of ridiculous nonsense of the French Socialist in relation to property, and the unintelligible jargon of the Northern fanatic about anterior or higher laws of paramount obligation in extenuation of his murder and treason? Both are equally shocking to common sense and common honesty.

Municipal law is the expression of the whole public mind or conscience, either through the legislative department of the Government, or by the acquiescence of the people themselves, manifested by their acts and conduct. In the enactment of the written law the Legislature is the organ of the public mind; the unwritten or customary law is silently adopted by the people themselves. The law-making power is so inherent in the people that it never has been and never can be entirely wrested from them even by the most unmitigated despotism;

for although the despot may, to a great extent, pervert and misrepresent the public mind, he cannot completely silence it.   The history of every nation is replete with evidence of this important fact.   When, for instance, under the regal government of Rome, arbitrary and oppressive laws were enacted, repugnant to the public sentiment, the kingly power was subverted, and the Tarquins had to fly for their lives!   When, at a subsequent period, the patricians oppressed their fellow-citizens by unequal and tyrannical laws, the plebeians rose upon their oppressors; resumed the legislative power; abolished those odious distinctions which the usurpation of the aristocracy had introduced into the laws; and adopted that series of profoundly wise plebiscita, which still challenge our admiration!   Even in her decrepitude and decay, when Rome was ruled with an irod rod, by the worst monsters that ever disgraced humanity, the public mind found an organ in the writings of those great lawyers, whose opinions obtained the force of law, and who built up and perfected that admirable system of jurisprudence which, by the common consent of mankind, has been honored by the appellation of written reason.   Papinian was the contemporary of Caracalla, and was assassinated by that wretch, whose hands were still reeking with the blood of his brother, Geta, for refusing to write an apology for fratricide.   The public mind of France was energetically, though silently, expressed in its customary laws, during the worst and most absolute tyranny of its kings.   An attempt to stifle the expression of the public mind in its laws, brought Charles the First to the block.   The same effort on the part of the narrow-minded and obstinate George the III, lost him the brightest jewel in his crown.   Within our own recollection, we have witnessed two crowned heads driven into exile by the same cause; Charles X and Louis Phillipe of France.   These examples might be multiplied to an almost indefinite extent; but a sufficient number has been cited to fortify my position.   Hence, it is obvious that no individual, or set of individuals, can be permitted to oppose their conscientious scruples to the binding force and effect of a law, without a total subversion of the whole social fabric.

All the serious concerns of life resolve themselves into rights, duties and obligations.   It is the province of the law to define and protect legal rights, and to enforce the performance of legal obligations.   The terms legal rights and obligations, are used in contra-distinction to that class of imperfect rights and duties defined and inculcated by the precepts of morality and religion, but of which jurisprudence takes no notice. To illustrate,--when I inure your property, I incur the obligation to pay the damages which I have caused, and you acquire the right of invoking the aid of the law to compel me to indemnify you; this is an example of a perfect or legal obligation and corresponding right.   On the other hand, am under the moral obligation to be grateful to my benefactor; but if I neglect the discharge of that duty, the law cannot coerce me to perform it; and, therefore, the obligation is an imperfect one.

Legal rights are either personal or general: they are called personal when they have their origin in a corresponding legal obligation, incurred by a particular person, or a designated number of persons; they are general when they exist independently of any personal obligation, and equally against the whole world. Thus, when I borrow a thousand dollars of you, your right to the return of the money arises out of the obligation which I have contracted in borrowing the money; consequently it is a personal right to be exercised against me alone. But if I am the owner of a house, you are bound to respect my right of property, and to refrain from doing any act that would be an infringement of my right of property, but this duty or obligation is not limited to you--it is equally binding on all other persons; my right is therefore general--<u>erga omnes</u>.

There are four essential elements in every legal right:

Firstly. A person to whom the right belongs, or who is its active subject.

Secondly. A thing which forms the <u>object</u> of the right, or with reference to which it exists.

Thirdly. A fact or event which is the source or origin of the right, or by the happening or occurence of which the right is created; and

Fourthly. A judicial action to protect and enforce the right, and to make it efficacious and perfect.

The law regards persons only with reference to their capability of acquiring legal rights, and of incurring perfect obligations, if, therefore, a human being should be destitute of this capacity, he would not be considered as a legal person. Hence every natural individual is not necessarily a person, for without the capacity of acquiring rights, and of incurring obligations, there is no legal person. This definition of what constitutes a legal person, of course, applies only to the civil law terminology, for in the eye of the criminal law, every human being is viewed as a person, without any regard to the capacity of acquiring rights or incurring obligations.

Persons are either natural, or merely juridicial or fictitious. Juridical persons are created by the law; they are legal abstractions, to which the law communicates the capacity of acquiring rights, and of incurring obligations: to this class of persons, belong all private corporations, such as banking institutions, insurance companies, as well as the <u>hereditas jacens</u>, and many others.

Natural persons are divided into free persons and slaves, though the latter are legal persons only in a limited sense of the term, inasmuch as a slave can incur no civil obligation, nor acquire any legal right, with the exception of the right to his freedom.

Free persons are sub-divided into those who are in the untrammeled exercise of all their legal rights, without the intervention of any other person or authority; and those, who, on account of age, infirmity of body or mind, or in consequence of the relation in which they stand towards another person, are not permitted to exercise their legal rights, without the co-operation, and in some cases exclusively through the agency of another person. The latter class embraces minors, married women, and those who have been interdicted.

A distinction is likewise made between such slaves as have acquired the right of becoming free at a future time, or on the happening of a condition, and such as are slaves for life: the former are denominated statu liberi, and can acquire rights prospectively, to be exercised when they become free, and which in the mean time, are preserved for them by a curator appointed for that purpose: they can also claim the protection of the law, if an attempt should be made to remove them out of the State, with the intention of depriving them of their anticipated freedom.

After having formed a general idea of persons, we must next direct our attention to the consideration of things, as the second essential element of rights. The law generally treats of things only so far as they are the object of legal rights, or as we observed before, a person is the subject, and a thing the object of every legal right.

In the same manner as persons are characterised by their capacity to have or acquire rights, so the term things comprehends whatever is susceptible of forming the object of a right. Here again the law exercises its power of abstraction, and creates things that have no existence in the physical world--things that are neither visible nor tangible.

In this last category of things, are included all obligations by which property is not directly and immediately transferred from one person to another. These things are called incorporeal: hence the great division of things into corporeal and incorporeal.

Whatever can be used to satisfy the wants, or conduce to the convenience or pleasure of man, is susceptible of forming the object of legal rights.

We have thus glanced at the subject and the object of legal rights; and this brings us to the inquiry how they are formed? It is evidently not sufficient that there should be a person with capability of becoming the subject, and a thing to be the object of a legal right, in order to create or give existence to that right: something else is requisite to call it into being; and that is the happening of some fact or event, which is the immediate or proximate cause of its creation or formation. Thus rights are acquired by contracts, quasi-contracts; offences, quasi-offences; inheritance, &c.

These are all facts, acts or events, without the occurrence or happening of some one of which no legal right can have any existence. It is therefore evident that there can be no question of law unconnected with a certain state of facts. When we say that a case presents nothing but a question of law, we only assume that the facts on which the law is to operate are admitted, or not disputed; for otherwise the assertion would involve a

contradiction in terms.   It is absolutely impossible that
any practical question of law can arise without a
particular state of facts.

This distinction between questions of fact and
questions of law seems to be plain enough, and no lawyer
who has studied his profession as a science, and whose
knowledge of law is not exclusively empirical, can ever
experience any difficulty in perceiving the obvious line
of demarcation which divides them.   Yet the Supreme Court
of this State, in the case of Cammayer, decided in the May
term of 1853, confounded a clear, unmixed question of law
with a supposed question of fact.   The case was briefly
this;--Cammayer was prosecuted for the crime of larceny;
after the evidence for the prosecution was closed, his
counsel requested the District Court to charge the jury,
that the facts proved, did not, in law, constitute the
offence charged, i.e., larceny.   This charge the judge
refused to give, and a bill of exceptions was taken to the
refusal, in which all the facts proved were incorporated,
and certified by the District Judge.   On the trial of the
appeal, the only question to be decided by the appellate
tribunal was, whether the state of facts set forth in the
bill of exceptions, constituted the crime of larceny?
That this was a dry, naked question of law, unmixed with
any question of fact, would seem to be too evident to
admit of controversy.   Nevertheless, the Court determined
the contrary, and observed--"the jurisdiction of this
Court extends to criminal cases on questions of law alone,
and if we were to examine the facts on which the jury
found the verdict, in order to determine whether the Court
below erred in refusing to charge them that those facts
did not constitute larceny, we would certainly be
exceeding our jurisdiction, and deciding on the facts as
well as the law."   That so glaring an error should have
been committed by that high and enlightened tribunal is
passing strange; that it should have been pertinaciously
persisted in, when pointed out, is to be deplored.

But the concurrence of these three elements of
rights, (person, thing, fact,) would frequently be of
little avail if there were no means of effectually
protecting and enforcing rights; this fourth and last
element, which gives force and efficacy to the others, is
called action.   Legal action in its enlarged sense, means
the exercise of the power of government through the
judiciary for the vindication of rights and the
enforcement of obligations.   The definition of actions of
the Roman law has been copied almost literally into our
Code--"actio autem nihil aliud est, quam jus persequendi
in judicio, quod sibi debetur."   An action is the right
given to every person to claim judicially what is due or
belongs to him.

The history of actions, their various forms and
ceremonies, in the gradual growth and development of the
Roman jurisprudence, is one of the most curious and
interesting subjects of inquiry.   We shall have occasion
to discuss this important matter in the progress of our
labors; for it must be our constant endeavor to unite the
theory with the practice of the law.

All rights may be classed under one of four divisions:

First--Family rights.
Secondly--Rights in and to things, or real rights.
Thirdly--Rights arising from obligations; and
Fourthly--Succession rights.

In the first division are included all those rights arising from the domestic relations, such as husband and wife, parent and child, master and servant &c., &c.

The second comprises titles and claims of every description to things, whether moveable or immoveable.

Every obligation necessarily produces a co-relative right; hence the relation between debtor and creditor. This class of rights constitutes the third division.

The last category of rights embraces those which have their origin in inheritance, either legal or testamentary.

Three of the elements of rights which have been thus faintly and imperfectly sketched, are developed and expounded in the Civil Code, and the last is treated of in the Code of Practice.

The Civil Code is divided into three books; each of which is devoted to one of these elements. The first, treats of persons; the second, of things and of the different modifications of the various rights that may be acquired in things; and the third, of the different modes of acquiring the property of things, or as we have stated, of facts, acts or events, by which rights are created.

Such is the simple and logical arrangement of the great heads of jurisprudence, adopted in the Code of Louisiana, which is the repository of the modern Civil Law, as contra-distinguished from the Common Law which prevails in England, and in the other States of the Union.

A sort of rivalry seems to be carried on between ignorance, prejudice, and arrogance, for the purpose of depreciating the merits of the Civil Law. Indeed, most of these critics, while indulging in their unbounded and extravagant admiration of the Common Law, at the expense of the Civil Law, dogmatically deny that the latter has any merit at all. Lord Mansfield, whose great legal mind and splendid judicial labors contributed so largely to give something like shape and symmetry to the uncouth and rude materials of the Common Law, was vilified and abused by Junius, for resorting for instruction, to that pure fountain of legal science--the Roman Civil Law. Among other charges which he urges against him, he says--

"I see through your whole life, one uniform plan to enlarge the power of the crown, at the expense of the liberty of the subject. To this object, your thoughts, words and actions, have been constantly directed. In contempt or ignorance of the Common Law of England, you have made it your study to introduce into the Court, where you preside, maxims of jurisprudence unknown to Englishmen. The Roman Code, the law of nations, and the opinions of foreign civilians, are your perpetual theme; but whoever heard you mention Magna Charta or the Bill of Rights with approbation or respect? By such treacherous arts the noble simplicity and free spirit of our Saxon laws were first corrupted. The Norman conquest was not complete until Norman lawyers had introduced their laws, and reduced slavery to a system. This one leading principle directs your interpretation of the law, and accounts for your treatment of juries, &c."

The attractive and classic style of Junius has given currency to this groundless aspersion; but instead of being confined to the individual against whom it was directed, it has become fashionable to apply it to the Civil Law itself.--Now, Junius, with all his varied attainments, was either profoundly ignorant of the Roman private Civil Law, or he was guilty of wilful misrepresentation.

Those who object to the Civil Law on the ground of its repugnancy to the principles of liberty, are evidently unacquainted both with its letter and spirit: the public or constitutional law of the Roman Empire, and the Senatus-Consulta, as well as the imperial rescripts in relation to the organization and administration of the Government, have never been in force in Louisiana, nor in any other country since the destruction of the imperial government: what has been preserved and handed down to our time, is the private law; and I should like, to be informed in what respect, that part of the Roman jurisprudence is hostile to the spirit of liberty. The admirers of the Common Law are justly proud of that feature in it which secures the trial by jury; but some of them do not seem to know the fact, that the trial by jury formed a constituent part of the Roman Law, three centuries before Julius Caesar conquered England; and at least six centuries before the Common Law had any existence.

The term judices designates in general, says Bonjean, in his Treatise of Actions, vol. i, p. 164, § 72, the jurors to whom the Roman magistrates referred the cognizance and consideration of cases, and to whom was delegated the power to decide them. During the period of the Republic, these juries were known by the names of judex unus, arbiter, recuperatores, centumviri. As the modern expression judge conveys the idea of a public functionary, we shall without hesitation use the word jury: there exists besides a striking analogy between the judices and our juries, for Cicero himself designates them by the appellation of judices jurati. De Lege Agraria. In the Common Law they are called juratores, an expression of doubtful Latinity.

As our juries, the Roman judices were simple citizens, called upon to decide cases submitted to them; their functions were essentially temporary and limited to the case in which they were empanneled and sworn: when the suit was decided, they disappeared and were lost in the crowd of their fellow-citizens. They generally only decided questions of fact, though in some instances they were authorised to judge of the law as well as of the facts. The Praetor or other magistrate laid down the rules of law applicable to the case, and directed the judices or jury to condemn or absolve the defendant in accordance to the state of facts which they might ascertain to exist. Our judges charge the jury as to the law, after the evidence has been closed and the argument heard: the Roman Praetor informed them of the law, before the inquiry into the facts was commenced. With us the judge presides at the trial of the case and decides incidental questions of evidence, &c., but is not present at their deliberations, nor has he even a casting vote in the rendition of the verdict: under the Roman Law, after the judge had stated the law to the jury in writing, he did not participate any further in the trial of the case, but left its decision entirely to them. Gaius 4.46, 104, 105, 109, 141. Now, let me ask, what is the substantial difference between the trial by jury according to the Roman Law, and that of the Common Law? Is it the cabalistic number twelve? But, how do we know what was the precise number of the recuperatores or of the centumviri, empanneled and sworn in each case? We know that the judex unus and the arbiter, acted generally alone, though the twelve tables speak of tres arbitri; but we have no reliable information of the number of recuperatores or centum viri who acted in each suit.

Another of the boasted excellencies of the Common Law is the habeas corpus, which was recognized by statute in the reign of Charles the Second; but this invaluable protection for the personal liberty of the citizen is derived from the Civil Law, and was familiar to the Romans, more than two thousand years before its permanent introduction into England, by the name of Interdictum de libero homine exhibendo, which was a laconic and stern command addressed by the judge to any individual who detained a free man, to produce him instantly, "Quem libero dolo malo retines, exhibeas." This writ was granted forthwith on the application of any person. D. 43, 29. 1 et seq.

No doubt the few fragments of the Twelve Tables that have come down to us, are stamped with the harsh features of their aristocratic origin. But the jus honorarium, established by the Praetors and other magistrates, as well as the Customary Law, which was built up principally by the writings and opinions of the prudentes, are founded essentially on natural equity and justice, and breathe the most liberal spirit of equal rights in every line.

The Roman jurists always assume that the law-making power belongs to the people: the Emperors attempted to justify its exercise on the ridiculous pretext, that the people had voluntarily surrendered the legislative power and vested it in them by the lex regia, by which they pretended the imperium was conferred on them. But this is a contemptible fiction invented by the flatterers of power.

It is an historical fact, that the CIvil Law prevailed in England, and was publicly taught in her Universities, for more than three centuries. Nay, all the leading principles of the Common Law, except those relative to the titles and rights to real estate, can be traced to the Roman Law. The complex and artificial rules concerning titles and conveyances of immoveable property, had their origin and foundation in the feudal system,

which has never been considered a distinguished for its
tendency to promote or encourage the spirit of liberty.

But why was the Civil Law superseded in England? Why
were its professors silenced in the University of Paris?
Why was its quotation prohibited under the penalty of
death in Spain? Surely not because its principles were
repugnant to liberty; for when these events took place,
England, France and Spain, were equally groaning under
oppression and despotism.

Comparative anatomy is one of the most important
branches of study to the physician; and I have often
thought that the study of comparative jurisprudence would
be of equal usefulness to the lawyer and the legislator.
It seems to me that every Law School should have a chair
to teach this special branch of legal learning.

Far be it from me, however, to say a single word in
disparagement of the Common Law. It is, in the eloquent
language of Judge Story, the law of liberty, and the
watchful and inflexible guardian of private property and
public rights. In a practicable point of view it is
almost as necessary for a Louisiana lawyer to be
acquainted with the doctrines of the Common Law as to be
familiar with those of the Civil Code. Questions
depending for their solution on the former arise daily in
our tribunals, and the practitioner, who is a mere
civilian, is only half qualified for the efficient
exercise of his profession.

Eclecticism has been adopted in many of the other
departments of the moral sciences; why should the student
of jurisprudence not avail himself of its advantages? Why
should we not profit by the illustrious example of a
Story, a Kent, a Mansfield, and a host of others? It is
time that the narrow-minded and petty bickerings about the
superiority of one system over the other should cease;
sectarianism can find no permanent place in the science of
jurisprudence.

It would be a great mistake to suppose that a
knowledge of the Civil Law can be acquired by the study of
the Louisiana Civil Code alone. Let us, therefore, direct
our attention for a moment to the consideration of the
best sources of information to assist us in our proposed
course of study.

When Louisiana was colonized by the French, in the
early part of the eighteenth century, the custom of Paris
was introduced as the Private Law of the colonists. At
that period the northern part of the kingdom of France was
governed by a great variety of customs, none of which had
been reduced to writing before the year 1510, during the
reign of Louis XII. In the south of France, the written
law (droit écrit,) or Roman Law prevailed. But even in
those provinces of the kingdom, governed by customs, the
Roman jurisprudence was resorted to as a subsidiary system
to afford rules for the decision of cases not provided for
by the customary law. About 1769, after the cession of
the province of Louisiana by France to Spain, the Spanish
Law was introduced by the celebrated Don Alexander
O'Reilly. That system of laws is substantially identical
in its leading general principles with the Roman Law as

found in the compilations of Justinian. The Spanish Law
was collected shortly after the dawn of the revival of
learning into a number of Codes of different degrees of
merit.   By far the most perfect and complete of these
Codes is that compiled under the auspices of Alphonso el
Sabio, the Learned, known as the Siete Partidas, published
in 1263, but which was not authoritatively promulgated as
the law of the land until 1348, in the reign of Alphonso
XI.

Alphonso the Wise succeeded his father Ferdinand III,
on the throne of Leon and Castille, in the year 1252. He
was entangled in a contest with Rodolphe of Hapsburg, for
the German Empire, in which enterprise he failed.   But
during his competition for the imperial crown, and
consequent absence from his kingdom, the Moors invaded his
territories, and to add to his misfortunes, he was
dethroned by his own son Sanchez. He died broken hearted
at Seville, in 1282.

Mr. Schmidt, in his excellent Historical Outlines of
the Laws of Spain, justly observes, that "this Code is one
of the most remarkable monuments of legislation of the
middle ages, and which the Spaniards regard with the
highest veneration, and as a model both of style, method
and precept." It still continues to govern Spain, Mexico,
and the whole of South America. But it cannot be denied
that Alphonso borrowed nearly all that is really valuable,
at the present day, in his collection, from the Roman Law.
Many of its provisions bear the distinct impress of the
age in which they were written, and refer to matters which
are entirely foreign to a Code of Laws.

Although the Roman Law, as has been observed, was the
original source whence nearly all the really and
permanently important portions of the Spanish Law was
extracted, yet instead of gratefully acknowledging their
obligation, it has been asserted by some writers, that the
Spanish law-makers had the egregious folly to prohibit
their judges and lawyers, on pain of death, to quote or
refer as authority to the fountain of their legislation.
I have not been able to find, in the law containing the
prohibition, the dreadful penalty for its violation. But,
be this as it may, the absurdity of the prohibition
defeated the object which it was intended to
accomplish--for the fear of death itself could not deter
the Spanish jurists from availing themselves of the
accumulated wisdom of ages.   Every effort to quench by
force or fear the intellectual light which the human mind
has once made its own, has been alike unsuccessful. When
Galileo was released from the dungeons of the Inquisition
because he had retracted his alleged heresy, he whispered
to his friends who met him at the prison door--"But the
earth turns notwithstanding."

To the general student, the Siete Partidas are highly
interesting, as evincing the early development and
perfection of the Spanish language. The ordinary Spanish
scholar experiences no difficulty in understanding the
phraseology and diction of Alphonso the Wise, written in
the middle of the thirteenth century. Few persons indeed

can boast of being able to read with facility the English, French or Italian authors of the same period.

In 1808, a meagre and incomplete digest of the existing laws was published by the territorial government of Louisiana, which is known by the name of the Code of 1808, or the "Old Code." Notwithstanding this work, however, the Spanish Law continued in full force, in every particular, not differently provided for by positive legislative enactments. For the purpose of enabling the citizens generally to acquire a knowledge of these laws, the legislature passed an act on the 3d March, 1819, authorizing the printing and publication, at the expense of the State, of an English translation of that portion of Las Siete Partidas, which was considered as having still the force of law in Louisiana. This translation was executed by Louis Moreau Lislet and Henry Carleton, both gentlemen of the New Orleans Bar, of respectable legal attainments: it was published in 1820, and is known as "Moreau and Carleton's Partidas." Though on the whole a tolerably faithful translation, it is not safe to place implicit confidence in its version, without comparing it with the original.

On the 14th of March, 1822, the Legislature passed a resolution, appointing three distinguished lawyers, namely, Edward Livingston, Louis Moreau Lislet, and Peter Derbigny, to suggest and propose additions and amendments to the Code of 1808, and report the same to the General Assembly. The jurists thus appointed presented the result of their labor in the incredibly short period of one year; for their report was printed in 1823: the Legislature displayed equal zeal and diligence, in the discussion and adoption of nearly all the additions and amendments as proposed, during the Session of 1824. On the 12th April of that year, an act was passed to "provide for the printing and promulgation of the amendments made to the Civil Code of the State of Louisiana." It became the law of the State on the 20th June, 1825. This extraordinary precipitancy, is, no doubt, the cause of many serious defects which are to be found in the work. One of the most serious of these defects is the imperfect and frequently incorrect translation into English of those articles which have been copied form the Napoleon Code: indeed the whole English text of the Code ought to be re-written. The Louisiana Code has, in a great measure, been transcribed from the Civil Code of France: it contains, however, many of the peculiar features of the Spanish Law. By the 3521st article of this Code, it is provided that—

"From and after the promulgation of this Code, the Spanish, Roman and French Laws, which were in force in this State, when Louisiana was ceded to the United States, and the acts of the Legislative Council, of the Legislature of the territory of Orleans, and of the Legislature of the State of Louisiana, be, and are hereby repealed in every case, for which it has been specially provided in this Code, and that they shall not be invoked as laws, even under the pretence that their provisions are not contrary or repugnant to those of this Code."

So that the Roman, Spanish and French laws, still remained in force, as to all cases not specially provided for in the Louisiana Code. But in 1828, the Legislature passed an act expressly repealing those laws. It provides, that all the Civil Laws which were in force before the promulgation of the Civil Code, lately promulgated, be and are hereby abrogated, except so much of title tenth of the old Civil Code as is embraced in its third chapter, which treats of the dissolution of communities or corporations. Sessions Acts of 1828, p. 160.

Notwithstanding the general and sweeping character of this repealing act, the Supreme Court decided in the cases of Reynolds vs. Swain, et al. 13 L.R. 198. Waters vs. Petrovic & Blanchard, 19 L.R. 591, that for the purpose of expounding legal principles and developing the doctrines of jurisprudence, the writings of the Roman and Spanish jurists might be consulted as safe guides, and their authority was entitled to respect.

From this imperfect sketch of the legal history of the country, it is evident that the principal foundation of the laws of this State, in civil matters is, the Roman Law: indeed, there are but few principles enunciated in the Code, the origin of which cannot be traced to the Roman jurists. Hence it has always been conceded by all intelligent members of the profession, that the study of the Roman Law, in connection with our own Code, is indispensably necessary for a thorough understanding of the laws of Louisiana.

Besides, there are other advantages to be derived from the study of the writings of the Roman lawyers: in them alone do we meet with that admirable union of theory and practice; that concise yet clear exposition of principles, forcibly illustrated by their application to striking cases, for which we look in vain in the works of other writers.

Troplong, one of the greatest jurists and most philosophic minds of the age, observes, in speaking of the comparative excellence of the Roman Law and the Civil Code: --

"Ulpian, Gaius, Papinian, and their compeers, will always stand at the head of the science of their excellent logic and their profound views. Their comprehensive decisions, the firmness of their judgment, the delicacy and sagacity of their perception, the analytical power of their minds, elevate them above all of whom I have any knowledge: and there is not perhaps in the Code a single article which can be compared, for precision, for force, and for beauty of style, with the innumerable fragments which Tribonian has extracted from their writings. Nor can we too highly appreciate their efforts to give predominance in the Roman Law, to those enlarged, generous and liberal views which have their origin in natural equity, to which the Constitution of Rome was so long inaccessible. But that which they could only attempt, the Code has fully realized. The Code, by a movement more active and more rapid, has gone beyond the progressive impulse which they originated. To them belongs the

artistic perfection -- to the Code, the philosophic
perfection; and it is the latter, which most concerns the
citizen. Between the law which they have handed down to
us, and that which is embraced in the Civil Code, there is
all the difference which exists between Paganism and
Christianity -- between stoicism and Christian morality."
     In the course of study which we propose to pursue, it
is intended to combine, as far as possible, the
dogmatical, the exegetical and the historical methods of
teaching, for it is of equal importance to be acquainted
with the text of the law, to understand its meaning and
philosophy, and to know its origin and the modifications
which it has undergone.
     We shall therefore assiduously and diligently study
the Code, in connection with the Roman, the Spanish, and
the French Laws; we shall endeavor to ascertain the reason
and intention of the law, and show its practical
application to the concerns of life; and we shall trace as
succinctly and clearly as possible the sources and
development of the great principles of law.
     In the execution of this plan, much assistance will
be derived from the jurisprudence of the State, as settled
by the decisions of the Supreme and other Courts.
Jurisprudence, in the acceptation of the term as here
used, consists in the concurrent and uniform exposition
and application of the law by Courts of Justice; it
exhibits, as it were, the whole vast and complicated
machinery of the law in actual operation; and it has not
been inaptly styled the living law. But while we
acknowledge the great importance of this branch of legal
learning, we must take heed not to lose sight of
principles, in following the easy and beaten track of
precedent. A mere case lawyer is like a third rate
player, who repeats the words of others, without troubling
himself whether he is uttering sense or nonsense. A well
considered and well written judicial opinion, resting on
sound and clearly developed legal principles, is a more
efficacious method of communicating legal knowledge than
any other that can be devised. But such is not always the
character of the decisions of Courts of Justice: judges
sometimes unwittingly indulge in freaks of fancy, or
paradoxical propensities, to the utter disregard of the
plainest principles of law; and then, their decisions,
instead of being safe guides are deceitful but solemn
delusions, leading the confiding mind into error and
confusion. The decisions of Courts should, therefore, be
always studied in subordination to sound doctrine and
correct principles.
     Little or no advantage can be derived from the study
of any work on the Roman law written in the English
language. We have not even a translation of the Pandects;
the English version of the Institutes is inaccurate and
imperfect. Strahan's translations of Domat's Civil Law in
its Natural Order, is a work of great merit, though I
cannot but think that the praise bestowed on it by
D'Aguesseau is exaggerated. I would recommend it to your
careful perusal as one of the best introductions to the
study of the Civil Law. A new edition has lately been

published of this work under the editorship of Professor Cushing of Harvard University. It is neatly printed, but it has lost much of its value by the omission of the texts of the Roman Law, which are interspersed in the original work as well as in the translation as published by Strahan. Editors frequently take great liberties with the productions which they edit, both in the way of omission and addition; but it is a custom more honored in the breach than the observance.

At a more advanced stage of his course, the student cannot select a safer guide than Pothier, who was one of the first authors by whom jurisprudence was popularized, and who has had the glory of furnishing a large portion of the materials for the Napoleon Code.

The best Commentaries on that Code, and at the same time on our own, are those of Toullier, Troplong, Marcadé and Duranton, all in the French language.

One of the best Commentators on the Spanish Law is Gregorio Lopez, whose views and opinions have always commanded great respect. He has written in Latin, and elucidates the Spanish Law, by constantly referring to the Roman jurisprudence.

The German legal literature has been enriched, during the last half century, by some of the greatest productions on the modern Civil Law, to be met with in any language. Savigny, Hugo, Glück, and others, have conferred imperishable glory on their language and country, by their works on the Roman Law.

Nor ought he who is desirous of acquiring eminence at the Bar, neglect to invigorate his mind, by the study of the great writers of the sixteenth century, such as Cujacius, Donellus, Duaremus, &c.

I trust, gentlemen, that it is not necessary to urge any thing further, to satisfy you, that the study of jurisprudence is not so dry and uninteresting, as is generally imagined by those who are unacquainted with the subject. How can the study of that science be tedious or irksome, which embraces almost the whole circle of human knowledge?

"Jurisprudentia est divinarum atque humanarum rerum notitia, justi atque injusti scientia." Jurisprudence is the knowledge of things divine and human; the science of what is just and unjust.

But where is the mind it may be asked, of sufficient grasp and power to master this universal science? Candor compels us to confess that no such mind has ever existed, and in all probability never will exist. Excellence in the science of jurisprudence is only relative; no man ever was a perfect master of it. Human life is too short -- the powers of the human mind are too weak, to acquire a thorough knowledge of every thing a lawyer ought to know. The studies requisite to secure a respectable standing in the ranks of the legal profession, are long and difficult; the exertions of him whose aim is loftier, must be proportionably greater. I would recommend to your careful consideration and faithful observance, the following general rules: --

1. Permanent success in the profession of law cannot be hoped for without serious and persevering study and application. The aspirant to eminence in our profession should never forget that Themis is a jealous mistress, who will not permit her votaries to worship at any other shrine. He must also bear in mind, that the course of study and labor to which he devotes himself, is not limited to a certain number of years, but must be persisted in, without any interruption, to the last day of his professional life. From the first moment he enters on the arena of forensic strife, he will find himself surrounded by hundreds of competitors, eager to outstrip him in the race; while those who have the start of him will use their utmost exertions not to be overtaken.

2. Without proper method and system in his studies, no one can obtain any proficiency in the knowledge of the law. An irregular and superficial course of reading will never make a lawyer. In the science of law, as in all others, we must commence at the beginning; make ourselves familiar with general principles; understand the reason of every rule of law, and discover the connection and harmony existing between every part of the system.

3. The reading of books and listening to lectures will be of little or no advantage, unless the student digests what he reads or listens to, by thought and reflection. The mind, like the stomach, may be surfeited by being overloaded. Many a man, and especially among members of the legal profession, has made himself absolutely stupid by too much reading. Reading, is the means; thought and reflection, the end; the former furnishes the materials on which the latter exercise themselves.

4. An indispensable requisite for the practising lawyer, is business habits. In a large commercial city, particularly, it is necessary for the practitioner at the Bar to be familiar, at least, with the manner in which commercial transactions are conducted; he ought to be acquainted with accounts, book-keeping, &c. Unless he possess this knowledge, he will frequently be at a loss to understand the case stated to him by his client, and, of course, utterly unable to argue it to the court or jury, as an advocate.

5. Ministering at the altar of justice, the moral character of the lawyer must not only be without a stain, but should be, like Caesar's wife, above suspicion. Weight of character is frequently of more advantage in the argument of a cause than the greatest power of intellect. Judge Story truly observes, "even the lips of eloquence breathe nothing but an empty voice in the halls of justice, if the ear listens with distrust or suspicion."

But the question will naturally occur to all who have made choice of this arduous profession, what probability is there of attaining an elevated rank in it? You may perhaps be discouraged by the reflection, that many are called, but few are chosen. My answer, gentlemen, to those objections is, that success depends almost exclusively on yourselves. If you resolve to become good lawyers, and use the requisite exertions to accomplish

your end, depend upon it, you cannot and will not fail.
Every thing depends on a firm, unfaltering, indomitable
will:--let the word impossible be expunged from your
vocabulary so far as your professional studies are
concerned, and your efforts will be crowned with success.
If, on the other hand, you feel a lack of that energy and
determination of which we have just spoken;--if you prefer
a life of listlessness and ease, the sooner you abandon
the idea of studying and practising law, the better: turn
your attention to some other and more congenial pursuit;
and save yourselves from the mortification of remaining
briefless lawyers all the days of your life.

In conclusion, gentlemen, I will quote the
encouraging language of Prof. Story on a similar occasion:

"Enough, has been said, perhaps, more than enough, to
satisfy the aspirant after judicial honors, that the path
is arduous and requires the vigor of a long and active
life. Let him not, however, look back in despondency upon
a survey of the labor. The triumph, if achieved, is worth
the sacrifice. If not achieved, still he will have risen
by the attempt, and will sustain a nobler rank in the
profession. If he may not rival the sagacity of
Hardwicke, the rich and lucid learning of Mansfield, the
marvellous judicial eloquence of Stowell, the close
judgment of Parsons, the comprehensive reasoning of
Marshall, and the choice attainments of Kent, yet he will,
by the contemplation and study of such models, exalt his
own sense of the dignity of the profession, and invigorate
his own intellectual powers. He will learn that there is
a generous rivalry at the Bar; and that every one there
has his proper station and fame assigned to him; and that
though one star differeth from another in glory, the light
of each may yet be distinctly traced, as it moves on,
until it is lost in that common distance, which buries all
in a common darkness."

– 16 –

Montague Bernard

Notes on the Academical Study of Law
(1868)

There is opportunity, I think, at the present moment for some short remarks on the Academical Study of Law. My general object in making them is the improvement of the study of Law in England; my particular aim is that my own University should do such service in this respect as may reasonably be expected from a University. Having during sixteen or seventeen years been in practice myself, and had pupils in my chambers, -- having been an Examiner, and for eight years a teacher, here, -- having acted for three years as one of the two Examiners in Jurisprudence for the University of London, and for a considerable time as the Examiner in Jurisprudence for the Civil Service of India, I have had some opportunities for forming the opinions which I shall venture to express.

For an advance in this way we have to look --
1. To the Inns of Court.
2. To the Universities.

THE INNS OF COURT.

I take it to be the opinion of every one who has seriously considered the subject, that more systematic preparatory study is desirable, if it can be had, for persons intending to practise at the Bar, and for the whole class who, with various aims, apply for and obtain licence to practise. Whatever, then, can reasonably be done to promote this by the authorities having control over calls to the Bar, ought to be done. The most obvious way of promoting it is to assign, among the qualifications for a call, a definite and substantial place to proof of having gone through a systematic preparatory course. The only practicable proof is the certificate of an examining body. The authorities of which I speak might obtain this proof by exacting a certificate from an examining body of their own, under their own immediate control, or by accepting the certificates of other examining bodies ascertained to be competent, or by a combination of both methods. There are reasons, I conceive, for accepting, at least in the

alternative, the certificates of independent examining
bodies.   Such preparatory study as I speak of may be
pursued elsewhere, and tested elsewhere, as well as, in
some respects better than, in London.   It may be worked
into a regular course of academical study, amongst other
studies calculated to enhance its value; it may be tested
by ordinary academical examinations, and such examinations
have considerable advantages, which I need not enumerate
here.   I may add that as regards this stage, as it may be
called, of Legal Education, it is not only a harmless
thing, but a good thing, that some freedom and variety
should be allowed in the methods of study and examination,
and that all should not be reduced to one uniform standard
under one uniform control.

     I shall not attempt to speak more precisely on this
head.   The present arrangements of the Inns of Court
respecting calls to the Bar are evidently experimental,
and not destined to be permanent.   They are a compromise
between requiring definite and very substantial
qualifications, (as is done in France and Germany,) and
requiring none at all, (as in the State of New York,) -- a
compromise so little satisifactory that it could not
possibly be sustained if public attention were seriously
directed to the subject.   But whatever form they may
hereafter take, whatever conditions may be imposed,
whatever securities exacted for professional knowledge,
and whether proof of having read in the chambers of a
practising barrister be or be not required, (as I am
inclined to think it ought,) I am earnestly desirous to
secure in future a definite value and substantial
encouragement for what I must call, wanting a better
phrase, elementary scientific study, for the elementary
study of Law in a scientific way.

SUBSTANCE OF A PREPARATORY COURSE.

I will attempt a rough enumeration of the things (not all
of them essential) which an elementary Course should, in
my view, aim at imparting to the student.
     a.   Elements of General Jurisprudence, -- i.e. some
acquaintance with the principles common to systems of Law
in general;
     b.   Some acquaintance with legal method or
arrangement, and with legal reasoning, and especially with
the application of principles to cases;
     c.   Some acquaintance with the history of Law,
especially of English Law;
     d.   Some acquaintance with the general scheme of
English Law, and with its special principles, so far as it
has special principals.   This would include the principles
of Criminal Law, and of the Law of Criminal Procedure;
     e.   The Constitutional History of England;
     f.   Elements of the Theory of Legislation, -- in
plainer words, some acquaintance with such simple
principles as can be laid down for the making of laws in
general;

g.   The principles of International Law.   What is
miscalled "Private International Law" belongs in part to
General Jurisprudence, in part to Comparative
Jurisprudence, and should be treated accordingly.   I
should wish to see Comparative Jurisprudence itself so far
taught as to warrant the setting of a paper in this
subject.   In his excursions in that immense field, the
student must of course depend much on the guidance of the
teacher.

For the first three heads of this list, Roman Law is
an instrument so useful as to be practically almost
indispensable.   It is true that English Law is not, as the
law of continental countries generally is, Roman
throughout, more or less, in both form and substance, and
that, to an English lawyer, Roman Law has and must have
far less of direct importance than it has to a French or
German lawyer: it is true also that the elementary
text-book used through-out Europe, the Institutes of
Justinian, contains a quantity of obsolete technicalities,
of details in themselves valueless to the student, and of
matter valuable only as throwing light on classical and
medieval history, and on literature; that its method is
imperfect, and its definitions often worthless, whilst
from its structure as an elementary text-book it affords
comparatively few specimens of those just and ingenious
reasonings from principles to cases which abound in the
huge and slovenly compilation called the Digest.   And yet,
with all its faults, its educational value, and the light
it throws on modern law, are such that he who knows
nothing of it can hardly be said to know even the law of
England otherwise than empirically, and must be quite
unprepared to deal with any system of law but his own.   It
needs, however, judicious teaching, and judicious
examining.

The want of good English text-books is undoubtedly
the chief difficulty of this whole branch of study.   Other
studies are not free from a like difficulty.   Among
ourselves the want is supplied, in the case of studies
long established in the place, by the process of dipping
into a large number of books under the direction of a
tutor, and by a mass of traditional teaching which varies
from one generation of tutors to another.   In the case of
Law it needs to be supplied by --

a.   Oral Teaching;
b.   Selections from time to time of books covering
particular portions of a field too large to be entirely
covered.   Such portions would be specimens, and a careful
study of them would imprint on the mind, pro tanto, the
elementary knowledge required.

There is another reason, and an important one, for
which such selections are desirable.   They combat the
tendency to get up books and subjects by rote, by means of
second-hand abstracts, and by the help of a kind of cram,
which runs always in the same groove and becomes throughly
mechanical.

The reason why we are so ill supplied with
institutional books is that we have hitherto had no
elementary scientific teaching of Law, and therefore no

demand for such books.   Another reason lies in the
undigested and unmethodical state of English Law, a matter
to which I shall have occasion to refer hereafter.   The
introduction of elementary scientific teaching would
remove the first reason, and would indirectly but
powerfully tend to remove the second.

LAW EXAMINATIONS OF THE UNIVERSITY OF LONDON.

The Examinations for the Degree of Bachelor of Laws in the
University of London are spread over three years, and
comprise the following books and subjects.
    1st Examination, -- Austin (the whole of the three
volumes); Justinian's Institutes, with Ortolan's
Commentary and Introduction in French; Maine's Ancient
Law; Constitutional History of England.   The papers in
Roman Law must include passages in Latin for translation,
one, at least, to be from the Digest.   No candidate is
allowed to pass who does not shew a competent knowledge of
Latin.
    2nd Examination (two years later), the following
subjects - Common Law, Equity, Real Property Law, Law and
Principles of Evidence; a portion of the Digest, to be
announced two years before, and the History of Roman Law
to the time of Justinian.
    For the Degree of LL.D. there is an Examination of a
higher kind, which it is unnecessary to describe here.
    This course is, in my opinion, somewhat too
ambitious, and otherwise open to criticism.   But it is
framed on an intelligible plan; and under this system of
examinations, as well as under that which it superseded
about two years ago, I have seen some very careful, able,
and intelligent work done by successful candidates.   If
such a test of preparatory study as I have spoken of were
to be exacted by the Inns of Court, the course itself and
the standard of attainment actually reached would
substantially satisfy it.   In some respects they would
more than satisfy it.
    The University of London excercises no educational
function except that of holding examinations, and
therefore, though an institution of great and increasing
public importance, it is not, strictly speaking, a
University at all.   But, exacting no residence at any
particular place, and extending its examinations over the
whole Empire, it evidently possesses the means, if it
chooses to use them, of raising its Degrees, as
certificates of attainment, to a very high standard value.
Examining is but a part of the services which a University
like Oxford or Cambridge ought to render to learning and
education.   Yet the current value of our Degrees, as
certificates of attainment, is of material importance to
us, and that importance will increase with the growing
tendency, outside the Universities, to attach weight to
examinations and to multiply their number.   Degrees, which
purport to be certificates, are more strictly scrutinized
than they were, and are likely to be more strictly
scrutinized hereafter than they are now.   It is out duty

to take care both that our Degrees are <u>bonâ</u> <u>fide</u>
certificates of attainment as well as of residence, and
that they are so arranged as to embrace, as far as
possible, all true academical studies, though it is not
our duty to bid against other examining bodies, nor to
regulate our standards by theirs.

Of the Cambridge Examinations I say nothing, because
I have no personal knowledge of them, and because I
believe that they are undergoing, or likely to undergo,
revision.

LAW EXAMINATIONS AT OXFORD.

The Law Examinations which exist at Oxford would not, in
my opinion, satisfy such a test as I have adverted to, nor
would the actual standard of attainment by any means
satisfy it. I shall not describe here the examination for
the degree of B.C.L., nor that in the Law and History
School. We know them, or have the means of knowing them.

ACADEMICAL STUDY OF LAW SUITABLE TO OXFORD.

Ought the University of Oxford to have a Law Course, and
if so, what relation should this study hold to the other
studies of the place?

The classes educated here are chiefly clergymen,
barristers, and men without a profession, of whom many
engage in politics, and many more act as magistrates or
otherwise take part in public business. A few leave us
for the Civil Service of the State, a few for commerce.
Speaking generally, we educate men whose actual
circumstances and intended pursuits in life make a
prolonged education and residence in a University town
matters of no extreme inconvenience to them or their
families. For attracting and retaining such men the two
ancient English Universities have extraordinary
advantages; and this constitutes their political
importance, which is great, but which they will gradually
lose if they fail to keep pace with the general advance of
higher education. If such a course as I have suggested be
proper for any University, it is proper, I think, for
Universities of this character, possessing these
particular advantages, and doing this particular work.

ITS RELATION TO OTHER ACADEMICAL STUDIES.

A.   It Needs Concentrated Attention.

Such a course as has been suggested above ought to occupy
a substantial portion of time, during which the student
should be able to concentrate his attention on his work.
The minds of very young men are capable of grasping legal
principles, and of understanding the methods of applying
those principles; but it is not easy work to them; it is
dry; it demands close exactness; and it has not, I think,

for any class of minds, attractions such as those which
speculative philosophy, classical literature, and natural
science present in different ways to young minds of
different types and habits. A good teacher can do much,
it is true, by careful illustration, and by giving to the
early study of Law that strong historical colour which it
ought to possess; but the difficulty will always be
considerable, and it will betray itself in the natural
tendency to escape from an effort of thought to an effort
of mere memory (in youth the readiest of our faculties,
and the most exercised by constant use,) and to neglect,
where this is possible, a rugged subject for one which is
more agreeable. In the School (as it is called) of Law
and Modern History at Oxford, this tendency is constantly
at work; and it is, inevitably perhaps, rather encouraged
than checked by the arrangements of that School, and by
the mass of historical details which a candidate for
Honours is expected to have mastered. The consequence is,
that the young men who go into that School -- men of whom
a large proportion have, as boys, been comparatively idle,
and are therefore peculiarly averse to the trouble of
thinking -- whilst they read their History with a fair
amount of attention and interest, too commonly yield to
the temptation of "cramming" their Law. The University of
London now exacts Law, and nothing but Law, from its
candidates for the degree of LL.B. during the three years
which must elapse from the passing of the matriculation
examination, (a period which may be shortened to two years
in the case of persons who are Masters of Arts of any
other University). In the two years' Course through which
the selected candidates for the Civil Service of India
have to pass, it is impossible for them to escape from
devoting a great deal of their time to Law, and that in a
prescribed order and method; but it is necessary for them
also to work simultaneously at several other subjects,
including Oriental languages, and their general standard
of attainment, though tolerably good, is certainly
inferior to what it would be if they could concentrate
their attention more.

B.   It Should Aim at a High Standard.

We ought not to shrink, if we adopt Law as a study, from
aiming at a high standard of attainment -- high, I mean,
in point of accuracy, method and intelligence, not as
regards quantity or range of knowledge. This remark
applies indeed to all University studies. The specific
service which Universities render to education consists in
keeping up a high standard of teaching and attainment; and
they act upon their own students by this means, and by
making them feel (as young men of one or two and twenty
have a right to expect to feel) that they are doing what
is really of use to them, far more than by more direct
influences - by punishments, which the men have outgrown,
by importunity of exhortation, or even by multiplying
rewards. The University, if it chooses to adopt Law, must
do so with other aims than that of merely offering a more

varied choice of occupations to indolent or undecided men,
only desirous of obtaining a Degree or an Honour at a
minimum cost of time and labour.

  C. It Should not Be Incompatible with the Pursuit of
      Other Academical Studies.

It is not to be desired that the study of Law should
preclude a man from following other studies: it is much
to be desired that other studies should not preclude men
from studying Law.
  Of the studies now pursued in the University, some
are obviously germane to Law, such as History, Ethics,
Logic. Psychology, Political Economy, the Classical
Languages, and Literature, Mathematics and Physical
Science have points of connection with it more or less
remote. Latin it demands of course, but not Latin as it
ought to be studied at a University, not Latin literature
nor philology.
  I should wish, for my part, that a man should be able
to pursue with distinction any study for which he has
aptitude and inclination, and should yet have opportunity
and inducement to study Law. There are several large and
important classes of men for whom legal study is useful;
it is not to be wished that these classes should be cut
off from the different branches of higher general
education which Universities have to offer, but rather
that they should be able to take advantage of them freely;
that they should exhibit not one uniform mental type, but
as wide a variety of types as there are lines of study
which can be pursued with advantage to the mind.
  At present, of the ablest men who come hither, a
large proportion go into the School of Literae Humaniores.
Why? Because it has the advantage of old traditional
esteem, because it commands most Fellowships and prizes,
and also because to such men it appears, and in fact is, a
natural continuation of the studies which they have
already pursued with success and distinction at school.
To these men, more than any others in the University, I
should like to offer good elementary study of Law. There
University will continue to offer, as it does now, a
higher general education, branching into several
independent lines, without direct reference to this or
that profession. If there should be change in this
respect, and we should run more into Fach-studien than
there is any immediate prospect of, one consequence would
be that Law as an academic study would acquire a larger
development than I contemplate in this paper.

  D. It Should Have an Independent Place Side By Side
      with Other Studies.

Is it desirable that a further step should be taken, that
Law should not only be disengaged from other studies, but
placed side by side with them as an independent avenue to
distinction, and to the privileges of the M.A. degree?

Yes, I think it is, and that this is necessary, if it is to be seriously adopted at all. A study which should come in only for such remnant of time and labour as men could be induced to spare for it after their substantial University work was done, and before migrating to London (as they are naturally impatient to do) or otherwise embarking in the pursuits of adult life, might possibly gain a footing here, especially if the Inns of Court would recognise our Law Degree, amongst other tests, as assisting to qualify for a call. But it could hardly, I fear, maintain a sufficiently high standard, and the footing would probably be a precarious one. In a School placed in such a position, work has a tendency to be hasty, and examiners have only too plausible excuses for being indulgent. The time consumed at the University is already too long, and a study which must necessarily be deferred until the regular Academical course was over, would be at a serious disadvantage in more respects than one. Nor can it be justly said that a course of elementary jurisprudence, strengthened by history and moral philosophy so far as these are germane to the matter, is an inferior instrument of mental training for young men from twenty to two or three and twenty than mathematics pure and applied, or than ethics and metaphysics with the histories of Greece and Rome. I have adverted before to some difficulties which might arise from the want of good text-books. But experience amply shews us how strong is the tendency of all important subjects, when once fairly recognised and in the hands of good teachers, to grow, deepen, and expand, to make larger demands for time, and compete more vigorously for attention. We see this, for example, in the case of speculative philosophy, of history ancient and modern, of chemistry, of physiology, of physics. The Germans feel it more than we do in their great schools as well as in their Universities. It constitutes, and always will constitute, the chief difficulty in the regulation of academical studies, whilst it is the natural symptom of their vitality, and the great influence which moulds them into conformity with the state of knowledge and the wants of society. It is the part of a good teacher, as of a good judge, "ampliare jurisdictionem suam," though in both cases the tendency may need some correction beyond the self-acting check which is furnished by the co-existence of a body of teachers or a number of judges.

PARTICULAR SUGGESTIONS

In suggesting exactly what I want the University to do, I have a difficulty like that which I feel in stating exactly what I want the Inns of Court to do, and for a like reason. Our whole system of studies is in an unsettled state, from circumstances peculiar to ourselves, and is also threatened with changes more extensive than we can at present foresee. Arrangements which would fit into our existing system might be thrown out of joint by an alteration in that system. The difference is that we have control over our own arrangements, and have no control over those of the Inns of Court.

1.   I have no doubt whatever that the University ought to take the simple, intelligible, reasonable, and straightforward step of making its examination for the B.C.L. degree a real test, and the degree itself a real certificate, of a man's having passed through a good elementary course of legal study.   I wish that the title of the degree were "Bachelor of Laws," instead of "Bachelor of Civil Law," but that is of minor consequence.

2.   I think this Degree should entitle the graduate to all the privileges conferred by the Bachelor's Degree in Arts, and that the examination for it should form a separate School, to preparation for which the student may, if he will, devote himself after passing the First Public Examination.

3.   I think that the subjects of examination in this School should not be settled in detail by Statute, but should be left, in part at least, to the direction of a Board of Legal Studies, which might correspond, when necessary, (through the Vice-Chancellor or otherwise,) with the Council of Legal Education in London.

4.   I should be content with such a standard that the Degree might be attainable by an intelligent man accustomed to Academical work -- accustomed, that is, to arrange and retain his knowledge, to think a little, and to profit by good instruction -- after at least a twelvemonth's steady reading.   I should hope, however, to get some higher work out of the School than a twelvemonth's reading could possibly be expected to yield, and this is a reason why (as has been explained before) I think it should be an independent School.   Candidates, however, who had not already qualified themselves for the Degree of B.A. might be required to pass, or have passed, in additional subjects cognate to Law.   Such, for instance, are Ethics and History.

5.   I should be content that the School should be what is called an Honour School, that is, one in which every man who passes is classed, and none can pass without reaching a creditable level of attainment.

I shall not attempt to define the standard nor the curriculum, the general scope of which I have tried to indicate above.   Reasonable freedom of choice within the range of the curriculum should be allowed to candidates. The student should be encouraged to use French and German books, and should be allowed the full advantage which he may gain from his knowledge of those languages.   The University of London exacts from every candidate for its LL.B. degree a knowledge of the three volumes of Ortolan in French.   It is not necessary to go so far, at least, at present.   Every candidate ought to be so far master of Law-Latin as to be able to translate correctly into English tolerably easy passages from the Digest or Code.

I do not anticipate any difficulty in finding Examiners.   On this head I have only one observation to make.   While it is certain that the expenditure of the University on examinations must increase, and must somehow be provided for, examining ought, I think, to be reckoned, more distinctly than it is now, among the duties of Professors.

HISTORY

It is a corollary of what has been said, that the subsisting connexion between Law and Modern History ought not to continue. The reasons which may make it desirable that a man should apply himself to the Academical study of Law would not necessarily or commonly lead him to the Academical study of History (with the school-boy study of it I have no concern); and it is not reasonable or convenient that to gain distinction or pass creditably in the former should be impossible without also gaining distinction or passing creditably in the latter. If the views expressed above as to the proper range and dimensions of a Law Course, as to the demand it makes for concentrated attention, as to the expediency of opening it to men of different intellectual habits and pursuits, be correct, it follows of necessity that these two lines of study cannot remain tied together as they now are. They are allied, by no means remotely; each throws frequent lights on the other; a knowledge of History, within certain limits, is helpful -- is more than helpful -- to a knowledge of Law: but to say this is very different from saying that both ought invariably to form parts of one Academical Course. Let a man, if he will, devote himself to History and Law: many, I hope, will do so. But is there any sufficient reason why he should not be able, if he prefers it, to devote himself to Mathematics and Law, or to Ancient Literature and Law?
       History is in some respects a good academical study. It accustoms men to grasp and arrange masses of facts relating to human life and conduct, to deal with facts accurately and carefully, to trace the sequence of events, to generalize cautiously but on a considerable scale. Superficially or mechanically read, it tends, I am afraid, to nourish mental habits which are just the reverse of these. But I am speaking of it as read methodically, with the help of good teaching, and under the check of examination. It affords abundant food for thought. It has the advantage of being interesting. How, in the event of such a divorce as I recommend, the School of History should be dealt with, is a question for those who have a more special interest in the subject than myself. Whether, under the superintendence of a Board of Studies or otherwise, the Course might not be varied and re-arranged from time to time, so as to embrace fields which now are hardly touched at all -- whether Oriental History should not have a more distinct and important place -- whether Political Philosophy, International Law, and Political Economy, should not be regularly included in it -- are questions which I only venture to indicate. Can even convenience be pleaded in favour of always maintaining the rude bisection into two "periods?" It is absolutely inadmissible, certainly, in regard to the Constitutional History of England.

COMPARATIVE BREVITY AND SCANTINESS OF THIS COURSE HERE
CONTEMPLATED.   REASONS FOR THIS

The Course contemplated in this paper and the time
assigned to it are undoubtedly brief and contracted, in
comparison with what is attempted in continental
countries, or even (to look nearer home) at the University
of London.   The chief omission is that of a comprehensive
study of English Law, such as a French or German advocate
is supposed to have made beforehand of the whole field of
French or German Law.   No doubt that is a large omission.
An English lawyer, for the most part, is not only ignorant
of the laws of other countries than his own; he commonly
knows little of those parts of English Law itself which
lie outside of his own line of practice.   He studies Law
as an art, not as a science; he acquires the habit of
picking up learning as he wants it, looking about for a
principle or rule when he has occasion for one, and
applying it with a mechanical dexterity and quickness
which are cultivated by use to an admirable pitch of
perfection.   The theory is, that a man learns English Law
in London whilst reading in chambers.   The fact is, that
he learns so much of English Law as he comes into contact
with whilst reading in chambers.   Now what is the reason
why English Law is not read systematically?   It is the
unsystematised, undigested state of English Law.   English
Law, so far as it has been made by judges (which is true
of the greater part of it), is generally equitable,
sensible, and justly reasoned, and shews everywhere
innumerable marks of the patient care with which it has
been hammered out by accumulated arguments and decisions.
But it is disorderly and unmethodical in the highest
degree.   No text-writer could make it orderly, even if he
were content to write for learners and not for
practitioners, as our text-writers always do.   The French
Codes, it is true, are becoming overloaded with a mass of
commentary, but it is material to observe that a mass of
commentary which is compelled to follow a symmetrical plan
never becomes absolutely unmanageable.   An immense work
like that of Demolombe, which has reached the 23rd volume
without exhausting more than half of the Code Civil, is
indeed somewhat appalling; a treatise like Larombière's
Théorie et Pratique des Obligations affords evidence of
the vast quantity of law which can be spun out of a small
number of apparently simple propositions arranged in a
Code: yet what has just been said will, I think, have
struck English lawyers who may have had occasion to look
into such books as these, and still more those who may
have glanced at good popular text-books -- the latest
edition, for example, of Zachariä's Droit Civil Français,
or institutional works like those of Delsol or Mourlon.
Now this difficulty, which has hitherto met and
disconcerted students of English Law who wished to know
something of it as a whole before embarking in practice,
presents itself in the way of those who would make English
Law a subject of Academical study.   It is not absolutely
prohibitory; something may be done in spite of it; but it
is a great difficulty.   Another obstacle of a practical

kind arises from the fact that it is the established custom in England to leave school late, and enter on the pursuits of life rather early, and to regard the Universities wholly as places for prolonging general education, in the case of those who can afford it, and carrying it to a higher level. But setting aside these difficulties, it may well, I think, be doubted, whether, in a country where all judicial proceedings are public, and so many opportunities exist of seeing the whole machinery of law, in all its departments, in action, it is really desirable in the majority of cases that a lengthened course of preliminary or scientific study should be interposed before the entrance on regular professional training. An intelligent man who goes into chambers feels at once the life and interest infused into his reading by actual contact with business. He does this at present for the most part with little or no preliminary study. I wish regular preliminary study to be the rule. I wish it to be careful and thoughtful, but not as a rule to be long.

EARLIER GENERAL INSTRUCTION

I wish in this paper to keep clear of that competition, real or supposed, between general and special instruction, about which we hear so much, especially in Universities. For the profession of Law, as for Medicine, education, when complete, naturally arranges itself into three stages, -- the stages of general education, of special scientific study, and of practical professional training. They do not distinguish themselves by precise lines; and that which from one point of view, or in reference to one profession, is special teaching, may become a part of general education from a different point of view, and for persons outside of that profession. Particular callings may require some special branch of instruction in youth, or make special claims for some one branch of general instruction. Thus modern languages are a part of general instruction, but to a physician French and German have a specific value which they have not to a lawyer, for this, if for no other reason, that medical science being of no country, a physician who is ignorant of those languages is debarred from access to a great part of the common stock of professional knowledge, -- knowledge which is exactly as applicable and valuable in London as it is in Paris and Berlin. The Medical Council have therefore reason for insisting that in the general instruction of persons who are to be physicians or surgeons, French and German shall have a recognised place. But although it may be difficult in several ways to draw with exactness the dividing lines between different stages of instruction, the divisions themselves are not unsubstantial, and it is desirable that they should be maintained and respected, -- that the young should be educated to be men before they begin to learn to be physicians, lawyers, magistrates, or legislators, and that the business of imparting general education should be distinct, and should be carried on by persons who make

this their business, and in places where those whose paths
are hereafter to diverge may get their earlier training in
mind and character together. It is to be desired that the
professions should interfere as little as possible in the
work proper to places of general instruction. But these
places can prevent such interference with their proper
work only by educating up to the mark which the
professions require. To recur to my former example, the
Medical Council ought not to examine in French and German,
nor to meddle in such examinations. These things belong
to early general instruction -- the work of boyhood and
youth. But the Medical Council may have to do so, if it
cannot be assumed that the necessary proficiency in one at
least of these languages is really acquired in places
which profess to give, and really tested in examinations
which profess to test, the early general instruction
suitable to boyhood and youth.

I assume in this paper that early general instruction
-- all the proper work of boyhood and youth -- has been
gone through and tested before the student thinks of
entering on the academical study of Law. With the earlier
examinations of the University I am at present no further
concerned than to ask that they should not be so arranged
as to carry on school-work into the time which ought to be
given to academical study. With this view it is that I
have always urged, in the interest not only of the
scientific study of Law but of other scientific studies,
that the time at which our First Public Examination can be
passed should be advanced, and that the examination itself
should undergo revision.

SUMMARY

I will sum up what has been suggested in this Paper. It
is as follows: --

1.   That among the qualifications for a call to the
Bar a definite and substantial value should be assigned to
elementary scientific study of Law.

2.   That a University Degree should be accepted as
a certificate of such study, on reasonable evidence of the
sufficiency of the examination, and the competence of the
examining body.

3.   That the general character of a Law Course
confined to elementary scientific study should be such as
has been suggested above.

4.   That the University of Oxford should institute
a Law Course.

5.   That with reference to other University
studies it should be so arranged as --
a. To allow and encourage concentrated attention, as well
as steady work, during a certain period of time.
b. To secure a reasonably high standard in respect of
accuracy, method, and intelligence.
c. To be compatible with the free pursuit -- I do not say
the simultaneous pursuit -- of other University studies on
the part of men who may desire this.
6. That, with these objects, --

a.   The Degree of B.C.L., or Bachelor of Laws, should be put on a new footing, and be conferred after a general examination in the proper subjects of an elementary Law Course.

b.   The subjects of examination should be (mainly at least) left to the superintendence of a Board of Legal Studies.

c.   The Degree should entitle the successful candidate to all the privileges conferred by that of B.A., including that of being admitted to the M.A. Degree at the usual time.

d.   The standard might be such as to enable an intelligent man, accustomed to academical work, to obtain the Degree with (at the least) a twelvemonth's steady reading. Candidates who had not qualified themselves for the B.A. Degree by passing a sufficient examination in some other School might be required to pass, or have passed, creditably in additional subjects, such as Ethics and History. The student should be encouraged to use French and German books, and should be allowed the full advantage which he may gain from a knowledge of those languages. He should be able in all cases to translate correctly into English tolerably easy passages of the Digest or Code.

7.   That the time at which the First Public Examination can be passed should be advanced, and the scheme of examination re-considered.

All Souls College,
March 5, 1868.

indispensable to a good schoolmaster, but we do not
therefore warrant that our prizemen and classmen shall be
good schoolmasters.   If any one holds our Classical
Schools cheap for not being, as of course and without
more, an _officina_ of successful teachers of the classics,
the same greatly misconceives both the function of the
university and the dignity and difficulty of the teacher's
office.   What, again, of our relation to those other arts,
eminently so called, which more visibly adorn and elevate
life?   Why have we saluted Mr. Herkomer as a colleague,
and why do we receive Dr. Joachim and Dr. Richter not only
as the welcome and familiar guests of England, but as
partakers of the honourable degrees of our ancient English
Universities?   Surely it is not that we expect to send out
into the world, from hence or from Cambridge, a certain
number of painters and musicians.   It is indifferent
whether we send out any.   The significance of our action
is a different and independent one: that the humanities
are not limited by an one form of expression.   Because
Michael Angelo and Turner not less than Homer, Bach and
Beethoven not less that Plato, had the secret that bids
the immeasurable heavens break open to their highest,
therefore we do honour, in the name of the Muses whom we
serve, to the masters and ministers of their art.   The
witness of our various activities here, of the new studies
which some regard with suspicion from within, and some
with contempt from without, is that the humanities have
their part in all science whatever; that a profession,
above all a learned profession, is not an affair of
bargain and bread-winning, but the undertaking of a high
duty to mankind.   We do not say that in our schools we can
make a man a skilled physician; but we can show him what
is the tradition inherited by the science and art of
medicine, and how intimate its connections with the whole
of man's knowledge of nature and of himself.   Neither do
we say, perhaps even less ought we to say, that we can
make a man a skilled lawyer.   But we can endeavour to
impress on him those larger and more generous notions
which, if not planted betimes, are apt to wither in the
dust of technical detail and the heat of forensic
business.   We can help him to regard law not merely as a
regulated strife, or a complex machine for securing and
administering property, but as the greatest, the most
interesting, and in one word, the most humane of the
political sciences.   We can show him how legal ideas,
legal habits of thought, oftentimes even legal
controversies of the most distinct and technical kind,
have entered into the very marrow of our political
history, and may do so again.   We can guide him to the
distinction of that which is accidental and local from
that which is permanent and universal; we can map out for
him the analogies and contrasts between our own system and
that of the Roman law, with whose descendants and
successors our Germanic law, broadly speaking, divides the
civilised world.   Most chiefly, we can help him to fix in
his mind that there are such things as general principles
of law; that the multitude of particulars in which he must
inevitably be versed as a practical students and worker

– 17 –

Frederick Pollock

Oxford Law Studies (1886)

That the profession of the law is necessary in a civilised commonwealth, and competence therein by no means to be attained without study, is matter of common knowledge. In speaking here of that study we have to consider more closely how it stands with us, not only as English citizens, but as scholars in this University. To what end is our study and teaching of law? Shall we say that we aim at producing successful lawyers? That would be a facile answer, if tenable. But it will not hold on any side. The university would justly refuse approval to it, as the world would justly refuse credit. Speaking as from the world to the University, I should feel constrained to say that such is not our competence; we could not achieve this if we would. Speaking as from the University to the world, I would say that such are not our aspirations; we would not undertake this if we could. Nay more, the undertaking is not within any resources of human teaching; it is in its own nature beyond them. Success in a profession depends, at the last, on a man's self and not on what he has received from without. All that his friends can do for him, or any teaching or training institution whatever, is to furnish him forth with such equipment that he may be ready for opportunities when they come, or for the one critical opportunity. And we cannot make even this our business to the full extent or for its own sake. We are no more called upon to make our graduates accomplished advocates or draftsmen than to make them accomplished engineers or railway directors. What really does concern us is that there is a science as well as a practice of law; a science inseparable from the practical art, or separable only at the cost of ceasing to be versed in real matter, but still a science of itself. And we shall find that in this there is nothing strange to our traditional habit, or alien from our dealing with other arts and sciences which have a practical side. If we consider the most obviously academical, and certainly not the least noble or strenuous of professions, we shall find the same distinction in force. The humanities are

are not really a chaos; and that, if he sets out with good
will and good faith, he need have no fear that the search
for a true art founded on science,   , will lead him
into the wilderness where blind and erring tribes worship
routine justified by rule of thumb, the
    denounced by Plato and by all sound philosophy.
    So much we offer to the student, and it is not a
little.   If proof be needed that the offer is no vain
boast, it shall presently be forthcoming.   But a
University has regard to the mature worker as well as to
the novice.   We shall send forth our students warned and
strengthened, as we trust, for the toil of their strictly
professional training, and prepared to fill up and enrich
with active experience the general notions they have
already formed.   For some years, perhaps for many, the
larger would will claim them; many will belong to it
irrevocably.   Yet some will return to us, meaning to
attach themselves to the science rather than the art of
their profession, but with fresh interest, wider scope of
knowledge, and a firmer grasp of intellect, derived from
contact with the living affairs of mankind.   These will
not find their pursuits uncared for.   We have here, in
well devised order and easily accessible, all the needful
appliances of legal work and research.   In one way the
apparatus of our science is simple; we share with moral as
distinguished from natural philosophers the convenience of
working mainly with books.   But the amount of books a
working lawyer must have within reach, whether his work be
for the sake of practice or of science, is beyond the
means of most private men.   Our colleague Mr. Freeman can
write a history without leaving his Somersetshire
country-house.   To write a law-book under such conditions,
a man would need an exceedingly well filled purse or a
singularly capacious and accurate memory, unless in other
respects he were more than man or considerably less than a
sound lawyer.   To say, therefore, that serious workers in
the law will find here an adequate and well-ordered law
library -- in some respects a better one than those of the
Inns of Court in London -- is to say that of which every
lawyer will perceive the importance.   I need not add that
the means to which I refer are those placed virtually at
the disposal of the University by the care and liberality
of All Souls College.   Moreover, opportunities for oral
discussion (a way of improving knowledge and clearing up
doubts which is often and justly commended by our writers
of authority) are in no wise wanting.   In All Souls we
have a centre of legal thought and work fitted to produce
results that shall be academical in the best sense, and as
far as possible from academical in the disparaging sense
of having no relation to real facts in which the word is
sometimes used.   I will be so bold as to say that we have
gone far to solve, as regards our own Faculty, the problem
which some years ago was current, even to weariness of
ears and vexation of spirit, under the name of the
Endowment of Research.
    It may be said to us, and fairly: These are your
assertions on behalf of your own speciality; these are
your professions of what the Oxford Law School can do;

such intentions may be very good, but can you produce any visible fruit whereby men may judge your work?   Now, considering the moderate number of years for which our Law School has been in existence in its present form, we think we can show fairly acceptable results.   Fifteen or twenty years ago there was hardly to be found in the English language a good elementary introduction to any part of jurisprudence.   I speak of elementary text-books, of works fitted to the apprehension of an intelligent but as yet untrained beginner.   Books were then in just repute, as they still are, which were and are invaluable repertories of learning for the trained lawyer; but such books presuppose familiarity with the very forms of speech and order of thought wherein the novice finds his difficulties.   They are meat for men.   And if elementary guidance was scanty even in the common lines of English law, there was almost a total lack of it in the region of public and constitutional law; and we shall scarcely find the law of nations to be an exception in this category, notwithstanding the bulk of its English and American literature.   In Roman law we had simply nothing deserving of serious mention.   What do we find now?   I have no mind to exaggerate our merits, but neither will I use the language of false humility because I have to speak of the work of colleagues and friends.   Mr. Poste, and more lately Mr. Moyle, have made accessible to English readers (for English students who can use German books without difficulty are still the minority) the results achieved in Roman law by the Continental scholarship of this century. We can now welcome the excellent contributions of Mr. Muirhead from Edinburgh or Mr. Roby from Cambridge without feeling that our own hands are empty.   Last of all, our colleague Dr. Grueber has for the first time, in his exhaustive monograph on the Lex Aquilia, exhibited to us in our own language the very form and method of the leading modern school of Roman law: and this, be it remembered, with direct and definite relation to our University course.   Not less are the benefactions of Professor Holland and Dr. Markby to the beginner in search of an introduction to the general principles of law.   It was Blackstone, teaching in this University, who, in the words of Bentham's frank admission, "first of all institutional writers taught Jurisprudence to speak the language of the scholar and the gentleman."   The crabbed involution of Bentham's own later manner, and the still more repulsive formlessness of his successor Austin, who could never forgive Blackstone for writing good English, deprived a later generation of these advantages.   In following the technical divisions of the law (with partial amendments, not always felicitous) Blackstone was at any rate intelligible to lawyers.   The terminology of Bentham and Austin inflicted on us a mass of new technicalities, little better in themselves, if at all, than Blackstone's, and intelligible to nobody.   Dr. Markby and Mr. Holland have delivered us from this state, and furnished us with lucid and readable expositions of the elementary (though not always easy) conceptions which underlie the detail of the law.   Passing from these generalities to our

particular system, we find ourselves indebted to the
Warden of All Souls -- and I am only repeating what I said
some years ago, before I had any standing here -- for a
model introductory text-book on a special subject of
English law.
     These results, I conceive, are somewhat. But there
is more yet; there is that which we may claim as not only
service to professional students, but direct service to
the Commonwealth. It is going, perhaps, to the verge of
what is permissible in this place to refer to the
constitutional argument lately addressed to the House of
Commons by my friend Professor Bryce, an argument which
faced the highest and most difficult questions of modern
politics. I refer to it only to say that, whether or not
we agree with its aim and conclusions, no competent person
can fail to admire in it the combination of learning and
subtilty with sincerity and highmindedness; and that
generous adversaries were to my own knowledge among the
first to bear witness to its merit. The Warden of All
Souls, however, and Mr. Dicey have been elucidating the
principles of our public law within strictly academical
bounds, and their labours belong to our Law School in the
full and proper sense. Professor Dicey's book, designed
for peaceful uses, has become an armoury for political
combatants; whether the untried weapons snatched out of it
by untrained hands are altogether safe for those who wield
them, it is for the captain and not for the armourer to
consider. Sir William Anson's exposition of the law of
Parliament has been only these few days in our hands. It
is at least an excusable ambition to hope that work of
this kind, addressing itself to all capable citizens, and
executed by persons of verified competence who are removed
from the stress and disturbing influences of active
politics, may do something to enlarge the horizon of
English political thought, and mitigate the crudeness and
bitterness of English political controversy. In no
generation of English history has the solid framework of
law and custom on which the English Constitution is built
up stood more in need of plain, definite, impartial
exhibition than it does this day. At no time has it been
fitter for us to be put in mind that the effective power
of law is not only the work but the test of a civilised
commonwealth, and that law, as a great English writer has
said, is in its nature contrary to such forces and
operations as are "violent or casual." It may be now and
again inevitable that the casual fortunes of political
strife determine resort to violent experiments for whose
consequences we have no warrant. There may be such
junctures brought about in the fates of nations, or by the
improvidence of their rulers, that good citizens must
acquiesce in desperate remedies rather than expose their
country to yet worse evils. We who believe that law, like
all other human sciences, and politics, like all other
human arts and faculties, rest at bottom on the nature of
things, and that the nature of things cannot be deceived
and will not forgive, may submit to such things if the
need for them is proved; but we will not praise them, nor
the men who have made them needful. The learning which

practical men affect to despise shall help us, at least,
to know whither we are going, and what we risk.

It is time to come back from justifying ourselves to
the world to considering, here among ourselves, how we
shall best further our work. There are some kinds of
technical study (I have already hinted) which cannot well
be undertaken here, or not so well here as elsewhere. In
what lines, then, is it wise to guide our students, having
regard both to the abundance and to the limitations of our
resources? Let us consider for this end the general forms
of an English lawyer's knowledge. They may be laid out in
a threefold division of things necessary, things useful,
and things of ornament. Some knowledge is necessary to a
lawyer, in the sense that it should be always in his mind,
and capable of being instantly called up into active
apprehension, and that a good lawyer would be ashamed of
not having it at command. Much is useful, but not in this
way necessary. A good lawyer will be glad to have the
full and actual command of as many departments as he can.
but no man can thus occupy the whole field of such a
science; and as a rule, both in practical and in
speculative work, one must choose one or two departments
for minute acquaintance, and in others be content with a
sort of index-knowledge. Outside his own special branch,
a sound lawyer will know where to look for full
information, and have a fair notion of what he may expect
to find. But it will be no shame to him not to be ready
with an off-hand answer. Then we have the matters which
are rather of delight and curiosity than of immediate
profit, and are the ornaments of professional knowledge.
Familiarity with them is the mark of the lawyer who is
learned in the eminent sense, as distinguished from him
who is merely competent. Now and again they become of
importance, even of capital importance, in practical
application: witness, for example, the masterly
historical investigation of the jurisdiction of Justices
of Assize delivered as a judgment in Fernandez's case by
Willes J. But to be thus applied, they must have been
acquired for their own sake: they cannot be "got up" like
the facts of a brief. Bearing these distinctions in mind,
it is in our power here in every one of these kinds to
start a learner on the true path. We cannot usefully
attempt to give him even so much of the details of law as
will ultimately be indispensable to him; but we can give
him a clear vision and a firm grasp of elementary
principles which, being called to mind as occasion
requires, will save him from being oppressed and confused
by the multitude of particulars. Much less can we teach
him all that is useful for a lawyer; but we can aid him to
form the scholarly habit which makes the difference in
practice between sure-handed and slovenly execution. We
cannot make him a profound jurist or an accomplished legal
historian; but we can aid him to form tastes which, after
the inevitable stress of purely technical training has
been endured and has done its work, will lead him to enjoy
the fruits of the higher learning, it may be to add to
them.

In particular, the course of our Law School -- and I
refer more especially to the course prescribed for the
Civil Law degree -- gives an opportunity, which may not
recur for years after, for imbuing the mind, at the stage
when it is just ripe for appreciation, with the classics
of English legal and political science. A student will
hardly lose sight of the larger bearings of jurisprudence
who has been grounded betimes in Hobbes, in Blackstone, in
Burke's great constitutional speeches and writings, in the
best parts of Bentham's work, and in the lines of research
opened by my predecessor in this Chair, Sir Henry Maine.
Herein I assume a genuine pursuit of knowledge. There is
no kind of sound doctrine which may not be -- and I fear I
must say, which is not -- perverted by shortsighted
learners and unscrupulous teachers, who substitute for the
pursuit of knowledge the pursuit of examinations. For
such as these their place is prepared, according as they
have desired and deserve. The Muses will deal with their
blasphemies in their own good time, showing perhaps some
mercy to the dupes, but none to the sinners against light.

Again a man may learn here better than elsewhere, and
certainly better than by perfunctory reading snatched from
the time which is none too much for his practical
training, to appreciate the Roman law as a real and living
system, different from our own but of kindred spirit, and
presenting the most instructive analogies even in detail.
It is neither possible nor desirable for an English lawyer
to know the Corpus Juris in the way that a German
professor does; and a compulsory smattering of undigested
Roman law rules and terminology is worse than worthless.
But the original authorities of the Roman system are,
compared with our own, compendious; and a moderate amount
of systematic application under proper guidance will give
a man a range of legal ideas more complete in itself and
more conducive to orderly thinking than he is likely to
get from any other form of legal study at present
practicable. In the Common Law we have outgrown
Blackstone's work, and we are not yet ready to replace it.

And this brings me to a not unimportant
consideration: that the invaluable habit of first-hand
work and constant verification can be formed and exercised
in a limited field no less than in an unlimited one, and,
for the beginner, even better so. We no longer make and
transcribe notes and extracts, with infinite manual
labour, in a huge "commonplace book," as former
generations were compelled to do by the dearth of printed
works of reference. But, since the law is a living
science, no facilities of publishing and printing can ever
perfectly keep pace with it. A student who intends to be
a lawyer cannot realise this too soon. There is no need
for him to make voluminous notes (indeed there is a great
deal of vain superstition about lecture notes); but those
he does take and use ought to be made by him for himself,
and always verified with the actual authorities at the
first opportunity. Another man's notes may be better in
themselves, but they will be worse for the learner. As
for attempts to dispense with first-hand reading and
digesting by printed summaries and other like devices,

they are absolutely to be rejected. No man ever became a
lawyer by putting his trust in such things; and if men can
pass examinations by them, so much the worse for the
examinations.   It is of course needless to say this to
scholars; I now speak of purely professional experience.
And in order to form the habit of first-hand work it is
not necessary to possess many books, or even to have
constant access to libraries. There is nothing to prevent
any student of average means from having in his own copies
of good modern editions the whole of the authentic texts
of the Roman law. If, however, the Corpus Juris appears
too formidable, the use of select parts of the Digest has
been greatly facilitated by the publications of this
University. English authorities are less manageable, but
the selections of leading cases which have been published
on both sides of the Atlantic (I may specially mention as
the latest and one of the best Mr. Finch's, on the Law of
Contracts) will go some way towards enabling the student
to practise real search and verification without so much
as leaving his own rooms. At the same time it is good to
learn, as early as may be, the use of public libraries,
catalogues, and books of reference generally. Facility in
such things may seem a small matter, but much toil may be
wasted and much precious time lost for want of it. To the
working lawyer these things are the very tools of his
trade. He depends on them for that whole region of
potential knowledge which, as I have said, must bear a
large proportion to the actual. And where can one learn
the mechanism of scholarship, general or special, better
than at Oxford?

It is somewhat old-fashioned, though there is plenty
of authority for it in our legal literature,to offer
general good advice for the student's conduct of life.
Such advice is apt to fall upon a dilemma. If you have
had the experience on which it is founded, you do not need
it; if not, you will not believe it. And after you have
forgotten the advice and the adviser, and discovered the
truth of things at your own charge, you will say to
yourself quite innocently, Why did not some one tell me
this before? Yet a few hints of warning and encouragement
may fall on kindly soil and ripen. And therefore I would
say to the student going forth into the heat of the day,
Trust your own facilities and the genius of your
University, and beware of the idols of the forum. You
will meet those who will endeavour to persuade you that it
is "unbusinesslike" to be a complete man; that you should
renounce exercises and accomplishments, abjure the liberal
arts, and burn your books of poetry. Do this, and the
tempters will shortly make you as one of themselves. You
will steadfastly regard your profession as a trade; you
will attain an intolerable mediocrity, the admiration of
crass clients, and the mark of double-edged compliments
from the Court; you will soberly carry out the rule laid
down in bitter jest by a judge who was a true scholar, of
attending to costs first, practice next, and principle
last; you will stand for Parliament, not as being minded
to serve the common weal, but as thinking it good for you
in your business; and if you are fortunate or importunate

enough, you may ultimately become some sort of an
Assistant commissioner, or a Queen's Counsel with
sufficient leisure to take an active part in the affairs
of your Inn, and prevent its library from being encumbered
with new-fangled rubbish of foreign scientific books. But
if you be true men, you will not do this; you will refuse
to fall down and worship the shoddy-robed goddess
Banausia, and you will play the greater game in which
there is none that loses, and the winning is noble. Let
go nothing that becomes a man of bodily or of mental
excellence. The day is past, I trust, when these can seem
strange words from a chair of jurisprudence. Professors
are sometimes men of flesh and blood, and professors of
special sciences are not always estranged from the
humanities. For my part, I would in no wise have the oar,
or the helm, or the ice-axe, or the rifle, unfamiliar to
your hands. I would have you learn to bear arms for the
defence of the realm, a wholesome discipline and service
of citizenship for which the Inns of Court offer every
encouragement, and for learning to be a man of your hands
with another weapon or two besides, if you be so minded.
Neither would I have you neglect the humanities. I could
wish that every one of you were not only well versed in
his English classics, but could enjoy in the originals
Homer, and Virgil, and Dante, and Rabelais, and Goethe.
He who is in these ways, all or some of them, a better man
will be never the worse lawyer. Nay more, in the long run
he will find that all good activities confirm one another,
and that his particular vocation gathers light and
strength from them all.
     And what is to be the reward of your labour, when you
have brought all your best faculties to bear upon your
chosen study? Is it that you will have more visible
success and prosperity than others who have worked with
laxer attention or with lower aims? Is it that the world
will speak better of you? Once more, that is not the
reward which science promises to you, or to any man.
These things may come to you, or they may not. If they
come, it may be sooner or later; it may be through your
own desert, or by the aid of quite extraneous causes. The
reward which I do promise you is this, that your
professional training, instead of impoverishing and
narrowing your interests, will have widened and enriched
them; that your professional ambition will be a noble and
not a mean one; that you will have a vocation and not a
drudgery; that your life will be not less but more human.
     Instead of becoming more and more enslaved to
routine, you will find in your profession an increasing
and expanding circle of contact with scholarship, with
history, with the natural sciences, with philosophy, and
with the spirit if not with the matter even of the fine
arts. Not that I wish you to foster illusions of any
kind. It would be as idle to pretend that law is
primarily or conspicuously a fine art as to pretend that
any one of the fine arts can be mastered without an
apprenticeship as long, as technical, as laborious, and at
first sight as ungenial as that of the law itself. Still
it is true that the highest kind of scientific excellence

ever has a touch of artistic genius. At least I know not
what other or better name to find for that informing light
of imaginative intellect which sets a Davy or a Faraday in
a different rank from many deserving and eminent
physicists, or in our own science a Mansfield or a Willes
from many deserving and eminent lawyers. Therefore I am
bold to say that the lawyer has not reached the height of
his vocation who does not find therein (as the
mathematician in even less promising matter) scope for a
peculiar but genuine artistic function. We are not called
upon to decide whether the discovery of the Aphrodite of
Melos or of the unique codex of Gaius were more precious
to mankind, or to choose whether Blackstone's Commentaries
would be too great a ransom for one symphony of Beethoven.
These and such like toys are for debating societies. But
this we claim for the true and accomplished lawyer, that
is, for you if you will truly follow the quest. As a
painter rests on the deep and luminous air of Turner, or
the perfect detail of a drawing of Lionardo; as ears
attuned to music are rapt with the full pulse and motion
of the orchestra that a Richter or a Lamoureux commands,
or charmed with the modulation of the solitary instrument
in the hands of a Joachim; as a swordsman watches the
flashing sweep of the sabre, or the nimbler and subtler
play of opposing foils; such joy may you find in the lucid
exposition of broad legal principles, or in the conduct of
a finely reasoned argument on their application to a
disputed point. And so shall you enter into the
fellowship of the masters and sages of our craft, and be
free of that ideal world which our greatest living painter
has conceived and realised in his master-work. I speak
not of things invisible or in the fashion of a dream; for
Mr. Watts, in his fresco that looks down on the Hall of
Lincoln's Inn, has both seen them and made them visible to
others. In that world Moses and Manu sit enthroned side
by side, guiding the dawning sense of judgment and
righteousness in the two master races of the earth; Solon
and Scaevola and Ulpian walk as familiar friends with
Blackstone and Kent, with Holt and Marshall; and the
bigotry of a Justinian and the crimes of a Bonaparte are
forgotten, because at their bidding the rough places of
the ways of justice were made plain. There you shall see
in very truth how the spark fostered in our own land by
Glanvill and Bracton waxed into a clear flame under the
care of Brian and Choke, Littleton and Fortescue, was
tended by Coke and Hale, and was made a light to shine
round the world by Holt, and Mansfield, and the Scotts,
and others whom living men remember. You shall understand
how great a heritage is the law of England, whereof we and
our brethren across the ocean are partakers, and you shall
deem treaties and covenants a feeble bond in comparison of
it; and you shall know with certain assurance that,
however arduous has been your pilgrimage, the achievement
is a full answer. So venerable, so majestic, is this
living temple of justice, this immemorial and yet freshly
growing fabric of the Common Law, that the least of us is
happy who hereafter may point to so much as one stone
thereof and say, The work of my hands is there.

– 18 –
O.W. Holmes, Jr.
The Use of Law Schools (1896)

Oration Before the Harvard Law School Association,
at Cambridge, November 5, 1886, on the
250th Anniversary of Harvard University

It is not wonderful that the graduates of the Law School of Harvard College should wish to keep alive their connection with it. About three quarters of a century ago it began with a Chief Justice of the Supreme Court of Massachusetts for its Royall Professor. A little later, one of the most illustrious judges who ever sat on the United States Supreme Bench -- Mr. Justice Story -- accepted a professorship in it created for him by Nathan Dane. And from that time to this it has had the services of great and famous lawyers; it has been the source of a large part of the most important legal literature which the country has produced; it has furnished a world-renowned model in its modes of instruction; and it has had among its students future chief justices and justices, and leaders of state bars and of the national bar too numerous for me to thrill you with the mention of their names.

It has not taught great lawyers only. Many who have won fame in other fields began their studies here. Sumner and Phillips were among the Bachelors of 1834. The orator whom we shall hear in a day or two appears in the list of 1840 alongside of William story, of the Chief Justice of this State, and of one of the Associate Justices, who is himself not less known as a soldier and as an orator than he is as a judge. Perhaps, without revealing family secrets, I may whisper that next Monday's poet also tasted our masculine diet before seeking more easily digested, if not more nutritious, food elsewhere. Enough. Of course we are proud of the Harvard Law School. Of course we love every limb of Harvard College. Of course we rejoice to manifest our brotherhood by the symbol of this Association.

I will say no more for the reasons of our coming together. But by your leave I will say a few words about the use and meaning of law schools, especially of our law school, and about its methods of instruction, as they appear to one who has had some occasion to consider them.

A law school does not undertake to teach success. That combination of tact and will which gives a man immediate prominence among his fellows comes from nature, not from instruction; and if it can be helped at all by advice, such advice is not offered here. It might be expected that I should say, by way of natural antithesis, that what a law school does undertake to teach is law. But I am not ready to say even that, without a qualification. It seems to me that nearly all the education which men can get from others is moral, not intellectual. The main part of intellectual education is not the acquisition of facts, but learning how to make facts live. Culture, in the sense of fruitless knowledge, I for one abhor. The mark of a master is, that facts which before lay scattered in an inorganic mass, when he shoots through them the magnetic current of his thought, leap into an organic order, and live and bear fruit. But you cannot make a master by teaching. He makes himself by aid of his natural gifts.

Education, other than self-education, lies mainly in the shaping of men's interests and aims. If you convince a man that another way of looking at things is more profound, another form of pleasure more subtile than that to which he has been accustomed -- if you make him really see it -- the very nature of man is such that he will desire the profounder thought and the subtiler joy. So I say the business of a law school is not sufficiently described when you merely say that it is to teach law, or to make lawyers. It is to teach law in the grand manner, and to make great lawyers.

Our country needs such teaching very much. I think we should all agree that the passion for equality has passed far beyond the political or even the social sphere. We are not only unwilling to admit that any class or society is better than that in which we move, but our customary attitude towards every one in authority of any kind is that he is only the lucky recipient of honor or salary above the average, which any average man might as well receive as he. When the effervescence of democratic negation extends its workings beyond the abolition of external distinctions of rank to spiritual things -- when the passion for equality is not content with founding social intercourse upon universal human sympathy, and a community of interests in which all may share, but attacks the lines of Nature which establish orders and degrees among the souls of men -- they are not only wrong, but ignobly wrong. Modesty and reverence are no less virtues of freemen than the democratic feeling which will submit neither to arrogance nor to servility.

To inculcate those virtues, to correct the ignoble excess of a noble feeling to which I have referred, I know of no teachers so powerful and persuasive as the little army of specialists. They carry no banners, they beat no drums; but where they are, men learn that bustle and push are not the equals of quiet genius and serene mastery. They compel others who need their help, or who are enlightened by their teaching, to obedience and respect. They set the examples themselves; for they furnish in the

intellectual world a perfect type of the union of
democracy with discipline. They bow to no one who seeks
to impose his authority by foreign aid; they hold that
science like courage is never beyond the necessity of
proof, but must always be ready to prove itself against
all challengers. But to one who has shown himself a
master, they pay the proud reverence of men who know what
valiant combat means, and who reserve the right to combat
against their leader even, if he should seem to waver in
the service of Truth, their only queen.

In the army of which I speak, the lawyers are not the
least important corps. For all lawyers are specialists.
Not in the narrow sense in which we sometimes use the word
in the profession -- of persons who confine themselves to
a particular branch of practice, such as conveyancing or
patents -- but specialists who have taken all law to be
their province; specialists because they have undertaken
to master a special branch of human knowledge -- a branch,
I may add, which is more immediately connected with all
the highest interests of man than any other which deals
with practical affairs.

Lawyers, too, were among the first specialists to be
needed and to appear in America. And I believe it would
be hard to exaggerate the goodness of their influence in
favor of sane and orderly thinking. But lawyers feel the
spirit of the times like other people. They, like others,
are forever trying to discover cheap and agreeable
substitutes for real things. I fear that the bar has done
its full share to exalt that most hateful of American
words and ideals, "smartness," as against dignity of moral
feeling and profundity of knowledge. It is from within
the bar, not from outside, that I have heard the new
gospel that learning is out of date, and that the man for
the times is no longer the thinker and the scholar, but
the smart man, unencumbered with other artillery than the
latest edition of the Digest and the latest revision of
the Statutes.

The aim of a law school should be, the aim of the
Harvard Law School has been, not to make men smart, but to
make them wise in their calling -- to start them on a road
which will lead them to the abode of the masters. A law
school should be at once the workshop and the nursery of
specialists in the sense which I have explained. It
should obtain for teachers men in each generation who are
producing the best work of that generation. Teaching
should not stop, but rather should foster, production.
The "enthusiasm of the lecture-room," the contagious
interest of companionship, should make the students
partners in their teachers' work. The ferment of genius
in its creative moment is quickly imparted. If a man is
great, he makes others believe in greatness; he makes them
incapable of mean ideals and easy self-satisfaction. His
pupils will accept no substitute for realities; but at the
same time they learn that the only coin with which
realities can be bought is life.

Our School has been such a workshop and such a
nursery as I describe. What men it has turned out I have
hinted already, and do not need to say; what works it has

produced is known to all the world.   From ardent coöperation of student and teacher have sprung Greenleaf on Evidence, and Stearns on Real Actions, and Story's epoch-making Commentaries, and Parsons on Contracts, and Washburn on Real Property; and, marking a later epoch, Langdell on Contracts and on Equity Pleading, and Ames on Bills and Notes, and Gray on Perpetuities, and I hope we soon may add Thayer on Evidence.   You will notice that these books are very different in character from one another, but you will notice also how many of them have this in common -- that they have marked and largely made an epoch.

There are plenty of men nowadays of not a hundredth part of Story's power who could write as good statements of the law as his, or better.   And when some mediocre fluent book has been printed, how often have we heard it proclaimed, "Lo, here is a greater than Story!"   But if you consider the state of legal literature when Story began to write, and from what wells of learning the discursive streams of his speech were fed, I think you will be inclined to agree with me that he has done more than any other English-speaking man in this century to make the law luminous and easy to understand.

But Story's simple philosophizing has ceased to satisfy men's minds.   I think it might be said with safety, that no man of his or of the succeeding generation could have stated the law in a form that deserved to abide, because neither his nor the succeeding generation possessed or could have possessed the historical knowledge, had made or could have made the analyses of principles, which are necessary before the cardinal doctrines of the law can be known and understood in their precise contours and in their innermost meanings.

The new work is now being done.   Under the influence of Germany, science is gradually drawing legal history into its sphere.   The facts are being scrutinized by eyes microscopic in intensity and panoramic in scope.   At the same time, under the influence of our revived interest in philosophical speculation, a thousand heads are analyzing and generalizing the rules of law and the grounds on which they stand.   The law has got to be stated over again; and I venture to say that in fifty years we shall have it in a form of which no man could have dreamed fifty years ago. And now I venture to add my hope and my belief, that, when the day comes which I predict, the Professors of the Harvard Law School will be found to have had a hand in the change not less important than that which Story has had in determining the form of the textbooks of the last half-century.

Corresponding to the change which I say is taking place, there has been another change in the mode of teaching.   How far the correspondence is conscious, I do not stop to inquire.   For whatever reason, the Professors of this School have said to themselves more definitely than ever before, We will not be contented to send forth students with nothing but a rag-bag full of general principles -- a throng of glittering generalities, like a swarm of little bodiless cherubs fluttering at the top of one of Correggio's pictures.   They have said that to make a general principle worth anything you must give it a body; you must show in what way and how far it would be applied actually in an actual system; you must show how it has gradually emerged as the felt reconciliation of concrete instances no one of which established it in terms.   Finally, you must show its historic relations to other principles, often of very different date and origin, and thus set it in the perspective without which its proportions will never be truly judged.

In pursuance of these views there have been substituted for text-books more and more, so far as practicable, those books of cases which were received at first by many with a somewhat contemptuous smile and pitying contrast of good old days, but which now, after fifteen years, bid fair to revolutionize the teaching both of this country and of England.

I pause for a moment to say what I hope it is scarcely necessary for me to say -- that in thus giving in my adhesion to the present methods of instructions I am not wanting in grateful and appreciative recollection (alas! it can be only recollection now) of the earlier teachers under whom I studied.   In my date the Dean of this School was Professor Parker, the ex-Chief Justice of New Hampshire, who I think was one of the greatest of American judges, and who showed in the chair the same qualities that had made him famous on the bench.   His associates were Parsons, almost if not quite a man of genius, and gifted with a power of impressive statement which I do not know that I have ever seen equalled; and Washburn, who taught us all to realize the meaning of the phrase which I already have quoted from Vangerow, the "enthusiasm of the lecture-room."   He did more for me than the learning of Coke and the logic of Fearne could have done without his kindly ardor.

To return, and to say a word more about the theory on which these books of cases are used.   It long has seemed to me a striking circumstance, that the ablest of the agitators for codification, Sir James Stephen, and the originator of the present mode of teaching, Mr. Langdell, start from the same premises to reach seemingly opposite conclusions.   The number of legal principles is small, says in effect Sir James Stephen, therefore codify them; the number of legal principles is small, says Mr. Langdell, therefore they may be taught through the cases which have developed and established them.   Well, I think there is much force in Sir James Stephen's argument, if you can find competent men and get them to undertake the task; and at any rate I am not now going to express an opinion that he is wrong.   But I am certain from my own experience that Mr. Langdell is right; I am certain that when your object is not to make a bouquet of the law for the public, nor to prune and graft it by legislation, but to plant its roots where they will grow, in minds devoted henceforth to that one end, there is no way to be compared to Mr. Langdell's way.   Why, look at it simply in the light of human nature.   Does not a man remember a concrete instance more vividly than a general principle?   And is

not a principle more exactly and intimately grasped as the
unexpressed major premise of the half-dozen examples which
mark its extent and its limits than it can be in any
abstract form of words? Expressed or unexpressed, is it
not better known when you have studied its embryology and
the lines of its growth than when you merely see it lying
dead before you on the printed page?

I have referred to my own experience. During the
short time that I had the honor of teaching in the School,
it fell to me, among other things, to instruct the
first-year men in Torts. With some misgivings I plunged a
class of beginners straight into Mr. Ames's collection of
cases, and we began to discuss them together in Mr.
Langdell's method. The result was better than I even
hoped it would be. After a week or two, when the first
confusing novelty was over, I found that my class examined
the questions proposed with an accuracy of view which they
never could have learned from text-books, and which often
exceeded that to be found in the text-books. I at least,
if no one else, gained a good deal from our daily
encounters.

My experience as a judge has confirmed the belief I
formed as a professor. Of course a young man cannot try
or argue a case as well as one who has had years of
experience. Most of you also would probably agree with me
that no teaching which a man receives from others at all
approaches in importance what he does for himself, and
that one who simply has been a docile pupil has got but a
very little way. But I do think that in the thoroughness
of their training, and in the systematic character of
their knowledge, the young men of the present day start
better equipped when they begin their practical experience
than it was possible for their predecessors to have been.
And although no school can boast a monopoly of promising
young men, Cambridge, of course, has its full proportion
of them at our bar; and I do think that the methods of
teaching here bear fruits in their work.

I sometimes hear a wish expressed by the impatient,
that the teaching here should be more practical. I
remember that a very wise and able man said to a friend of
mine when he was beginning his professional life, "Don't
know too much law," and I think we all can imagine cases
where the warning would be useful. But a far more useful
thing is what was said to me as a student by one no less
wise and able -- afterwards my partner and always my
friend -- when I was talking as young men do about seeing
practice, and all the other things which seemed practical
to my inexperience, "The business of a lawyer is to know
law." The professors of this Law School mean to make
their students know law. They think the most practical
teaching is that which takes their students to the bottom
of what they seek to know. They therefore mean to make
them master the common law and equity as working systems,
and think that when that is accomplished they will have no
trouble with the improvements of the last half-century. I
believe they are entirely right, not only in the end they
aim at, but in the way they take to reach that end.

Yes, this School has been, is, and I hope will be, a centre where great lawyers perfect their achievements, and from which young men, even more inspired by their example than instructed by their teaching, go forth in their turn, not to imitate what their masters have done, but to live their own lives more freely for the ferment imparted to them here. The men trained in this School may not always be the most knowing in the ways of getting on. The noblest of them must often feel that they are committed to lives of proud dependence -- the dependence of men who command no factitious aids to success, but rely upon unadvertised knowledge and silent devotion; dependence upon finding an appreciation which they cannot seek, but dependence proud in the conviction that the knowledge to which their lives are consecrated is of things which it concerns the world to know. It is the dependence of abstract thought, of science, of beauty, of poetry and art, of every flower of civilization, upon finding a soil generous enough to support it. If it does not, it must die. But the world needs the flower more than the flower needs life.

I said that a law school ought to teach law in the grand manner; that it had something more to do than simply to teach law. I think we may claim for our School that it has not been wanting in greatness. I once heard a Russian say that in the middle class of Russia there were many specialists; in the upper class there were civilized men. Perhaps in America, for reasons which I have mentioned, we need specialists even more than we do civilized men. Civilized men who are nothing else are a little apt to think that they cannot breathe the American atmosphere. But if a man is a specialist, it is most desirable that he should also be civilized; that he should have laid in the outline of the other sciences, as well as the light and shade of his own; that he should be reasonable, and see things in their proportion. Nay, more, that he should be passionate, as well as reasonable -- that he should be able not only to explain, but to feel; that the ardors of intellectual pursuit should be relieved by the charms of art, should be succeeded by the joy of life become an end in itself.

At Harvard College is realized in some degree the palpitating manifoldness of a truly civilized life. Its aspirations are concealed because they are chastened and instructed; but I believe in my soul that they are not the less noble that they are silent. The golden light of the University is not confined to the undergraduate department; it is shed over all the schools. He who has once seen it becomes other than he was, forevermore. I have said that the best part of our education is moral. It is the crowning glory of this Law School that it has kindled in many a heart an inextinguishable fire.

Select Bibliography

The history of legal education in the Eighteenth and Nineteenth Century has not attracted as much attention as one might have expected. Three classic general works touch upon it: A.Z. Reed, Training for the Public Profession of Law (1921), A. Harno, Legal Education in the United States (1953), and R. Stevens, Law School: Legal Education in America from the 1850s to the 1980s (1985). In addition, A.H. Chroust in his The Rise of the Legal Profession in American (1965) and C. Warren in his A History of the American Bar (1913) both devote chapters to the subject. A bibliography of these subjects has also been published; D. Djonovich, Legal Education: A Selective Bibliography (1970). On the English profession and its education in general R. Cocks, Foundations of the Modern Bar (1983) is particularly useful. Also, important is F.H. Lawson, The Oxford Law School 1850-1965 (1968).

On the early history of the profession in England (including education) the work of J.H. Baker, W. Prest, and P. Brand stands out; see, J.H. Baker, The Legal Profession and the Common Law (1986); W. Prest, The Rise of the Barristers (1986), W. Prest, ed., Lawyers in Early Modern Europe and America (1981), P. Brand, "The Origins of the English Legal Profession," Law and History Review, v. 5, pp. 31-50 (1987); see, also, for contemporary accounts, J.H. Baker, ed. The Reports of Sir John Spelman, Selden Society, vv. 93 and 94 (1977-78) and J.H. Baker, ed. The Notebook of Sir John Port, Selden Society, v. 102 (1986).

Blackstone's contribution to the development of modern legal education is analyzed in a number of books and articles. Chief among them is H.G. Hanbury, The Vinerian Chair and Legal Education (1958); P. Lucas, "Blackstone and the Reform of Legal Education; English Historical Review, pp. 456-489 (1962); D. Nolan, "Sir William Blackstone and the New American Republic: A Study Intellectual Impact," N.Y.U. Law Review, v. 51, pp. 731-768 (1976). Also helpful is Blackstone and Oxford

(1980), an exhibition catalog from the Bodleian Library which includes descriptions of a number of items relating generally to Blackstone's law teaching at Oxford.

On the reform of legal education in Nineteenth Century England two articles are especially helpful; P. Stein, "Legal Theory and the Reform of Legal Education in Mid-Nineteenth Century England," Educazione Giuridica, v. 2, pp. 185-206 (1977) and M.H. Hoeflich, "The Americanization of English Legal Education in the Nineteenth Century," Journal of Legal History (1987). Also helpful is P.A. Smith, A History of Education for the English Bar (1860).

On the apprenticeship model of legal education, see, especially, P. Hamlin, Legal Education in Colonial New York (1939) and C. McKirdy, "The Lawyer as Apprentice: Legal Education in Eighteenth Century Massachusetts," Journal of Legal Education, v. 28, pp. 124-136 (1976). A number of Eighteenth Century lawyers kept diaries in which they recorded their educational experiences. Chief among these which has been published is the diary of John Adams; see K. Wroth, & H. Zoebel, edd., The Legal Papers of John Adams, v. 1, pp. 1-25 (1964).

An extremely interesting study of European legal education in the Eighteenth Century which provides a useful comparative perspective is E. Bussi, "Die Lehrmethoden des Reichrechts im 18 Jahrhundert," in A. Fink & H. Becker, edd., Rechtsgeschichte als Kulturgeschichte. Festschrift für Adalbert Erler zum 70 Geburtstäg (Aalen, 1976). Also helpful in drawing the connections between Eurpean and Anglo-American thinking is M.H. Hoeflich "Law & Geometry: Legal Science from Leibniz to Langdelll," American Journal of Legal History, v. 30, pp. 95-121 (1986).

On early Nineteenth Century American law schools, see, especially, C. Warren, A History of the American Bar (1913). Also very helpful is the series of articles on leading American law schools published in the early issues of the periodical The Green Bag. On one of the earliest of American law schools, see, too, M. MacKenna, Tapping Reeve and the Litchfield Law School (1986).

A number of Nineteenth Century periodicals are rich in articles about legal education and legal method. In the United States the American Jurist (1829ff.) gives much information on legal education in the Northeast. In the South, most important are the Southern Review (1828-) and the Southern Literary Messenger (1835ff.). for the period after 1850 in the American Midwest, the Western Jurist (1875ff.) is also quite useful. In England perhaps the most important periodical source is the London Law Magazine and Review (1829ff.).

Several Nineteenth Century works on legal education not included in this collection merit special attention. Especially interesting are: D. Hoffman, A Course of Legal Study, 2 vv (2d ed., 1836); W. Wirt, "Letter to a Law Student," Souther Literary Messenger, v. 1, n°. 2, pp. 1-2 (1834); B.G. Baldwin, Introductory Lecture Before His Law School in Staunton (1831); S. Greenleaf, "Law as a Liberal

Science," Huntington Library Ms. LI 2530; W.G. Hammond, "Legal Education and the Study of Jurisprudence in the West and North-West, in Proceedings of the Conference of Charities, pp. 165-176 (1875).

Notes on Authors and Essays

Notes on Authors and Essays

1. Roger North, <u>Discourse on the Study of the Laws</u> (London, 1824).
  Roger North (1653-1734) spent two years as a student at Jesus College, Cambridge without receiving the degree, then entered Middle Temple in 1669 and was called to the Bar in 1675. He carried on a successful career until the accession of William and Mary. After 1690 he retired to the country where he began his literary career. The <u>Discourse</u> reprinted here was completed sometime before his death in 1734 but was first published in 1824.

2. Thomas Wood, <u>Some Thoughts Concerning the Study of the Laws of England in the Two Universities</u> (London, 1708).
  Thomas Wood was a graduate of New College, Oxford, where he took the degrees of B.C.L. and D.C.L. and was called to the Bar of Gray's Inn <u>ex gratia</u> in 1692. One of the greatest jurists of his age, he was also a prolific author. In addition to the essay reprinted here, he wrote the <u>Institutes of the Laws of England; or the Laws of England in their Natural Order</u> (1720), one of the earliest and best attempts at systematization in England, as well as the <u>A New Institute of the Imperial or Civil Law</u> (1704), one of the most important Civilian treatises of his age.

3. William Blackstone, <u>A Discourse on the Study of the Law</u> (Oxford, 1759).
  Sir William Blackstone (1723-1780) was a fellow of All Souls College, Oxford and the first holder of the Vinerian Chair. He was the greatest jurist and law teacher of his period. His greatest works are his <u>Analysis of the Laws of England</u> (1754) and his magisterial <u>Commentaries on the Laws of England</u> (1765-1770), which remain in print after two hundred years and which served as the main introductory text for law students in England and the United States for over a century after their publication.

4. Frederick Ritso, <u>An Introduction to the Science of the Law, Shewing the Advantages of a Law Education, Grounded</u>

on the Learning of Lord Coke's Commentaries upon Littleton's Tenures . . . (London, 1815).

Frederick Ritso took his B.A. at Christ's Church, Oxford in 1792 and was called to the Bar at Lincoln's Inn in 1814. This appears to have been his only substantial published work.

5.   James Hooper Dawson, A Practical Treatise on the Law Relative to Attornies, Solicitors, and Their Agents . . . (London, 1830).

Dawson was a member of the Inner Temple. This appears to have been his major work.

6.   Thomas J. Hogg, An Introductory Lecture on the Study of the Civil Law (London, 1831).

Hogg (1792-1862) studied at University College, Oxford where he became an intimate of Shelly. He was called to the Bar in 1817. He devoted himself primarily to literary activities and had only a modest success at the Bar. Lord Brougham promised him a professorship at the University of London, but the chair was never established for want of funds. The lecture reprinted here was intended at his inaugural.

7.   Nathaniel Beverley Tucker, "A Lecture on the Study of the Law; Being an Introduction to a Course of Lectures on that Subject in the College of William and Mary [Richmond, 1834]," Southern Literary Messenger, v. 1, pp. 145-154 (1834-5).

Beverley Tucker, the son of St. George Tucker, was a well-known Southern lawyer who was appointed to the Chair of Law at William and Mary in 1834 and served in it until 1853.

8.   Simon Greenleaf, A Discourse Announced at the Inauguration of the Author as Royall Professor of Law in Harvard University (Boston, 1834).

Simon Greenleaf (1783-1853) was admitted to the Bar of the State of Maine in 1806 and became reporter of the Maine Supreme Judicial Court in 1820. He was appointed to the Royall Chair at Harvard in 1833 and, after Story's death, became Dane Professor. He is best known for his Treatise on the Law of Evidence.

9.   Daniel Mayes, An Address to the Students of Law in Transylvania University (Lexington, Ky., 1834).

Daniel Mayes had a distinguished career as a Kentucky state legislator and judge and then as a professor and dean of the law school at Transylvania University in Lexington, Kentucky.

10.   Benjamin F. Butler, A Plan for the Organization of a Law School in the University of the City of New York (New York, 1835).

Benjamin Butler (1795-1858) was admitted to the Bar in 1817 and had a rapid rise in politics. He became Attorney-General in President Jackson's Cabinet in 1833

and remained in office for five years. He subsequently
became U.S. Attorney for the Southern District of New York
and then a private practitioner. During his
Attorney-Generalship he attempted to start a law school at
New York University, but it closed its doors after only
one year.

11.   Samuel Warren, A Popular and Practical Introduction
to Law Studies (London, 1835 [2d ed., 1845]).
      Samuel Warren (1807-1877) studied medicine at
Edinburgh University and was called to the Bar at the
Inner Temple in 1837. Neither the practice of law nor
medicine alone attracted him; he sought a literary career
as well. He was a prolific author and wrote one of the
biggest best-sellers of the Nineteenth Century, Ten
Thousand a Year (1841).

12.   Anon., Study of the Law, Southern Literary Messenger,
v. 3, pp. 25-31 (1837).

13.   Anon., The Legal Profession, The Law Reporter, v. 1,
pp. 209-215 (1839).

14.   Christian Roselius, An Introductory Lecture (New
Orleans, 1854).
      Christian Roselius (1803-1873) was born in Bremen,
Germany but immigrated at age 20 to the United States. He
studied law in New Orleans and was admitted to the
Louisiana Bar in 1828. He became Attorney-General of
Louisiana from 1841-1843 and was a member of the Louisiana
Constitutional Convention of 1845. He was appointed
professor of Civil law at Tulane in 1850 and dean of the
Law Department in 1865.

15.   Montague Bernard, Notes on the Academical Study of
Law (Oxford, 1868).
      Montague Bernard (1820-1882) was called to the Bar in
1845 and became the first Professor of International Law
at Oxford in 1859. He was a prolific author on
international law.

16.   Frederick Pollock, "Oxford Law Studies," in F.
Pollock, Oxford Lectures and Other Discourses (London,
1890).
      Frederick Pollock (1845-1937) was an Oxford graduate
and was called to the Bar in 1871. He became Corpus
Professor of Jurisprudence at Oxford in 1883 and was
founding editor of the Law Quarterly Review from
1884-1919. He was a Privy Councillor and Judge in
Admiralty as well as a prolific treatise writer.

17.   O.W. Holmes, Jr., "The Use of Law Schools," in O.W.
Holmes, Jr., Collected Legal Papers (Boston, 1920).
      Oliver Wendell Holmes (1841-1935) graduated from
Harvard in 1861 and was admitted to the Bar in 1867. In
1881 he published The Common Law, arguably the greatest
work of jurisprudence published by an American since

Story's <u>Commentaries</u> of the 1830's. He became
successively a Justice and Chief Justice of the Supreme
Judicial Court of Massachusetts and then, in 1902, was
appointed Associate Justice of the U.S. Supreme Court, on
which he served until 1932.

Index

About the Editor/Compiler

MICHAEL H. HOEFLICH is Dean of the College of Law at Syracuse University. He is coauthor of *Texts and Materials on Deferred Compensation,* and the author of numerous articles relating to legal history, real estate law, tax, and finance.